DATE DUE			

being human:
the psychological experience

being human: the psychological experience

elton b. mcneil
the university of michigan

canfield press ⌀ san francisco
a department of harper & row, publishers, inc.
new york • evanston • london

BEING HUMAN: THE PSYCHOLOGICAL EXPERIENCE

International Standard Book Number: 0-06-3854406 (paper edition)

International Standard Book Number: 0-06-012902-6 (hard cover edition)

Library of Congress Catalog Card Number: 72-6266

73 74 75 10 9 8 7 6 5 4 3 2 1

Editor: *Theodore Ricks*
Editorial and design supervision: *Brian Williams*
Production and manufacturing supervision: *Christine Schacker*
Illustrations: *Jim Goldberg*
Copyediting: *Linda Harris*

contents

preface

Being human means we are forever engaged in a restless quest for some meaning in life. The human condition—troubled or serene—is marked by the need for certainty in our search for an answer to being here now in these times. Mankind has always been a troubled species whose social inventions produce as much pain as pleasure and whose personal problem-solving is burdened with as much agony as ecstasy.

Psychology is an adolescent science that, with the courage typical of all adolescents, has ventured beyond those safe limits carefully defined by the past. It has soared and it has stumbled and fallen, but it has never abandoned the urge to explore further. This is an account of the adventuring of psychology today focused on where we have been, where we are now, and where we are going. It is akin to taking the pulse of humanity or of measuring the fever of its involvement with current, critical social issues. And, it bears a simple message—psychology has no magic wand to wave over the troubled brow of mankind to ease its pains or solve all its problems. But, psychology offers new hope—hope that man studying man will finally comprehend the basic nature of mankind and one day substitute reason for instinct and emotion.

e. b. mc neil

being human:
the psychological experience

parascience

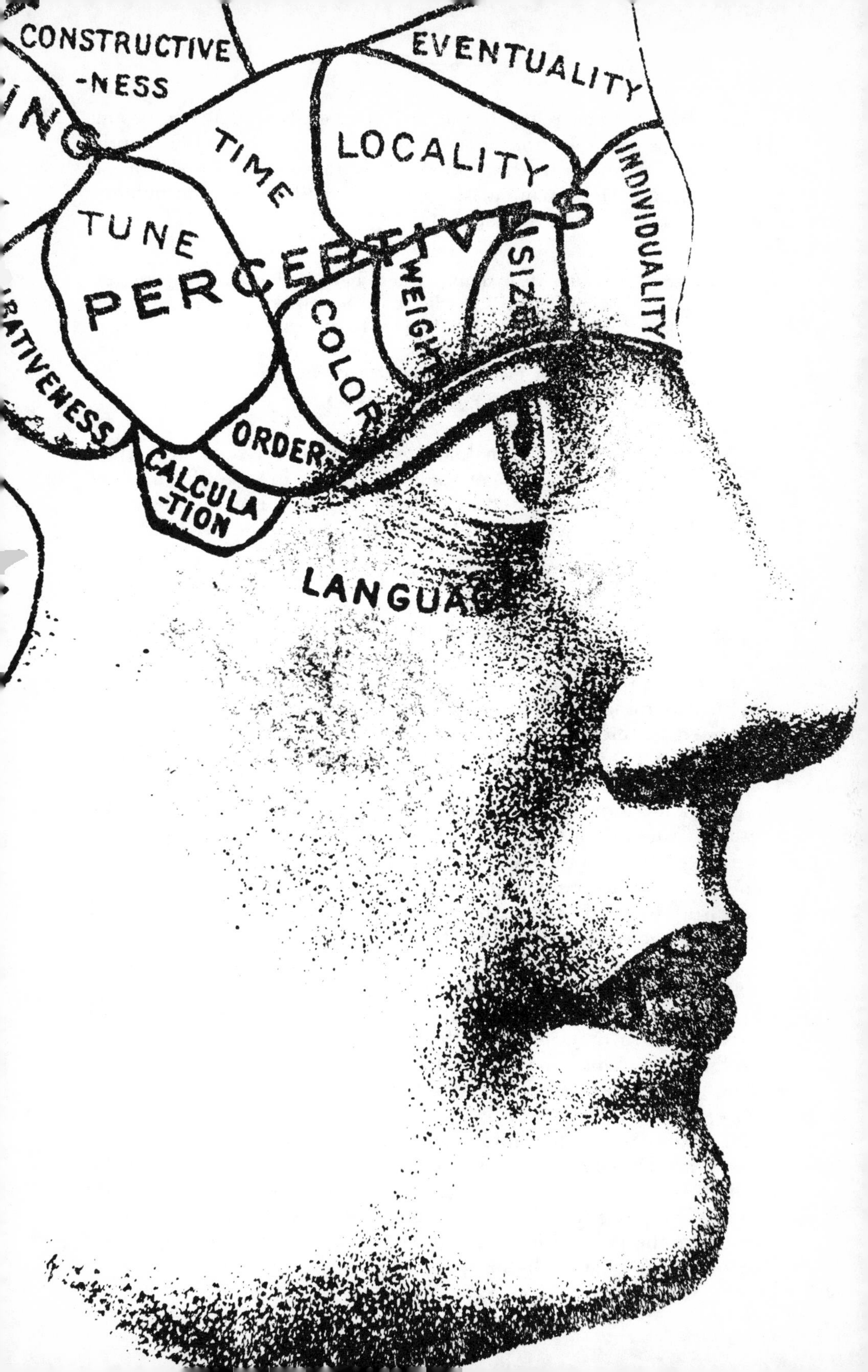
CONSTRUCTIVE-NESS
EVENTUALITY
TIME
LOCALITY
TUNE
PERCEPTIVES
INDIVIDUALITY
WEIGHT
SIZE
COLOR
ORDER
CALCULATION
LANGUAGE

The world of sorcery, mysticism, and the occult operates according to premises different from those of the "rational," "scientific" world most of us think we live in. Consider, for instance, the world of the Yaqui Indian Don Juan in Mexico, as described by anthropology graduate student Carlos Castaneda:

> At first I saw don Juan simply as a rather peculiar man who knew a great deal about peyote and who spoke Spanish remarkably well. But the people with whom he lived believed that he had some sort of "secret knowledge," that he was a "brujo." The Spanish word *brujo* means, in English, medicine man, curer, witch, sorcerer. It connotes essentially a person who has extraordinary, and usually evil, powers.

Castaneda entered Don Juan's world for five years and learned of a "nonordinary reality" generally alien to us in scientific Western civilization. Which is the true reality? Our certainty may never go beyond the fact that the worlds of different peoples have different shapes.

In other, different worlds a Westerner must also suspend his beliefs before he can enter the worlds, for instance, of psychedelic drugs, astrology, the Tarot, and the I Ching or Book of Changes. It is not just that these worlds contain unfamiliar ideas and concepts, but they require, as one psychologist put it, a fundamental difference in life experience and outlook. It is for this reason that communication between the scientific and, as we shall call it, *para*scientific viewpoints has so often been a "dialogue of the deaf," with both speaking persuasively but neither listening.

As a modern scientist I am biased on the side of science as the establishment defines it, but I am aware that at this stage in history we have many more questions than answers. Thus, I use the term *parascience* (the prefix *para* means "beside, beyond, apart from, or accessory to") rather than the more traditional and derogatory label *pseudoscience* (*pseudo* means "false, counterfeit, not genuine").

In his progress from the cave to outer space, man has relentlessly sought knowledge and yearned to know the meaning of life. He has scattered the entrails of slaughtered animals and searched for meaning in the pattern they made on the ground; he has studied the lines on the palm of his hand; he has looked to the stars, and, in historical times, he has invented science. As the psychologist H. Kaufmann observed, "Some aspects of science itself developed out of magic, and whatever the dissimilarities, it shares with magic the urge to know the physical (as opposed to the metaphysical) world, and the belief that Man can be more than a passive, uncomprehending thing in it." The modern argument between science and parascience, then, concerns the method used and the kind of facts that are considered evidence for what we believe.

4

In recent times, interest in astrology, numerology, witchcraft, satanism, Ouija boards, Tarot cards, and a multitude of other parascientific approaches to the mystery of man, has been revived. Ninety percent of all American newspapers carry daily astrological forecasts, and as many as two million Ouija boards are purchased each year. We are living in the Age of Aquarius—an age of the occult, the mystic, and drug-induced hallucinations of reality. Increasingly, people are turning to supernatural explanations or solutions to problems. The link between anxiety and the belief in magical solutions to human problems was first explored some years ago by anthropologist Bronislaw Malinowski, who observed that magical thought is evoked in primitive tribes when highly risky or uncertain events are impending. In his study of 50 societies, sociologist Guy Swanson detected a relationship between the occurrence of witchcraft and the presence or absence of legally instituted social controls and moral bonds among persons in the society. When the legal means of social control are absent or no longer operating effectively, the belief in magic and witchcraft increase accordingly. Insofar as we are eager to believe, there will always be a ready market for miracles. As the Harvard psychologist S. S. Stevens stated: "Creatures in saucers are not likely to stop their visitations upon us as long as they can home in on the glowing beacon of human faith. Perhaps it is too much to say that man believes without evidence, but the evidence ... may often be flimsy indeed." The nature of the evidence—or lack therof—is precisely what concerns us about parascientific endeavors. As long ago as 1865, French physiologist Claude Bernard insisted that, "If the facts used as a basis for reasoning are ill-established or erroneous, everything will crumble or be falsified; ... it is thus that errors in scientific theories most often originate in errors of fact." The disagreement over what is or is not "fact" triggers most of the hostile dialogue between scientists and the parascientists.

One writer uses the example of the stage magician to illustrate our limited abilities to perceive the facts—all the facts, and nothing but the facts. The professional magician depends upon the shortcomings of human perception and upon his ability to fool people by making them perceive the "facts" wrongly. Magicians know that, in addition to seeing what actually takes place, most of us embellish what we see by filling in details according to what we *believe* or *think* we know. Our expectations and our knowledge from past experiences alter or twist what we actually see. For these reasons, scientists mistrust some of the "facts" that enthusiastic parascientists are anxious to accept. Tales of riding in flying saucers guided by little green men, chilling accounts of an impending disaster, or declarations of the astounding accuracy of the daily horoscope do not qualify as scientific evidence. Facts are always suspect when heavily laden with human hopes or emotions.

5

The scientists may seem stubborn, but as one observer pointed out, this very stubbornness "forces the scientist with a novel view to mass considerable evidence before his theory can be seriously entertained. If this situation did not exist, science would be reduced to shambles by having to examine every new-fangled notion that came along. Clearly, working scientists have more important tasks." This same writer paints an unflattering portrait of the parascientist, claiming that some parascientists consider themselves geniuses, regard those who disagree with them as ignorant, or believe they are persecuted. Indeed, many scientists, whether rightly or wrongly, maintain a deliberate neutrality in regard to all experimental findings and particularly in regard to findings that have yet to be replicated under the controlled conditions of scientific method.

Recent times have also witnessed the proliferation of "psycho quacks" who borrow the cloak of psychological thought and method but are untrained in the discipline. Tough-minded personnel managers, for example, are often taken in by "psychological testers" who falsely promise to deliver results that any properly trained psychologist would view as inconceivable. It is important to admit, however, that as a science, psychology still has some distance to travel. Koch, an outstanding critic of theoretical systems in psychology, suggests that the study of man has not yet accumulated many triumphs: "Here and there the effort has turned up a germane fact, or thrown off a spark of insight, but these victories have had an accidental relation to the programs believed to inspire them, and their sum total is heavily overbalanced by the pseudo-knowledge that has proliferated."

the parascientific method

Before considering specific popular approaches that man has used in his endeavor to understand himself, let us examine the parascientific method that is common to all of them. The parascientist satisfies certain needs experienced by all of us. We are all curious about ourselves and want to know about those qualities that escape our understanding. Since the parascientist offers answers that are free of the crippling doubts so frequently characteristic of scientific statements, he is able to satisfy our need for certainty.

Another facet upon which the parascientific method rests is the fact that almost every known psychological trait can be observed to some degree in everyone. This is the key, for instance, to the apparent accuracy of horoscopes. Personality traits can be conceptualized as distributed along a continuum ranging from strong to weak; in other words, each of us could be placed somewhere along a scale marked "stingy" at one end and "generous" at the other. When interpreting one's character, the parascientist uses general terms that could apply to almost anyone. Furthermore, if the personality analysis is flattering, the interpreter will find himself increasingly favored by the eager listener.

Psychologists have developed experiments to demonstrate the effectiveness of using generalized personality interpretations. The experimental procedure is quite simple. Research subjects take a "personality test" and then receive an interpretation of what the test supposedly revealed about them. The catch is that all subjects receive identical interpretations worded in a manner that would fit most persons. Such an analysis might read as follows.

> You are not a stubborn person, but once you have examined the relevant facts you make up your own mind and stick to your guns. You pride yourself on being an independent thinker and are not likely to accept others' opinions without satisfactory proof. You need to have other people like and admire you but you won't go to excessive lengths to win their approval. While you have some personal shortcomings, you are usually able to compensate for them, and you have a great deal of unused capacity which you have not yet turned to your advantage. At times you are extroverted, affable, and sociable, but at other times you are more reserved and wary. Some of your aspirations tend to be unrealistic, and you are not always certain you have made the right decision or done the right thing. You have a need for a certain amount of change and variety and become frustrated when hemmed in by too many restrictions and limitations.

Incredibly, a high percentage of people respond to such a meaningless conglomeration of personality statements as if the interpretation contained precise, insightful views. The parascientific method, then, rests upon (a) our need to have certain knowledge and (b) the fact that most everyone possesses almost every known psychological trait. Keeping these aspects of the method in mind, let us now examine some of the many faces of modern parascience.

PHRENOLOGY

The premises of phrenology are fairly straightforward. The brain is the physical organ of the mind; the shape and size of certain parts of the growing brain represent the over- or underdevelopment of personality traits or characteristics; and the bumps and hollows of the skull reflect the shape of the brain it contains. Accordingly, the phrenologist need only measure head bumps to determine the shape of the brain and to diagnose the personality of his client.

Phrenology began with the work of Franz Joseph Gall (1758–1828). As a child, Gall surmised that the boys in his class who had unusually good memories also seemed to have bulging eyeballs. Gall became curious about a possible relationship between physical and psychological characteristics, and after finishing medical school he began a series of investigations to prove his beliefs. Gall used the questionable research method of selecting persons known to have some outstanding psychological characteristic and then looking for bumps on the head. In one instance, Gall visited prisons, measured the skulls of convicted pickpockets, and then reported that all these subjects demonstrated an overdeveloped region called the "Propensity to Acquisitiveness."

Gall believed that the mind is composed of 37 powers or propensities. Firmness, reverence, acquisitiveness, and combativeness are a few examples. He located these powers in specific parts of the brain. When he published his phrenological theory and reported his "scientific" findings, Gall was attacked by his professional colleagues who then refused to grant him membership in the French Academy of Sciences. Gall's cofounder of phrenology, German physician Johann Kaspar Spurzheim (1776–1832), fared somewhat better. Spurzheim modified some of Gall's theories, made a number of further observations, and was invited to America in 1832 to lecture before the medical faculties at Harvard and other noted universities.

By 1840 phrenology had become a widespread craze that offered a quick, "scientific," inexpensive way to secure vocational guidance, bring personal improvement, and ensure happiness. Phrenology parlors were scattered across the country; traveling phrenologists crisscrossed the nation on lecture tours; and phrenological literature was available everywhere. In a very short time, amateurs everywhere were eager to measure the bumps on one's head and to furnish—for a price—a full analysis of one's personality. Soon every carnival had a phrenological side show, and waves of transient phrenologists exploited every small town in America. The fad did not die easily. Store-front phrenology parlors, filled with intriguing "scientific" objects and trappings, existed as late as the 1930s and early 1940s.

Phrenology is just one episode in the long history of beliefs that people have accepted uncritically. Ironically, we find it easy to scoff at human gullibility in the past while subscribing to a similar set of "modern," yet equally unscientific, convictions. In its own day and age, phrenology had a reasonable ring to it, despite the fact that today's scientists reject the notion that the brain is like a muscle which becomes weak or strong depending upon how much it is exercised.

Although phrenological theory was inaccurate, the recommendations made by phrenology theorists read very much like the conclusions some modern theorists have reached. As one writer has described it,

> Phrenologists urged a short school day, together with physical training and a good deal of free play; they were opposed to drill and the use

8

of punishment; they advocated "learning by doing"; they objected to training in the classics exclusively and urged the training of all the mental faculties—always with the metaphorical model before them that learning was simply the proper exercise of the muscles.

Obviously, whether they be scientists or parascientists, theorists can be right for the wrong reasons.

GRAPHOLOGY

Graphology, or the analysis of handwriting, occupies a special niche in the halls of parapsychology since its practitioners are still very much alive and well. As graphologist D. S. Anthony maintains, "I am convinced that in the hands of a skilled practitioner graphology can assist corporations in the selection of productive and reliable employees, can aid therapists in evaluating their patients, and can help youths choose their careers by pinpointing talents and personality traits. I believe that graphology could aid in difficult medical diagnoses."

In addition to a few self-styled "expert" graphologists, diploma mills grind out thousands of graduates who advertise inexpensive personality analyses by mail. Although Anthony insists that graphology is a legitimate subdiscipline of psychology, few psychologists would agree with him. Furthermore, few psychologists know enough about handwriting analysis to do effective research on the claims made by graphologists. What little psychological research has been accomplished is not favorable to the graphologists. In one methodological survey of past experiments, possible reasons for the relatively stagnant state of research in the area of handwriting and personality was explored. A number of weaknesses were revealed: some of the handwriting analyses failed to consider whether the individual's handwriting was consistent or whether the judgments of the raters were reliable. In other cases, the criteria used to evaluate handwriting samples were vague or not specified. Another weakness was the rather dubious nature of some of the personality variables used.

The classic work by psychologists in the area of graphology was that of Allport and Vernon as long ago as 1933. In their investigations of human behavior, these psychologists included handwriting on the assumption that (a) personality is consistent, (b) movement is expressive of personality, and (c) the gestures and other expressive movements of an individual are consistent with one another. They had no intention of confirming or disconfirming the claims of graphology, but their studies are often cited by graphologists as evidence that human expressive activity of all sorts—including handwriting—is reliable and consistent.

Psychological research in graphology continues to languish, but

popular fascination has not diminished accordingly. This public interest has, in fact, "been parlayed by the shrewd clip artist looking for
a panacea for his personal and financial frustrations. The easy art of
handwriting analysis has answered the needs of the drawing room
psychologizers who seek a dramatic new path to personal popularity."
An unusual resurgence of interest in graphology has occurred among
many of the members of the younger generation as a part of their
all-enveloping search for answers to questions such as "Who am I?"
or "What kind of person am I?" Their interest in graphology is only
one aspect of their willingness to explore the mysterious. Astrology,
another area of increasing fascination to young people, may be an
even more mystifying realm.

ASTROLOGY

For centuries the peoples of Asia have planned life events with one
eye to reality and the other to the stars. Now, the ancient art of astrology
has entered the computer age. Computer-cast horoscopes are available
for anywhere from 5 to 30 dollars, and the charge can be taken care
of by another technological breakthrough, the credit card. Astrology
has long captivated the interest of persons of all ages in our society,
but recent attention has taken a new twist. The modern astrological
preoccupation leans toward a popularization of the simplest elements
in astrology—that is to say, the position of the sun, the planets in
the zodiac, and their transits over the important points in the natal
chart. This trend toward popularization seeks to blend the fundamental
methods of ancient and Medieval astrology with the broad psychological notions that are now widespread throughout the United States.

The prevalence of a glib and superficial familiarity with
psychoanalytic and psychological theory soon inspired an astrological
innovation called astroanalysis. Unblushingly, astroanalysts publish
claims such as those in the following advertisement.

> Your talents and tendencies, your personal assets and your "danger
> zones," the strengths and weaknesses that operate in your work-life,
> your love-life and your social-life—find out *all* there is to know about
> yourself through the amazing techniques developed by astrologer Ilya
> Chambertin. Astroanalysis is the new scientific way to a happier,
> healthier, more successful self!

Ilya Chambertin dedicates her book to the memory of the Swiss
psychiatrist Carl G. Jung, whom she describes as the theoretical father
of astroanalysis—a system combining the ancient wisdom of astrology
with the modern interpretations of psychiatry and psychoanalysis. As
a short cut to the analysis of personality, character, and behavior,
astroanalysis furnishes "instant-glance charts" to help its readers find

10

the proper marriage mate. In my case, I am a Capricorn married to an Aries. According to Chambertin, ours is an impossible relationship, "doomed to failure." I was greatly surprised at learning this, since during the last 30 years my wife and I have lived with the impression that we are more than simply compatible.

Chambertin's astrological system claims to probe both conscious and unconscious personality traits. As a Capricorn, consciously I should be the most tenacious, perservering human being on the face of the earth; I should be a grave, hard-working, determined individual who approaches all tasks in a single-minded manner. I should be practical, realistic, and ambitious, but not very magnetic, even if somewhat overwhelming to others. Unconsciously, I should be rigid, unbending, inhibited, defensive, and ridden with anxiety over defeat or failure. Allow me to say that, for this sample of one, I hope astroanalysis is not accurate.

The difficulty posed by such a global analysis of personality (by astrological or any other means) is that at different times, in different situations, with different people, it is all true and it is all false. As long as analyses of this sort are couched in vague and undefined terms, they will always be neither right nor wrong. Instead, the analysis will appear to the beholder in whatever form he or she most desires. Astrology superficially invites the believer to relax and to accept his personal fate passively; if one's future has been determined by the position of the planets at the moment of birth, what is to be will be despite determined efforts to alter the course of destiny.

The reassurance astrologers offer their believers is often rooted in mysterious, ancient wisdom amassed over the centuries. Precisely what this wisdom was and exactly what the ancients achieved through their knowledge is never discussed. The facts are probably not even relevant if a man believes that the ordered patterns he observes in the sky signal an end to the apparent chaos and confusion of his daily life.

Obviously, I do not regard astrology as seriously as it seemingly regards itself, nor do I give credence to exotic accounts of miraculous happenings which believers claim to have seen or heard about. I sense a subtle, ego-gratifying philosophy among those who read their daily horoscope and find in it a meaningful message to guide one's personal behavior; indeed, astrology is one way to convince ourselves that we are not alone and unnoticed in this life. The belief in astrology or any parascientific phenomenon is an *emotional* rather than a rational event. What *feels* right to an individual is truth to him, and no massive accumulation of so-called "scientific" data can shake the foundations upon which such belief is based.

The belief itself is comforting and probably harmless if it does not become the sole focus of existence. One might get carried away, however, in the bizarre expressions of belief in astrology. At least one astrologer, for example, is convinced that the position of the stars at the time of a woman's birth is the key to her fertility and indicates the days on which she may conceive for the rest of her life. Astrological charts might even become the newest form of birth control, although their use would probably be limited to those persons who unquestioningly accepted astrology as a true science.

NUMEROLOGY

The parascience of the meaning of numbers is another of the ancient psychic arts. Numbers are thought to represent psychic power, and certain digits have long had magical qualities ascribed to them. As long ago as the year 1533, numbers were accorded human psychological characteristics. One, for example, is the number signifying aggression, action, and ambition (qualities which begin with the letter *a*, the number one letter in the alphabet). Four is the number that stands for steadiness, solidity, and endurance (the square, the four seasons, the points of the compass, the elements of fire, air, water, and earth). Seven is the number of the mysterious and the unknown (the days of the week, the notes of the musical scale, the seven planets).

Each of the numbers 1 through 9 is considered a primary number and is said to have its own particular characteristics and qualities. For numbers beyond these primaries, individual digits are added until a primary number is reached. Thus, 1924 (1 + 9 + 2 + 4) when added equals 16. When added again, 16 (1 + 6) equals 7. In the same fashion, dates can be added by combining the date of the month, the number of the month, and the figures that compose the year. Thus, the date July 4, 1776 can be reduced to its "vibrational" number, 5. Certain numerologists have noted that "no numerical vibration could be more expressive of the hazard and uncertainty that went with the signing of that momentous document [the Declaration of Independence]. The risk assumed by all the persons involved, as well as the launching of a new ship of state upon uncharted waters from which there could be no return, reflected to full degree the number 5, symbol of adventure." For numerologists the important issue is how each individual is affected by the "vibratory" influences attributed to numbers and how the individual can use these numbers to personal advantage.

One of the most vital numbers in life is the birth number. Thus, a person (such as myself) born on January 1, 1924 would have a vibratory number of 9. Since the birth number is unalterably set at the moment of birth, it holds a fixed vibratory influence which may shape the individual's character and future. The number 9, numerologists say, is the symbol of universal achievement and the greatest of all primary numbers since it combines the features of many other numbers. For example, in the form of 3 × 3, it turns versatility into inspiration.

In much the same fashion, a name can be reduced to a vibratory number. Thus, when translated into a number by assigning a digit to each letter in the alphabet, Elton B. McNeil turns out to be 7—a truly psychic number. The number 7 means I have a scholarly, poetic nature, inclined toward the fanciful—though analytical as well. Intuition should be a strong part of my nature, and I should be highly imaginative. As a name number, 7 is thought to have "grand possibilities," and I can look forward to attaining greatness as a leader or teacher of other persons since I possess deep understanding and inspire loyalty in others.

One can also find a vowel vibration (by adding the numerical value of the vowels in one's name), or the birth number and the name number can be added to the number of any particular day of the year to learn the degree to which one's psychological vibrations harmonize for the day. Numerologists also delight in drawing historic parallels. Two numerologists, for example, suggest that if Napoleon had studied numerology he would have avoided the Battle of Waterloo. Although numerology is fun to play with, there is not one shred of evidence that it possesses any psychological validity. Why, then, do so many people play the game? For the most part, they play it jokingly, but their casual interest may conceal a belief in the magical capacity of numerology to reveal destiny and guide actions in uncertain times.

some parascientific odds and ends

If some omnipresent power is indeed attempting to communicate with man to help him through the difficult times in life, these cryptic messages could be transmitted in a variety of forms. The question is: why are such elaborate degrees of subtlty and mystery needed to communicate with the human species? The range of media being employed for the apparent reception of such messages is astounding. In this section, we shall review some of these parascientific offshoots.

TAROT

Playing cards, probably since their invention, have been used to forecast the future. The first packs of cards were called tarots, and there were originally 78 cards. Of these, 56 were suit cards similar to those of the modern card pack. The suits in former times were swords, cups, coins, and rods; there were four court cards to each suit—namely, king, queen, knight, and knave. The spot cards ranged from ten to ace. The other 22 cards included jugglers, an empress, lovers, the devil, stars, the fool, the hermit, justices, and others. When card games were invented the deck was reduced to 52 cards of four suits. Only the fool has survived in the modern deck of cards, as the joker. This development did not, however, destroy the ancient art of cartomancy; card readers simply reassigned meanings to the cards in the new-fangled decks. Each card was given a specific meaning. The nine of hearts, for example, became the "wish card," the card of fulfillment which promises harmony and success to projects delineated by cards falling alongside it. But, if the nine is a spade, it is the worst card in the pack, representing misery, loss of money, and illness. In much the same fashion, hearts point toward success; clubs symbolize friendship and influence; and diamonds indicate difficulties on the practical side of life.

The variations in methods of fortune telling are enormous since each *artiste* has added to the standard, mystic formula. One usual method is the mystic cross. Thirteen cards are laid in cross rows of six and seven (in order to balance bad and good luck). The mystic cross is read vertically from the bottom followed by the three cards in the left arm and then the three cards in the right arm of the cross. On the face of it, the shuffling, dealing, and reading of cards should be questionable means of determining one's character, personality, and future, but the popularity of this method is growing enormously. It is particularly paradoxical to witness well-educated young people deeply engrossed in fortune telling with Tarot cards. It does not quite ring true when they dismiss this pursuit as no more than a parlor game played for the fun of it.

THE OUIJA BOARD

The strange name *Ouija* (pronounced *wee-juh*) is a combination of the French *oui* and the German *ja* and literally means "yes-yes." The Ouija board has the letters of the alphabet, the words *yes* and *no*, and the numbers one through ten printed on its surface. The tiny Ouija table (a small surface with three peg-like legs) responds to pressure from the finger tips of the participants by moving about the larger board from letter to letter, spelling out words, answering yes or no, or adding up numbers. True believers claim that the answers to their questions are furnished by a supernatural force that guides the participants' fingers. Nonbelieving psychologists are convinced that the phenomenon amounts to little more than a simple physical expression of the unconscious wish for some superior guiding force that cares for the participant and that communicates messages about current fears and desires.

Spending an evening with a Ouija board among friends ready to suspend disbelief and entertain the possibility of supernatural forces

14

can be fun, if somewhat spooky. Indeed, a certain intimacy can be gained from sharing this kind of mystic adventure with others. This unique quality pervades many mystic experiences and allows them to be harmless fun, if not taken seriously.

PALMISTRY

Cherio is representative of the many hand readers who pretend to scientific authority. With perhaps too little modesty, Cherio notes:

> The success I had during the 25 years in which I was connected with this study was, I believe, chiefly owing to the fact that although my principal study was the lines and formations of hands, yet I did not confine myself alone to that particular page in the book of Nature. I endeavored to study every phase of thought that can throw light on human life; consequently the very ridges of the skin, the hair found on the hands, all were used as a detective would use a clue to accumulate evidence.

Cherio further assumes that the brain is directly in touch with the nerves of the hand and the corpuscles in the tips of the fingers. Thus, the study of the hand—long practiced by every ancient civilization—is, in some ways, said to be like the study of the brain.

A typical interpretation of personality that palm readers make is that of the inner life line or the line of Mars. To the palmist, the extended length, depth, and clarity of this line denotes a robust person with a fighting disposition, inclined to rush into quarrels. A weak line of mentality stretching out from the line of Mars is a sure sign of a craving for drink and intemperance of all kinds. Other lines such as the line of destiny or line of fate are of great importance since they may make some of us helpless children of fate,

Cherio offers one of the most comforting—yet maddening—explanations of the relationship between hand lines and the unknown future that I have ever encountered. This palmist simply says that, although the why and wherefore of such a relationship may escape easy explanations, there are so many mysteries in life itself, one more does not seem to matter. This dismissal of scientific questions may be irritating to scientists, but perhaps they are envious of the glib assurance palmists display in regard to the mysteries of life.

PHYSIOGNOMY

The study of heads and faces to determine personality characteristics is a pastime first detailed by a Swiss mystic named Johann Kaspar Lavater. His works, published at the time of the American Revolution, became a basic text for those interested in the study of faces and features. Size of head, shape of face, placement of the features in relation to one another, and the details of the features (size of ear lobe and the like) all had individual meanings which could be combined into a general personality sketch by an artful face reader.

In the sixteenth century, metoposcopy, or the study of the lines of the forehead, became a popular subspeciality of physiognomy. Jerome Cardan developed a system in which the lines of the forehead were named for the planets and then interpreted in astrological terms. Wavy lines crossing the longer horizontal lines meant travel at sea, while straight crossing lines meant travel by land. Lines that crossed and then turned up signified nothing—perhaps because there was little air travel in 1558!

For physiognomy students interested in specializing even further, there was the field of moleosophy—the study of the location, shape, and color of moles. Light colored moles, for example, brought the bearer a better fate and fortune than did dark moles. Mole location was of even greater significance to the moleosophist. While an ankle mole indicated a fearful nature in the male, the same mole on a female suggested courage, a sense of humor, and willingness to share love with others. Belly moles were particularly bad signs since they revealed a tendency toward self-indulgence, overeating, and excessive drinking. Finally, in these days of the population explosion, it would be well to check for a mole on one's navel, since this portends the desire to have many children.

THE MYSTICISM OF COLOR

The colors in the spectrum have been numbered and interpreted in systems of numerology and have been assigned zodiacal signs and treated in astrological terms as well. (Gold is the sun; silver is the moon; and red is Mars.) Colors have different physical vibrations which are said to affect the life and character of the individual. For example, we "have the blues" or get blue; cowards are yellow; we see red; we are green with envy, and so on. In addition, we all prefer certain colors as a life theme. Blue is said to mix sensitivity with fervor; red responds to warm primitive urges; and those of us with literary, artistic, or dramatic ability have a "violet aura."

Colors are also said to shape the spirit of individuals and nations. Did you know, for example, that all of the Allied forces in World War I had flags colored red, white, and blue? Not one of the enemy had a red, white, and blue flag! In World War II the same situation prevailed; not one of the Axis powers had red, white, and blue colors.

Another uncanny phenomenon realted to the mysticism of color is "Kirlian" photography. Semyon and Valentina Kirlian of the Soviet Union have reportedly developed special photographic techniques that reveal the existence of a luminescent aura surrounding all living tissue. This aura diminishes in cases of a disease that has not yet reached the symptomatic stage. This aura is said to emanate (in a variety of colors, twinkles, flashes, and sparkles) from so simple a form of life as a leaf. The Kirlians have also reportedly invented a transparent screen that can make the aura surrounding all living things visible to the naked eye.

Even more mysterious is the Kirlian claim that a second human body is detectable in these luminescent patterns of life energy. Apparently, in addition to our ordinary physical body, we each possess an additional semiphysical body that is the source of the aura. The "energy body" or "plasma body" concept has long been a favorite theoretical speculation among spiritualists and mediums seeking an explanation for how consciousness can continue after physical death. In addition, psychic theories have long maintained that human auras of lights and colors reflect the mood or state of mind of the individual. Psychic persons gifted with inner sight can clearly see the emanations of others, and even some less sensitive persons can have brief glimpses of such auras or sense their existence and influence.

THE OPEN CULT

The flying saucer phenomena of the 1950s provide additional insight about the emotional and social aspects of belief in the occult. In H. T. Buckner's analysis of flying saucers, excitement about unidentified flying objects (UFOs) began in 1947 and produced a period of public concern about the notion that mysterious objects might be flying around our planet. During the months of April to July, 1952, *Life* magazine carried a series of articles about flying saucers, which increased the number of saucer sightings by about tenfold. Before long the flying saucer craze entered a new phase which Buckner calls occult colonization—people began to report UFOs landing and making contact with humans. By the mid-1950s a publication explosion had taken place and the possibility was suggested that we were being watched by aliens from outer space. Flying saucer clubs were formed, national UFO conventions were held, and a lecture circuit was established. As Buckner observed:

> The social world of the occult "seeker" is a very unusual one. The seeker moves in a world populated by astral spirits, cosmic truths, astrologers, mystery schools, lost continents, magic healing, human "auras," "second comings," telepathy, and vibrations. A typical occult seeker will probably have been ... a member of four or five smaller specific cults. The pattern of membership is one of continuous movement from one idea to another. Seekers stay with a cult until they are satisfied that they can learn no more from it, or that it has nothing to offer, and then they move on.

Much of the parascience that some young people are "into" today is an open rather than closed cult. That is to say, the believer need not adhere to a fixed dogma or doctrine. He or she need only respect the mystic beliefs of others and share a common mood of mystery. This is, perhaps, as concise a statement as we can make of the psychological view of the modern resurgence of the occult. Indeed, the current prosperity of parascience may be a direct consequence of the terror of our times.

parapsychology

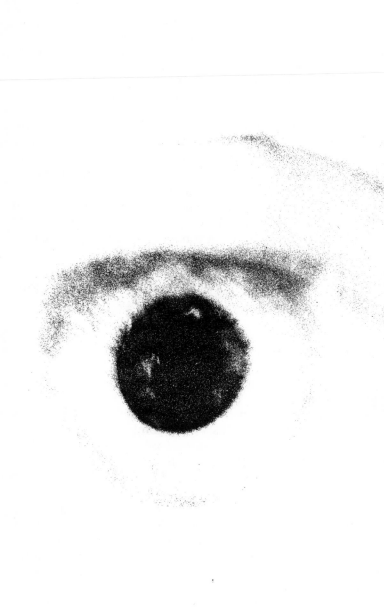

The present state of parapsychology is probably much the same as it was when Gardner Murphy, the "grand old man" of psychology, appraised it more than a decade ago:

> A large number of people, especially in the lower educational levels, believe themselves to have received impressions regarding distant realities which did not reach them through their sense organs, or through their normal processes of drawing inferences. They report that they have caught impressions of distant catastrophes to loved ones, or have had curiously exact and detailed premonitions of future events.

Parapsychology, or psi phenomenon, includes clairvoyance (in which extrasensory perception allows one to perceive an object or event without employing the usual five senses), telepathy (being aware of another person's thoughts without communicating through the familiar sensory channels), precognition (either knowledge of another person's future thoughts—precognitive telepathy—or knowledge of future events—precognitive clairvoyance), and psychokinesis (the ability to influence a physical object by a sheer exercise of will). Of this catalogue of parapsychological possibilities, ESP (extrasensory perception) is currently the most fashionable concern. An extended network of research avenues are being pursued by those interested in probing the innermost secrets of psi phenomena.

the range of research

Reporting all of the existing avenues of research would be too great a project for our purposes here, but we can sample some of the various approaches now being pursued. The American Society for Psychical Research has reported that ESP tests were conducted with graduate students in psychology before and after a swami delivered a lecture on meditation and breathing exercises. The "before" results on the ESP tests could be predicted on the basis of chance, but the researchers declared that the "after" scores were significantly above chance expectation. Among other research efforts, Stevenson is exploring the possibility that some individuals have precognition of disasters involving multiple fatalities, and Stanford is laboring to discover whether ESP could, without the individual's awareness, exert an influence on the details of what that person can recall. ESP may, for example, influence the substitution of correct for incorrect detail in the memory of events.

The hypnotic state has been included in the armamenterium of ESP experiments. Teams of hypnotized and nonhypnotized subjects have been studied to determine whether hypnosis could facilitate telepathic rapport. To date, the results have been inconclusive. Great distances have also been used in testing extrasensory perception.

22

Researchers arranged for a group of persons in Los Angeles to "transmit" their personal reactions to programmed emotional episodes to "receivers" in Los Angeles, New York, and Sussex, England; but, here again, the results were mixed and offered only marginal proof to psychologists.

The most startling example of experimentation with extrasensory perception across unusual distances was the attempt of astronaut Edgar Mitchell of the Apollo 14 moon flight to send mental messages back to Earth. Mitchell took time out on six successive days of the mission to transmit readings of ESP cards to a recipient in Chicago. Although the experiment failed, its success or failure is less important than the credibility it lent to the legitimacy of the mysterious "extra sense." Long distance experimentation with ESP is not really novel; it was first attempted in 1933 by the Pearce-Pratt Distance Series of ESP tests. Certainly, if ESP exists, it is logical to assume that it could surmount obstacles such as time and space.

On a more mundane level, even the lowly fungus has felt the possible influence of parapsychology. One investigator, for example, studied the effect of human thought on the growth of fungus. In 15 minute bursts of concentrated thinking, experimenters tried to inhibit the growth of fungus samples placed in a laboratory environment. According to their evaluations, the experiments were usually successful. The skeptics among us, however, would attribute greater credibility to these reported findings had objective, nonbelieving researchers calculated the degree to which the experimental fungus samples grew less than the control samples. In the scientific world it is not exactly cricket for the researcher to appoint himself both judge and jury. Fungus has not been the only target of experiments in parapsychology. Similar attempts at determining the influence of extrasensory forces have been carried out with particle flow in a cloud chamber, the flow of sand in an hourglass, and the speed at which tablets dissolve in solution.

Even when dreaming we may be a part of the world of extrasensory perception, according to psychologists M. Ullman and S. Krippner. More than 20 years ago, these researchers were intrigued by the notion that telepathic communication might fashion the content of dreams. To explore this possibility, a dream laboratory was established in 1962 at the Maimonides Medical Center in New York; in the years since that time, eight formal experimental studies have been completed, and five of these have yielded statistical results supporting the theory of telepathic influences on dream content. The researchers reported:

> We are convinced that the effect is real, and have been conducting a number of pilot studies to determine new directions for telepathy

research and to investigate the influence of many related variables. We want to know, for example, whether telepathic messages are received more easily in one stage of sleep than another.

Research into extrasensory perception has also invaded the animal kingdom. Morris has surveyed a series of reports on animals mysteriously homing, thinking, or displaying other evidence of Anpsi (animal psi phenomenon). Efforts to test for Anpsi began as early as the 1920s when the Russian neurophysiologist Bechterev reported telepathically influencing the behavior of Pikki, his fox terrier. Other reports have appeared concerning a horse named Lady that answered questions by pointing to lettered blocks with her hoof. In this last instance, as in every other situation where an animal might give advice to human beings, the experimenters concluded that the beast was responding to subtle cues emanating from its master and possessed no extrasensory capacity of its own whatsoever. Additional research on Anpsi phenomena includes: psi trailing (when animals follow "loved ones" into totally unfamiliar territory; for example, when dogs or cats track families over hundreds of miles); death reactions (when animals inexplicably react to the death or impending death of their master); animals that signal the approach of some natural disaster (when dogs howl before earthquakes and so on); homing (for example, the salmon's ability to detect the particular stream in which it was spawned); and awareness of approach (when animals anticipate the time of their master's return by assuming a favorite position to greet him, even when he returns unexpectedly).

the origin of esp

Assuming that perception of an extrasensory sort can and does occur, some investigators have suggested that ESP is related to some as yet unknown quality of brain tissue, which is slowly emerging as the human species plods along the path of continuing evolution. While this possibility offers hope for some eventual improvement in the human race, a more common theory is that psi abilities were originally a part of the natural endowment of all living things. This heritage, it is said, has deteriorated over the centuries of human evolution as our ordinary sensory capacities developed. Another observer has suggested that a loss in the capacity for extrasensory perception accompanies the loss of innocence that inevitably occurs in the process of growing up. Thus, preschool children are considered more likely to exhibit ESP than are older children since the young have "greater extrasensory rapport" with their parents and can often express aloud parental thoughts and feelings. To some inves-

24

tigators, ESP is viewed as a perfectly normal capacity—but one that diminishes as life's harsh realities begin to intrude upon the individual.

Theories about the origin of ESP are highly speculative; and, of course, there is a larger degree of skepticism in the scientific community about whether ESP even exists in the first place. These scientific doubts are not shared by the average citizen, however, and parapsychology has become a significant part of the culture of our times.

esp for everyman

Popular support for the possibility of ESP has expanded explosively among the members of recent generations seeking new answers to age-old problems. Sensationalized books on ESP have exploited and further expanded this renewed fascination with extrasensory phenomena. One such book offers "a battery of mind-blowing scientific experiments designed to reveal the psychic forces in you!" The author insists that the results from such "scientific" explorations "can be more solid than those achieved with a battery of computers." The claims of this and other popularized accounts of ESP are suspiciously extravagant. Another book, for example, claims that "everyday, thousands of people show uncanny ESP abilities—and don't even realize it." Such books imply that the capacity for ESP is an ability common to us all and is not limited to famous clairvoyants or any select group. Thus, if ESP is not welcomed in the halls of science, it can at least be used for party games; one might plan an "ESP bee" in which the player sits down when he cannot guess the color of a card drawn at random from the deck. The last remaining player, by virtue of having been the last to miss, might put on a special demonstration of his exceptional capacity for ESP.

As writer Martin Ebon has suggested, you can do ESP experiments on your own, using simple experimental materials. Take, for example, 20 playing cards (5 of each suit); shuffle the cards; place them face down on the table; remove one card at a time and guess which card was removed. Record the guess; compare it with the actual card drawn; and then compare the results against chance (a distribution of hits and misses that could have happened by accident). Tables such as the following allow you to calculate the odds.

No. of guesses	Chance score	20 to 1 odds	100 to 1 odds
100	25 correct	34 correct	36 correct
200	50 correct	62 correct	65 correct
300	75 correct	90 correct	93 correct

What if your experiments were to exceed the laws of chance but in a negative direction? ESP researchers regularly report that some subjects consistently score significantly below chance expectations. The researchers insist this may be considered as clear an indication of ESP as a high score of correct "hits." In other words, people who score below chance unconsciously use their ESP to perceive what the correct answer is, but they block out the proper answer and give an incorrect one. Obviously, such assertions are difficult either to prove or disprove.

the scientific controversy

In the late nineteenth century, a group of scholars at Cambridge University in England organized the Society for Psychical Research and undertook a systematic investigation of supernatural events. This organization and its counterpart, The American Society for Psychical Research, soon acquired a reputation for hardheaded, objective evaluations of reported phenomena. Several standard references espousing the cause of parapsychology now exist. In particular, the reader might see G. Murphy's book, *The Challenge of Psychical Research;* J. B. Rhine and J. G. Pratt's *Parapsychology: Frontier Science of the Mind;* and J. B. Rhine's *Parapsychology Today.* In addition Louisa Rhine in *ESP in Life and Lab* has assembled more than 12,000 reports by laymen of parapsychological experiences.

The psychologist Helmholtz (1821–1894) stated many years ago a sentiment that still seems evident among present-day psychologists. When asked in the late 1800s what evidence would convince him of the reality of extrasensory phenomena, Helmholtz replied that neither the testimony of all the members of the British Association for the Advancement of Science nor what he saw with his own eyes would convince him of telepathy. To Helmholtz, extrasensory phenomena were manifestly impossible. ESP has never lost this taint of scientific unrespectability, and the few hardy psychologists who continue to believe have had to swim upstream throughout their professional careers.

Gardner Murphy is one of the few psychologists who display the exceptional tenacity necessary to study an unpopular topic. Writing in a 1963 book entitled *Taboo Topics,* Murphy confesses that, "As a matter of fact, I have had the pertinacity to persist for more than forty years in examining these phenomena, during which time the phenomena have increasingly proved to be out of touch with all basic, decent, scientific modes of thought." The taboos that apply to the study of parapsychological phenomena today are reinforced by professional derision, academic dismissal, or, even worse, bemused toleration by one's peers. As the psychologist J. B. Rhine says "Parapsychology is treated like a ragged little urchin tagging along, an urchin Psychology doesn't want to be photographed with."

Psychologists are expending very little scientific effort on ESP. If a diligent, honest, and dedicated psychological scholar enters the laboratory today to test parapsychological claims scientifically, he must bear up under accusations of being a charlatan, stage magician, or amateur pretender to scientific status. The parapsychologist can expect little support or recognition from fellow psychologists. A survey conducted more than 20 years ago concluded that fewer than 3 percent of all psychologists felt ESP was an established fact and as many as 10 percent believed ESP was impossible. There is little likelihood that the attitudes of psychologists have changed since then. As one observer recently noted, "A glance at the Psychological Abstracts indicates that by the criterion of number of published articles, parapsychology is only a minor topic; and ESP is only one of its subtopics."

THE PROS AND THE CONS

Because so many diverse and barely understood influences act on normal sensory perceptions, it seems to believers only a small speculative leap to the possibility that some human perceptions do not require traditional forms of sense organ stimulation. Psychologists, however, have grouped forces, with heat and passion, to deny the reasonableness of this position.

Those who argue most vehemently against ESP insist that this so-called phenomenon is no different than the superstitious beliefs of all primitive and nonliterate people and that scientific inquiry into the nature of ESP is of no more value than the ghost hunting that has preoccupied unscientific man for centuries. Most American psychologists barely maintain an open mind to the issue. They are willing to become believers only if confronted with an inescapable, incontrovertible body of absolutely undeniable evidence—a "scientific" prerequisite they seldom apply stringently to the many personal convictions and persuasions they endorse in other spheres of their professional life.

Believers consider the demand for this degree of scientific rigidity excessive and unrealistic. One believer in extrasensory phenomena is R. A. McConnell, a biophysicist long active in parapsychological studies. McConnell questions the credibility of scientists of all sorts. He insists that no one has the necessary know-how to determine whether our trusted fellow scientists are perpetrating a fraud or social hoax in "respectable" research. Most social scientists, however, seem to have reached such a conclusion about ESP experimenters. McConnell points to the example of scientific belief about meteorites before the year 1800. The reasoning of the scientists of that day was impeccable. There are no stones in the sky, so how can stones fall out of the sky? As we know, this thoughtful, seemingly rational conclusion was a common-sense mistake; it follows that we have no way of knowing what other logical mistakes our modern textbooks contain. Our present-day knowledge simply does not give us an easy way to judge the accuracy of belief or disbelief in ESP.

As McConnell has regretfully concluded,"Most of this research on ESP has been done by people who were not psychologists. From this fact and from the usual psychology textbook treatment of the subject as well as from private discussion, we know that psychologists are *not* interested in ESP. This raises a question—: Why are psychologists not interested in ESP?" Some scientists have provided answers to this question: For one, it is easier to demonstrate something that is highly plausible than it is to find adequate evidence for something that is implausible. Supporting evidence for plausible findings comes from many directions, while the implausible finding must hang upon the slender thread of nonrandomness until certain systematic relationships can be found. The very implausibility of the idea of ESP (given the state of modern psychological knowledge) is enough to deter most social scientists from choosing this area of knowledge as the target for a scientific life.

Perhaps what psychologists fear, according to their critics, is finding themselves in a position similar to that of the seventeenth-century church fathers who compelled Galileo to renounce his conviction that the sun was the center of the solar system. Although the scientific burden of proof belongs to those who put forth the hypothesis (not those who are expected to believe), it has been evident that, with regard to ESP, something akin to bigotry exists among psychologists. For the typical psychologist, dabbling in implausible parapsychology is a high-risk venture best fueled with the high octane of rebelliousness and antiestablishment sentiment. The one who does choose to venture needs to see himself as an undaunted pursuer of truth, an independent thinker, and a mystic searcher who goes beyond science as we know it. For those of us who do not possess this particular combination of personality traits, ESP is a professional dead-end street.

THE STATISTICAL CASE

The discovery of reliably sensitive ESP subjects is rare. Between 1938 and 1954 (despite active research in the field) no such subject appeared in America. In England researchers would credit only three persons with the capacity to maintain their ESP ability over a sustained period of time. Even this "sustained" ability often was a marginal one—the ability, for example, to guess 7 out of 25 ESP cards correctly compared to the chance expectation of 5 out of 25 correct. This is an exceptionally thin margin of scientific safety upon which to base extended theorizing about the existence of forces unknown to man.

The conclusions from parapsychological experimentation most often rest on statistical evidence, but, when parapsychological experimenters fail to confirm their hypotheses, they may manipulate their statistics in ways that lack scientific credibility. Although scientists are trained not to twist nature's arm in order to make it conform to personal beliefs, among parapsychologists this admonition has at times gone unheeded.

Let us consider an experiment performed in parapsychologist J. B. Rhine's laboratory at Duke University. Rhine was trying to determine whether a subject might, through some combination of ESP and will power, influence the positions of cards in a mechanical shuffler. In all, 50 persons predicted the order in which cards would come out of the mechanical shuffler ten days later. The experiment was performed carefully and in more than 50,000 trials the results were at chance level—just 11 hits in excess of expectation. This seeming failure was deemed unacceptable, and further statistical analyses were made. Two more of these analyses (based on the division of the trials into segments) failed to yield significant results, but a fourth analysis (based on a complex statistic called a covariance of salience ratio) finally produced a better than chance effect. As other scientists have commented, "When belief in bizarre effects is carried this far, it is no wonder that the unconvinced scientist begins to question the statistics, even though all the computations are accurate." Psychologists are naturally suspicious of any research findings in which additional experimental sophistication and better experimental control result in a decrease, rather than an increase, in significant results. In the case of parapsychology, a steady loss of consistency in research findings has been demonstrated over time.

Another unsettling observation stems from the work of psychologist Gertrude Schmeidler and biophysicist R. A. McConnell. They separated research subjects into the two categories of sheep (believers in ESP) and goats (nonbelievers in ESP). Their findings showed that in experiments the sheep regularly scored beyond chance expectation, while the goats scored with equal consistently at, or a little below, chance expectation. This discovery led to a frenzy of scientific review, criticism, and analysis during the late 1950s. To the many goats among professional psychologists, these research findings suggested that the study of ESP (traditionally conducted almost exclusively by sheep) had been unwittingly biased in its design, execution, recording, and analyses. The sheep, of course, held views to the contrary. This scientific debate raged for a while and then subsided—unresolved, as most great debates are. By the 1960s the arena of conflict was abandoned by most of the combatants, leaving only a few die-hards flailing in all directions. Although the parapsychological statistical case is much more complicated than the brief and biased account presented here, hopefully we have underscored the complex emotions that ESP stirs up among scientists who must decide which side of the fence they are going to sit on.

THE PROBLEM OF REPLICATION

To a scientist such as research psychologist J. C. Crumbaugh, the statistical argument is futile, since it begins with the premise that ESP exists and its proof awaits only some demonstration of the human capacity to violate the laws of mathematical expectancy. Crumbaugh feels that an experimental reply is the only solution to a crucial question that must be answered before the great bulk of scientists will swing over to acceptance of the ESP hypothesis. The question is why ESP experimenters have failed to produce a truly *repeatable* experiment which can be replicated in any laboratory with the same results. Repeatability has always been the cornerstone of sound methodology in all experimental sciences, but it has yet to be accomplished by parapsychologists.

In Crumbaugh's experience only 25 to 50 percent of the experimental replications attempted in parapsychological experiments have been successful. In addition, he criticizes the tendency among parapsychologists to allow research to be conducted by persons without adequate scientific training. Crumbaugh also deplores the practice of failing to report experimental instances in which disconfirming results were obtained. In his own research in parapsychology, he reports meeting with almost constant negative results; over the years, he has been startled to learn that reports which made the most convincing case for ESP were conducted and published by researchers whose reputations among working parapsychologists were less than trustworthy. Crumbaugh has concluded that scientists cannot possibly decide the merits of the case for ESP solely on the basis of published reports of its success—a conclusion that reflects precisely the view of most psychologists.

Obviously, if extrasensory perceptions exist in meaningful intensity, some of the ideas we hold most precious in psychology will become somewhat doubtful. We would for example, have to rethink the trustworthiness of some of our experimental findings involving interactions between two human beings. The reality of ESP would not make all the psychological efforts of the last century a total loss, however. Even the most ardent believer in ESP is unwilling to suggest that this talent is distributed equally among all human beings. To the contrary, believers have always stressed the extraordinary capacities of a "gifted" few, while maintaining that most persons seem dulled to this class of barely understood sensations. Thus, past experiments involving human subjects would not all be rendered invalid by the existence of this mysterious force in so few people.

the esp revival

Scientific concern about experimental evidence has had almost no impact on the younger members of our society seeking answers to the riddle of life. ESP and several varieties of occult experience thrill the young and offer hope that life is not really what it appears to be. This romantic attachment to the occult is symptomatic of the crisis the young face. In other times, such a widespread retreat from reality would have been considered pathological. But these present-day symptoms resemble desperate attempts to discern order in apparent chaos.

A massive cultural shift in attitude and feeling on the part of the elite, white, middle-class college students has revived these dormant issues and infused them with life once again. Thus, the revitalized concern with ESP is occurring along new and less scientific lines. Experience and feeling are being accorded a higher priority than that given to cognitive and statistical "facts." Emotions and intuition have been infused with a new importance, and sometimes drug-induced visions are credited with revealing the underlying truth of a situation. Thus, for some, the nature of reality rests on a kind of evidence that is alien to the halls of science.

This sudden resurgence of interest in astrology, witchcraft, ESP, palmistry, hypnosis, and so forth, can in part be attributed to the predictability with which every generation reinvents the wheel, convinced that it is the first to have done so. This recent interest in occultism may be a psychological reaction which occurs when a generation discovers that Santa Claus is a myth. When the beliefs and convictions that sustained and nourished previous generations begin to disintegrate, the young reach for supernatural guidance in their search for new ways to assemble the puzzle of life. This return to the irrational may well dissipate if our social reality assumes a more rational form. Hopefully, interest in ESP will wane when new purpose and meaning appear. Perhaps, as Gardner Murphy has so wisely observed, "The evidence tends to suggest that the normal and the paranormal are as a rule found under somewhat different conditions; the paranormal does not appear if the normal is doing its work well." Ideally, the 1980s will witness a return to reality—and a reality as defined by social scientists.

hypnosis

3

Thanks to Hollywood's brand of sensationalism, for many of us hypnosis suggests images of sinister figures with piercing eyes bent on enslaving someone's mind for some evil purpose. As one observer has stated: "The execution of posthypnotic suggestions by an unwitting subject, the unusual memory feats of the hypnotized patient, the reexperiencing of childhood behavior under hypnotic regression, the denial of pain under hypnosis, and the demonstration of hypnotic hallucinations strike the uninitiated as magical, as supernatural." The mysterious aura that surrounds hypnosis is rooted deeply in its long association with malevolent, supernatural forces. Skin anesthesia (demonstrated by sticking pins in hypnotized subjects who have been told they will feel no pain) was considered by some early Christians to be *stigmata diaboli* (the devil's marks) that identified people who were possessed by the devil; hypnotic phenomena of all sorts were believed to be signs of possession by the devil. Indeed, the fear that supernatural forces will gain control of the mind has always flourished in religion and superstition.

A wild assortment of myths has surrounded hypnosis. Many people thought that only unintelligent, weak-minded, or emotionally unstable persons could be easily hypnotized, and it was believed that continuous exposure to hypnotic influence would destroy the subject's free will. On this point, we can be reassured by the words of F. L. Marcuse, a psychologist specialized in hypnosis: "No evidence whatsoever has been found to support this point of view. Individuals who have been deeply hypnotized over 500 times have shown no harmful effects as a consequence of their repeated hypnotic experience."

Despite the fact that hypnosis appears to produce profound effects on behavior, psychologists and other professionals have neglected its study. In a way, this neglect is an historical accident. Physicians first used hypnosis as an anesthetic but discarded it as soon as more efficient chemical means were perfected. Freud initially relied upon hypnosis to assist his patients in recalling early traumatic experiences, but he also abandoned the technique in favor of the method of free association. During these early years, in the hands of charlatans, stage magicians, and entertainers, hypnosis acquired an increasingly bad name, becoming too controversial for conventional scientists. In the present analysis, we shall try to dispel the cloud of mystery surrounding hypnosis by tracing its origins, examining the phenomenon itself, and exploring its contribution to human psychology.

the evolution of hypnosis

The word *hypnosis* is from Greek and means sleep. The history of its application to human problems is several thousand years old.

Ancient records indicate priests used suggestion as one of many therapeutic tools in the fourth century B. C. The history of hypnosis in more recent times begins with the fascinating, but controversial, work of Franz Anton Mesmer (1734–1815), an Austrian doctor best described as an odd mixture of saint and sinner. To quote Marcuse's account, Mesmer was a man who "spoke of animal magnetism (an emanating fluid, visible to some!), of universial fluids, of the proper distributions of these fluids in the healthy body, of the magnetization of inanimate material such as wood, metal, and water, of the importance of bodily stroking (passes), of the influence of the planets on man, and of many other strange and mysterious things." To Mesmer, there was only one universal disease—the obstruction of the free flow of animal magnetism and its consequent improper distribution throughout the body. His theory became a fad, and for the sake of efficiency, he began to treat patients in groups assembled around a *baquet,* or tub of magnetized water with iron rods protruding from it. Mesmer was finally forced to abandon his lucrative practice and leave Paris following an investigation by a royal commission of his peers.

Serious investigation of animal magnetism was initiated in England in the 1830s by another controversial physician, John Elliotson (1791–1868). When Elliotson's colleagues would not permit him to continue experimentation with mesmerism in the hospital he resigned in anger. He paid a heavy price for his faith in animal magnetism; he was ostracized by the medical profession, and his career was ruined.

In the 1840s a Scottish physician and surgeon named James Braid (1795–1860) began experimenting with mesmerism on his friends and concluded that the phenomenon was actually "nervous sleep" or neurohypnotism. He discounted theories of mysterious fluids coursing through the body and described hypnosis as a combination of physiological and psychological mechanisms such as the power of suggestion and the role of intense mental concentration. At the same period a Scottish surgeon named James Esdaile (1808–1859) used mesmerism (or hypnosis) to perform more than 1000 minor and 300 major operations in India. His work was the moving force behind the establishment of several mesmeric hospitals in the United Kingdom. At this moment in history, however, chemical anesthesia was discovered, and the less reliable mesmeric techniques were soon abandoned.

In the last quarter of the nineteenth century, scientific interest in hypnosis was rekindled in France by the work of the distinguished neurologist Jean-Martin Charcot (1829–1893). Even his considerable genius, however, did not lead him to the correct theoretical path. Charcot concluded that hypnosis was a pathological state much like an hysterical attack. His erroneous conclusions were due to a mixture of observational error, the unfortunate selection of subjects from a population of hysterical patients, and stereotyped behavior by patients who had learned to react in the way they thought hypnotized persons were supposed to act. In the winter of 1895–96, Freud studied with Charcot and tried hypnosis on his patients. Freud was attempting to remove symptoms, and he was also seeking, in the memories of his patients, the traumatic event that was believed to have caused the symptoms in the first place. Not all of Freud's patients could be hypnotized, and some of those whose symptoms had been removed through hypnosis soon redisplayed the symptoms or had them replaced by a new set of symptomatic disorders. Faced with these problems, Freud abandoned hypnosis as a therapeutic tool.

the nature of hypnosis

As will be seen, hypnosis is a broad field of inquiry, offering interested students many different avenues of thought and experience, yet to be adequately explored. In the present section, we shall review some of these areas. One topic over which much confusion still exists is animal hypnotism. Although there seems to be a resemblance between hypnosis in animals and in human beings, the similarity is a superficial one. Other topics to be covered here are susceptibility to hypnosis, induction of the trance state, and phenomena such as age-regression and certain physiological effects.

ANIMAL HYPNOSIS

What is called animal hypnosis is an immobility, lasting from seconds to hours, that can be induced in a variety of species of animals including the horse, lion, octopus, lizard, guinea pig, chicken, cockroach, rat, frog, snake, and monkey. The literature on animal hypnosis spans 40 species and more than 300 years of recorded observations of trance-like behavior in animals. Darwin interpreted this immobility as an adaptive response which is made for the purpose of survival; in other words, animals feign death to escape attack from predators.

The phenomena of animal hypnosis are familiar to anyone in close contact with animals. When chickens are lain on their sides, they will stare fixedly at a chalk line drawn away from their beaks; frogs will remain passive when placed on their backs and their stomachs stroked; rabbits will become immobile when suddenly upended and then firmly held down; and, of course, possums will play possum. Four principal methods can produce hypnotic-like reactions in animals —restraint, pressure on body parts, repetition of stimuli, and inversion of the animal. One common method in all such "hypnosis" seems to be restraint of movement (by hand, in a harness, or by hooding a bird's eyes). The hypnotic state can be terminated by the animal itself or by any of a variety of external stimuli (a loud noise, electric shock, and so on).

Over the years, theoretical explanations of animal hypnosis have ranged from conceptualizing it as a reflex that inhibits brain function to viewing it as a kind of paralysis induced by fear. One investigator who reviewed the research on animal hypnosis concluded that this trance-like response is most often produced by an apparently threatening stimulus (usually restraint). First, the animal struggles to escape. When escape fails, immobility and unresponsiveness are the only remaining alternatives for the animal, and an hypnotic-like state results.

SUSCEPTIBILITY TO HYPNOSIS

Some of us are more susceptible to hypnosis than others. An effortless response to hypnotic suggestion seems to have its origin in the early childhood experiences that establish our basic psychological make-up. Some researchers theorize that being a good hypnotic subject requires the capacity to become deeply involved in imaginative experiences of any and all kinds and that this capacity is learned from parents who are themselves so inclined. Another experience which may lead to a susceptibility to hypnosis is enduring severe punishment in childhood. Scientists conjecture that a history of punishment may produce hypnotizability in two ways. First, a habit of automatic and unquestioned obedience may be instilled, and, second, a tendency to escape harassment by entering a realm of imagination may develop, thereby instilling the dissociations that are later used in hypnosis.

Being willing and able to be hypnotized also depends on personal motivation and an understanding of what being hypnotized means to the individual. For some persons, being hypnotized is simply one more expression of an exhibitionistic style of life in which anything will be done to keep the social spotlight focused on the self. For others, hypnotic susceptibility may reflect the passive need to be dominated and controlled. If the hypnotist is viewed as a powerful and awesome figure, surrendering one's self to his influence may be a way to share indirectly a part of his strength and power. If susceptibility to the "powers" of the hypnotist involves such a deeply personal psychological relationship, it is not surprising that hypnotists do not always agree about who will or will not be susceptible to hypnosis.

THE INDUCTION OF HYPNOSIS

Many years ago I and another psychology student, Paul Sparer, attempted to automate the process of hypnosis by recording the induction of the trance state on long-playing records. (In that day, each record was a cumbersome 16 inches in diameter.) The hypnotic "spiel" was recorded by a professional actor; after the subject was hypnotized, control of the trance state was transferred to the researcher, who could then conduct a series of experiments with the hypnotized person. The "hypnotic record" was also used successfully to induce hypnosis in small groups of persons. Traditionally, however, the induction of hypnosis is a less mechanical and much more personal relationship between two persons ready to play their prescribed roles. The process has been described as follows:

> ... The hypnotist creates the conditions for entering hypnosis by any of a number of methods that relax the subject, exercise his imagination, and lead him to relinquish some control to the hypnotist and to accept some reality distortion. A common method is for the hypnotist to ask the subject to fix his eyes upon some small target, such as a thumbtack on the wall, concentrate on the target, detach his thoughts from other things, and gradually become relaxed or sleepy. The suggestion of sleep is a convenient one because it is familiar as being a relaxed state, out of touch with ordinary environmental demands.

In the hypnotic state, the hypnotized subject appears to abandon the planning function he exercises in his everyday life and passively attends to the hypnotist's instructions. This seems to occur partly because the subject selectively focuses on the hypnotist's voice and suspends his usual tendency to examine critically the reality of what is happening to him. The subject willingly accepts reality distortions (hallucinations, illusions, improbable beliefs, and so on) as a consequence of his heightened suggestibility.

While there is great diversity in the techniques and circumstances of inducing hypnosis, a common element is the hypnotist's ability to manipulate the subject, making him compliant and responsive to suggestions. Suggestions of relaxation are particularly common since relaxation allows the subject to retreat from other sources of stimulation and focus attention on the suggestions made by the hypnotist. The hypnotist commonly asks the subject to act and react in unusual ways, and this feat is best accomplished when the subject is disconnected from his usual view of reality. Thus, most hypnotists have their subjects close their eyes to eliminate distracting visual stimulation that might interfere with concentration.

The reasons for individual differences in susceptibility to hypnosis are still a matter of speculation and theoretical inference. In one investigation, for example, researchers were struck by the fact that the conditions surrounding induction of hypnosis seem very much like those used in experiments involving perceptual and sensory deprivation. Following this lead, other investigators exposed ten persons who had initially resisted hypnosis to six hours in a sensory deprivation cubicle. Approximately one week later another attempt was made to induce hypnosis in each of the subjects. The experimental subjects who had been perceptually deprived were reported to be significantly more susceptible to the induction of hypnosis, when compared with a control group. Apparently, then, by simply reducing sight and sound to a minimal level in a perceptual deprivation cubicle, an individual's resistance to hypnosis can be changed. Furthermore, this change was shown to persist for at least a week following the experience of perceptual deprivation.

The erroneous notions most of us have about how persons are hypnotized are based on exaggerated versions of the event shown in movies, on stage, and on television. Stage hypnotists rely on waking suggestibility more than they do on hypnosis and achieve their effect by dramatically defining the situation as hypnotic as much as they do by actually inducing hypnosis. The important fact to keep in mind is that the trance state is a result of psychological processes occurring within the individual rather than an outcome of actions by the hypnotist.

HYPNOTIC PHENOMENA

Reference is frequently made to the apparent similarity between hypnosis and other shifting states of consciousness each of us normally experience (day dreaming, hypnosis of the road while driving, and so on). This analogy, however, is a forced one; these states of consciousness are similar but hardly identical. The phenomena of hypnosis are substantially more varied. Almost every motive, attitude, belief, or behavior can apparently be manipulated during this altered state of consciousness—physical feelings, moods, awareness, and response to physiological experiences can all be altered under hypnosis. While in the hypnotized state, posthypnotic suggestions can be made that will be followed long after the subject has returned to a normal state. In one case, a posthypnotic suggestion was reportedly carried out five years later.

The full range of hypnotic phenomena cannot be detailed in the limited space here, but for purposes of illustration hypnotic age-regression can be discussed and some of the physiological effects of hypnosis can be described.

HYPNOTIC AGE-REGRESSION.   When subjects are hypnotized and told they will return psychologically to an earlier time in their life, they may manifest behavior that seems appropriate to that age and stage of their existence. This age-regression, however, may be more apparent than real and could be an instance of creative role playing in which an adult acts the part of a young person.

Obviously, no adult can completely reinstate the condition of his infancy or childhood, but a number of researchers have attempted to prove that the phenomenon is "time regression" by searching for physiological responses known to be present only at certain stages of life. Hypnotized subjects have been instructed to regress to the first few months of life, but when this occurs experimenters have not been able to demonstrate that EEG (electroencephalogram) or brain wave patterns undergo a corresponding shift toward an infant-like stage. In studying age-regression, subjects have been asked and have reportedly answered with startling accuracy questions such as the day of the week their birthdays occurred at ages four, ten, and seven. In most cases, however, these original findings have not been confirmed by subsequent studies. Researchers have used optical illusions (which are responded to differently at different ages), intelligence tests standardized for levels of performance at different ages, drawing tests, and ink-blot (Rorschach) tests to probe the meaning of hypnotic age-regression, but the total scientific yield has thus far been less than convincing.

A reasonable summary of the present state of hypnotic age-regression would seem to be as follows. When told to regress, a good hypnotic subject vividly imagines what it was like at the designated age and tends to behave in a convincing, childlike manner. Such persons are capable of equally convincing performances without the aid of hypnosis. They can be hypnotically progressed to age 70 or 80 or returned hypnotically to before birth in the womb. Few reputable theorists would suggest that hypnosis can probe the future accurately, and, of course, we have no way to attest to the reality of life before birth. At this moment in scientific history, we can only conclude that age-regression is a fascinating topic but hardly a reliable fact.

THE PHYSIOLOGICAL EFFECTS OF HYPNOSIS. If a quality of magic characterizes hypnosis, it is most visible in the exceptional range of physiological alterations that seem to accompany it. Unquestionably, a wide variety of physiological functions can be influenced by hypnotic suggestion. The heart can be accelerated or decelerated; functional color blindness can be induced; subjective deafness can be produced; emotions and their bodily manifestations can be evoked; the reaction to sweet or sour substances can be depressed; the rate of salivation can be increased or decreased; visual activity can be improved; reaction to painful stimulation can be suppressed; objects can be made invisible; and even allergic reactions can be suppressed. The list is endless. Through hypnosis imaginary pain can be made to appear; labor in pregnant women can be induced or inhibited; skin temperature can be changed; blood-glucose levels can be modified; gastric secretion can be increased or decreased; cold sores and blister can be made to appear; and warts can even be removed. Yet, despite this massive evidence of the peculiarities of hypnosis some theorists remain unimpressed. On the basis of comparisons between hypnotic inductions and direct, waking suggestion, they insist that these startling mind-body interactions can be elicited with or without hypnosis—if individuals who have a natural, easy access to the physiological systems involved are carefully selected. We know, for example, that certain persons respond to stress and interpersonal pressure by displaying psychosomatic symptoms; they have, throughout their lives, found the path between emotion and physiology easily available whether hypnotized or not. Unquestionably, hypnosis has provided us with an invaluable tool for the exploration of the mysterious and uncharted regions of mind-body interaction. At the same time, the hypnotic state has probably been oversold as the only route to comprehending the little understood nature of psychological man.

hypnosis and morality

The aspect of hypnosis most frightening to the average person is the possibility that the subject will lose self-control and the ability to resist demands of an evil hypnotist. The issue of the moral limits of hypnotic control has been debated vigorously over the last three decades. The continuing question is whether we can be induced through hypnosis to humiliate or injure ourselves or to commit crimes revolting to our conscience. Dramatic instances of immoral and antisocial behavior while hypnotized have been reported. In the notorious Heidelberg case, a young lady gave money to her hypnotist, engaged in sexual relations with him and with his friends, and made several attempts on her own as well as her husband's life. One report tells of a subject induced to rob a bank and captured only after he had killed two men. In another case, a schoolteacher was induced to shoot himself after committing criminal acts.

After a careful review of the experimental literature dealing with evil uses of hypnosis, one researcher concluded there was little reliable evidence supporting the notion that anyone would engage in antisocial behavior that was clearly contrary to his or her wishes. In cases where hypnosis was apparently used to stimulate criminal activity, it was found that an intense emotional relationship existed between hypnotist and subject. The existence of such a relationship throws doubt on the role of hypnosis, since the consequent behavior, whether criminal or not, can be explained as the attempts on the part of one individual to please another.

Evaluating such bizarre stories scientifically is difficult, but a rough attempt has been made in which hypnotized subjects were instructed either to throw nitric acid at a research assistant or handle an apparently deadly poisonous snake. The subjects complied without hesitation. Other researchers have tested to see whether hypnotized persons would risk injury to themselves or commit antisocial acts. During the trance state, the hypnotized subjects were informed that they would be unable to resist the hypnotist's suggestions. Subjects were than ordered to pick up a harmless but wicked looking lizard in their bare hands, to remove a coin from concentrated nitric acid, and to throw acid in the face of the experimenter. In each instance, the real risk of damage was eliminated, unbeknownst to the subjects. The hypnotized persons followed the instructions to the letter.

As dramatic as these reports may be, the experimenters made the even more interesting observation that nearly identical compliant behavior can be elicited from persons who are not hypnotized. Acting the role of a hypnotized person is not after all, a particularly difficult task since the nature of hypnotic phenomena is widely known. It is probably not possible to make a truly valid laboratory test of the issue of morality and hypnosis under controlled experimental conditions. Had some hypnotist managed to induce unmistakably antisocial behavior in hypnotized subjects in a laboratory setting (senseless murder, for example), he would hardly be willing to confess such an ethical and legal violation by publishing it in the scientific literature! One may also reasonably assume that if the researcher fervently believes antisocial behavior *cannot* be induced under hypnosis, he may subtly transmit cues to his subjects that contradict his consciously given suggestions. The subject may please the investigator by producing behavior he knows the experimenter really wants. The hypnotized person is not just the passive recipient of the wishes of the hypnotist; he is an active participant who continuously interprets what the hypnotist has in mind. Thus, two scientists may report quite different findings, although each has applied carefully controlled experimental procedures.

the dissident theorists

During the major part of the history of psychology, hypnosis was assumed to be an altered state of consciousness, and psychologists invested most of their efforts in exploring the details of this condition and theorizing about the dynamic mental mechanisms that might account for it. For some, hypnosis is a vague and confusing term referring to a wide range of altered states of consciousness. Hypnosis is not a clearly defined condition even though many investigators have used the term as if there were general agreement about its exact meaning. One scientist maintains that a careful examination of the variability from subject to subject and from laboratory to laboratory suggests that there are probably several kinds of altered states of consciousness produced by the "induction of hypnosis." Differing internal experiences can have similar external manifestations and that has contributed to our confusion about what hypnosis is.

In recent years, there has been a growing criticism of psychodynamic explanations and an insistence that "hypnotic" phenomena are not uniquely different from "normal" behaviors. Among the most outspoken critics is Theodore Xenophon Barber who, with his co-workers, has launched a series of attacks on traditional views of hypnosis. Barber maintains that both the popular and professional literature have created the mistaken notion that a unique condition called the hypnotic trance really exists. He contends, however, "There is almost no scientific support for it. It has been assumed that the hypnotic-trance state is real—that there is some reliable way to tell whether a person is hypnotized or not, some simple physiological measure—brain waves, eye movements, pulse rate or galvanic skin response, for example—that would clearly distinguish a hypnotized person from a normally awake person. Unfortunately there is no such test."

The critical issue for Barber is the fact that, although hypnotists have claimed to be able to produce or inhibit allergic reactions and labor contractions, improve vision or to change heartbeat rates, evidence shows that the same effects can be obtained in about the same proportion of subjects by suggestion alone *when no attempt is made to induce hypnosis.* Barber's position is that if hypnotic phenomena can be produced in the waking state then we have no need for the vague theoretical construction called hypnosis.

While Barber is probably the most outspoken critic of hypnosis, other theorists have questioned some of the psychological conclusions reached in the past. In 1960 and 1961, for example, one researcher observed that persons who reported they felt no pain while hypnotized still displayed the physiological responses usually associated with the experience of pain. The conclusion was that hypnotic subjects must be deluding themselves psychologically. Perhaps, then, hypnosis itself is no more than a calculated delusion—a psychological pretense that requires no mysterious trance-state for an explanation.

Finally, two other investigators suggested that hypnosis can be explained by role-playing behavior—that is, behavior that follows the traditional laws of imagination, expectant attention, and heightened motivation. It is not felt that the hypnotized person fakes the trance state; rather, the difference between hypnosis and the waking, suggestible state is believed to be in the degree to which an individual can involve himself in playing the role of the hypnotized person. For working hypnotists, this theoretical argument is highly academic since they know that something called *hypnosis* happens under special circumstances in the relationship between two persons. These phenomena may be "no more than" a degree or extension of what can be attained in the normal waking state, but the incontrovertible fact remains that startling patterns of behavior can and do issue from the simple transaction of one person talking to another. Whatever its source, hypnosis is a challenging and yet little known phenomenon.

hypnosis and therapy

When hypnosis was first used in therapy, direct suggestion was most often employed. Patients were hypnotized and told that their symptoms would disappear or at least cease to be disturbing. The apparent difficulty with this method was that most hypnotic cures were not permanent and suggestions had to be repeated at frequent intervals under hypnosis. The height of interest in hypnotic therapy was in the 1890s and early 1900s, but professional involvement sharply declined by the 1920s. As Robert White, author of a standard work on abnormal psychology, has stated:

> As we look back on this rise and decline of hypnotic therapy it is easy to see what was the matter. The whole thing was conceived too much along the line of a doctor giving medicine to a patient. . . . The hypnotist gave doses of suggestion, he implanted ideas in the patient's mind, he set certain automatisms in motion. Such concepts are inappropriate, we realize today, for describing the known facts about hypnotism. Hypnotic behavior is produced by the patient, not forced upon him by the hypnotist.

The principal drawback to the use of hypnosis in therapy today is (as it always has been) the fact that not everyone is hypnotizable, nor are all persons equally susceptible to hypnosis. Despite this limitation, some therapists still use hypnotherapy as a technical aid and one aspect of a larger, comprehensive therapeutic plan. Thus, for example, when the therapeutic goal is to bring the patient temporary relief of symptoms, direct posthypnotic suggestion may be used. The patient is hypnotized and told he will be free of his symptoms when he recovers from the trance. Often, psychological symptoms do disappear after hypnosis, and in some instances even symptoms with an organic basis have been altered. Posthypnotic suggestion has been used to relieve pain during childbirth, surgical operations, and dental work.

Hypnosis may also be of diagnostic value in psychotherapy if the subject can be helped to remember events he has repressed. The therapist may be able to induce the patient to relive troublesome or terrifying experiences of the past, or the therapist may obtain information that would be useful in other aspects of the treatment. When hypnosis is used for diagnosis, the patient may be instructed to regress psychologically to the age at which the symptom first appeared and describe the circumstances surrounding its formation. By this method, symptoms may be connected with the early traumatic experience that produced them.

As a closing note it is worth reporting what is probably the most optimistic experimental therapeutic use of hypnosis ever made. It is possible, in theory at least, to assume that death is a psychosomatic condition—in other words, that the time of our death is in part determined by our attitudes and beliefs about living and dying. To test this possibility, researchers gave hypnotic suggestions to 50 undergraduate students, intimating that they would live to be at least 120 years old while maintaining full control of all their physical and mental capacities. A control group of randomly selected students were given no such suggestions. The results are not yet in, but the investigators anticipate the findings should be ready for publication by the year 2070! To sum up the shifting status of hypnosis in psychotherapy, let us quote clinical psychologist Claude Moss, who observed that it has generated "a curious, fluctuating ambivalence, resulting in a waxing and waning of enthusiasm and frequent, sometimes vitriolic, differences of opinion."

education

With the exception of sex, there has probably been no more interesting pastime over the years than criticizing our educational system. In recent times, the tempo of the assult on education and the seriousness of the accusations have escalated markedly. The attack on our schools, however, may be misguided simply because schooling comes too late in the process of development. Research on the learning process suggests that early childhood education by the parents may be both more important and more demanding than any instruction that follows. Evidence shows that half of the level of intellectual capability young people will achieve by age 17 is determined by the age of 4; another 30 percent of one's intellectual ability is predictable by 7 years of age. Thus, it may be that the issue is not really better schools but radical alternatives to the idea of school itself. To set these criticisms in perspective, let me repeat something I wrote in 1967: "What analysts of education seem regularly to overlook is that the American Public School System is a daring social experiment which may well be recorded either as a monumental failure or as the most magnificent of achievements in functional democracy. No other society has had the courage to regard education as the individual responsibility of its fifty states and, further, to accept relegation of this authority to the citizen members of more than 40,000 local school boards. We as a nation are committed to a vast social and educational experiment with our children."

In the colonial period of our history school was in the home and teaching a child a little reading and writing was enough for all practical purposes. Although schools today have professionally trained teachers, special equipment, and special buildings, it is still true that most "modern" advances in education were invented and applied 100 years ago or more. In education there seems to be surprisingly little that is new under the sun. In 1848 we began to use one teacher per grade; in 1862 we experimented with ungraded elementary schools; in 1873 there were separate tracks for brighter students; in 1888 instruction was "individualized"; in 1895 pupils were promoted to higher grades all during the school year; and in 1898 talented students were given "enriched" curricula. Work-study-play programs, ability grouping, and team-teaching are only a few of the innovations we reinvent every half century.

America once educated only an elite few who would advance beyond elementary and secondary school, but we seem now to have taken seriously the dream of education for all people. Unfortunately, the schools, the teachers, and the curriculum were never designed for all the people, and the inability of the system to adapt to these demands is perhaps at the base of our modern educational upheaval. Certainly, it is easy to be critical, and one probably sees only what one wants to see. The situation has been described with a good deal

48

of accuracy by Goodlad: "Put on one pair of glasses and the schools appear to be moving posthaste toward becoming centers of intense, exciting learning, marked by concern for the individual. Put on another, and they appear to be mired in tradition, insensitive to pressing social problems, and inadequate to the demands of learning."

For Goodlad, education should start where the students are; it should be directed toward learning how to learn and reach beyond the classroom to encompass all of life. The process should take place in a setting rich with educational materials and be adapted to individual differences. It should be flexible enough to be able to respond to the crises of the era. The sad fact is no such educational enterprise is available to most of us. The approximately 12,000 hours a child spends in school is overshadowed by the 15,000 hours he spends being informally "educated" by the television set in his home.

The educational task of every society has always been first to decide what kind of adults will best contribute to and fit into the society and second to decide how to go about producing such persons. Those who attack the present system fault it on both counts. In the following section we shall look at some of these criticisms of American education.

the critics

The list of modern-day critics who attack our educational system is seemingly endless, and a catalog of all the charges leveled against education would be an impossible task here. A fair sampling of dissident opinion, however, will be presented. In an article entitled "The Seven Deadly Myths of Education and How They Mangle the Young," D. W. Allen has discussed the damage done by certain misconceptions that have thrived in our schools.

The myth of Original Stupidity is one such fiction suggesting that children are stupid until the teacher makes them smart. A second fiction is the myth of Pure Rationality by which it is believed that the body and emotions are dangerous and must always be kept under the strict control of the mind. This myth leads to the false conclusion that education proceeds best when it can ignore the student's emotional needs. A third myth is the One Best Way, according to which the best curriculum, the best way to teach reading, or the best college program depends upon the winds of fad and fashion. The myth of Stable Knowledge perpetrates the belief that knowledge is certain, sacred, fixed, and can be gained simply by accumulation. Finally, there are the myths that all critical learning takes place in school or that learning can be a mechanical process bereft of the human touch. In the conclusion of his article, Allen states that these and a host of related myths must be dispelled if we are to humanize the educational system and make it responsive to people rather than theory.

In an article entitled "Fostering Self-Direction," A. W. Combs, another critic, contends that there is no longer a common body of information that everyone must have. According to Combs, authoritarian schools are as out of date as the horse and buggy. Such schools cannot achieve our purposes and may even contribute to our defeat. Instead of the present system, we need self-starting, self-directing citizens capable of independent actions and responses.

Learning is a unique experience and a personal matter that can be accomplished only with the cooperation and involvement of the student. Providing students with information is simply not enough. To produce self-directed students, we must believe independence is important and we must trust the human organism. If the natural basic striving of the organism is toward physical and mental health then we must experiment with ways to enhance rather than retard this urge. Combs maintains that in order to produce more self-directed people, we must give them the opportunity to practice self-direction, even if some of us must give up our traditional prerogatives. In short, Combs believes education must deal with real problems and student decisions must count.

"Emotional Barriers to Education" is the title of an article written by another critic, psychologist R. E. Farson. In this article, Farson contends that our educational system is confronted with a new set of human values and a new technology. We must change both our educational methods and our basic concepts of education. Farson states that for generations little in education has changed in any fundamental way, and our allegiance to tradition may be our undoing as we face tomorrow. Education must not be limited solely to activities that seem to involve thinking. We must develop the dimensions of the senses, our feelings, and our emotions. We must cultivate taste and judgment and an understanding of how human beings relate to one another. We seem to want creativity in the young but only if it follows all the rules. Children must not be too noisy; they must please the adults and be careful not to rock the social boat. These conditions, however, as Farson asserts, are certain to kill all creativity in our offspring.

D. P. Ausubel, an M.D. and Ph.D. psychologist, is the author of an article entitled "Some Misconceptions Regarding Mental Health Functions and Practices in the School." In this article, Ausubel focuses on the schools' responsibilities to the whole child, including personality development and the state of the child's mental health. The author suggests that educational responsibilities extend beyond the development of intellectual skills and the transmission of subject-matter knowledge. The school has these undeniable responsibilities simply

50

because it is where children spend much of their waking hours. School is the setting where children perform much of their purposeful activity, obtain a large share of their status, interact with adults and age-mates, and confront the demands of society. Ausubel argues that, since the organizational, administrative, disciplinary, and interpersonal aspects of the school environment inevitably affect the mental health and personality development of our future citizens, society would obviously benefit from arranging these matters as constructively as possible. As a professional mental health worker, however, Ausubel deplores the rigidity with which psychological difficulties are increasingly used by educators to absolve the child from any moral accountability for behavior. Contrary to some popular practices, mental health is not composed solely of warm, loving, uncritical acceptance of every behavior of the child.

In a book called *How to Survive in Your Native Land*, J. Herndon, a teacher in California ghetto schools, takes up the issue of threat and compulsion. Herndon contends that when threat is employed, one cannot be sure whether children are interested in what they are supposedly learning, whether they will actually learn, or whether they will continue to learn when the threat is withdrawn. Herndon puts it simply: "You cannot tell. You cannot tell if the kids want to come to your class or not. You can't tell if they are motivated or not. You can't tell if they learn anything or not. All you can tell is, they'd rather come to your class than go to jail."

Another recent book entitled *Celebration of Awareness: A Call for Institutional Revolution* was written by social critic I. D. Illich and deals with the inequities of our various educational systems. Illich reports that it would cost an additional 40 billion dollars a year to give every citizen of the United States the level of schooling now enjoyed by an affluent one-third of the population. But, obviously, no country is rich enough to afford this. Trying to improve the existing schools is not enough; rather, we need to question the assumptions on which the school system itself is based. If done objectively and honestly, this might mean the disappearance of schools as we know them. Illich warns us that we have made no real effort to adapt the schools to a changing society and that the schools may well be left behind as we move on.

In another book entitled *Deschooling Society*, Illich suggests we abandon schooling. This does not mean the discarding of education—but of schooling. According to Illich's definition, "schooling" makes the student confuse teaching with learning, grade advancement with education, a diploma with competence, and fluency with the ability to say something new. We worship our schools as though they were sacred cows, but schools teach us to use the wrong yardsticks for measuring the quality of life and they are failing to meet our individual needs. Our institutions of higher education have become social instruments to recruit personnel for a consumer society; some are selected to engage in the on-going competition, while others who are judged unfit to expand society in its present form are disposed of. We need alternative means of learning, acquiring skills, or becoming educated—alternative means that are outside the graded school system. In Illich's opinion, we must disestablish schools so people can learn once again and make schools totally voluntary.

P. W. Jackson, a psychologist specialized in the study of classroom learning problems, wrote an article entitled "The Student's World," in which he discusses many of the problems of our educational institutions. One of the major problems is the kind of teacher who serves as a supply sergeant for a cramped classroom, who dispenses special privileges to certain students, or who plays the role of official timekeeper of classroom life (starting, stopping, and switching activities). For the student, school may be a continuous experience of delay, denial, interruption, forming straight lines, or waiting for the teacher to check his work. Students may have some vague sense of the boredom of school, but they may find it difficult to translate their feelings into appropriate words

In a book entitled *Teaching as a Subversive Activity*, education professors N. Postman and C. Weingartner emphasize that, while constant, accelerating change is a basic fact in modern society, our educational system studiously ignores this reality. The educational establishment is not sufficiently daring or vigorous to furnish ideas for a new approach to education; it needs a kind of shock therapy if it is to abandon its present "veneration of crap." Schools need to teach children how to think and learn in the present and also throughout life. The authors of this book insist that we have devoted our attention almost exclusively to equipping the educational system with gadgets to speed up the process without asking where it is we want to go. They believe that change is requisite:

> The institution we call "school" is what it is because we made it that way. If it is irrelevant, as Marshall McLuhan says; if it shields children from reality, as Norbert Wiener says; if it educates for obsolescence, as John Gardner says; if it does not develop intelligence, as Jerome Bruner says; if it is based on fear, as John Holt says; if it avoids the promotion of significant learnings, as Carl Rogers says; if it induces alienation, as Paul Goodman says; if it punishes creativity and independence, as Edgar Friedenberg says; if, in short, it is not doing what needs to be done, it can be changed; it *must* be changed.

One final work to be mentioned here is a book by R. Gross and Beatrice Gross, entitled *Radical School Reform*. This book provides a fitting summary to the current criticism, of our educational system.

We have bungled badly in education. Not merely in the ways noted by most school critics: too little money for education, outdated curricula, poorly trained teachers. But in more fundamental ways. It isn't just that our schools fail to achieve their stated purposes, that they are not the exalted places their proponents proclaim. Rather, many are not even decent places for our children to be. They damage, they thwart, [and] they stifle children's natural capacity to learn and grow healthily.

plans for change

Criticizing the educational system along vague, abstract lines may be an engaging exercise, but it is not an adequate substitute for designing new systems which might succeed where other approaches fail. Not surprisingly, the critics outnumber the designers many times over.

One plan for change, which has been hailed by some as the best hope of American school reform is the open classroom, a concept pioneered in Britain. Indeed, much of the American reform literature is dominated by reports from British infant and primary schools. As defined by one educator, the open classroom tries to keep open as many avenues of learning as possible by letting children pursue their interests, work alone or in groups, move freely from one area to another, explore, test, and join other children and teachers.

In Harlem, Herbert Kohl put into practice his concept of an open classroom and experimented until he gradually found ways of teaching that were not based on compulsion, grades, tests, or curriculum, but on pursuing what interested the children. Kohl learned that in an open classroom the teacher must be himself, which means that if the teacher is angry he ought to express his anger; if he is annoyed at someone's behavior, he ought to express that too. According to Kohl, in an "authoritarian classroom annoying behavior is legislated out of existence. In a 'permissive' classroom the teacher pretends it isn't annoying.... In an open situation the teacher tries to express what he feels and to deal with each situation as a communal problem."

In his class a math lesson on probability theory could lead to a crap game or a study of the origins of dice. A discussion of the French Revolution might lead to a study of instruments of execution, to an examination of penal institutions, or to a consideration of how laws are used in an unjust society. Kohl learned to go with the class and to respond to the students' desires to learn about things—wherever it might lead. He became an adult resource, available if needed, but not a director, a judge, or an executioner.

The open classroom has been tried experimentally in some American cities in the past few years, but a number of experts, even those who are sympathetic to the new trend, have begun to issue storm warnings about its application. The critics point out that American theorists are notorious for trying to accomplish instant reform with a form of education that has taken many years to achieve in England. Furthermore, not everyone is convinced that a situation in which children do their own thing is inevitably constructive. Discarding the formal structure of traditional schooling will improve education only if the teachers and children have important, useful things to do with their freedom.

The so-called free schools reflect one attempt to relieve education of the strangle-hold of a rigid, oppressive curriculum. However, the average life span of such free schools has been about nine months. Jonathon Kozol, a Harvard B.A. in English and Oxford Rhodes Scholar who taught in a predominantly black school in Boston, has examined the reasons why such child-centered, open-structured, individualized education never fulfills its initial promise. In part failure has been the fate of these experiments because its zealots have begun with a "naïve, noncritical acceptance of the unexamined notion that you cannot *teach* anything. It is just not true that the best teacher is the grownup who most successfully pretends that he knows nothing or has nothing to suggest to children. It is not true, either, that the best answer to the blustering windbag teacher of the old-time public school is the free-school teacher who attempts to turn himself into a human version of an inductive fan."

It has become evident that abandoning every aspect of the public school system in favor of letting children learn if and when they are "ready" for it is a romantic dream that is little suitable for the poor, black, urban child in need of basic educational skills if he is to survive at all in our society. The young, well-educated white critic of existing educational forms is enjoying a luxury ill-affordable by the poor desperate to establish a minimal economic foothold in America.

In addition to the open classroom, other solutions to the current educational dilemma have been suggested. One solution has been proposed by education critic John Holt, who tackled the question of what steps would move American schools toward a better tomorrow. Holt has stated:

> It would be to let every child be the planner, director, and assessor of his own education, to allow and encourage him, with the inspiration and guidance of more experienced and expert people, and as much help as he asked for, to decide what he is to learn, when he is to learn it, how he is to learn it, and how well he is learning it. It would be to make our schools, instead of what they are, which is jails for children, into a resource for free and independent learning, which everyone in the community, of whatever age, could use as much or as little as he wanted.

It follows for Holt that we should abolish compulsory school attendance or at least modify it by giving children a large number of authorized absences every year. It is important to get people out of the school and give them a chance to learn what the would is all about. Surely, it is insane to try to teach young people about the world by shutting them up in brick buildings isolated from life. We need to let children work together, helping and learning from each other, especially since children are often the best teachers of other children.

Learning while teaching is a concept also advocated by A. Gartner, Mary C. Kohler, and F. Riessman, three investigators who ran a project where children taught children. These researchers report that the peer-teaching task provides reassurance and confidence for the young people who are given this opportunity to enact an adult role. When children requiring special attention are matched with those who need to learn how to assume responsibility, a rewarding, mutually beneficial relationship emerges. Along with these changes, some educators feel that the fixed, required curriculum and educational testing should be abolished since they do more harm than good by distorting and corrupting the learning process.

Some educational theorists believe we must initiate change by striking at the very root of the system—by changing the teacher-learner relationship completely. These theorists suggest that the structure of the classroom be redesigned by adopting an inquiry method of teaching and learning. A teacher who asks the question, "Who discovered America?" would answer with another question, "How do you find out who discovered America?" Thus, learning how to learn would be the major objective. Teachers would be required to practice a new stance in the classroom; they would abandon formal lesson plans, search for problems that would interest students, and listen to students rather than talk at them. As students learn to seek their own education, they will develop active, innovative, creative, and inquiring minds.

summerhill

When the book *Summerhill* was published in 1960, the author, A. S. Neill, felt its enormous impact could be attributed to the fact that the book voiced what so many young people felt but had not intellectualized or made conscious. The theme of the book was freedom in education so all could grow at their own pace, freedom from indoctrination, and freedom for children to live in their own community making their own social laws. This freedom would have abolished nearly every school subject in favor of creative pursuits such as art, music, or drama.

Writing in a foreword to Neill's book, Erich Fromm described this radical approach to education and child rearing in terms of the following principles: (a) a firm faith in the essential goodness of children; (b) a belief that education must be both emotional and intellectual and must have happiness as its aim; (c) a conviction that punishment creates fear and fear creates hostility; (d) a declaration that freedom does not mean license; (e) a belief that education must help the child cut his primary ties to parents and other authority figures if he is truly to become an individual; and (f) dedication to rearing children to become happy human beings rather than to fit into the existing social order. Neill's children at Summerhill were not required to do things they did not wish to do. No one was required to attend any classes; and they were allowed to do almost anything they wished as long as they did not infringe upon the rights of others.

Among those who took note of the Summerhill project, New England teacher E. Bernstein wondered if, given such freedom, children could ever accept the responsibilities and limits of society. Bernstein asked: "Could the products of such a permissive atmosphere adjust to the realities of life: a job, marriage, parenthood? Could they learn to cope with the authority of a traditional school?" Bernstein bought an old motor scooter and a map of London and began visiting the former Summerhill students. After having seen 50 Summerhill products, he concluded from the interviews that, although some students found Summerhill ideal, it failed to meet the needs of others. Of his interviewees, ten former students seemed to have benefitted most by acquiring the confidence and maturity needed for a fulfilling way of life. However, seven former students felt Summerhill had been harmful to them, had not helped them grow, and had led them into more difficulty in life than they otherwise might have experienced. Most of the 50 interviewees felt academic subjects were deemphasized too much, and they complained of a lack of good teachers. In general, Bernstein observed that gregarious, aggressive people seemed to benefit the most. The school seemed to have a negative effect on withdrawn, quiet students.

When Bernstein tabulated the positive remarks made by the 50 former students, the following items were mentioned most often: a healthy attitude toward sex, good relationships with the opposite sex, a natural confidence, ease with authority figures, and a natural development in line with personal interests and abilities. Ranked closely behind these benefits was the feeling that Summerhill helps one grow out of the need to play continuously, making it possible to settle into more serious pursuits. Surprisingly enough, however, of the 11 former students who had become parents, only three had sent their own children to Summerhill.

No one of the foregoing plans for change in education may be the final answer, and most likely none of them will be accorded a full-scale experimental test. The inescapable fact is that flexible class-room life contradicts a great many fixed educational traditions. One commentator has succinctly described the present circumstances:

> Schools have chosen a course that little resembles the relaxed, unscheduled flow of life in the home and, as in no other element of society, schools are organized fiercely and formally by age and grade. Time is made the master of people, and even student responsibility and extracurricular participation are organized rigidly by age. No other aspect of normal social life is divided into such rigid periods of time as is the school day yet, astonishingly, this slavery to clockwork can claim only a remote kinship to the facts of child development. Rigid age-grading is a function of tradition and administrative convenience; its cost to education has yet to be calculated and probably the price will be very dear.

schools for the poor and the black

It has been stated that the critical psychological variable in the poor or black child's encounter with the educational system is that every educational experience further discourages the child. Over a period of time the discouragement deepens until its victim never expects to win a battle, solve a problem, or have confidence about his chances in life. Encouragement is not given where it is most needed, and even many sincere people who try to encourage these children fail miserably because of their misconceptions about the process. Due to their lack of skill or ability to encourage, they may actually be discouraging the child.

Discouraged and hopeless, the students drop out as soon as they can, only to be met by a barrage of threats and appeals to drop back in. The Office of Education has spent millions of dollars to locate dropouts in our major cities and persuade them to return to school. Virtually all such appeals suffer from the same basic weaknesses. The school officials who mount these efforts are often more concerned with their own image than they are with the reality of the efforts to help dropouts. Radio and television caution students not to drop out, while principals in the schools are sending new dropouts into the streets of the cities by the thousands. Even if the dropout does sheepishly return, he may be confronted with hostility, endless red tape, and constant reminders that he failed once and not much more is expected of him the second time around.

It makes no sense to get the victim back into school, if no significant change has taken place in the school to keep him there—and usually nothing has changed. What, after all, makes a high school diploma truly meaningful when the awaiting job market discriminates against one because of the pigmentation of one's skin? If a student does not succeed in high school, this failure, when coupled with limited economic and cultural resources, makes moving up the status ladder exceedingly difficult.

The fundamental problem has been succinctly summarized by R. L. Green who noted that we have *interracial* schools (in which students of varying racial backgrounds are found), but we have yet to achieve *integrated* schools (where students of varying racial backgrounds experience mutual interactions). Even though minority group students may be brought into the school population, there has never been a guarantee that group segregation will decrease voluntarily. Because the culture has conditioned people to feel and react in specified ways, white students see black students as different, and black students see themselves as different since they are placed in special tracks and classes. Moreover, the white student population feels that the black group members are intellectually inferior. Teachers also regard an assignment to a racially imbalanced school as a loss in status, since the greater the number of blacks in such schools, the lower the school ranks on the academic totem pole.

Unquestionably, what the schools teach reflects, directly or indirectly, the generally held concepts of a good life, a good man, and a good society. C. E. Silberman, director of the Carnegie Study of the Education of Educators, is one observer whose views of our schools and the ideals perpetuated therein are dismal indeed. As he gloomily observes:

> It is not possible to spend any prolonged period visiting public school classrooms without being appalled by the mutilation visible everywhere—mutilation of spontaneity, of joy in learning, of pleasure creating, of sense of self. The public schools—those "killers of the dream," to appropriate a phrase of Lillian Smith's—are the kind of institution one cannot really dislike until one gets to know them well. Because adults take the schools so much for granted, they fail to appreciate what grim, joyless places most American schools are, how oppressive and petty are the rules by which they are governed, how intellectually sterile and esthetically barren the atmosphere, what an appalling lack of civility obtains on the part of teachers and principals, what contempt they unconsciously display for children as children.

Worse yet, Silberman is convinced that a great deal of what is taught is not worth knowing, while the triviality of the curriculum in schools is beyond belief.

In Colin Greer's 1972 book *The Great School Legend* the point is made that it is fashionable these days to talk of the decline of the public school, as if there were some golden past when schools made equal opportunity available to children of every economic and social class. The truth is that our public schools have always failed the lower classes—both white and black. Current educational problems stem not from the fact that the schools have changed, but from the fact that they continue to do precisely the job they have always done.

This Great School Legend is a Great Myth. Studies made as early as 1898 indicate that more children have always failed than succeeded in urban public schools. In school systems with large numbers of immigrant or poor children the failure rate was always exceptionally high. Academic work has simply never been very relevant to the American poor, and the urban poor in particular; the public schools did then as they are doing for the black poor today. The truth is, the public schools have never done what they are now expected to do.

Our schools have simply failed to meet up to a commitment to opportunity and equality. Culturally deprived children are unprepared to compete in schools that insist on maintaining middle-class goals and middle-class values. Some critics believe that schools fail not only the disadvantaged student but all intellectually capable students. Other critics feel that even the apparently successful students are damaged in our schools. One disturbing fact is the way schools mold youth to fit passively into the culture. By threatening to fail students, schools are most efficient in destroying youth's individuality and creative potential. One observer contends that, if the fear of failure were removed, American education "would stop as if its heart had been cut out." Some are even more critical, pointing out that one of the most obvious functions of school is to train prospective employees for private enterprise at public expense; schools teach the niceties of corporate conduct and compile dossiers of children's social or antisocial tendencies.

Some critics still have hope that children can succeed in ghetto schools, but the formula that they seemingly must follow is not a simple one. Students who do succeed have to learn to behave in ways that are acceptable socially and at school. The school wants pupils to be polite, to listen to the rules and follow them, and be passive. This pattern of behavior must be begun early since after the third grade hardly anyone makes it to the top if he was not in the top classes previously. As clinical psychologist B. Mackler has noted:

> Relatively early in life a successful pupil looks upon himself differently from the way average or failing youngsters look upon themselves. He is proud of himself and wants to learn to get ahead, to go to college, to become a teacher, doctor or lawyer.

Educators operate the schools as if they knew all the fine details of man's capacity to learn. When students do not learn, these same educators look to see what is wrong with the children rather than what might be wrong with the school. Equal educational opportunity will require more rather than less educational resources for the students from poor homes, but we seem to be doing just the opposite by spending more money educating well-off children that we are in educating poor children. The funds are available, of course, if we are really committed to the creation of excellence in our ghetto schools systems. But throughout history, the powerful and the wealthy have resisted demands to educate the children of the lower classes and have yielded only under great pressure.

According to Milton Schwebel, dean of the New York University School of Education, education for the poor and the socially disenfranchized in America can be improved if we will put up the money, change the composition of local boards so as to give a voice to the poor, improve teacher training and quality, and broaden the concept of school by making it a community center for citizens of all ages. Finally we must involve parents directly in education itself. This is a utopian dream, of course, and Schwebel realistically expects it will take years of disorder and travail before we finally respond to the obvious fact that education has failed to educate all the people.

When signs of alienation appear in a student it is important to determine the source of the symptoms. To what extent do the symptoms arise from the individual, and to what extent do they stem from the school system? Certainly, every child experiences failure and success long before he reaches school age. But alienation may be related to the fact that achievements, or lack of them, do not really become official until the child enters the classroom. From then on, he accumulates a public record of his progress. If the student is alienated it will be apparent in his refusal to accept personal responsibility and to attribute his gains or losses to what others have done to him. When he reaches this point, he no longer feels pride in his achievements or shame in his failures.

Special education programs designed to improve the academic performance of "disadvantaged children" proliferated during the 1960s. These "compensatory education" programs sought to make up for presumed deficits in the pre-school socialization of poor children. Those who have worked professionally in compensatory education programs are uniformly enthusiastic about their achievements with disadvantaged children, but research appraisals of the outcomes seldom produce evidence of a general improvement in academic performance. One observer has noted that, before such efforts can become fully effective, teachers must come to understand—and really believe—that impoverished children, given appropriate learning experiences, can indeed learn effectively. Professional staffs will then have to learn to relate to the parents and to the members of the local

60

communities while developing curricular content that truly relates to the lives of the disadvantaged learners. The lock-step, recitation teaching methods that exist now must be supplanted by individualized, small-group approaches that are based on an accurate diagnosis of the varying needs of pupils.

Some educators feel it is still possible to design schools that beat the present system and that overcome the expectation of substandard performance which pervades the atmosphere of most slum schools. It must begin by breaking the shackles of modern education. In other words, we must do away with situations where principals are bound by irrelevant or obstructive regulations imposed by administrators who are conscious merely of cost and public relations. These same administrators, constricted by regulations, often constantly watch teachers who then feel bound to unimaginative and poorly designed curricula. Unfortunately, under the present system, innovators at any level find it difficult to pursue their experiments through to the logical conclusions. A solution to these problems, as proposed by one educator, would be the creation of a new national complex of privately managed inner-city schools, completely divorced from the public educational establishment.

Success or failure in school reform is not likely to be a matter of gimmicks but one of assembling in the schools a preponderance of people who care deeply about their students, believe in them, and demand much from them. Equality in education cannot be achieved unless the poor schools are funded well enough to compensate for the unequal start "disadvantaged" children have had. One plan for achieving this is a system of vouchers for education—an unconventional program which involves giving money directly to poor children (through their parents) to assist them in paying for their education. Essentially, the plan calls for creating a meaningful competition among schools that serve the poor, while providing the means for meeting the extra costs of teaching. The voucher system supports open discrimination in education in favor of the poor child by giving him money (in the form of a coupon) to take to the school of his choice to be enrolled. The school could use the "grant" as it saw fit. Such a plan would mean that, for the first time in history, parents of poor children would have the power to choose the kind and quality of education they wanted their children to receive. Hopefully, the proposed competition for the educational dollar would eliminate inferior schools and listless personnel.

Before long, new schools would be created to capitalize on this new financial bounty, just as new programs in higher education arose to service the veterans of World War II. Only those curricula which met the real educational needs would show a profit and survive. As the recent controversy about busing has made clear, however, poor children might still need to be transported from their ghetto neighborhoods to places where quality education is provided. Proponents claim that the voucher experiment would (a) expand the public system by the inclusion of formerly private schools; (a) make all schools accessible to all children; (c) provide educational alternatives for low-income parents; (d) allow parent control over the education of their children; (e) permit the development of new community schools; and (f) accelerate economic and racial desegregation.

This plan has not been received with open arms by all parents. Some complain that a voucher system could deepen the segregation of the schools and place an even greater burden on public school systems by adding students not now enrolled in public schools. (These students would receive funds if they chose to attend a voucher school.) Others complain that education for profit will encourage a new "hucksterism" that will promise more than it can deliver.

Experiments employing profit-making private business have not, to date, quite achieved all that public-relations flacks have promised. Indeed, the grinding, leveling fact of day-to-day contact in the classroom punctures a great many rosy dreams of how education ought to be conducted. In Gary, Indiana, for example, an entire school was furnished for an experiment; honoring the assumption that the child cannot be taught but learns for himself, the program provided little supervision of the children. In the first year of the experiment chaos prevailed, and a tightly controlled system was shortly substituted. When reading and math became the sole subjects of study in any one day, both students and teachers grew bored and restless.

For certification purposes, other subjects were soon added to the curriculum, but attendance and discipline continued to be unsolved problems. Only vandalism was reduced, but the entire project began to emanate an overripe odor with conflicting reports about the extent of progress that was made with private industry at the helm. Grades that were lagging behind national norms have remained nearly as far behind as they had been before the instigation of the experiment. In summary, the only business-run school in the nation has not failed, nor has it succeeded. And one can safely predict that a miraculous cure to the problems will not occur. The company servicing Gary has made a 4 percent profit on the first year of operation. However, by 1974—the year of final reckoning—the profit margin may well have shrunk.

higher education

Going to college is not what it used to be, since today it may involve deep political concern, protest, and revolt on the part of the students.

Students and professors alike have recently become the target of outrage by the "average American, tax-paying citizen." Those of a rightest
political persuasion have been most vocal about the "revolutionaries,
vandals, arsonists, and terrorists" whom they feel are now attending
college. Some citizens believe that, in the space of an exceptionally
few years, the academic society became the cause of all the troubles
of our society—the breeding ground for riot, rebellion and members
of the Radical Left.

The fact is that the overwhelming majority of college campuses
have been peaceful, orderly, and oriented toward getting and giving
an education. The mass media exploited the image of a rowdy,
obscenity-shouting student body that is of one mind on social issues;
but three-quarters of our campuses have experienced only peaceful
protests or no protests at all. Of the incidents that did occur, fewer
than 10 percent involved violence. Americans reacted to the actions
of 1 percent of the student population and mistakenly understood
those actions to be a reflection of the sentiment of the other 99 percent.
It was not long before a hue and cry arose to exclude "protest-prone"
students from residence in the ivory towers of higher education. Two
researchers, K. Keniston and M. Lerner, have discussed the issue
of protesting students. They contend that the students to be kept out
would include many of the best students in the country. Studies have
shown that students involved in protests tend to be above-average
students; they do well on aptitude tests, are intellectually independent,
and stress values like serving their fellowman, acquiring a good education, and expressing their convictions and feelings directly.

Keniston and Lerner conclude that protest-prone students are
young men and women that most American families take pride in.
American high schools consider these students some of their best
products and colleges believe they are lucky to attract them. If American higher education were to turn these students away, colleges would
have to accept students who do *poorly* on aptitude tests, who *lack*
intellectual independence, who have *little* interest in serving their
fellowmen, who do *not* express their convictions, and who are *not*
interested in solving the problems of the country. Prohibiting potential
protesters from entering college would deprive our society of the
desperately needed talents, ability, and idealism of these young men
and women. But, of course, even if colleges decided on this course
of action, they could not make it work. From academic aptitude and
skill, there is no way to judge who may become a protester.

Dissenting students are intelligent and idealistic, but, as Keniston
and Lerner have observed, they are also rotten psychologists. Young
people regularly underestimate the pain involved in producing
changes in large masses of humanity. They have yet to acquire the
wisdom that can only be accumulated through extended experience

with people. Young, white, affluent, bright, educated, middle-class citizens must yet learn that they are a minority group in a society ruled by the majority.

In response to the ferment on American college campuses, the Carnegie Commission on Higher Education recommended a major overhaul of the system of university education by 1980. The plans included reduction of the time required to earn all degrees, calling for "less time, more options" in education. Accordingly, a bachelor's degree would require only three years, and an M.D. or Ph.D. would take one or two years less than what is now required. A new degree, Master of Philosophy, would be established for those who get stalled in the middle of advanced educational efforts, and a D.A., Doctor of Arts, would be granted to those more interested in teaching than research.

One of the intriguing ideas in the commission report was the recommendation that two years post-high-school education would be "banked" for every person in the society. This educational deposit could be withdrawn by the potential student whenever further education seemed necessary or worth pursuing. A pipe dream? Perhaps. But it seems clear that too many of us at the wrong stage of our life spend too much time "attending school" rather than "getting an education." Thus, between attacks from the Left and attacks from the Right, our colleges have served as a battleground for one of the most extensive social turmoils to engulf our society in recent years.

education tomorrow

Buck Rogers, Flash Gordon, and other prophets of times past may have the last word, and tomorrow all of us may do our learning at home. Facsimile reproducers, teleprinters, electrowriters, flashbacks by wire, and similar inventions may one day render the classroom obsolete; sound systems and video tapes may be substituted for the crude lecture halls of today. The cost will be less, the convenience greater, and the learning as great. Or, as educator R. L. Schwitzgebel has speculated, the ultimate outcome of school reform may resemble a situation where the school child of the future spends part of his day in a nine-foot opaque spheroid "learning center" at home. "Inside the spheroid will be a two-way T.V. set, a teaching machine with a typewriter connecting the student to the school's computer center, food and token dispenser, 360° color-variable lighting, temperature regulator, microfilm encyclopedia and reference library, tactile communication pad, and stereophonic speakers."

In the future, man may be integrated with the machine early in the educational process. A few years ago there was a similar widespread hope that educational technology might succeed where all else seemed to be failing. For a while the "teaching machine" was oversold and prematurely applied as an educational panacea. The result, however, was that educational hardware turned out to be much more primitive than anyone had previously realized. Unreliable and expensive devices are gathering dust in a classroom corner, now that their novelty has worn off. Moreover, knowledge about how to apply the technology is even more primitive, with teaching methods and curriculum contents remaining virtually unmodified.

As it turns out, the greatest obstacle to rapid and effective introduction of technology into the schools is the incredible capacity of the American school system to resist any kind of change. Perhaps this recalcitrance will even keep tomorrow from being different. As I've summarized it elsewhere, "For too long in the history of American education, innovation and progress has been the responsibility of outsiders to education—outsiders whose grasp of the process is based more in theory than on practical experience. A new conception of the educational process is desperately needed if we are to give the lie to the statement that nothing fundamentally new in education had occurred in the last quarter century and nothing new can be expected until after 1984."

drugs

Once upon a time it was possible to write an essay on drugs in a modest number of pages. But, that was before the American Drug Scene—before the chemical alteration of body and mind became a major preoccupation in our society. Now, the flood of social comment on drugs is overwhelming, and the task of sifting and sorting seems almost insurmountable.

Throughout history and in nearly every culture people have taken chemical substances to change their mood, perception, and thought processes. *Soma*, the magic mushroom of the Aryan invaders of India, is praised in hymns in the Vedas; the use of wine by the Egyptians was described about 1500 B.C.; and records of the opium poppy appear as early as 1000 B.C. The ancient Indian civilizations of Mexico and South America used mind-altering chemicals, and the natives of the Pacific islands used betel and kava kava. Men have always sought chemical methods to alter their minds, and this urge has continued and spread in modern times.

In the nineteenth century the psychedelics of choice were chloroform and ether. The college students of those days held chloroform parties until they became aware of its toxic dangers. Ether was safer, and for a while it was used in the same way modern psychedelic drugs are used. In addition, nitrous oxide (laughing gas) was widely used after the discovery that it released inhibitions producing strange new sensations and fantasies. S. Cohen, a researcher and writer concerned with drugs, stated: "Visions of Paradise, universal truths and enormous insights were all experienced and duly reported. On college campuses and at certain dinner parties, laughing gas was the fashionable, the only genteel way to become 'potted,' to lose one's inhibitions. At sideshows and county fairs nitrous oxide inhalations were dispensed for a quarter." Marijuana, the most popular of the currently illegal drugs, was brought to America by laborers in the Southwest in the 1930s. Initially, it was a drug for jazz musicians. Then, as Cohen has reported, "Nezz Mezzrow spread it around Harlem, and it became a favorite of minority groups. During the past decade it has extended to the campus, the arty set, and beyond."

The history of drug use has also had its less serious moments. When drug usage among the young was just beginning (before supply-and-demand networks were established) the fabled "high" was sought in whatever was close at hand. As one researcher noted, "Among the more bizarre products that have been reported from time to time as having psychedelic properties are dried banana peels, dried hydrangeas, chlorinated lettuce leaves, and rotting green peppers. The smoking of dried scrapings from the inner portion of banana peel (bananadine or mellow yellow) has received the most national publicity." No "bad trips" were reported, but more than one user experienced nausea, dizziness, a sore throat, or coughing from smoking banana scrapings. Scientifically, the only active ingredient in bananadine was the suggestibility of the smoker—in other words, his expectation of a high. The great banana hoax was a laughable forerunner to similar, but less humorous, events; soon every conceivable chemical preparation was being pushed on unsuspecting drug users—but at the price of the real thing.

Around 1960, communities in different parts of the country began to report a relatively high incidence of youth sniffing plastic cements, airplane glues, paint thinners, cleaning fluids, gasoline, industrial solvents, and other products. When inhaled, these chemicals produced effects that range from mild intoxication to disorientation, coma, and death. The practice became most common among elementary or junior high school students and maladjusted adolescents of less than average intelligence.

The rate of illegal drug usage among students today has clearly changed from what it was 20 or so years ago. A 1970 study indicates that 28 percent of the freshman students surveyed had some form of contact with drugs; this compares with a figure of 12.8 percent of the students from all levels who had contact with drugs in years past. It is impossible, however, to estimate percentages in a drug scene that changes week by week. The percentage of experienced marijuana users rises with each survey taken of college students. In 1967, for example, a Gallup drug survey reported that only 5 percent of all college students said they had tried marijuana. By 1969, this figure had risen to 22 percent, and by 1970 the percentage had almost doubled (42 percent). By December 1971, 51 percent of the college students reported they had tried marijuana. About 5 percent of the college population were described as "heavy users" who smoked pot almost every day. More men than women were marijuana users.

The only incidence of "prohibition" comparable to the present sanctions against drug use was the attempt by the Volstead Act to prevent alcohol use from 1920 to 1933. During this time, Americans experienced a period of changing moral standards in which sanctions against smoking, drinking, courting, and hemlines were relaxed. Trapped by a primitive set of restrictions regarding alcohol, most of the adult drinking population chose to ignore or flaunt the law.

The drug problem of today is not identical to the problems of the prohibition era. Young people today must deal with a conflict between the informal norms of their peers and the official norms imposed by the laws of their elders. Like their adult counterparts of yesteryear, when confronted with this conflict of interests, they choose to resolve the impasse by ignoring or flouting the official norms. We should not forget, however, that during the 1950s pollsters

69

reported, with alarm, the serious drinking problem among college students. Now, it has become the drug problem—or, more properly, the marijuana problem. The only thing new about the use of peyote, marijuana, opium, and comparable substances is the exceptional incidence of young people using drugs.

The outcry for acceptance and legalization of marijuana began in 1945 when Mayor LaGuardia of New York City appointed a special commission to review the effects of marijuana. From a limited sample of only 77 prisoners, the commission concluded that marijuana was not significantly associated with crime, delinquency, or insanity. This report, a quarter of a century ago, was vehemently denounced by the American Medical Association. As recently as 1964–65, the use of marijuana was mainly a matter of history. Now the matter of widespread concern is whether marijuana should be equated with the social use of alcohol, or whether it should be considered an equivalent to cocaine and a stepping stone to heroin.

Older persons now in their fifties have lived with alcohol and its abuses so long that they accept it as a way of life. They do not seem particularly disturbed that 20,000 people die every year from cirrhosis and other diseases closely linked to excessive alcohol use. Apparently, for this older set, the fact that half of the 53,000 traffic deaths which occur each year are connected with drinking is only a moderately interesting statistic. We are equally unperturbed by the fact that 9,000,000 people are medical problems because of their alcoholism. Indeed, the modern history of drug use in America is complicated by the fact that we seem to have become a population of addicts living in a drugged society.

the addicted americans

Some observers assert that the drug habits of the young are no more than an extension of the general American addiction. L. H. Farber has presented the following analysis of the situation:

> Believing, as we do, that we should be able to will ourselves to be calm, cheerful, thin, industrious, creative—and, moreover, to have a good night's sleep—they [the drug innovators] simply provide the products to collaborate in such willing. If the satisfactions turn out to be short-lived and spurious and if their cost in terms of emotion, intellect and physical health is disagreeable, these scientists are ready to concoct new drugs to counter this discomfort. In other words, they offer us always new chances—virtually to the point of extinction—to will away the unhappiness that comes from willing ourselves to be happy.

The young have witnessed the hypocrisy of adults who are dependent on chemicals to add or subtract from their lives; youth have consequently caricatured the adult state with their own absorption in the drug culture. The question is: in an addicted society, how does one determine which addict should be labeled pathological?

When we speak of the *addicted* American, we employ a graphic but imprecise use of the term, since a variety of drugs can cause the kind of physical dependence where the body tolerates ever-increasing doses and reacts with withdrawal symptoms when deprived of the drug. It is also easy to confuse the terms *addiction* and *habituation*. Addiction involves tolerance and psychological or physical dependence; it is a compulsion to continue using the drug and implies detrimental effects on the individual or the society. Habituation involves repeated consumption of a drug with little or no evidence of tolerance, some psychological dependence, no physical dependence, and a desire (but not compulsion) to continue taking the drug for a feeling of well-being. The terms *addiction* and *habituation* are frequently and erroneously used interchangeably, further confusing discussions and understanding of the drug abuse.

We are a drug-dependent society that cannot sleep, wake up, or feel comfortable without drugs; yet we will not admit we are "hooked." As R. H. Berg has indicated, "Contrary to claims of indescribable delights by some drug takers, most people abuse drugs to relieve anxiety. They're not pursuing pleasure, they just hurt less on drugs. This is true also of hard-narcotic users. A heroin addict told a reporter, 'You don't even know what I'm talking about; you feel okay all the time. Me, it costs me $100 a day just to stop hurting so much.'" The statistics make the problem clear. There are more than 900 drugs listed as mood-altering (psychotropic) by the National Institutes of Mental Health. In the United States, in 1969, 90 million new prescriptions were issued for minor tranquilizers; 17 million new prescriptions were given for antidepressive drugs; and 12 million people reported using marijuana at least once. In addition, there is an enormous consumption of diet pills, stimulants, aspirin, sleeping compounds with scopolamine, and other psychotropic drugs.

Since psychotropic drugs were introduced for the treatment of mental illness, physicians and psychiatrists have been inundated with commercial advertisements pushing psychotropic drugs as the treatment of choice for emotional disorders of all kinds. The drug industry spends nearly a billion dollars a year advertising directly to doctors; as one critic insists, the epidemic of legal drug abuse is just what the doctor ordered:

> Depression, social inadequacy, anxiety, apathy, marital discord, children's misbehavior, and other psychological and social problems of living are now being redefined as medical problems, to be solved by physicians

with prescription pads. Psychiatrists as well as physicians of every other specialty now prescribe a wide variety of mood-altering drugs for patients with emotional, motivational and learning problems, and even the mildest psychological discomforts.

Problems which should be coped with are now circumvented through drugs—a new and worse kind of living through chemistry. In one report, the drug scene was projected into the year 1990; it was suggested that by that time almost every individual will be taking mood-altering medicines regularly. Some critics believe that the way for future drug use is being paved now. Physicians who treat children have moved from an initial stance of completely opposing tranquilizers for very young people to their present position of excessive use and over-reliance on the drugs. Drugs have been proven a less painful emotional drain on parent and physician, since an impersonal pill may quiet a child and short-circuit years of grappling with faulty parent-child relationships.

Drug dependence may begin much earlier than this; pregnant women take drugs and pass the effects to the newborn baby. Different effects are manifested at different times on different organs or systems during pregnancy. The nervous system is most apt to be damaged by drugs during the fifteenth to twenty-fifth day of pregnancy; the eye is most vulnerable during from the twenty-fourth to thirtieth day; the legs from the twenty-fourth to thirty-sixth day; and the heart from the twentieth to the fortieth day. Another kind of prenatal drug effect may be the breakage of human chromosomes. Breakage occurs just before an abnormal chromosome develops, and, if these breaks do not heal they may lead to defects in genetic content. Rearrangements in cells may result in abnormalities and maldevelopments of the human embryo, causing the infant to be deformed at birth.

the drug users

In recent times we have refurbished the ancient stereotype of the drug pusher, making it into a modern myth. Drug researcher Richard Blum has described this mythological figure in the inflammatory terms used so well by middle America: "Who is more malignant, more evil than the drug peddler? Can there be a criminal more loathed and feared than the pusher who is thought to seduce children into a life of slavery? He is the demon who spreads crime and corruption in the slums, who controls the minds and bodies of others by exploiting the cravings he has himself created." According to Blum's study of drug dealers in the San Francisco Bay area, this good guy-bad guy dichotomy between pushers and users is not quite correct. The evidence shows, rather, that drug dealers and drug users are one and the same, and if you know a user you probably know a dealer. Blum's study of 450 dealers discounted the notion that they were manifestly different from the rest of us, and he made the point that few dealers planned pushing drugs as a life-long occupation. Half of the dealers were worried about the extent of their own drug use, and two-thirds reported unpleasant life events that happened to other drug dealers. Interestingly, fewer than 10 percent of the dealers would want their own children to follow in their footsteps.

The inaccurate but fearsome image of the drug pusher is matched by the older generation's vision of the dope addict.

> Before the 1960s few people, including the drug users themselves, protested against the stereotype of the "dope addict" as the epitome of an outcast. He was pimply-faced, emaciated, perhaps black, but certainly swarthy, and probably illegitimate—with an alcoholic or criminal father and a prostitute mother. His use of heroin was the culmination of a long criminal history. He was untrustworthy, fluctuating between sudden violence and whining cowardice, willing to break every commandment to get his drug—even sending his loving girlfriend out to hustle for his drug money. He made the meaning of virtue absolutely clear to the rest of us: it was the opposite of himself.

It was this imagery which came to the minds of many older people when drug usage spread to the younger generation, and this is still the image that lurks in the minds of those who favor severe punishment for the erring young. Although gathering accurate statistics of drug use is impossible, it has become particularly apparent that the problem is no longer one of adult criminal types skulking in the dark alleys of our major cities. The problem is one that has an early beginning among our children. An investigation of drug use among 4220 white, middle-American adolescents in grades 8 through 13 showed that, although drug use begins early, overall usage rates were relatively low. Marijuana was the most extensively consumed drug. Although boys reported more experience with all types of drugs, both sexes showed similar patterns of consumption.

Most drug studies published to date have dealt with college populations or those who live in metropolitan areas. Three researchers, D. L. Hager, A. M. Vener, and C. S. Steward have, however, reported on the use of marijuana, hallucinogens (LSD, STP, mescaline), amphetamines (benzedrine, dexedrine, methedrine) and hard drugs (heroin, morphine) by public school students in grades 8 through 12 in white, nonmetropolitan, noncollege communities of the Midwest. They found that drug use begins as early as age 13; 5 percent reported early experiences with marijuana, and smaller percentages reported experiences with other types of drugs. Between the ages of 15 and

16, there was an increase of all types of soft drug use (marijuana, hallucinogens, amphetamines). A fairly high intercorrelation of the usage of different drugs suggests that drug users may form a subculture in which the use of one drug greatly increases one's opportunity to use other drugs.

In the 1960s, the times were ripe for a changed world view, and drugs became the lubricant that made change and dissention less difficult. Some of the young withdrew from the political process and turned their energies inward in a search for creative satisfaction; drugs became the means to this end. One could compose a long list of the reasons for drug experimentation among the young; possible motivating factors are: (a) curiosity; (b) the feeling of missing something—of not being "with it"; (c) a need to prove one's intellectual depth and emotional maturity (particularly among shy students who do not relate easily with others); (d) a search for meaning (when an unambiguous answer cannot be found in the outside world, the quest turns inward); (e) escape from feelings of inadequacy (the hope for a magical cure for personal, emotional turmoil without the embarrassment of sharing one's weaknesses with others); and (f) an end to isolation (drugs may give the feeling of having cleared channels of communication to permit greater closeness with others).

It is important to note that no single effect is attributable to any drug; all drugs have multiple effects and no specific effect is completely reliable or predictable. Drugs are chemicals that interact with the biochemical system that is the living organism. This system varies from individual to individual and from time to time in the same individual. It varies with age, sex, and in sickness and in health.

marijuana

One of the first records of marijuana use was made in 400 to 500 B.C. And according to one author, "even then there were those who felt that the road to Hades was lined with hemp plants, and others who felt that the path to Utopia was shaded by the freely growing *Cannabis sativa*." The reputation of marijuana was not aided much by Marco Polo's report (about the year 1300) that hashish was used to bolster the courage of professional assassins. But throughout its long history marijuana has never produced quite as much social discord as in modern times.

THE EFFECTS OF MARIJUANA

Drugs alter the state of consciousness in characteristic ways. The shift in consciousness may involve: (a) disturbances in thinking—altered attention, memory, and judgment; (b) a changed sense of time—time may speed up, slow down, or seem suspended; (c) feelings of loss of control—the helpless kind of feeling where, as in a nightmare, you run but never seem to get anywhere; (d) alteration of emotional expression—unexpectedly intense or primitive emotional outbursts; and (e) distortions of perception—illusions, hyperacute perceptions, or hallucinations. Drugs may also produce changes in the meaning or significance of events. One may experience a sense of profound insight or discovery of ultimate truth that is impossible to communicate to others. These drug-induced "insights" may trigger a sense of rejuvenation or rebirth of hope. Reportedly, some persons become hypersuggestible while drugged, and their critical faculties falter. These persons come to depend on others when they can no longer depend on themselves. Drugs may also produce a sense of depersonalization in which the usual perception of the body image is distorted. Parts of the body may seem shrunken, enlarged, or floating, or there may be sensations of numbness, weakness, dizziness, tingling, and so on.

Solomon Snyder reported an experiment in which he gave naïve subjects cigarettes containing moderate amounts of marijuana, large amounts, or no marijuana at all. Nine naïve subjects could not tell which cigarette they were smoking, but a control group of experienced marijuana smokers got high on the heavy-dose cigarettes. The experiments confirmed the folk wisdom of the drug subculture that experienced users get stoned more readily than do novices. Experienced marijuana smokers can smoke less and enjoy it more because it seems that the active metabolites in marijuana—when properly ingested—can last for several days.

The variations of marijuana products are numerous. In India a preparation called *bhang* (legal in some provinces) is consumed at social gatherings and is prescribed by physicians. Growers harvest the tops of cultivated plants to make a potent drug called *ganja*; a more potent preparation is obtained by scraping resin from the leaves of cultivated marijuana plants to make hashish—about ten times as powerful as marijuana and outlawed in India since 1956.

To understand marijuana intoxication one must take into account the personal and physiological idiosyncrasies of the user as well as his expectations and hopes about what will happen while smoking. The setting in which marijuana is smoked also makes a difference. The users of marijuana know that the effects of the drug are influenced by these factors—that is, the physiological characteristics of the individual, his psychological makeup, his reasons for using the drug, and his expectations about the experience. It has been reported that in a neutral setting persons who are new to marijuana do not have powerful experiences after smoking either low or high doses of the drug, and the effects the new users do report are not the same as those described by regular users who take the drug in the same setting.

Regular users of marijuana get high when smoking in a neutral setting, but they do not show the same degree of impairment of performance on various tests as do naïve subjects. In some cases, the performance of regular users even appears to improve slightly after smoking marijuana

Studies of marijuana intoxication have concluded that getting high on marijuana is a much more subtle experience than getting drunk on alcohol. If you pour enough alcohol into someone who has never had much before, he will be aware that he is intoxicated and he will know that he is behaving in an abnormal fashion. With marijuana, a novice smoker can consume substantial amounts without any observable mental effects at all. Unlike alcohol, marijuana has no general stimulative or depressive action on the nervous system and produces no clear effect on centers that control the mechanical aspects of speech and coordination. Being "high" and being "drunk" are simply not the same.

An objective appraisal was made by researchers who noted that marijuana requires no sophisticated technology for its production or distribution, and, unless we become incredibly repressive, it will probably remain a low-cost drug, available from numerous, relatively unorganized sources. More critical, psychologically, is that drug use and involvement in the drug-using subculture among teen-agers can be a vital, ego-forming experience. We need to examine the young person's motivation for taking drugs with as much care as we assess the drug-taking experience itself.

THE MOTIVATION

Young people are the first to admit that much experimentation with marijuana is motivated by the fact that it is illegal. Smoking marijuana is simply much more exciting when there are heavy pressures exerted against it by adults. Now that the pot culture seems to have spread to those of all ages in the straight society, some of the thrill has gone; the marginal ones who smoked in defiance of the system must turn to a more visible and effective means of communicating their unrest and psychic dissatisfaction. The straight society, as it inevitably does, smothered the protest by absorbing it and adopting it as their own. Like pornography in Denmark, marijuana has been made so commonplace that it has been stripped of its defiant and faddish elements. As one team of researchers suggested, many of the young wanted "the prize located at the top of the Cracker Jack box, not at the bottom." Drugs act precisely in that fashion for those who are unwilling to drop out but who are not yet turned on by the world. They drift into drugs from boredom more than they do from inner turmoil.

Two researchers divided drug users into three groups. One group is made up of dependency-prone persons whose personality problems fated them to become heavily immersed in drug use and the drug subculture (the heroin and barbiturate addict, the speed freak, the multiple drug user, and some chronic marijuana users). For these persons, personal and social maladjustments are expressed via drugs; other means would be employed for self-destruction if drugs were not available. A second group (erroneously confused with the first group by the general public) differs markedly in motivation and drug choice. A decade ago this group did not exist, but the recent psychedelic and marijuana explosion thrust them into a different group of drug experimenters who use marijuana and sometimes LSD or the amphetamines; they are mostly young people. A third group is composed of disturbed young people who appear, at first, to be part of the drug-experimenting group but who use drugs solely to escape their difficulties. For them, the drug subculture is a way of life that comforts and supports them.

Four levels of use have been defined by other researchers studying the personality characteristics of marijuana. These levels are: frequent users, occasional users, nonusers, and principled nonusers. The researchers found that users were "socially poised, open to experience, and concerned with the feelings of others. Conversely, they also seemed impulsive, pleasure-seeking, and rebellious. In contrast, nonusers were responsible and rule abiding; however, they also tended to be inflexible, conventional, and narrow in their interests. Both frequent users and principled nonusers appeared less than morally mature on two scales designed to predict moral behavior."

For some theorists, drugs are tools used in the quest for identity. In an article entitled "Drug Use and Student Values," psychiatrist and social commentator Kenneth Keniston said: "Among today's self-conscious college students, the statement, 'I'm having an identity crisis' has become a kind of verbal badge of honor, a notch in the gun, a scalp at the belt. . . . Since academic pursuits, on the whole, tell the student so little about life's ultimate purposes, students are turned back upon their own resources to answer questions like, 'What does life mean? What kind of person am I? Where am I going? Where do I come from? What really matters?' " Other researchers relate the use of marijuana to a new "hang loose" ethic in which the future is left open; the young do not invest their emotions in establishment values but look for a new and more meaningful combination.

Getting good grades or making it in the academic world may have relatively little to do with answering these "ultimate" questions; as some students turn away from academic pursuits in a private quest for identity, they search for experience with an emphasis on the present, the here-and-now. Immediate pleasure and satisfaction are substituted for the traditions and virtues of the past such as planning, saving, waiting, control, and postponing. These ethics are abandoned for the adventure, openness, spontaneity, and genuineness of drugs. In addition to these reasons, and as was mentioned previously, some observers have drawn a parallel between the motivations for marijuana use among the young and alcohol use among their elders.

OF POT AND BOOZE

The comparison of alcohol to marijuana is mistaken since their active ingredients are entirely different substances with different mental and somatic effects. Marijuana is a stimulant and hallucinogen; alcohol is a depressant. Marijuana, unlike alcohol, is usually consumed until intoxication is produced. In this country, most experience has been with marijuana containing a low concentration of the active ingredient tetrahydrocannabinol, since hashish is expensive and the lower grades of marijuana are often diluted with inert materials to turn a higher profit. Legalization of marijuana would invite the importation of more refined and potent products than are commonly obtainable—namely, hashish and perhaps pure tetrahydrocannabinol.

If marijuana is legalized because we feel unable to control its illicit use, we must then face the possibility that it will pose social problems that are even worse than those posed by legalized alcohol. If pot becomes legal, then why not legal LSD, legal peyote, mescaline, or any other drug? Almost every country in the world has laws against the use of marijuana, and the taboo against pot is not simply a result of our Puritan ethic. The sanctions against pot results from a world-wide conviction that its prolonged use is harmful.

The prime argument used by those who support legal marijuana rests upon the disastrous consequences of the use and abuse of alcohol in our society. There are perhaps nine million people in America who are psychologically dependent on alcohol. "Moreover, the long-term physical effects of alcohol are more dangerous than those of almost any other pleasure giving drug. Alcohol, coupled with a disregard for health, can produce serious physical difficulties, including brain and liver damage. The total destructive reach of alcohol is, in fact, impossible to calculate. According to some estimates, about 15,000 deaths and 200,000 injuries are associated with drunken driving in the United States each year. Absenteeism, job loss, and accidents together produce an estimated annual loss of about $500 million in our economy." It is easy, however, to support the myth of harmless social use. Since 80 percent of the physicians in this country drink alcohol, they may, as a consequence, be less willing to condemn their fellow drinkers. But, of course, legalized pot will not solve the alcohol problems; it will simply add a new dimension to our difficulties.

78

lsd

LSD is one of a collection of chemicals which have variously been called the Utopiates or the Nightmare Drugs. LSD-25 (lysergic acid) produces a profound alteration of sensory, perceptual, cognitive, and emotional experiences that defies description. The words of one writer, however, come close:

> They [colors] swirl around the individual with great vividness. Fixed objects fuse and diffuse; there is often a perpetual flowing of geometric designs and one sensation merges into another and one sense into another so that the individual may say he can taste color; touch sound. The body image is distorted and ordinary sounds increase profoundly in intensity. There is a sense of intense isolation and depersonalization so that "me" as an individual disappears and the user feels he is fused with all humanity and with his environment. Time stands still and many give themselves up to what they describe as an experience of inexpressible ecstasy.

According to the impressions of another author this experience involves "the capacity of the mind to see more than it can tell, to experience more than it can explicate, to believe in and be impressed with more than it can rationally justify, to experience boundlessness and 'boundaryless' events, from the banal to the profound." After experience with LSD, the user may try to convey to others what he believes to have been a revelation. His self-centered mystical or religious feelings may appear in the form of pseudoprofundity or a belief in personal omniscience—even when these characteristics are objectively judged by others to be philosophical naivete, impulsive judgment, or inadequate foresight.

The problem posed by discussing LSD is that every word carries a biased connotation. Dr. Joel Fort, in an article, "The Semantics and Logic of the Drug Scene," has examined this problem. The word *hallucinogenic*, which is one of the most common, implies that the characteristic effect of LSD is to produce hallucinations. *Psychotomimetic* is a term implying that LSD imitates or mimics psychosis. *Psychedelic* or *consciousness-expanding* are terms which imply that one can expect a positive or beneficial creative consciousness-expanding, or mind-expanding experience.

Realistically, there is no consistent effect from the use of any given drug. At a cocktail party, for example, people of the same age and body size may consume the same amount of alcohol during a fixed period of time; yet they may behave in quite different ways. For every person who becomes boisterous or aggressive, another may become amorous, and yet another may become quiet and withdrawn.

79

No drug produces the same effect in everyone or even the same effect in the same person at different times.

Before the recreational use of LSD by the young became a critical social issue, the drug was employed primarily in research designed to find solutions to other social problems. LSD has been used with alcoholics to help them stop drinking; it has been used as a psychotherapeutic aid to increase insight and lift repressions; and it has been used with autistic children to increase their contact with people in the real world. LSD has also been administered to persons dying of cancer to produce greater tolerance of acute pain and a calmer acceptance of death. For some persons, it produces a dramatic improvement; in other instances, it worsens their plight. Pain relief is the most obvious benefit of the drug, but for some patients LSD also relieves various degrees of depression, anxiety, or feelings of psychological isolation. Pain relief in itself may be a sufficient justification for the use of LSD, since, for the terminal patient, severe pain may become the focus of his remaining time. When the use of LSD is successful, narcotic dosage can be reduced and there seems to be improvement in the patients depressed view of certain death.

LSD has been the most prominent and newsworthy of the psychedelic drugs, but there are other substances that produce related psychological effects. Peyote is one such substance; it contains alkaloids, one of which is mescaline. These alkaloids act in rough sequence to produce, at first, an unpleasant sensation which upsets the stomach but dies in about a half hour; the face then begins to flush; the pupils dilate; salivation increases, and there is a sense of exhilaration something like the effect of swift intakes of pure oxygen. This is followed by a period of withdrawal, intense color awareness, and successions of hallucinations when the eyes are closed. After a few hours, reflexes seem heightened; time is overestimated; spatial perception is altered; hearing and sight seem intensified; and ideas flow rapidly. Some Indian tribes have used mescaline (derived from the Mexican cactus, peyote) for centuries in religious ceremonies. Mescaline is available as a cyrstalline powder in capsules or as a liquid in ampules; it may also be obtained as whole cactus "buttons," chopped "buttons" in capsules, or as a brownish-gray cloudy liquid. The drug is usually taken orally despite its bitter taste.

Another drug, psilocybin, is derived from mushrooms that have been used in Indian religious rites dating to pre-Columbian times. This drug is not nearly as potent as LSD, but similar hallucinogenic effects are produced. Psilocybin too is available in crystalline, powdered, or liquid form. DMT (dimethyltryptamine) is a synthetic hallucinogenic that is also a natural part of the seeds of certain plants found in the West Indies and South America. Powder made from these seeds is used as a snuff by some Indian tribes of South America.

80

DMT produces effects similar to those of LSD, but much larger doses are required.

A word should also be said here about the dangers of LSD. History books describe mass epidemics of "insanity" occurring in Europe during the Middle Ages. One theory holds that these epidemics could have been caused by the ergot derivatives found on mouldy wheat. (This is the same type of fungus that first led to the discovery of LSD in 1943.) It has been reported that a similar epidemic occurred in a small town in France not too many years ago. The irony is that a drug which has been shown to cause severe mental derangement and was considered as a potential chemical warfare agent in the 1950s is hailed by some as the source of expanded consciousness, wisdom, and delight in the 1960s and 1970s.

Clinical psychologists and psychiatrists have been alarmed about the possibilities of psychological damage linked to the use of LSD. It has been found, for example, that delusions are quite common among young people who have taken LSD as are severe depressions accompanied by suicidal thoughts. Another symptom is anxiety to the point of panic, confusion, and wandering about. In one extreme case, a young girl who took LSD stayed on a bad trip for four months. This "bummer" was halted only after 15 electroconvulsive shock treatments, where electrodes were attached to the scalp and electrically induced seizures produced in the patient.

Studies reveal that approximately 70 percent of the persons who have bad experiences with LSD have had previous psychiatric care. In one study, 44 percent of those hospitalized by bad trips had previously received psychiatric treatment. In a related study of 20 LSD takers, most chronic users had long-standing personality disorders which preceeded the use of the drug. During the two to three years of LSD use, these psychological problems were not made worse, but there was no evidence they got any better. These studies of chronic use regularly report that involvement with LSD seems to be self-limiting; in other words, there is a clear tendency to decrease its use over time.

In addition to a high incidence of previous psychiatric treatment, a high incidence of psychopathology among LSD users has been reported. Half of the LSD users studied had been treated previously for psychological disturbances, and these users showed far greater psychological disturbance than nonusers. LSD users were described as more escapist, socially alienated, and self-alienated than were nonusers, and they reported experiencing more family discord and authority problems in life than did nonusers.

When LSD was used for psychotherapeutic purposes a decade ago (before its use was limited to experimental efforts only), it was hailed as a breakthrough that promised an end to a variety of mental conflicts. In a ten-year follow-up study of such patients, however, it was concluded that no lasting personality, belief, value, attitude, or behavior changes were produced.

As regards the illegal use of LSD among young people anxious to experiment, the fear of psychological damage was not sufficient to deter exploration and the tasting of forbidden fruit. LSD lost its status as an "in" drug only with the discovery that it might produce chromosomal breakage or abnormality. Steady users then had to look beyond their own immediate pleasure and consider its cost in malformed generations yet unborn—even though the scientific reliability of the studies performed was questionable. Indeed, serious question could be raised about the research on which the LSD genetic scare was based. But, even the remote possibility of chromosomal damage, cancer, or birth defects was sufficient to allow users to stop taking the drug without losing face with one's peers. The "scare" became an easy way out for many users who had ceased regarding the drug as a meaningful part of life.

A review of studies and case reports covering a four-year period suggests that the LSD dosage necessary to produce chromosomal damage is far in excess of what most human beings could possibly ingest safely. Furthermore, the amount of damage sustained would resemble that produced by any of a number of common chemicals—aspirin being one example. The scientific studies reported used a pure form of LSD, uncontaminated by impurities such as strychnine. The damages which had been reported initially could have been caused by such impurities, rather than by LSD.

The studies linking LSD to genetic damage were done on flies, and those studies connecting it to birth defects were based on populations of rodents. What human evidence exists is limited to women who used illicit LSD. The problem with such evidence, however, is one of quality control; one cannot be sure of the purity of drugs obtained on the street from unscrupulous pushers. In addition, users who get drugs in the street are seldom taking one drug exclusively, and there is no way to account for the possible interaction of a variety of drugs differing in purity and dosage.

There are still those who "believe" in LSD and expect that the laws regulating LSD will one day be relaxed or abolished and that life will then be better for everyone. They claim that alcoholism will decline, organized religion will be revitalized, the mental health problems of the nation will be drastically reduced, and the gifted in our society will become more creative and productive. In order to subscribe to such a chemical Utopian dream, however, it is necessary to pretend that the pre-adolescent runaway who sits alone drugged and hallucinating in a strange city simply does not exist. It is unlikely we will build a chemical heaven. The search for a safer psychedelic is probably a waste of scientific time since the effects of such drugs —the loss of ego controls, euphoria, and disappearance of rational thought—are precisely the outcomes which make it a danger.

drugs and tomorrow

Perhaps, as has been suggested, what this country needs is a "safe, five-cent intoxicant." At first, alcohol would seem to fit this prescription, but obviously alcohol is too dangerous for some people. Indeed, no drug in existence is perfectly safe or adequate to the psychological tasks we set for it. Looking to the future, some have argued that, once a drug is introduced into a culture, it seldom disappears; but it is nevertheless true that the sudden widespread youthful experimentation has had a faddish quality to it. One writer has stated:

> One of the consistent historical observations about drug using behavior is that excessive use flourishes during periods of social upheaval. Where family, community, and cultural structure are strong, abuse is low; when wars, massive migrations from rural to urban settings, unemployment, and breakdown of family influence occur, abuse tends to be high. In short, lack of structure, discipline, and involvement are conducive to patterns of excessive drug use. If one projects a future society in which large segments of the population are unemployed or otherwise alienated and uninvolved, then a high rate of drug abuse can be anticipated.

Other writers predict that the use of mind- and mood-altering drugs will continue to increase in the next two decades. Marijuana may in some fashion be legalized; but, according to some observers, we will most probably continue to prohibit its use and distribution. Our efforts to deal with the "drug problem" have been characterized by panic, and there are fears that the coming years will see more of the same.

The future is a mixed promise, carrying with it the threat of new memory drugs, amnesia chemicals, dream-producing agents, pills to increase suggestibility, and all manner of other chemicals to alter life. Some have even suggested that elderly persons should be allowed, on weekends or special occasions, to experience the excitement produced by a stimulant, a psychedelic compound, or an amnesic drug! Why, one writer has asked, should their lives be a constant, grey boredom waiting for death? Despite the anxiety of the older generation about the future of drug use and abuse, it is obvious that this social issue will ultimately be resolved by the drug experimenters of today as they grow older in the next two decades, ascending to positions of power and prominence. In the light of their own experiences with drugs, they will decide the fate of future generations.

Clearly, the issue that citizens must resolve is moral and political rather than medical. The problem was clearly defined by John Stuart Mill in his essay *On Liberty* many years ago. Mill insisted that the only reason for the members of a civilized community to exercise power is to prevent harm to others. The government of the people, for and by the people, should not legislate our personal independence over body and mind. In the more modern view of T. S. Szasz, a psychiatrist, this principle has been rephrased: "In an open society, it is none of the government's business what idea a man puts into his mind; likewise, it should be none of the government's business what drug he puts into his body."

Szasz argues that regardless of the inherent danger, all drugs should be legalized and not regulated by medical prescription, if we are to be consistent with the principles of personal liberty on which our society was founded. At the moment we do reserve such liberty for alcohol. As Szasz stated:

> Our present practices with respect to alcohol embody and reflect this individualistic ethic. We have the right to buy, possess, and consume alcoholic beverages. Regardless of how offensive drunkenness might be to a person, he cannot interfere with another person's "right" to become inebriated so long as that person drinks in the privacy of his own home or at some other appropriate location, and so long as he conducts himself in an otherwise law-abiding manner. In short, we have a right to be intoxicated—in private.

Our attitude toward alcohol—forged the hard way over years of social dispute—should, Szasz argues, be our attitude toward all other chemicals. We sell poisons of various sorts and "push" cigarettes with no more than a warning on the label. In an even more paradoxical manner, we have failed to solve the problem of gun control in our violent society. The inconsistency of our national attitude was underscored by Szasz when he observed: "As everyone knows, it is still possible in the United States to walk into a store and walk out with a shotgun. We enjoy this right not because we believe that guns are safe but because we believe even more strongly that civil liberties are precious. At the same time, it is not possible in the United States to walk into a store and walk out with a bottle of barbiturates, codeine, or other drugs."

There is no simple or easy answer to the drug problem. It has produced in this decade enormous public expense and psychological furor. What is evident is that the drug issue has driven an additional wedge between the generations. When the issue is resolved—as it ultimately will be—it will reach beyond the drug question, having meaning for the direction in which our society chooses to go.

race

It began with slavery; it evolved into chaos, and it remains a social crisis. The future of the racial issue has now become the future of American society. "America has had an almost perpetual racial crisis for a generation. But the last third of the twentieth century has begun on a new note, a change of rhetoric and a confusion over goals. Widespread rioting is just one expression of this note. The nation hesitates; it seems to have lost its confidence that the problem can be solved; it seems unsure as to even the direction in which a solution lies."

The first legal recognition of slavery took place in Virginia in 1661, and by the time of independence a substantial body of law defined chattel slavery, in which the slave received none of the protections of organized society because he was not considered to be a person. He was property, and could expect society's consideration only to the extent that a citizen's property must be protected. The slaveholder maintained absolute power over his property. Under this system of chattel slavery, approximately nine out of ten American blacks were slaves until the slave trade was officially abolished in 1808. From that year until shortly after World War I, there was unrestricted white immigration from Europe and other areas, and the proportion of blacks in our population declined until about 1930. When a quota system was established for white immigration, the proportion of blacks began to rise steadily.

Commentators have often contrasted the American history of slavery with slavery in Brazil, suggesting that the peculiar institution of slavery in the United States accounts in part for the current bitterness and strife we are experiencing. Interestingly, Brazil did not abolish slavery until 1888, about 25 years after the United States did. It then moved rapidly to a society in which acceptance was to be based entirely on personal achievement and education—not color. In this country, slavery was abolished only after a long and bitter civil war, the effects of which are still with us. In Brazil, abolition was achieved entirely by legislation; Brazil has never had a civil rights movement—obviously because its blacks never felt the need for one.

Although there appears to be racial harmony in Brazil, discrimination still exists but in a form that differs slightly from discrimination in America. Whites are dominant in both societies, and even those members of the Brazilian middle class who are of African descent tend to be light skinned. The darker the skin, the greater the likelihood they will have low-level, marginal occupations and live in the slums of the major cities.

racism

Americans were outraged when the 1968 Commission on Civil Disorders labeled the U.S. racist. Most of us consciously deny racial bias, but to the victims of racism it matters little whether racist acts and attitudes are intentional or the result of indifference. The pain is just as real. To suggest that the United States is a racist society does not mean that all individuals living in the society are racist, or that all regions and institutions are equally racist, or that no significant differences exist between the United States and other countries in which racism is present. The problem is not that all whites are racist, but rather that most racists are white. As psychologist Lloyd Delany, who has worked with black delinquents, has observed, a "society in which racism is a major theme quickly establishes a network of institutions to perpetuate its racist actions and attitudes. And eventually racism affects all the society. Such is the nature of American bigotry."

Racism in America is not limited merely to the delusions of a bigoted and ignorant minority. It is a set of beliefs whose "structure arises from the deepest levels of our lives—from the fabric of assumptions we make about the world, ourselves, and others, and from the patterns of our fundamental social activities." Indeed, it is impossible to be white in our culture and grow up free of any taint of racism. And, now, racism has become a critical problem for our culture. "For the first time in our history almost all of the submerged groups in our country ... are demanding entrance into the major institutions of our society. And, in addition, they are demanding admission on their own terms. They come often not as humble petitioners seeking boons, but as free Americans demanding what they regard as their stolen birthright. Sometimes they even ask for compound interest to cover past injustices."

As these demands for equality increase in frequency, they provoke racist reactions in the white population. Whites are stimulated to conjure up a series of justifications for the master-slave social structure that has existed for so long. In a book entitled *American Racism: Exploration of the Nature of Prejudice*, R. Daniels and H. L. Kitano outlined the incredibly ugly "logic" of the bigot.

1. There is little validity in the doctrine of racial equality; some races are demonstrably superior to others.
2. Races can be graded in terms of superiority. The Caucasian is presumed to be superior, and history is used to validate this claim. Caucasians have constantly shown their physical and mental superiority.
3. Nations and peoples who have interbred with the nonwhite races do not progress, and countries controlled by nonwhites do not progress.
4. Amalgamation means the wiping out of the superior Caucasian race, a process which leads to the eventual decline of a civilization.

The outcome of such prejudiced, racist thought has been the evolution of a series of assumptions justifying the continued separation of white and black citizens. Separatists, for example, maintain that each of the races feels awkward and uncomfortable in the midst of the other; each is more comfortable "with their own kind." T. F. Pettigrew of Harvard has called this "the comfortable assumption." The second assumption of white segregationists, as discussed by Pettigrew, is blatantly racist. Segregationists unashamedly maintain that Negroes are inherently inferior to Caucasians. This is "the racial inferiority assumption," every argument of which is seriously jeopardized by findings in social and biological science. An additional assumption, "the racial conflict assumption," follows from this conviction of racial superiority. This fourth assumption states that racial harmony can only obtain if the races do not mingle until each has reached a state of true equality with the other. Thus, what Pettigrew calls the "autonomy-before-contact" assumption proposes that there be segregation until blacks are ready to meet whites on equal terms—a time, unfortunately, that will be postponed indefinitely by means of continued discrimination, prejudice, and segregation.

If successful integration would work anywhere, it ought to work on the university campus where supposedly the enlightened, emancipated, and unprejudiced young gather together in common purpose. But, the black experience at white colleges has been reported as "a story of hope, frustration and disillusionment, of individual and institutional racism, and of defensive separatism." According to some social critics, there is in reality "no chance" for integration in the college situation.

Contrary to expectations, with increased enrollment of black students and, consequently, an increased number of black-white interactions, trust and confidence between the races has apparently decreased. For blacks, the social life on campus soon becomes limited to other blacks as a part of the trend toward separatism. Weekends are increasingly spent off campus in black communities and metropolitan centers. The problem of an adequate social life becomes particularly acute, if the size of the black student population on a predominantly white campus is quite small. In such a situation, the social life of the black woman suffers most severely since she less often dates interracially and is confined to her own racial group. If she is to date outside her racial group, she traditionally does not take the initiative herself. The white male must ask her for a date. The black male, however, is freer to operate as he sees fit. He has a variety of justifications for his white dating activity, although at the same time he may criticize his black sisters for dating white men and allowing the continuation of white exploitation of the black female. Surely, both races have a long way to go to interracial understanding.

One author concerned with the nature of prejudice was O.

Klineberg. He raises the question whether skin color is reacted to because it is highly visible, or whether it has such high visibility because we take it so seriously. As Klineberg makes clear, considerable evidence shows that the young do not classify people in this way. Furthermore, prejudice is equally possible when the pigmentation of the skin is irrelevant. (Examples are the Nazi distinction between Aryans and non-Aryans, Catholic versus Protestant warfare in Northern Ireland, the Belgian separation into Flemish and French-speaking segments, the French Canadian separatist movement in Quebec, the Indian-Pakistani conflict, and the apparently inevitable regional conflicts between north and south in every country.)

As a prime example of the prejudiced workings of the human mind, Klineberg cited the Eta or Burakumin of Japan. An estimated two million Burakumin scattered throughout Japan form an outcast population considered to be defiled, unclean, and fit only for certain undesirable occupations. The Burakumin most often live in slums or ghettos, and intermarriage with other Japanese is practically taboo. They form a sort of "invisible race"—a race visible only to the eyes of those prejudiced against them, as this description attests:

> Officially the Burakumin were emancipated in 1871, at which time they were free to discard the special prescribed garb they had been forced to wear and the occupations that had identified them for over a thousand years. Yet, despite recent radical economic and social changes that have placed Japan among the top four or five countries of the world, the condition of the Burakumin remains unchanged and they suffer the same indignity and lack of opportunity as the Negro in America.

The Eta, like U. S. blacks, score lower on I.Q. tests, achieve less in schools, and are more often truant and delinquent despite the lack of racial differences from the dominant culture. Conflict, thus, may occur with or without visible color differences.

The white race is by no means an established fact of nature; it is no more than an idea. What we in our culture think of as a white man is considered to be red by some New Guineans, and when did anyone ever really see a *white* white man? As one writer noted: "Most so-called white men are turned by wind, rain, and certain kinds of lotion to various shades of brown, although they would probably prefer to be thought bronze." In reality, there is a continuous grading of human skin color from light to dark with no sharp breaks. Obviously, then, it is difficult to establish what constitutes the American Negro. What degree of black African ancestry establishes a person as a Negro? Is 51 percent, or 50.1 percent, or some other statistical percentage necessary? The question is ridiculous because there is no way of estimating quantities of racial inheritance in terms of percentages. Moreover, there is also no good evidence that any human group differs from any other group in its genetic potential for mental or social development.

When black-white prejudice is complicated by the additional factor of religion, our stereotypes become harder and harder to maintain. Blacks of a certain religious persuasion have been described as looking upon Negroes with scorn and derision. In addition to adopting the Star of David as a symbol, they speak Hebrew and maintain manners, customs, and diet that are as orthodox as that of the most orthodox Jew.

American prejudice and stereotyping of blacks as well as almost every national group has had an extended history. According to the work of three researchers, however, there may be hope that these prejudiced attitudes are breaking down. These men studied and compared the social stereotypes reported by Princeton undergraduates in 1967, 1951, and 1933. They began by reviewing the pioneer investigation of verbal stereotypes conducted by D. Katz and K. W. Braly in 1933. These two pioneering researchers studied the five key traits used by 100 Princeton undergraduates to describe ten different racial and national groups. The results in 1933 showed an impressively high degree of agreement and yielded a distinctive set of popular labels —many of them highly derogatory—for each of the ten groups. Uniformity in stereotyping Negroes, Germans, and Jews was extremely high; certain traits were ascribed to those groups by more than 75 percent of the subjects. Since most students had no contact with members of the stereotyped groups, it was obvious that they had simply absorbed the images of their day and culture.

Almost 20 years later in 1951, a researcher named R. Centers presented the original Princeton norms to students at the University of California at Los Angeles and found that each of the trait lists was correctly identified by a large majority of students; 75 percent recognized the 1933 characterizations of Japanese, Chinese, and Turks; and 95 percent recognized the 1933 descriptions of English and Jews.

By this time, however, things had changed at Princeton. Another researcher, G. M. Gilbert, repeated Katz and Braly's 1933 experiment at Princeton; he discovered that uniformity in verbal stereotyping had lessened considerably. During the 18-year period a more favorable characterization of the Negro emerged. In 1933, "superstitious" and "lazy" appeared in one-third of all responses. The number of students checking "superstitious" dropped from a nearly unanimous 84 percent to 13 percent—the largest difference found in the study. The percentage of those who checked "lazy" decreased from 75 to 26 percent. In 1951, only a few students referred to the Negro as "ignorant" (11 percent) or "stupid" (4 percent), as compared to 38 percent and 22 percent, respectively, in 1933.

92

Despite the fact that tendencies toward stereotyping and prejudice may gradually be decreasing, we still have grave problems. And, even though images are changing, American blacks still face a long, difficult struggle. As one writer stated: "We have had in this country, and to our shame we still have, a number of prejudices against Negroes—probably stronger against them because of their number and their inferior condition than against other minority groups."

the black experience

A white man can only guess at what it means to be black in America, and even an educated guess is likely to be a case of "knowing the words but not the music." One white man tried it, but he was still white pretending to be black. Using an oral medication coupled with exposure to ultraviolet rays J. H. Griffin, author of *Black Like Me*, changed his skin color from white to black and traveled as a Negro in the Southern part of the United States. While his was a white man's experience of being black, in the 1950s it was a startling documentary about suddenly moving from the position of the oppressor to that of oppressed. Pettigrew has asked us to consider the past experiences of the 20-year-old Negro in 1971:

> He was born in 1951; he was only 3 years old when the Supreme Court ruled against *de jure* public school segregation; he was only 6 years old at the time of the disorders over desegregation in Little Rock, Arkansas; he was 9 years old when the student-organized sit-ins began at segregated lunch counters throughout the South; he was 12 when the dramatic march on Washington took place and 15 when the climactic Selma march occurred. He has witnessed during his short life the initial dismantling of the formal structure of white supremacy. Conventional wisdom holds that such an experience should lead to a highly satisfied generation of young black Americans; but newspaper headlines and social-psychological theory tell us that precisely the opposite is closer to the truth.

The black 20-year-old has found that his freedom to work and live has not improved, despite these social advances.

In a 1964 article entitled "Who Needs the Negro?" S. M. Wilhelm and E. H. Powell indicated that the black man may be less exploited now than he was as a slave, but, an even worse fate is developing where he finds himself economically irrelevant to modern society. The authors suggest that in the days ahead the black man might be less abused, but he might also be seen as unnecessary. If the black disappeared from American life tomorrow, he would hardly be missed. Blacks have fled the rural South for the prison of the northern city, and northern whites have fled to the suburbs to avoid them. The ghettos have become a new form of the Indian reservation—a new junk heap on which the economically worthless are thrown. As we automate our society, the authors warn, the junk heap will get larger.

Economic uselessness defines a part of the black work experience. There is, according to one author, a black subculture in our society whose members do not want to conform to the white culture's definition of work. This fact has produced untold friction between the two cultures. "The antiwork ethic is solidified by creatively practiced teen-age rituals: hanging around the candy store, cutting school, dropping out, stealing, playing the numbers, etc. The teen-ager who does these things is known to his friends as a 'player,' the exact opposite of 'worker,' which is the white culture's name for a 'good' boy." When the black goes to work in jobs defined by the white culture, it works well for a while; but the black is soon laughed at by his player friends and the black militant calls him Uncle Tom. Before long he reverts to old ways, is late for work, or does not show up at all.

In the black experience, religion has been a psychological mainstay, or compensation for the daily affronts that life offers. But, even in their churches, blacks have been constricted. White religion has been less than charitable to the blacks. Attitude surveys have regularly reported that white churchgoers are significantly more prejudiced about race than nonchurchgoers of the same age, educational level, race, and geographical regions. But, as one observer has pointed out, there are at least two types of church members—instrumental and devotional. Instrumental involvement in church can serve self-centered purposes such as status, business contacts, fellowship, and so on that are far removed from religious devotion. In a devotional orientation to church, emphasis is on the nature of the religious experience itself as a way of life.

In one study of a church in a small Southern city a dramatic split was found along the lines of racial issues. Those with instrumental beliefs about religion were more frequently strongly committed to segregation, while the reverse was true for devotional members of the church. Thus, it is not religious participation that is the culprit, but rather, the style of religious involvement that is related to one's racial prejudice. In this respect, the role of the churches has been especially remarkable in forming the black experience. Despite their traditional dedication to moral values, church's have had limited influence on the racial attitudes of their constituents and, on the whole, have reinforced the status quo.

Although the idea of "being black" is continuing to evolve, it is rapidly being associated with a particular attitude toward the self and others. The concept of Black Power is still a vague slogan that has yet to be identified with a full ideology or political program, but identifying with and acknowledging one's blackness increasingly means being free of shame and moving beyond the heritage of slavery. With new perceptions come new understandings of the self, a new comprehension of previous indignities, and greater awareness of the path that must be followed in the future. Blackness is a matter of degree and psychological attitude toward the self. It is a sign of psychological progress that this minority group no longer sees itself as "colored" or "Negro" and no longer hopes for progress based on white "good will."

The black psychiatrists W. H. Grier and P. M. Cobbs point out that "For a black man survival in America depends in large measure on the development of a 'healthy' cultural paranoia. He must maintain a high degree of suspicion toward the motives of every white man and at the same time never allow this suspicion to impair his grasp of reality. It is a demanding requirement and not everyone can manage it with grace." Often this urge to survival has sapped the black's assertiveness, self-confidence, and willingness to risk failure in an innovative venture. Sapped of his aggressive drive, he has been effectively castrated and rendered compliant to reduce the risk of white retaliation. Self-denigrating, self-destructive, and pessimistic, the black has indulged in an endeavor toward social and community suicide which has fueled the fires of white prejudice. For a long time, the black was compliant, suppressing his rage and aggression. Now, he must learn to reverse the process and abandon subservience and dependency, no longer bowing and scraping to be "a good nigger." No more shall he convert rage into a smile or a shuffle or drugged self-deception in an effort to deny the painful reality of a hostile world.

The black psyche has much to overcome. More than two decades ago, a Swedish social scientist was invited to America for the purpose of conducting probably the most thorough study of the race problem ever undertaken. The social scientist, Gunnar Myrdal, produced a monumental work entitled *An American Dilemma*. When Myrdal asked white Southerners to list, in the order of importance, the things they thought Negroes wanted most, he got responses such as (a) intermarriage and sexual intercourse with whites; (b) social equality; (c) desegregation of public facilities, buses, and churches; (d) political enfranchisement; (e) fair treatment in the law courts; and (f) equal economic opportunities. The curious thing about this rank-ordering of ambitions was that when Myrdal approached the blacks, they listed the same items as whites but with one major change—their list was in the reverse order. For their own special reasons both blacks and whites are seriously concerned about the sexual issue. Certainly, the sexual aspects of the race problem in America are as much a "thorn in the side" for blacks as they are for whites. The white man, and especially the Southerner, is obsessed by the idea of blacks desiring sexual relations with whites; and the black man is tormented by the presence of white women whom he cannot or had better not touch. Indeed the race problem is inextricably connected with sex.

Another powerful contributor to the American black revolution was Malcolm X—a man who, by his own admission, rose from a life of stealing, pimping, and dope peddling to be a leader in the Negro revolution; a man; brilliant and sensitive, described as "a giant in a sick world," who gave manhood, pride, and self-respect to blacks. He was a necessary catalyst in the churning, tortured times in which he lived, before—as he fully anticipated—he was assassinated while making a speech in New York in 1965.

Malcolm X gave many blacks a new vision of themselves and made the least among them feel capable of becoming the best. It was a critical moment in the race struggle in America and his death attracted world-wide attention as he was elevated to the station of martyr for a cause. It is difficult to estimate the impact of Malcolm X during the intervening years since his life was snuffed out by assassins. History will evaluate him, finally, but often history has a short and selective memory. He was a man needed by the time and he served his time well.

The black psychiatrist Franz Fanon lived a short but remarkably telling life before he died of cancer at the age of thirty-six. His experiences during the French-Algerian war in the late 1950s defined his awareness of the role of violence in producing revolutionary historical change in society. His book *The Wretched of the Earth* carried a stirring message to all the deprived inhabitants of what was called the Third World—those emerging from native status in under-developed countries, the poor and disenfranchised on the planet's surface. Fanon's was an angry call to arms that would allow the Third World to write a new history of man free of the taints, sicknesses, and inhumanities of white dominated Western history in Europe and America. The message of revolution came at a fitting time for soon-to-be militant blacks of the early sixties in America who viewed racism in our country as nothing more than a sophisticated form of colonialism in which the natives are exploited for white power and profit. Franz Fanon, born in Martinique and concerned more with Europe than America, became an integral part of the black struggle for freedom in this society.

The experience of being black has been recorded poignantly by those sensitive to its meaning and impact. G. Leinwand, the general editor of a book entitled *The Negro in the City* has made a collection of such comments. The following excerpt is from Richard Wright's 1945 novel, *Black Boy*.

> The white South said that it knew "niggers," and I was what the white South called a "nigger." Well, the white South had never known what

I thought, what I felt. The white South said that I had a "place" in life. Well, I had never felt my "place"; or, rather, my deepest instincts had always made me reject the "place" to which the white South had assigned me."

A second excerpt presented by Leinwand is from James Baldwin's *Notes of a Native Son*.

Waiting for a hamburger and coffee; it was always an extraordinarily long time before anything was set before me; but it was not until the fourth visit that I learned that, in fact, nothing had ever been set before me: I had simply picked something up. Negroes were not served here, I was told, and they had been waiting for me to realize that I was always the only Negro present."

A third excerpt has been taken from Dick Gregory's *Nigger: An Autobiography*.

It was the first really good beating I ever had in my life, a professional job. End to end, up and down, they didn't miss a spot. It didn't really start hurting until about midnight when I tried to touch my face, and I couldn't get my arm up that high. What the hell, if you're willing to die for Freedom, you have to be willing to take a beating. For a couple of days, though, I thought that dying was probably easier.

This is the black psyche that issues from the black experience—an experience incomprehensible to any white member of our culture.

violence in the ghetto

The 1968 report of the National Advisory Commission on Civil Disorders concluded that our nation is moving toward two separate and unequal societies, one black and one white. Further, white racism is essentially responsible for the explosive mixture which has been accumulating in our cities since the end of World War II. The report was triggered by violent racial disorders during the summer of 1967, and the charge of the commission was to find out what happened, why it happened, and what would prevent it from happening again. The members of the commission pointed out segregation and poverty have created in the racial ghetto a destructive environment totally unknown to most white Americans. What white Americans have never fully understood—but what the Negro can never forget—is that white society is deeply implicated in the ghetto. White institutions created it; white institutions maintain it; and white society condones it.

There was no "typical" riot in 1967. Neither was there an orderly sequence of events or a predictable social process. It was clear, however, that the riots involved blacks acting against local symbols of white American society, authority, and property in black neighborhoods—rather than against white persons. Out of 164 disorders reported during the first nine months of 1967, eight (5 percent) were major in terms of violence and damage; 33 (20 percent) were serious but not major; 123 (75 percent) were minor and undoubtedly would not have received national attention had the nation not been sensitized by the more serious outbreaks. In the 75 disorders studied by a Senate subcommittee, 83 deaths were reported. Eighty-two percent of the deaths and more than half the injuries occurred in Newark and Detroit. About 10 percent of the dead and 36 percent of the injured were public employees, primarily law officers and firemen. The overwhelming majority of the persons killed or injured in all the disorders were black civilians.

The commission reported that most rioters were young Negro males. Nearly 53 percent of the arrestees were between 15 and 24 years of age; nearly 81 percent were between 15 and 35. In Detroit and Newark, about 74 percent of the rioters were brought up in the North. In contrast, of those who were noninvolved, 36 percent in Detroit and 52 percent in Newark were brought up in the North.

According to the report, the rioters were seeking fuller participation in the social order and material benefits enjoyed by the majority of American citizens. Rather than rejecting the American system, they were anxious to obtain a place in it for themselves. Numerous black counterrioters walked the streets urging rioters to "cool it." The typical counterrioter was better educated and had higher income than either the rioter or the noninvolved person.

A study of the aftermath of disorder leads to the disturbing conclusion that, despite the institution of some postriot programs, little basic change occurred in the conditions underlying the outbreak of the disorders. Actions to ameliorate black grievances were limited and sporadic; with but few exceptions, tensions had not been significantly reduced. In several cities, the principal official response was to train and equip the police with more sophisticated weapons. In many cities, increasing polarization is evident, with continuing breakdown of interracial communication and the growth of white segregationist or black separatist groups.

An explosive mixture had been accumulating in our major cities for a great many years and incidents with police served to set off the outbursts. According to the Kerner Commission, there were several ingredients in the conflagration. One additive was frustrated hope that came from the unfulfilled expectations aroused by the judicial and legislative victories of the civil rights movement in the South. Another ingredient was a climate that tended to approve and encourage violence as a form of protest. This kind of climate was created by the white terrorism directed against nonviolent protest. Both state and local white officials have openly defied the law and Federal authority, resisting desegregation. Some white protest groups have turned their backs on nonviolence, gone beyond the constitutionally protected rights of petition and free assembly, and resorted to violence in an attempt to force an alteration of laws and policies with which they disagree.

The frustrations of powerlessness, a third ingredient in the outbursts, have led some blacks to the conviction that there is no effective alternative to violence when means are needed to achieve the redress of grievances and to "move the system." These frustrations are reflected in alienation and hostility toward the legal and governmental institutions controlled by the white society. The frustrations are also embodied in racial consciousness and solidarity reflected in the term *Black Power*.

A new mood has sprung up among blacks, particularly among the young, in which self-esteem and enhanced racial pride are replacing apathy and submission to "the system." The police are not merely a "spark" factor. To some blacks, police have come to symbolize white power, white racism, and white repression. And the fact is that many police do reflect and express these white attitudes. The atmosphere of hostility and cynicism is reinforced by a widespread belief among blacks that there is police brutality and the existence of a "double standard" of justice and protection—one for blacks and one for whites. We have probably not seen the last of ghetto violence. Little in the ghetto has changed, and nothing has changed for the better.

social science and race

When Martin Luther King addressed the American Psychological Association in 1968 he stated: "It is the historic mission of the social sciences to enable mankind to take possession of society. It follows that for Negroes who substantially are excluded from society this science is needed even more desperately than for any other group in the population." King also made it clear that if the blacks needed the help of social scientists, the white members of the society needed their help even more to learn about the depth of white racism and prejudice.

Many of the people bred in the ghetto are telling psychologists to take their psychology and go home. According to black psychologist Charles Thomas, white psychologists are sustained by and have contributed to white racist values since, as whites, they are equipped neither by temperament nor training to consider anything other than the correctness and universality of white cultural norms. Thus, a number of black psychologists have demanded that research which is to be conducted on black people first be examined for bias by black psychologists.

We cannot underestimate the degree to which white social scientists have been unable, unwilling, or uninterested in properly studying the black segment of our population. As Billingsley scathingly observed: "Students of human behavior, policy makers, and citizens who look to the body of knowledge about the human condition which has been generated and reflected by American social scientists will find no area of American life more glaringly ignored, more distorted, or more systematically disvalued than black family life. Thus, black families who have fared so ill historically in white American society have fared no better in white American social science, and largely for the same reasons."

Billingsley concludes that social science scholarship has failed miserably to meet the challenge of studying the black minority; further, it has contributed much misinformation and misinterpretation which, in turn, has perpetuated a number of stereotypes and myths about black families. Billingsley observed:

> There are four tendencies in the treatment of black families in social science scholarship. The first is the tendency to ignore black families altogether. The second is, when black families are considered, to focus almost exclusively on the lowest income group of black families, that acute minority of families who live in public housing projects or who are supported by public welfare assistance. The third is to ignore the majority of black stable families even among this lowest income group, to ignore the processes by which these families move from one equilibrium state to another, and to focus instead on the most unstable among these low income families. A fourth tendency, which is more bizarre than all the others, is the tendency on the part of social scientists to view the black, low-income, unstable, problem-ridden family as the causal nexus for the difficulties their members experience in the wider society."

R. D. Abrahams in his book *Positively Black* argues that, no matter how much energy, time, and money are devoted to the "Negro problem," nothing substantial can be accomplished until we have a greater understanding of black culture. "We have been so bent on educating Negroes in our ways that we have forgotten that they have their ways too, and we whites need to be educated about them. Because we know so little about Negro culture, we have wasted huge sums of money as well as millions of man hours because in developing programs we have often failed to take into consideration black attitudes toward leadership, energy, time, work, money. We know very little about these matters, even less about black aspirations and ideals."

100

Social science confronts a race problem even when interpersonal transaction is reduced to a bare minimum. One hardly need explain why a white therapist would find it difficult to maintain rapport with a black patient. But, difficult issues remain unresolved for the black therapist and his black patient. The black therapist–black client situation also reflects the larger American racial climate; the black therapist may over-identify with his client and lose some of the objectivity necessary to help the client solve his problems. The black as well as the white therapist must work through his own feelings about race before he can serve those who come to him. To say this is not to accomplish it, of course. It may be some years before therapists can truly become color-blind in the therapeutic role.

A most damning indictment was made by the psychiatrist Price Cobbs, who has concluded that:

> American bigotry is a malignant disease not yielding to the passage of time, the enactment of laws or the effects of education. Moreover, the disease is deeply ingrained into American life. The most virulent racism is rarely expressed openly, it is not openly taught by parents and teachers, and is not identifiable by geographic regions. More often than not, Americans acquire attitudes about blacks that are the result of a twisted and distorted group logic, a logic rarely examined critically. Society imposes certain attitudes of hatred. Whites and blacks—each in their own way—accept and incorporate this "programmed" hatred.

In what Cobbs calls "ethnotherapy," race and racism becomes a central focus of therapy for both blacks and whites in whom, he believes, this issue is critical to the conduct of daily life. His work with white and black groups in San Francisco over the years has confirmed for him the importance of all of us gaining new insight and understanding into the deep, unconscious reach of a prejudice born of hundreds of years of mutual misunderstanding, fear, and hatred. Reflecting on his experiences with such groups, Cobbs observes that "What facilitates the process and makes therapeutic change possible is the ability of the leaders to help participants jar loose, dissect and examine in fine detail the usual information about race that our society makes certain we all receive and incorporate. And what comes out is an astonishing variety of biases and fears and an appalling lack of knowledge."

As these black-white group encounters progress through predictable stages of attack and counterattack, new emotions and understandings emerge both in their personal and American feelings about identity. Perhaps this, or something like it, may be the answer to our continuing and growing racial fear of one another.

One focal concern of psychological research over the years has been the study of racial differences in intelligence. Until the late

1920s most of the interpretations of research findings supported the theory of white supremacy and suggested inherent intellectual differences between races. In the 1930s a series of more rigorous studies appeared which emphasized the influence of environmental factors on intelligence test scores. The environmentalist position was strengthened over the next several decades.

In 1969, California education professor A. R. Jensen published an article that reopened the heated debate in the academic community. Jensen argued that intelligence was primarily a function of genetic inheritance rather than environmental influences and that whites were intellectually superior to blacks. The vast majority of behavioral scientists do not support the idea of differences in native intelligence between blacks and whites, and they disagree with Jensen about the role of genetic versus environmental factors in determining intelligence.

Jensen questioned the central notions that I.Q. differences are a result of environmental differences and cultural biases of I.Q. tests. His actions caused a furor among social scientists that has been unequalled in several decades. Jensen's concept of "heritability" of intelligence was particularly provocative, since it implies that genetic factors are more crucial to I.Q. than are the environmental factors with which one is forced to grow up. A part of Jensen's argument was that the massive educational programs instituted for young children in recent years have failed to alter our social and intellectual condition in any visible way.

In the Spring 1969 issue of the *Harvard Educational Review*, seven psychologists offered comment and rebuttal to Jensen's arguments and thus initiated a controversy that has since enveloped nearly every social scientist. Harvard psychologist Jerome Kagan's conclusions, for example, described Jensen's claims as founded upon "inadequate evidence and illogical conclusions." The outcome of this battle among social scientists is still in doubt. Nonetheless, Jensen's conclusions and the storm of criticism that followed have had at least one salutary effect—psychologists and their social scientific colleagues have had a rude awakening. They have been forced to recognize the degree to which they have ignored the critical social issue of racial relations in America. They have also learned, the hard way, that for the culture-at-large there are few "neutral" social scientific "facts." Social scientists can no longer find refuge in the famous (or infamous) "ivory towers" that once protected them from involvement with the rest of society.

The scholar Otto Klineberg agrees with most contemporary scientists when he insists that innate psychological differences between ethnic groups have never been satisfactorily demonstrated. The sci-

102

ence of psychology can offer no support to those who see in skin color a reason for denying individuals full participation in American democracy. The assumption of innate social inferiority has been assaulted by social scientists for over four decades, and certainly these efforts have had some impact on American attitudes toward race. In two studies of attitudes toward desegregation, it has been reported that in 1942 only two of every five white Americans regarded Negroes as their intellectual equals. By 1956 almost four out of five whites no longer felt that as a matter of course they were intellectually superior.

The range of psychological research pertaining to race has been extensive over the years. It is a critical problem today because the results of many psychological assessment programs have been detrimental to the welfare of black Americans. Since blacks have not tended to score as well as whites on assessment tests, the scores have functioned to exclude black students from a variety of opportunities. This highlights the distinction that must be made between the results and the *utilization* of the results of psychological tests. "It would seem advisable to reassess the utilization of the results of psychological tests and propose quite stringent regulations for their dissemination and use. To simply boycott testing programs as the Association of Black Psychologists has proposed is to retard progress in the area of being able to more effectively assist students and others through counseling based on refined standardized testing programs."

The study of race by social scientists has become an increasingly delicate and sensitive area. As M. Brewster Smith observed in a foreword to E. E. Baughman's book, *Black Americans*: "Much has happened to suggest that America's obsession with race may have neared or passed the boundary beyond which the spirit of science, open-minded and evidential, can no longer contribute. When scientific disagreement leads to personal vilification, as it recently has in matters of race, we are dangerously close to the edge. As polarization heightens, facts become irrelevant. Motives become impugned, whole lines of evidence get read out of court." We can only hope this mutual distrust will dissipate and social scientists will once again be free to contribute to the solution of this critical problem.

a black and white tomorrow

The black attitude toward the future is not a very optimistic one. White America seems habitually to ignore social problems until they reach crisis proportions and then respond with "band-aid" remedies that do not change the basic institutions responsible for the problems. A. Pinkney, author of *Black Americans*, concluded:

> In the immediate future black Americans will continue to make greater demands on the society and ... resistance by white Americans to these demands is likely to intensify. The employment gap between black and white Americans is likely to increase. In both rates of employment and in earnings, Negroes will continue to lag behind white Americans. In housing, middle-class Negroes will find it easier to move from the slums, but the central cities are likely to become more segregated and the black community will probably expand with the increasing high birth rate.... It is perhaps in the realm of politics that the greatest changes are likely. Throughout the country black people are likely to participate in the electoral process in greater and greater numbers, electing an increasing number of black people to municipal and state offices.

The white perspective is more encouraging at least with regard to white attitudes toward black people. Some indications are given by surveys conducted by the University of Michigan's Institute for Social Research. The findings and trends indicate that (a) an increasing proportion of whites and blacks report having friends in the other race; (b) both whites and blacks feel contact is increasing at work, in the schools, and in public places; (c) a significant upgrading of educational achievement is occurring among younger blacks; (d) a growing number of blacks are moving into white collar employment; and (e) the most positive racial attitudes are held by people with some college education, particularly those whose college experience has been since World War II.

The future depends on one's point of view. But, as badly battered as it is, the American Dream has not disappeared. However long it may take and however bitter the struggle may be, humanity has no other course to pursue. Tomorrow must be black *and* white.

poverty

It is a pleasure to be able to report that poverty no longer exists; recently, poverty was officially transformed, by the bureaus of our government, into the "low-income" problem. According to the logic of this maneuver, all of us now and then suffer an attack of low income, but this temporary financial reverse is not really a state of poverty. Despite efforts to discount the severity of the problem, however, there were 17.5 million of us who fell below the "low-income" level in 1970.

The contemporary poor are the nonwhites, families with no wage earners, families headed by females, and males aged 14 to 25 or over 65 with "poverty-linked" characteristics. These characteristics are less than eight years of education, residence in a rural farm area, members of families in which there are more than six children under age 18, and residents of the South. Poverty is more complex than this, of course. There are Americans who are impoverished despite the fact that they work from 50 to 52 weeks a year. These "working poor," nearly invisible in our culture, are made up of service workers, laborers, farmers, clerks, and sales employees who require little training for the job. Unfortunately, their plight is seldom documented. In many cases the individual is ready and eager to perform in a more demanding position, but the local section of the economy is simply unable to provide an adequate wage for the needed task. One author has ably stated the critical issue.

> On the average, the poor in the United States have bad reputations. They are regarded as responsible for much physical aggression and destruction of property; their support is alleged to be a heavy burden on the rest of the community; and they are said not even to try very hard to meet community standards of behavior or to be self-supporting. Poverty, it is said, is little enough punishment for people so inferior and so lacking in virtue.

There are all kinds of poor and all kinds of reasons for being poor. Most people who die poor were born poor. In part, this happens because by the time the male reaches his mid-twenties the limits of his lifetime income have already in great measure been established. By this age, his fate in school will have been decided, and this decision permanently opens or closes the doors of his future. If he starts a family while he is young, this responsibility will tend to bind him to when he begins work and what he does for a living. Thus, by the time the breadwinner is 25 or 30 years of age, the fate of his family will more or less be sealed. Those families who will always be poor can easily be recognized since early marriage, child-bearing, incomplete education, and a poor first job destines the family to an excessive risk of poverty.

One outspoken professor of education, Arthur Pearl, insists that the public view of the poor as inadequate can, in part, be traced to the doorstep of psychologists. Pearl is convinced that "Psychologists and other social scientists contribute to at least four mythologies from which emerge programs and policies that prevent the poor from escaping from poverty. These myths assert that the poor are: (a) constitutionally inferior, (b) victimized by accumulated environmental deficits, (c) inadequately socialized, (d) encapsulated within autonomous cultures."

When these myths are translated into social policies, the policies themselves reinforce institutionalized social inequality and racism. As psychologists we have done almost nothing about investigating the institutions that keep poverty alive—our target has always been the poor themselves. And, we have viewed the poor as deviants from the acceptable middle-class society from which psychologists issue.

One dramatic instance of the interaction of social science and public policy can be found in the affair of the Moynihan Report.

In March 1965, Daniel P. Moynihan, the Assistant Secretary of Labor, completed a confidential report for President Lyndon Johnson entitled *The Negro Family: Case for National Action*. Publication of this report produced an explosion of bitter, negative reaction among those concerned with racial issues throughout the country. In brief, Moynihan's report questioned whether the removal of the barriers of social discrimination would be enough to assure blacks of equality with whites, since conditions in the Negro community and family life had deteriorated to the point that many black children were illegitimate, dependent on welfare support, and raised in one-parent households dominated by females. Moynihan labeled this condition a "tangle of pathology that has produced high delinquency rates, high rates of drug addiction, despair about achieving a stable life, and alienation of poverty-stricken black males from the larger society."

As critics L. Rainwater and W. L. Yancey pointed out:

> To sociologists and psychologists with a professional interest in the situation of Negro Americans, the report presented little that was new or startling. Rather, it presented in a dramatic and policy-oriented way a well-established, though not universally supported, view of the afflictions of Negro Americans. Indeed, the basic paradigm of Negro life that Moynihan's report reflected had been laid down by the great Negro sociologist, E. Franklin Frazier, over thirty years before. ... Yet, if there was "nothing really new" in the report, why should it have elicited such a positive response from the White House; why the uneasy and critical response within certain segments of the government; why the strong negative response from some in the civil rights movement and in academic social science circles? How, in short, does "nothing new" become both new national policy and a controversy?

The heat of controversy has diminished over the years, but social scientists began to face the inescapable fact that they have unrecognized scientific blind spots that prove to be most crippling when they enter the social arena and speak to the issues of how Americans of all sorts should lead their lives. Social scientists came up with simple answers to what obviously is an exceptionally complex problem in our society.

the culture of poverty

It is true, of course, that all poor people are not poverty stricken. Graduate students in a university, for example, may live in dilapidated housing, eat an inadequate diet, and suffer from low income, but they are not impoverished. In much the same way, the immigrants dwelling in ethnic slums had no intention of becoming inveterate slum dwellers, and they were not members of the culture of poverty. The concept of a "culture of poverty" (or more accurately a subculture of poverty) refers to a way of life or a design for living that is handed down across generations. The concept tries to account for the behavior of the poor by positing a self-perpetuating system of values that differs from the value system of the middle class. The culture of poverty supposedly transcends social, racial, regional, and even national differences, and the poor are expected to be much the same the world over. Oscar Lewis, in his article "The Culture of Poverty," states that slum children have acquired the basic values and attitudes of the poverty subculture by the age of 6 or 7. He identifies 70 traits comprising the culture of poverty including feelings of fatalism and belief in chance, present time orientation and short time perspective, impulsiveness or inability to delay gratification or plan for the future, concrete rather than abstract thinking, feelings of inferiority, acceptance of aggression and illegitimacy, and authoritarianism. If we pursue this notion, we would naturally conclude, as Michael Harrington did in *The Other America*, "The poor are not like everyone else. They are a different kind of people. They think and feel differently; they look upon a different America than the middle class looks upon. They, and not the quietly desperate clerk or the harried executive, are the main victims of this society's tension and conflict."

The idea of a subculture of poverty has been applied to other aspects of our society. Some observers hold that a distinctive culture and distinctive moral system characterize those who are brought up in the lower class world. If a child associates intimately with no one but adults and children from the slum, naturally he will learn only slum culture. Thus, social class—in this case the lower class—limits and patterns the learning environment, structuring the social maze

110

in which the child learns his habits and meanings. As an illustration, what the middle class would label as delinquent, unmotivated, or shiftless behavior may actually be a practical, realistic pattern of adaptation to slum life. We must acknowledge that a large and very real segment of our population exists whose life, patterns of behavior, and moral values do not match those of the middle class.

If a culture of poverty really exists, then neither full employment nor a federal income-maintenance program would make a fundamental change in the established way of life of those who are chronically poor. Thus, to offer ghetto residents what we call "opportunities" might only lead to the discovery that their aspirations are different from our own, their notions of success may not be a driving force for them, and they are less convinced of the virtues of hard work. It has been suggested that the poor may have any one of four reactions to a life in which television tells them what they should value, while street reality tells them they will never make it. One of these reactions (the lower-class alternative) might be to abandon middle-class patterns and develop a separate cultural way of life. Another reaction may be the middle-class alternative where the poor believe in middle-class values, even if they are unattainable. A third reaction might be the value stretch alternative, where they maintain middle-class patterns but stretch them to justify behaviors unique to the lower classes. The fourth reaction might be the pragmatic alternative, where one adheres to neither set of values. One learns to apply whatever set of values is most profitable at the moment. If you were a ghetto resident in any major American city, what alternative would you choose?

the ghetto

The meaning of the term *ghetto* is not the same as it was in the 1920s when sociologists used it to describe voluntary communities of ethnic group members. Today, the ghetto refers to an area of socially and economically deprived persons who suffer acute social disorganization and enforced segregation. In general, it is produced by the steady migration of blacks from rural to urban areas. The struggle for civil rights has reflected three major developments in the American black community: accelerated growth, increasing mobility, and rapid urbanization. Nearly half of the black population now lives in the North; our liberal response has been to mouth the proper sentiments while staging a mass exodus to the suburbs, assuring a marked increase in the rigidity of residential segregation.

In the twentieth century, the black population moved steadily from the South to the North and West. In 1910, 91 percent of the nation's 9.8 million blacks lived in the South, and only 27 percent of American blacks lived in cities as large as 2500 persons. By 1966, the black population more than doubled, reaching 21.5 million, and the number living in metropolitan areas rose from 2.6 million to more than 14 million. Even these numbers do not match the statistics for immigrants arriving in this country during that time. But unlike blacks, the immigrants were carefully screened to admit only the highly skilled. Many of these whites tend to exaggerate how easily and quickly they escaped from poverty. The fact is, however, that immigrants from rural backgrounds are only now, after three generations, beginning to move into the middle class.

Lee Rainwater, in a foreword to the book *Coming Up Black*, notes deprivation and exclusion as critical features of life in a lower class ghetto.

> The lower class is deprived because it is excluded from the ordinary run of average American working-and middle-class life, and it is excluded because it is deprived of the resources necessary to function in the institutions of the mainstream of American life. . . . The most basic deprivation is of course the lack of an adequate family income, but from this deprivation flows the sense so characteristic of lower-class groups of not having the price of admission to participation in the many different kinds of rewards that ordinary society offers, some of which cost money, but also a good many others (education, for example) that do not.

Economic deprivation and social segregation operate hand-in-hand to concentrate black members of the lower class in ghetto communities where they will feel the full impact of the indifference and exploitative attitudes of the rest of the society. It is no surprise, then, that a characteristic pattern of attitudes, beliefs, and behavior develops in ghettos and slum neighborhoods; this ghetto world is experienced directly by the lower-class child as he grows up. Indeed, it is abundantly evident that there is not much romance about the pain and suffering of family life in the inner city.

The problem of the ghetto, according to other observers, boils down to employment and income. The wage earner with a sparse education and primitive job skills is frequently unemployed and regularly underpaid when he does work. Unable to be a provider, he is held in low esteem by his wife and children and occupies a marginal position in the family. The not unexpected outcome is the development of a variety of alternative marital forms including consensual marriages, separation, and divorce. These family patterns are realistic, rational responses to the impossible circumstances of life. But even though these responses to poverty are adaptive in the short run, they are maladaptive in the sense that they run counter to middle-class values.

Everyone is ready to deplore the existence of the miserable ghetto in which so many black and poor people live, but unadmitted unwillingness to find financial resources for change remains and our institutions are not modified in any serious way. Solutions to the ghetto problem have ranged from the alternative of ghetto dispersal to the opposite alternative of ghetto enrichment. If the ghettos are dispersed, so the theory goes, the black and poor will move into predominantly white communities, join white institutions, and be provided the measure of services, jobs, and housing that have long been the privileges of the affluent. If the ghettos are enriched, the poor and the blacks will be kept where they are, but vital services and opportunities will help them develop to a point where they will be able to participate in the dominant culture.

To some critics, however, neither of these alternatives is an either/or proposition, since neither solution can work without the other. At the moment, our unfortunate national policy is to provide just enough enrichment to keep the poor in ghettos, while giving enough hope to keep them nonviolent. At the same time, we must recognize that any method of assisting the integration of ghetto residents into the larger society may be a less valuable gift than the givers realize. Recent research findings picture the birth of a new ghetto man: he is the black militant dedicated to destroying traditional racial restraints by open confrontation. Indeed, this new man is very different in his actions and sympathies from the Negro of the past.

Black militants, in particular, have begun to question whether integration into middle-class suburbia would accomplish much more than exposing blacks to a distorted, sterile, materialistic way of life. Accordingly, black radicals have concluded that participation in the existing American system has no real value for blacks. "Negroes, they argue, would be better off pursuing their own separate lines of development, organizing their own communities for radical change, and shunning involvement with the bulk of white society, at least until the day when it is so radically restructured as to be worthy of black participation." At the moment, however, this seems to be a romantic fantasy since study after study has reported that most black ghetto residents are dissatisfied and would like to move out.

We all played cops and robbers when we were young, and they still love the game today in the ghetto. The difference is that for ghetto dwellers the game is a matter of life and death; it is for real! For those of us in the middle class, the police are hired public servants who help old ladies, protect our property, and give directions when we are lost. To the ghetto resident, the policeman is a walking, talking, uniformed bundle of trouble who harasses and arrests you. In every slum, there is a vast conspiracy against the man who represents the forces of law and order. The cop is the enemy and everyone knows that the rules of warfare dictate no one give aid or comfort to the enemy—however virtuous their errand may be.

Since most of us do not live in the ghetto, we tend to believe that the gulf between blacks and the police in the urban ghettos would be narrowed if only more money were invested in police recruitment, inservice training, human relations for officers, and increased salaries. But those closer to the problem insist the problem is not as simple as merely a few "bad eggs" in the police department. The system is one that recruits a significant number of bigots, reinforces this biogotry through socialization by older officers in the department, and then assigns these officers to duty in the ghetto where they can act out their prejudice.

Ghetto blacks report that policemen are brutal, harsh, discourteous to blacks, do not respond rapidly to emergency calls, do not enforce the law, and do not protect people who are poor. In addition, they believe most white people are simply unwilling to accept that there is racial discrimination by police officers. This ghetto view of the police has existed for many years. In a 1957 poll, for example, fewer than one in ten white persons rated police service as "not good," while two-thirds of the Negro respondents referred to anti-Negro discrimination and mistreatment by police. Nor is this black hostility to the police limited to poor blacks; it is found in the ranks of black professionals and black policemen themselves.

It is evident that raising salaries or levels of police education has little effect on the broad spectrum of police attitudes or behavior. Attempts to hire more black police officers may be one answer, but this solution is theoretical since it has yet to be adequately tested on a large scale. Certainly some ghetto blacks must see the situation as one in which the police force is a white occupation army patrolling the neighborhood.

education and poverty

Terms such as cultural deprivation or cultural disenfranchisement are only variations on an ancient theme. Over the years, the children of poverty have been called problem children, retarded, slow learners, underprivileged, and under-achievers. The use of terms such as *disadvantaged*, in itself, contributes to stereotypes that are often applied to children who do not really fit such categories. Rather than labeling the child, we might better describe him for what he really is. As one writer stated: "He is no stranger to failure and to the fear that continued failure engenders. He knows the fear of being over-powered by teachers who are ignorant of the culture and mores of his society, and who may not expect success of him. He fears lack of recognition and understanding from teachers whose backgrounds are totally dissimilar and who either misinterpret or fail to recognize

114

many of his efforts to achieve and to accomodate himself to demands which are basically alien."

In the terms of F. Reissman, author of *The Culturally Deprived Child*, this child is slow at cognitive tasks but not stupid, learns most readily through a physical, concrete approach, is pragmatic rather than theoretical, feels alienated from the larger culture, blames others for his difficulties, and is deficient in many of the skills most suited to the educational system. The list stretches longer, but the principle is clear. The child of poverty will almost always fare badly in middle-class institutions and barely comprehend the alien ways of middle-class life. This cultural disadvantage will affect the child now and cripple him later. We can safely predict that the children of high-income professionals will reap almost the entire crop of Merit Scholarships; in fact, it was reported in 1961 that there were 234 merit scholars per 12,672 professional families, but only one merit scholar per three and one-half million laborer families.

Of greater immediate relevance is the fact that poverty-ridden families produced most of those persons who were unable to attain the minimum mental and physical standards needed to be a private in the United States Army. About one-fifth of those rejected by the military on educational grounds came from families which had received public assistance in the previous five years; nearly one-half came from families with six or more children. More than half of those rejected had fathers who had never finished grade school, and, worse yet, four out of five of the rejectees had dropped out of school. Even the army—the only social institution designed to educate and train members of the lower classes in our society—is unobtainable to those crippled by the ghetto.

For psychologists, the ghetto manufactures a collection of feelings, attitudes, and beliefs that alienate children and give them a lowered sense of self-esteem. In the words of one psychologist, the ghetto leads children to "question their own worth, fear being challenged, have a desire to cling to the familiar, and have many feelings of guilt and shame; there is a limited trust in adults; they tend to respond with trigger-like reactions, are hyperactive, and have generally a low standard of conduct; and they usually show apathy and lack of respon-siveness. It is difficult for them to form meaningful relationships." When this psychological orientation includes a negative attitude to school, teachers, and achievement and is coupled with a tendency to seek immediate gratification at the expense of long-term goals, the child is set to experience acculturation problems in the school. If he begins to perform poorly on the school's ability tests, he is quickly labeled a slow learner or low achiever. By such time, his educational fate is sealed.

Interestingly, such a child may be trapped not so much by his ethnic, cultural, or economic life as by his teacher's reactions to his background. Two researchers, R. Rosenthal and L. F. Jacobson, have raised the suspicion that teachers in our schools may be short-changing slum children by anticipating that the children will fail to be good students. To test this idea, the two investigators explored the "self-fulfilling prophecy"—a concept whereby the teacher's expectations for a pupil somehow gets realized despite the child's capacity. Teachers were led to believe at the beginning of a school year that certain of their pupils (late bloomers) could be expected to show a marked academic improvement during the year. The teachers assumed these predictions were based on tests administered to the student body during the preceding school year. In actuality, the children designated as potential "spurters" were chosen at random rather than on the basis of testing. Despite this random selection procedure, intelligence tests given several months later demonstrated that these "spurters" had improved more than the other children.

The same kind of effect can be produced in the laboratory. Rosenthal carried out experiments using rats that were reported to be either bright or dull. In one experiment, 12 students in psychology were each given five laboratory rats of the same strain. Six of the students were told their rats had been bred for brightness in maze running. The other six students were informed that their rats, for genetic reasons, might be poor at running a maze. The students were told to teach all the rats to run the maze. As you might have guessed, the rats thought to have a higher potential proved to be the better performers. If expectations alone can produce such positive changes, then it does not take much imagination to conclude that the reverse can happen for children labeled "slow."

Educator Hilda Taba has defined the problem with exceptional clarity. "As the percentages of the age groups attending school increase, school also draws increasingly from the 'bottom of the pile.' The able, the adjusted, and the motivated, the upper 30 percent in ability, have always been in school. Extension of school attendance can only add students from the lower end of the span: the emotionally and the physically handicapped, the less willing and able, and the less motivated, those less able to cope with the school culture and its expectations." This then is the crisis we face as we look at poverty and examine the educational facilities we have provided. America had a magnificent dream hundreds of years ago, and it is the present young generation that must work to make that dream come true.

poverty and retardation

The relationship between poverty and mental retardation was ignored, until recently, by most researchers. Yet, even though there is insufficient scientific evidence to buttress the argument, theorists now believe poverty has a destructive effect on mental ability. Furthermore, it is believed that this damage begins at the moment of conception, the child receiving the detrimental effects of his environment even during the reproductive cycle. If this is true and the damage is permanent, then no later alterations of the environment will erase this disfigurement of intellectual potential. A woman living in poverty is more likely than her middle-class counterpart to be very young when she has her first pregnancy. She is more likely to have a greater number of children, and she will be more likely to bear children until a later age. Evidence shows a high, positive correlation between poverty and the incidence of prematurity, mental deficiency, and gross maldevelopment.

The little research that has been done on this issue in recent years has focused on cases of severe malnutrition. Attempts have been made to unravel the complicated issue of the relative influence of social, biological, and environmental conditions that are associated with malnutrition. We cannot yet give an accurate answer to questions about how malnutrition affects intellectual performance, and we must also consider that hunger and malnutrition are not, technically, the same. The child who attends school without breakfast or lunch will be hungry, inattentive, and distractible in class, but he may or may not be significantly malnourished. Simple hunger makes a child restless, but the victims of long-term, protein-calorie malnutrition are most often apathetic and withdrawn with a low energy level. A perhaps premature summary of the problem would be that malnutrition if severe and long lasting in the earliest part of life can present the greatest disadvantage for the child seeking an education. Hunger, at any age, is enough to destroy any possibility of academic achievement.

the many faces of the poor

It is difficult for most of us to recognize the poor because most of the time they are invisible. When, for example, was the last time you were in close contact with a truly poverty stricken person? They are invisible mainly because they live in rural areas, they are members of minority groups, and usually they are old.

THE AGED POOR

The invisibility of the aged poor is due to the fact that they are physically and financially unable to move about much in our society. They may sit out their remaining days in rented rooms or in decaying houses in neighborhoods that have long ago changed from the character they

117

had in the old days. More so than any of the ethnic minority groups, white people who are impoverished and old and who live in the inner city are cut off from the familial supports necessary to sustain their waning powers. They are surrounded by people but suffer isolation, invisibility, and grinding poverty.

The modern problem of the poverty-stricken old people can be traced to the emergence of the modern, industrialized state. The state provides the circumstances for survival for its citizens over 65 years of age, but it fails to furnish gainful employment for them. The improved practices of medicine, public health, and public sanitation have let us live longer, but this has become a mixed blessing to the industrial state.

Between the ages of 65 and 75, a significant population shift occurs as women begin to outnumber men. These are usually husbandless women trapped by a low, fixed income and incapable of meaningful employment. For these women and for the aged men, the longer one lives the worse one's plight becomes, since old people are ignored and no longer needed in the industrial state. In 1890, 70 percent of the aged were gainfully employed, but this figure fell to less than 33 percent in 1960 and has declined steadily since that time. Today fewer than 20 percent of the aged continue to earn money. The problem of the aged poor has already become a critical social issue and will become an increasingly severe problem in the years ahead.

THE RURAL POOR

In the richest nation in history nearly 14 million rural Americans are poor, and a high proportion of them could be described as destitute. It surprises most Americans to learn that there is proportionately more poverty in rural America than in our cities. In metropolitan areas, one person in eight is poor and in the suburbs the ratio is one in 15. In rural areas, one of every four persons is poor. Only one in four of these rural families actually lives on a farm; most live in small towns and villages.

Rural low-income areas have steadily lost population through the migration of rural farm people. From 1790 to the present, the nation's population has shifted from being about 95 percent to 30 percent rural. As recently as 65 years ago, 33 percent of the entire population was living on farms, but this figure has dropped to only 6 percent. This mass exodus from rural areas means that those left behind are often worse off than before. The many old people and children are too heavy a burden for the few working-age members of the family to support, and the chances of escaping from poverty or avoiding deeper poverty are greatly diminished as the young take flight to the cities. The problems of the rural poor are compounded in a variety of additional ways. Large families are traditional in rural areas, and the result is that meager resources have to be stretched past the breaking point to feed, clothe, and educate the children. The rural household may include several generations of the family, since families take pride in caring for the old folks at home.

Since more than 19 million persons in rural America have not completed high school and more than three million have fewer than five years of schooling, even migration does not promise much increase in income. But years of schooling is an inadequate index to the skill or ability of the rural poor, since rural schools pay low salaries, do not attract the better teachers, and do not always deliver quality in education. It is evident that, in whatever direction the poor may turn, they confront only another obstacle to the escape from poverty.

The continuing problem of Appalachia is one illustration. This region of original American frontier covers 182,000 square miles extending from southern Pennsylvania to northern Alabama and is rich in natural resources. Yet, Appalachia is now raising its third welfare generation. It has counties in which as many as one-third of the inhabitants are unemployed—some of whom have not worked for decades. In Appalachia, the average adult has a sixth-grade education and three-fourths of the children are drop-outs before they complete the twelfth grade. The additional burdens of human pathology (tuberculosis, silicosis, infant mortality, and so on) are so high that they do not fit into our concept of the Western world at all. As each new generation is born it has only poverty to look forward to—the young grow, marry, go on welfare, have children and keep the cycle of poverty going.

The plight of children caught in the poverty trap is particularly tragic. Migrant children, for example, are in the deepest trouble of all. Each year 150,000 of them move across our land harvesting crops carrying with them poverty, disease, and ignorance of formal education. They are unwelcome in the communities where they serve as cheap labor, and, constantly on the move, they are not eligible for public assistance to relieve their misery. The longer they remain migrant workers, the greater will be their cultural and educational deprivation and the more certain it will be that they will never escape from poverty. It has become fashionable to speak of "pockets of poverty." The truth is that there are concentrations rather than "pockets" of poverty. Poverty refuses to stay isolated; it can be found anywhere in America.

SPANISH-AMERICAN POVERTY

A little recognized concentration of poverty can be found among the Spanish-Americans of the Southwest. The ancient romantic history of this region of our land set the stage for a serious social problem. "Colonization of what is now the Southwest was started more than

119

three centuries ago when this entire area, along with Mexico, was part of Spain's vast overseas empire. Santa Fe was an important urban settlement in 1609. By 1790 the white population of the Southwest was practically all Spanish and included an estimated 23,000 persons."

From these modest beginnings have sprung more than three and one-half million modern Spanish-Americans—and they have a problem. They rank as low or lower in education than any other ethnic group in America, with the singular exception of the American Indian woman. They are unemployed twice as frequently as are their counterpart Anglos and only slightly better employed than blacks in America. Thus, Spanish-Americans are just barely better off financially than are blacks. Further, if the Spanish-American has any advantage at all, it is to be found in his more cohesive family life, 75 percent of Spanish-American households have both husband and wife present.

Recent reports by the Census Bureau show evidence that persons of Spanish origin are gaining in income more rapidly than are blacks, but they still lag far behind whites. Spanish-Americans still have less education than others. An average of five or fewer years of education for 20 percent of the Spanish group may be compared with 14 percent among blacks, and 4 percent among whites. The contrast among whites, the 23 million black Americans and the more than nine million persons of Spanish origin (five million from Mexico, one and one-half million from Puerto Rico, and 700,000 from Cuba) includes a number of other dimensions. For one, the median age for Mexican-Americans, blacks, and persons of Spanish origin is substantially younger than that for the white population. Blacks are more likely than Spanish to work as laborers or service employees; and more black women work than do Spanish or white women.

These details indicate that the dominant white Americans are selectively and differentially prejudiced and discriminatory. The advances Spanish-Americans have achieved to date are a likely prophecy of things to come in the years ahead, but their impatience is as great as any minority group condemned to poverty.

help for the poor

The measures we have been taking to help the poor reflect the beliefs and attitudes we hold about poverty stricken people. Historically, with a very few exceptions, the more affluent members of our society have believed that the poor deserved their fate as a consequence of shiftlessness, lack of virtue, and absence of character. "Probably the most enduring attitude toward the problem of poverty was that the poor should not be made too comfortable in it. There was serious concern that any real kindness or generosity shown the poor would merely encourage poverty and that the poor would come to enjoy it. Thus, aid was to be grudgingly, even meanly, given."

In the nineteenth century, the public poorhouse was fashioned to remove from public vision a variety of social discards—the blind, the lame, the old, the feeble, and the orphaned. Housed all in one building and maintained at a bare minimum level of subsistence, poorhouses became pesthouses that soon evoked outraged cries for reform. The private charitable organizations of that time helped selectively—by choosing whom among the poor were truly deserving of assistance and deciding how much aid could be given without encouraging them to remain poverty ridden.

Today the view of poor people has become less moralistic as the list of reasons for poverty has expanded. Race, age, geographic area, technological obsolescence, sickness, separation, and many other factors contribute to poverty. Today poverty is inextricably bound up with welfare programs such as Aid to Families with Dependent Children (AFDC). But our society is foundering in its attempt to deal with the recent explosion of relief rolls. As one report revealed: "Between 1950 and 1960, only 110,000 families were added to the rolls, yielding a rise of 17 percent. In the 1960s, however, the rolls exploded, rising by more than 225 percent. At the beginning of the decade, 745,000 families were receiving aid; by 1970, some 2,500,000 families were on the rolls."

The rapid expansion of relief rolls in the 1960s occurred during the years of the greatest civil disorder in our history; the turmoil of the civil rights struggle, the outbreak of rioting in the cities, and the mass protests mounted by relief recipients compounded an already difficult situation. The welfare rise coincided with the enactment of Federal programs designed to restore calm to the ghettos. Among other benefits, these programs hired thousands of poor people, social workers, and lawyers who worked actively to get relief for more families. The result was a quick doubling of the welfare rolls. By early 1969, 800,000 families had been added to the relief burden—an increase over 1960 of 107 percent. Moreover, the welfare explosion, while generally an urban phenomenon, had its greatest impact in that handful of large metropolitan counties where political turmoil had been the greatest.

The relief rolls surged upward at an even faster rate beginning in 1969. By the end of 1970, only two years later, another 900,000 families were receiving aid. Then, in November 1971, welfare statistics revealed that 14.6 million persons received a total of $1.5 billion in cash and services; 10.5 million recipients were those in the Aid to Families with Dependent Children program. This incredible expansion of requests for financial aid has jeopardized the liberal concept of social care for the poor. In the past when mass unemployment produced social turmoil, programs of public relief were instituted to absorb and control the unemployed. Once the social disorders were smoothed out, however, the welfare system quickly contracted to service only the aged, crippled, or disabled who were unable to contribute to the labor market. The theory has been that mass unemployment weakens social and psychological constraints on the poor and undermines the established network of social control. Thus, government aid is forthcoming only so long as disorder seems probable.

To rationalize the increase in public welfare, a system of make-work for the dependent poor has always appeared to sooth the public's moral concern about supporting the indigent. During the depression of the 1930s, the immediate humanitarian response of the federal government was to appropriate billions of dollars for direct relief payments. It shortly became apparent, however, that no one was happy with direct relief since it seemed no more than a temporary expedient to keep body and soul together—if not one's dignity. Direct relief did little to renew personal pride or restore the dignity of a previous way of life. An ancient remedy was then reinvented—abolish direct relief and put the unemployed to work on subsidized projects that might dignify subsistence aid. If the past is predictive of the future, it is likely we will repeat history by shrinking relief rolls and services as soon as full employment exists.

Michael Harrington in his book *The Other America* argued that we have a new kind of poverty—a poverty of automation, a poverty of the minority poor, and a poverty that is almost hereditary, invariably transmitted from generation to generation. Harrington had a solution. He suggested instituting a G.I. bill in the war against poverty whereby we would pay people to go to school—paying for their tuition and their books and giving them a reasonble living allowance if they had a family. Convinced that the G.I. bill was one of the most successful social experiments this society has ever undertaken, Harrington asks why it requires a shooting war for us to be so smart. If our society really believes that the most productive thing young persons can do is go to school, then we ought to put up the money to make it possible for *every* youngster to take advantage of such opportunity. Over time, that person would be able to strike a blow against the seemingly unbreakable cycle of poverty.

The poverty issue may better be described as one of inequality, since the poor in our country are often rich by the standards of other cultures. Still, the very poor are clearly extremely unequal when compared to others in America. But this shift in terms redefines the problem and can lead us to study different issues and search for different kinds of solutions. Should we focus, for example, on "changing opportunity" or "changing conditions"? Much of the anti-poverty effort in the 1960s was designed to increase educational opportunity for the young in order to promote individual social mobility. It was a bitter theory since it encouraged a higher rate of movement out of the ranks of poverty, even if those left behind were as badly off as before.

We lack an adequate social psychological theory to specify the interdependence between our socioeconomic system and the individual's way of life. As a consequence, social scientists have invested most of their energy in studying the children of poverty since there was some degree of agreement that the forces exerted on early socialization are particularly critical for adult behavior. Following this line of thought, scientists assumed that the earlier they could remedy or influence the effects of poverty, the greater the impact they would have. In time, given the lack of public readiness to put money where the sentiments were, this hope was abandoned. One writer has stated: "The discovery of a relationship between background (i.e., poverty) and behavior is no longer very satisfactory as an end in itself. Much more worthwhile is an understanding of the specific variables and detailed means by which environmental conditions produce the psychological dispositions, which in turn are responsible for a particular behavior."

To measure exactly the effects of poverty, we must devise a means of subtracting out the influences of a host of related variables. To date, researchers have made only sweeping generalizations about poverty based on unsystematic and uncontrolled experiments. There seems to be no way to make poverty "popular" in the scientific world.

ecology

WARNING

ATER POTENTIALLY
POLLUTED BETWEEN

Few students of humanity have given much thought to man's incorrigible urge to contaminate everything he touches. As the dominant species, Homo Sapiens has become the worst enemy of this planet, consuming its resources and expelling waste products into the environment at an unbelievable rate. Even our oceans, long treasured as an ultimate and inexhaustible source of protein, are less fertile than we smugly assumed they would be. Science fiction accounts of future man subsisting solely on algae cultured in hydroponic tanks now seem wishful thinking. The Space Ship Earth may be headed for a miserable fate. Man's dream of a return to the land, to nature, and to simple values is now a vision contaminated by sewage treatment plants, chemical fertilizers, DDT, strip mining, and pavement that will one day produce a silent spring in which birds will no longer sing. Obviously, something must be done about mankind if he is to construct a society that resembles something other than a giant, poisonous garbage heap.

Environmental psychology makes sense only when it is fitted into the larger context of all the environmental sciences that study man's manipulations of his surroundings. Man, in great part, creates his social and psychological environment and is in turn influenced by his creation. In fact, as some thinkers suggest, in the long run the product may become the master, and man may have modified his environment in irreversible ways. Man has the capacity to predict the consequences of his behavior and this may be the saving grace by which he survives. If he can learn from his mistakes—and, hopefully, not repeat them again—man need not continue to be both the conqueror and victim of his environment.

All ecological problems can be reduced to issues of human behavior when we fully acknowledge that it is man who has had such a destructive impact on our planet. No adequate theory of human ecology exists today, but social scientists are moving rapidly to find an answer to the new questions being asked. As one observer put it, "There can be no effective movement toward utopia without including the entire ecosystem of community and environment." The multiplicity of problems generated by the headlong thrust of technology have, in the past, been regarded as accidental social by-products of industry's benevolent attempts to improve the general welfare of mankind. One writer, J. D. Frank, suggests these adverse outcomes of progress might better be described as social "diseases" than as social "issues" and one precursor of the disease is the American faith in the quick fix. We are so impressed by our long history of incredible inventiveness that we believe "some new technological invention can always be devised to correct the evils created by the last one, without causing anyone too much cost or inconvenience."

Traffic fatalities have become just one such social disease. When we were no longer able to deny the reality of the carnage on our highways, we loudly demanded safer cars (a quick technological fix); at the same time, however, we quietly resisted accepting personal restrictions that would make us safer drivers—driving at 25 miles per hour maximum speed, for instance. No more than 20 percent of all drivers are involved in 80 percent of our accidents, and studies have recorded that in 50 percent of the fatal automobile accidents one or both of the persons involved had been drinking. Thus, in all its aspects, human ecology is a psychological problem. As we busily recycle throwaway bottles, avoid cyclamates, and abandon phosphates, more than 50,000 of us are killed each year on our highways. Surely, this is irrational, but we cannot remedy the ills of technology until we learn more about the peculiar attitudes and patterns of behavior of the American populace.

One upsetting and discouraging aspect of the initial proposals for solving ecological problems has been their naivete and prematurity. Thus, as each of us steadfastly collects bottles and dutifully transports them to the recycling center, we experience a sense of contributing meaningfully to the task of cleaning up the earth. Then, to our chagrin, we are informed that a more urgent ecological priority is the conservation of the fossil fuel supply; we are told that recycling such trash unacceptably pollutes the atmosphere and further exhausts our limited fuel supply. In other words, bottle reclamation produces the very disease for which it was intended as a cure. It is not surprising, then, that in the mind of the average citizen ecology has become a hopeless tangle; today's remedy seems destined to become tomorrow's problem. The power consumed to recycle bottles today is the power that will be unavailable to run the air conditioner tomorrow.

The ecological idea is a splendid one—in the abstract. It loses a great deal of its splendor when the general public is faced with the hard alternatives of oil pipelines versus nature, automobile safety versus one thousand dollars added to the price tag on each car, or industrial pollution versus severe unemployment. Clearly, as long as the profit motive is dominant in our culture, the ecology battle will be an exceptionally prolonged war; the cost will be staggering and most of us will fight it only if we make certain we sustain no personal wounds.

the crowded planet

From the beginning of recorded history until the early nineteenth century, the world accumulated a population of one billion persons. Only another 100 years was needed to add the second billion; 30 more years were required to reach the third billion; and it will take less than 15 years to add the fourth billion. Although population prediction is a perilous game, the United States is expected to have a population somewhere between 271 and 322 million by the year 2000. Considering that such estimates are give-or-take 50 million people even for a short time span, one realizes how difficult it is to guess about birth rates. As recently as 1967, statisticians were predicting that we would number 361 million by the turn of the century.

One reason we do not know how many of us there will be is that we know too little about the attitudes, beliefs, and convictions that lead to parenthood. The "baby bust" is an excellent illustration. The 1970 census revealed we have just had the greatest decline in the number of children 5 years old or younger in the last 120 years. This population drop was nearly twice as much as the largest previously recorded drop in the 1930s at the time of the Great Depression. Remarkably, almost every decade since 1850 has registered an increase in preschoolers. Further, considering the fact that the number of young adults reached a new high during the 1960s, one concludes that a massive reevaluation of the morality of bringing children into this troubled world has taken place.

What contributes to a "baby bust" or "birth dearth"? Let us take the Detroit metropolitan area as an example. The fertility rate fell from 3.8 children during a woman's child-bearing years in 1957 to 2.2 children in 1971; the number of unmarried men and women below the age of 35 increased; married women in their twenties "expected" to have fewer children (3.03 children in 1965 as compared to 2.53 children in 1971); and despite an increase in women of child-bearing age, fewer births occurred than were predicted. Thus, during a "baby bust," the number of households increases, but the households are occupied by fewer persons. The consequences? To name a few, more apartment buildings; decreasing toy, baby food, and clothing sales; and empty school classrooms. If the declining birth rate continues through the seventies and beyond, the time will come when the young adults of today will have become elderly, and as they die an enormous boost in the birth rate will be necessary simply to keep the ratio of births to deaths on an even keel.

To have or not have children becomes a psychological issue for each of us at some time in life, and this question has increasingly caught the interest of psychologists during the last decade. The problems of crowding and living arrangements were studied initially some years ago by three researchers, L. Festinger, S. Schachter, and K. Back, and have once again begun to intrigue ecology-minded psychologists. More than a decade ago, three other investigators began to explore the new field of environmental psychology. As psychologists, the researchers were initially asked to undertake research that might assist in designing psychiatric facilities with a therapeutic atmosphere for treating institutionalized mental patients. This new field of scientific inquiry, born of social necessity, lacked a theoretical

128

structure adequate to define the meaning of an environment to human beings. Thus, it was impossible to design a warm, friendly, supportive, reassuring environment, if the meanings of these terms were not yet clear to psychologists. Modern psychology was simply not ready to cope with the problem. Psychologists knew something about human behavior, but they had yet to make explicit the relationship between behavior and man's environment. The environment—for those behavioral psychologists most attuned to it—consisted primarily of discrete, quantifiable stimuli taken one by one and never seen as a meaningful whole.

The question is not how many people the earth can support but how many can exist without destroying the good life. It is foolish to ask how many can be crowded onto our globe. The question must be what number can live here happily. In a now classic experiment on the effects of crowding, J. B. Calhoun confined a population of wild Norway rats in a quarter-acre enclosure. With an abundance of food and places to live and with natural enemies and disease eliminated, only the behavior of the animals remained a force in determining the increase or decrease in this rat population. After 27 months, the population stabilized at 150 adults, despite the fact that mortality among adult rats was so low that 5000 adults would normally have been expected at the observed reproductive rate. This large population did not materialize simply because the infant mortality was extremely high. With only 150 adults in the enclosure, the stress of rodent social interaction produced so great a disruption of maternal behavior that few of the young survived.

In a series of studies of other rat populations, it became apparent that behavioral pathology was most visible among the females. Many were unable to carry pregnancy to full term, and many failed to survive delivery of their litters. Others, after successfully giving birth, fell short in the maternal role. Among the males, behavior distrubances ranged from sexual deviation to cannibalism and from frenetic overactivity to a pathological withdrawal whereby they would eat, drink, and move about only when other members of the community were asleep. The social disorganization of all the animals was readily apparent. Social organization among animals is clearly dependent upon proper spacing among them. Lions will not attack unless a stranger intrudes upon their territorial space, and, as in human social orders, animals that occupy positions of high status are afforded more personal space. Like the chief baboon, the corporate executive has a suite of offices, while his secretary has a five by five feet space in which to conduct her business.

Every known animal species, according to the authors of *The Year 2000*, becomes disorganized if it is not destroyed by overcrowding. If man becomes as crowded on this planet as the experimental rats were, we will need new rules to govern mutual adjustment. In a jam-packed world, "drugs, other worldly religions, delinquency, crime, and mental disease (as a way of 'opting out') could increase significantly, requiring medical, social, and criminal sanctions to prevent or contain those forms of disturbance that are excessively dysfunctional for the social and political systems."

Despite the rising clamor about overcrowding, some thinkers are not certain about the deleterious effects of being surrounded by masses of human beings. It has been contended that research of the effects of population density has most often dealt with nonhuman subjects. These studies, while provocative, simply may not apply to human beings. Animal research is, at best, only suggestive of the complex human condition, despite the fact that every measure of human density is correlated with social, physical, and mental breakdowns such as crime, suicide, mental disorder, venereal disease, illegitimacy, and infant mortality. Human density is a complicated happening and people—a great many of them—seem to be able to live together without suffering all the consequences that accrue to rat populations.

In some of the experiments on human subjects, for example, people were placed in crowded or uncrowded rooms for up to four hours while their behavior was being observed. The crowded rooms had enough furniture for all, but no more than four square feet were alloted per person. Four hours does not constitute a lifetime, of course, but the conclusion reached was that people can function nearly normally under such circumstances. Perhaps strains other than simple crowding must be explored before we can decide what is good or bad for mankind. High concentrations of human beings in a limited space (our most likely future) may be manageable or even good for people. At this point we simply do not know.

If you were to herd half of America's more than 200 million people into the state of California, you would duplicate the kind of crowding that exists in present-day Japan. In the major cities of Japan, one can witness an immense river of people who never seem to shove, cut one another off, bump, or brush elbows. Throngs of people are constantly everywhere; yet this closeness seems to bring comfort rather than oppression. Somehow, 50 percent of Japan's 100 million citizens have learned to live on just 1.5 percent of their land without destroying one another. The residents of Tokyo, for example, feel uncrowded at densities that would produce an intolerable feeling in Americans.

Are the Japanese merely better able to tolerate crowding than we are? We do not know, since we have exceptionally sparse information about the density levels at which various people can still feel happy and comfortable, while performing tasks with the greatest efficiency. As summarized by two writers: "We do not know whether high density during one part of the daily routine (at work, for example) coupled with low density at another (at home) would have the same effects as medium density throughout the day. We do not know exactly what role high density plays in the incidence of stress diseases and mental health."

life in the big city

Psychology has a vital contribution to make to the understanding of the ecology of life in modern cities. Most certainly, special psychological insights will be needed if the new generation is to survive the density and heterogeneity of the population of tomorrow. Our cities will expand beyond belief, their sheer size and complexity will alter the urban atmosphere. The roles each of us must play will become incredibly complicated, and we may all suffer stimulus overload in which a swirling mass of information will assault us at a rate too overwhelming to be assimilated. Faced with an increasing barrage of urban stimulation it may be necessary to allocate less time and attention to each input or learn to disregard certain low-priority inputs. If these defenses fail, we may be forced to block off some stimulation (the unlisted telephone number) or filter intrusions on our life (the secretary who intercepts callers), allowing only manageable inputs to reach us or force our reaction.

The reported "coldness" of present big-city dwellers, for example, may represent an attempt at this kind of stimulus control. We refuse to become involved with other persons and withhold simple courtesies (offering a lady a seat) in order to reduce the personal input of strangers. Urban dwellers have learned to respect the emotional and social privacy of other persons. In the big city, "it is much harder to know whether taking an active role is unwarranted meddling or an appropriate response to a critical situation... The heterogeneity of the city produces substantially greater tolerance about behavior, dress, and codes of ethics than is generally found in the small town, but this diversity also encourages people to withhold aid for fear of antagonizing the participants or crossing an inappropriate and difficult-to-define line."

In situations of high urban density, if people involved themselves in the affairs of others they would continually be distracted or unable to achieve their own goals and purposes; turning others off becomes functional. A researcher named P. G. Zimbardo tested the hypothesis that big cities create a necessary anonymity and impersonality. He arranged for an automobile to be left for 64 hours near the Bronx campus of New York University, while another car was parked for the same number of hours near Stanford University in Palo Alto, California. The license plates on the two cars were removed and the

131

hoods were opened. The New York car was stripped of all movable parts within the first 24 hours and was a hunk of rubble by the end of three days. Interestingly, most of the destruction occurred during daylight hours under the scrutiny of observers; the vandals were well-dressed white adults. The Palo Alto car, by contrast, was left untouched.

The urban setting poses additional problems for the human being who inhabits it. One investigator has referred to two major dimensions of big-city ecology: experiential congruence (how well the environment fits the characteristics and behavior of human beings) and mental congruence (what the person believes or thinks are the kind of settings that will satisfy him). When urban settings are looked at in physical terms, one can refer to "physical distances" and the sense of "accessibility" of parts of the city to the individuals who live in it. In every city some places seem "close" and others seem "far" even though the distance may literally be equal. Often our sense of accessibility is a function of the time and trouble it takes to get there. It is possible to design cities, then, in terms of a "manipulated distance" that creates an illusion of near or far. Similarly, there are psychological differences in the kinds of human density each of us will experience. When one is in a festive mood, a mobbed cocktail party may not seem crowded at all; a modest line at a movie theater, however, may deter the potential viewer.

Our reaction to the physical world is a function of our life style, our stage in life, and the social status we pretend to. Cosmopolitan people react less negatively to the nearness of neighbors, while rural types may feel the urge to move if they can see smoke from the neighbor's chimney. Unfortunately, the issues of privacy, territoriality, identity, and crowding have barely been touched by social scientific research.

Imagine that the fantasy of Arnold Auerbach, author of "The Alternate-People Plan," were to come true. Auerbach envisions a future in which cities become so crowded that they are forced to adopt an Alternate People Plan. The population would be divided into two groups: Monday, Wednesday, and Friday people (MWFs); and Tuesday, Thursday, and Saturday people (TTSs). No one would be allowed to leave home for any purpose except on his allotted days. When MWFs went out, TTSs would have to stay home! Anyone caught OWOL (out without leave) would be arrested and placed on exhibition in a public "pound" where on-duty citizens could go to jeer. To relieve population pressure in cities, Auerbach proposed "Operation Ill Will"—a campaign calculated to drive people away by publicizing the city's most intolerable features. Schoolchildren, for example, might win prizes for essays on "Why I Hate Living Here" and traffic lights at busy intersections would boldly instruct people to LEAVE TOWN.

A less radical approach to city living is advocated by G. H. Winkel, who speaks of the "nervous affair between behavior scientists and designers." Building design involves more than esthetics; it must consider the needs and preferences of those who will live out their lives in such structures. Yet, architects and planners are disappointed when they get help from psychologists and sociologists. As it happens, these professional social scientists know very little about the human response to a city environment. Why, as Winkel asks, "do people return again and again to a place where disaster has struck? The hillsides of California, the coastline of New Jersey, the gulf towns of Mississippi: people return and rebuild, no matter how severe the destruction." In connection with this, we might also reasonably ask why so many people live in large cities exposed to every form of dehumanization known to man. The problems of the ecology of cities are best summed up in the words of architect Moshe Safdie: "We want to live in a small intimate community; yet we want to have all the amenities of the great metropolis. We want a dwelling with privacy, identity; yet we want the setting of a rich social life. We want to be near open country; yet we let the city spread endlessly. We want all the things suburbia has to offer; but we also want the amenities of the downtown area. What we really want is Utopia, but we are not clear about what Utopia is."

don't drink the water and don't breathe the air

Stuart Chase, author of *The Most Probable World*, indulged in an ecological vision of what is possible, if not probable, in the twenty-first century. Exposed as we are to so many prognostications of doom and destruction, Chase offers a refreshing fantasy of how most of us wish it might be. He envisions a planet where the sky is a deep, unpolluted blue and where there is no sound of thundering jets, sonic booms, grinding trucks, roaring motorcycles, or grunting bulldozers. Small, quiet, fumeless, easy to park, electric fuel cell cars abound. The water from the local nuclear desalting plant is cold, clear, and chlorine free, and the beaches are white and clean. Lake Erie breathes again. This new world has television with no commercials, streets that are safe at night, no wars, and a Sunday *New York Times* that weighs only one-half pound!

This is, of course, a wild dream—but a dream because each of us is hooked by consumer habits that make it impossible. Consider cars as an example. Detroit does not just make cars. Its assembly lines manufacture a way of American life, and if you do not believe it, try asking your fellow Americans to abandon the automobile for just one month.

In 1906, 78,000 cars bounced over our crude highways; today there are more than 90 million cars, accounting for 25 cents of each of our retail dollars. It is not just the cars themselves that have altered our way of life; 800,000 businesses are dependent on the automobile. Our landscape has been rearranged and our downtowns have emptied in a pell-mell exodus to the suburbs. Buses have consolidated our schools, altered the curriculum, and become the last remaining means of integrating our school system. Every day we consume 26 million gallons of motor fuel (93 billion gallons a year) and pour one million tons of sulpher oxide, twelve million tons of sulphur oxide, twelve million tons of hydrocarbons, and an additional million tons of poisonous matter into our atmosphere. We kill one another with cars at a rate which exceeds 50,000 deaths a year. Our love of our cars may be the end of us, as the concrete and macadam sprawl swallows up our country. The most shocking fact is that, while Americans constitute only 6 percent of the planet's population, we own one-half of its motor vehicles. California alone has more automobiles than all of Eastern Europe and Asia combined. If we live outside the central cities, nine out of ten of us use our cars to get to work. Indeed there has been no more expensive and destructive love affair in human history.

In addition to polluting the air, vehicles make noise, doubling the world's noise level every ten years. If noise continues to increase at its present rate, the downtown areas of larger cities will be nearly intolerable by the year 2000. Exposure to sounds up to 85 decibels is generally considered safe, but continuous noise above that level is known to damage the microscopic hair cells that carry sounds from the ear to the brain. Unfortunately, many commonplace sounds are above the safe level—traffic at a busy intersection, power mowers, rock bands, food blenders, and factory machinery being a few examples. Now scientists are discovering that virtually every human bodily function is affected by noise. Thus, workers in noisy factories develop abnormal brain waves and "hopscotch" heartbeats. Children living near factories and airports suffer from noise damage that may produce heart trouble and stunted growth. Even unborn fetuses may be permanently damaged by violent noises.

When the Industrial Revolution was just beginning, we gave manufacturers free access to air and water and they, unthinkingly, turned the biosphere into a giant garbage can. One observer has suggested that we can only remedy this past error by now listing pollution correction as a cost of production. If users and abusers had to pay for the privilege, the pollution problem would shortly be corrected even if the costs were passed on to the consumer.

134

R. Neuhaus, author of *In Defense of People*, thinks it is not nearly as easy as this. He views the ecology movement as a reactionary event that will further increase the already painful social injustice to those not rich enough to overconsume. The poor will hardly benefit; they will simply pay more for every necessary commodity in life, and they will not be able to enjoy the clean lakes or pristine national parks they cannot afford to visit on annual vacations. If we are ever to see a clean world, what we will need is a coalition of persons more interested in survival than in perpetuating the madness of overconsumption.

Anthropologist Rene Dubos has made the following ominous prediction. "The worst effects of environmental pollution are probably yet to come, since it is only during recent decades that certain chemical pollutants have reached high levels almost everywhere and that children have been exposed to these pollutants almost constantly from birth.... What will happen is that in 20 or 30 years, as a result of that slow, chronic response to environmental insult, these children will certainly suffer from some form of chronic disorder." Dubos does not believe man is on the road to extinction, however, since, as a species, he seems capable of adapting to almost anything. It is tragic that we adapt as well as we do, since our offspring may not be able to manage pollution as well as we do. Worse than extinction is the possibility that millions of lives will be exposed to a progressive degradation of the quality of human life.

ecology and human adjustment

Ecology is simple to define when it applies only to mechanical features of the environment. It becomes exceedingly complex when one includes human beings, who create their own ecology. Human beings interact with one another in so many spheres and along so many intricate dimensions that they have become a critical part of one another's environment. Yet, we have accumulated surprisingly little trustworthy data about ecological relationships such as man's response to his physical environment. We need to know much more about the accuracy of observations about the influences of weather. It has been suggested, for example, that the hot, summer months produce the most homicides. Others have observed that riots occur when the temperature is between 80 and 90 degrees or that there are more suicides from April to June than in the hotter months. It has also been reported that there is a peak in admissions to mental hospitals about 35 days following geomagnetic storms or sun spots.

Since man lives cheek-by-jowl with others, he is exposed to a social ecology that far outweighs the importance of his relationship to the physical environment. But there are variables in each individual's social ecology. To borrow an example, it is unlikely that we could create identical environments for handsome and homely children however hard we tried—the psychological and social ecology of each would be different. Parents are nearly always the first and most important social ecological force in the child's life. "Out of his interactions with his parents, the child will form his earliest and probably most persisting hypotheses about the world and about his place in it. Whether he comes to view the world as an orderly, dependable place or as a chaotic, untrustworthy one may depend in very large degree on the experiences he has with his parents. The child may be thrown into a predominantly loving, rewarding environment, into a negative, rejecting one, or into one which is nearly oblivious to his existence. The consequences will be of greatest importance." Parents are a living environment that punishes and rewards behavior directly and immediately in order to shape the child's existence. Since the child, in turn, will react to his parents and produce changes in them, it is evident that social ecology is always a shifting, dynamic affair.

As the child grows he will enter a new world of peers—a world with its own unique ecology. The characteristics of this new world will be determined in great part by the "accident" of one's place of birth. How well or how poorly the child relates to his peers will be vital to the psychological ecology of most of his later years. How much stress he will experience throughout life will be determined by how he interacts with his people-world. Unfortunately, psychologists know too little about very basic events in life such as deprivation, hostility, freedom, friendliness, social pressure, rewards, and punishments. We have exceptional records of volcanoes, tides, sun spots, and the behavior of rats and monkeys, but there are few scientific records on exactly how mothers care for their young, how teachers behave in the classroom, or how children respond to life day by day or hour by hour. Certainly, the raw material of human existence remains a mystery.

Some years ago, two psychologists, Roger Barker and Herbert Wright, designed a kind of psychological weather outpost to collect ecological data about children and their daily lives. The researchers wanted to know where children go, what they do, what they say, and with whom they interact. Barker and his associates treated behavioral events as natural units occurring in specific environmental settings of the psychological ecology, much as zoologists might observe animals in their natural habitats. The ecological psychologist studies the frequency of various kinds of behavioral events and the environmental setting in which these events occur. As he collects samples of actual events over a period of time, typical patterns of behavior can become apparent—patterns free of the artificialities of the laboratory, interview, or testing situation.

Human ecology is the study of man adapting to the circumstances of his life. Man has been exceptionally successful at this task because, as Dubos stated, "he is the least specialized creature on earth; he is indeed the most adaptable. He can hunt or fish, be a meat eater or a vegetarian, live in the mountains or by the seashore, be a loner or engage in teamwork, function in a free democracy or in a totalitarian state." Yet, our adaptive potentialities are not unlimited, and current technological developments may already have begun to exceed those limits. The dangers of this era are partially unknown, since they have no evolutionary or historic precedent. Man has never had to adapt to invisible toxic assault on all his senses at once.

psychology and ecology

Psychologists, along with the rest of us, have finally begun to worry about the quality of our physical environment and the effect civilization is having on man. Psychologists do not have any special gift of prophecy or foresight; and, despite the years they have devoted to studying the effects environment has on behavior, they have only now become aware of the seriousness of our ecological problems. Psychologists have responded predictably by establishing graduate training programs in environmental psychology and publishing a new journal, *Environment and Behavior*. Despite this less than astounding response to the problem, one can predict that psychologists will shortly rediscover the human environment.

The first explorers to take a close look at environmental psychology today have decided it is at best a "bucket of worms." At the federal level, for example, the ecological idea remains fragmented and scattered across a half dozen bureaus, services, and commissions that are studying primary environmental variables such as sound, area, light, radiation, inhaled gases, temperature-humidity, air movements, force fields, and atmospheric pressure. Unfortunately, these variables are most often studied one at a time rather than in their proper, total context. The findings, as a consequence, fail to account for the incredible complexity of the human social ecology. It is almost impossible, therefore, to establish a hard and fast rule for so simple an issue as the minimum temperature for safely performing manual work. We are equally unable to agree about what constitutes a "comfortable" temperature for human beings, even though it is, in part, a semantic problem—"cold" for you may be "warm" for me. Then again, a 70-degree day in summer may seem cool, while a 70-degree reading in the dead of winter feels warm. If these simple problems elude an easy answer, how are we to comprehend the intricate issues of radiation, a space environment, or sonic booms? How shall we approach questions such as the amount of plastic and pavement mankind can tolerate without losing its basic humanity?

The behavioral scientists of tomorrow must broaden their focus to include the role of socially and culturally determined habits, attitudes, and values. We need to know more about the long-term behavioral effects of the sensory world of urban ghettos, center-city freeway traffic, jet airports, and industrial plants. Oddly, we are better informed about the psychological hazards of prolonged isolation in the frozen wastes of Antarctica than we are about the megalopolis in which most of us reside. It is time psychologists looked at the condition of the physical environment closer to home.

One psychologist suggests that we might well begin by studying the American "psychology of more." Americans are addicted to the concept of Supergrow—the idea that our society can only be alive if it grows and expands constantly. If it is newer and bigger, it is better. Our attitudes are based upon a "more-is-good" philosophy that will be an obstacle to social survival if we cannot alter ourselves psychologically. We need help in moving to a "psychology of enough." The only "more" which we may find useful is described by anthropologist Loren Eiseley: "The need is not really for more brains, the need is now for a gentler, a more tolerant people than those who won for us against the ice, the tiger, and the bear."

Barry Commoner, one of the pioneers of American ecological concern, insists there is an urgent need to establish within the scientific community some means of estimating the critical balance of benefits and hazards of environmental interventions before we undertake them. Echoing this thought, J. F. Howard goes one step further: "We must stop applying technological innovations until we have come to understand a little bit more about their impact and have decided explicitly that we're willing to pay the price.... We can achieve, or at least move toward, a physical environment which will encourage human interaction, facilitate intimate interpersonal contacts, provide opportunities for individuals to assert themselves against their environment and get a sense of self-fulfillment."

Some contend, however, that it may already be too late for technological man. R. R. Landers proposes that we are becoming physically and mentally more mechanistic, and, while machines are not taking over, they may outlive the human species. In the meantime, machines may dominate man by "influence" or "persuasion," in a manner he would never accept from his fellow man. The Good Life in the future may be available only to those of us who learn to love the machine—to accept the synthetic as if it were organic. In a sense,

138

man has created new machines which will eventually create a new kind of man.

As long as psychological prescriptions for ecological problems are no more than broadly moralistic ("Let us all walk together"), they will provide little direction to assist us in determining the best move to make next. As one writer stated, "Specific proposals, however worthy as individual items, seem too partial, palliative, negative; ban the bomb, tear down the billboards, give the Hindus contraceptives and tell them to eat their sacred cows. The simplest solution to any suspect change is, of course, to stop it, or, better yet, to revert to a romanticized past: make those ugly gasoline stations look like Anne Hathaway's cottage or (in the Far West) like ghost-town saloons."

It is evident psychologists have their work cut out for them. As anthropologist Margaret Mead observed, it is the human attitude that will determine whether man will plant trees that take two lifetimes to mature, stop forests from being depleted, stop the soil from being washed into the sea, or prevent the gene pool from becoming exposed to excessive radiation. But, changing the mind of man about his way of life is no simple matter. What experts propose is often rejected by the citizenry when small but vocal groups feel their rights are being violated and when political leaders are indifferent. We need to expend more scientific energy to understand why some innovations are adopted and others resisted. We have long experienced conflict, for example, over the issue of flouridation of our water to reduce tooth decay. Even when experts agree about the benefits of this technological advance, 60 percent of the local referendums fail to support fluoridation.

Psychologists have been late in responding to the ecological challenge, but there is a growing awareness of the issues. Behavioral psychology, for example, has burst on the ecological scene as an ally in the war on litterbugs. It has been evident for some time that the human urge to smother the environment with trash cannot effectively be curbed by passing antilitter laws or furnishing more ugly trash cans. A new behavioral approach to the psychology of trashing is exemplified by studies conducted at the University of Washington in Seattle. The researchers focused on two movie houses in Seattle that held Saturday children's matinees. First, following a show, they weighed all the trash found in the theaters to determine the relative amount deposited in trash cans (19 percent at theater number one and 16 percent at theater number two). Then, they experimented with several approaches designed to discourage littering. Doubling the number of trash cans had no effect and showing an antilittering film before the regular movie increased the properly trashed yield by only 5 percent. Handing out personal litter bags in theater number one raised the deposited trash from 19 to 31 percent, and this figure rose to 57 percent when it was coupled with a special trash announcement.

Then they tried handing out litterbags and offering rewards for each bag of litter turned in after the show. The amount of trash turned in rose to new heights of 95 percent. Outdoor trashing of our national parks and public beaches is a problem much more irritating than the typical child clutter in Saturday movies, and it may well be that such behavioral modification techniques will be an important part of psychology's contribution to a new ecological balance for the planet. It is a beginning, at least, and with awakened psychological interest we may yet find answers in time. Perhaps the necessary psychological prescription has been described by E. T. Hall, author of the *The Hidden Dimension*.

> It isn't just that Americans must be willing to spend the money. Some deeper changes are called for which are difficult to define, such as a rekindling of the adventuresome spirit and excitement of our frontier days. For we are confronted with urban and cultural frontiers today. The question is, how can we develop them? Our past history of antiintellectualism is costing us dearly, for the wilderness we must now master is one requiring brains rather than brawn. We need both excitement and ideas and we will discover that both are more apt to be found in people than in things, in structure than content, in involvement rather than in detachment from life.

violence

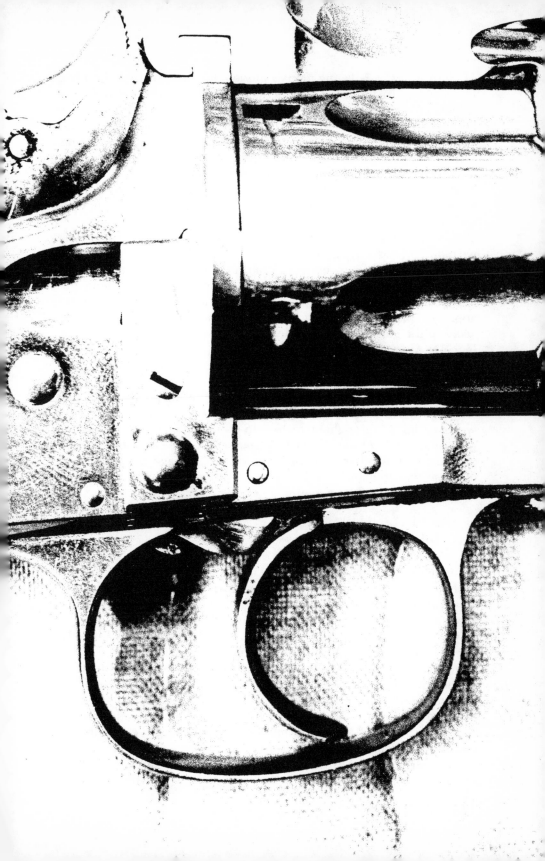

Modern America is facing a crisis of violence that has been building for decades. In the 126 years between 1820 and 1945, it has been calculated that 59 million people died at the hands of other human beings—in wars, in quarrels, or murders. The fact that for 126 years a man killed another man once every 68 seconds is indeed staggering. The present-day problems do not mean that Americans are more violent than in the past or more violent than the other people of the world. But today's violence has grown to such proportions that we are all threatened with extinction. "We build awesome instruments and institutions of destruction and bring reflections and portrayals of violence into every home. We all face the specters of nuclear weapons, a long and unpopular war, interracial riots, campus unrest, political assassinations, battered children, and unknown assailants." American "people and institutions are committed to it [violence] as a logical and useful style of life. American culture ... tolerates, approves, propagates, and rewards violence. The glamour of violent acts and the glorification of violent men create an idealization of violence in America."

In the face of such glorification of violence, it may be that birth control is the only way to limit violence. The human condition allows us to control violence in some of the people all of the time; and we can control violence in all of the people some of the time. But we have failed throughout history to control violence in all of the people all of the time. Even if fewer people are born and we kill off most of the others, we seem unable to manage the aggression of those who remain. Surely we need other explanations of man's inhumanity to his fellow man.

our violent history

Undoubtedly it began with the cave man, if not when Cain slew Abel. Some scientists are now convinced that our notion of a slope-shouldered, hairy, bent-kneed Neanderthal man is a pleasing but mistaken impression of early *Homo Sapiens*—an error based on the misinterpretation of the fossil skeleton of one old, arthritically crippled ancient man. Our concept of our forebearers as human brutes may have come about as a necessary confirmation of our current feelings of human superiority over all other forms of life. The Neanderthal man of 100,000 years ago had a brain as large as ours, a culture of sorts, and a survival-based willingness to kill others. In addition, he may have practiced cannibalism, not distinguishing the edibility of one species from another.

It has been suggested that warfare on a small scale must have existed as a part of the life of the very earliest human-like forms.

Almost all Neanderthal men disappeared about 40,000 years ago in what may have been the first genocidal war. In the 35,000 years of the history of modern man, we have done little to change from the ways of our very earliest practices. We simply have learned to kill our fellow man in a finer fashion. Consider, as an example, our 160 year love affair with violence in American literature. From Edgar Allan Poe to Mickey Spillane, blood, guts, and gore have occupied the American fantasy. This is not to say there is a direct or easy correlation between what we read and how we behave, but it does suggest that a sociology of the novel is revealing of the American character since sex and sadism has always sold books.

One kind of ideal man was the Western hero—aggressive, independent, nearly omnipotent, self-sufficient, and, often, beyond human law. "Removed from the complexities of adult love, family relations, or vocation, they [the Western heroes] were the perfect wish-fulfillment of the pre-adolescent mind. Instead of shaping their lives to distant goals, they lived for the present moment and according to an understood code of natural justice and good-natured generosity. Their independent existence implied a repudiation of sexual and economic responsibilities; yet even their violence retained a certain innocence, since it was devoid of social consequence." Bruno Bettelheim, noted child psychoanalyst and theorist, feels we have neglected the proper study of violence; he reminds us of Robert Warshaw's defense of the Western gunfighter as a moral hero. Perhaps only in this personage can we find some acknowledgment of the "value of violence." The Western hero is, for us, a hero with gun slung low on his thigh. He is not cruel but, again, not sentimental—in short, he is a man who believes in violence.

According to Bettelheim, we plant the seed of violence in the psyche of our children during the process of child rearing. We too often teach violence while attempting to control it in a violent manner. In Bettelheim's words, "Violence is the behavior of someone who cannot visualize any other solution to a problem that besets him." This sowing of the seed of violence is not, however, a recent phenomenon. If we are violent, we have not suddenly become more so in our recent history. We tend too easily to forget incidents such as Shays' Rebellion when in 1786 a group of hard-pressed, poor farmers in the western part of Massachusetts seized the law courts and refused to let justice be transacted. We forget the anti-Catholic, anti-Irish riots of the 1840s and 1850s, the Civil War draft riot of 1863 which killed 2000 people in five days, the anti-Chinese riots on the West Coast in the 1870s, the labor uprisings in the late 1800s which called for mobilization of 16,000 federal troops, the New York anti-draft riots of 1863, the great railway strike of 1887, the anti-Negro riots of 1919 and 1920, and the 1942 race riots.

The violence of the past nevertheless seems ancient history; the violence of today is what frightens most of us. In a recent survey, interviews were conducted with a nationwide sample of 1374 men who were representative of the male population as a whole but who were also selected to include a larger number of blacks than would normally have been sampled. The survey was aimed at unearthing the justifications we use to make different kinds of violence acceptable. A further aim was to discover just what levels of violence American men are ready to tolerate in various situations. Two types of violence were studied—violence used for social control and violence in the service of social change. The researchers concluded there is a significant number of Americans who feel that violence is necessary to bring about the needed changes fast enough. About 20 percent of the men questioned believed that protest involving extensive property damage or some deaths would be necessary to bring about social change. The 10 percent who believed in the necessity of severe violence are overshadowed by those who held the opposite view, but it should be noted that this percentage still represents some five million men. That is what frightens so many of us—the readiness of such vast numbers to resort to violence if things do not move fast enough for them. In response to these fears, our leaders give speeches about violence and the need for "law and order," but whenever public statements about violence are made, the speakers are always talking about someone else. One author has ironically described our refusal to see ourselves as the perpetrators of violence.

> When some national figure, a President, churchman or union leader, says that "we" are a violent people, he does not mean that we, the majority, are assassins or rebels, but that we have permitted criminality, assassination and revolt to flourish. Therefore, when he talks about "violent men," he does not refer to decent, respectable, middle-class white folk, but to the unruly, obstreperous mob of criminals, students, juvenile delinquents, Negroes, poor people and psychopaths who are now lumped together as lacking respect for law and order.

Not everyone is convinced that we have returned to savagery as a way of life. In a survey of the statistics of violent crime, two researchers dismissed the myth that Westernized culture is suffering from the sickness of increased violence. After a careful review of reported crimes the investigators concluded: "The crime and arrest data ... indicate no substantial increase in aggressive crimes during recent years. Robbery and forcible rape rates show moderate increases. Aggravated assault rates show the greatest increase but are far below the increase in rates shown for property or nonviolent crime." Making such conclusions from statistical studies of reported crimes is always a little suspect, however, since the rules of reporting are constantly changed. New regulations tend to produce a "paper" crime wave of staggering proportions. The basic problem is that offenses are reported by category, without any trustworthy indication of *degree* within the category. According to the statistics, an assault remains an assault, and if assaults have become more violent across the face of the nation it is difficult to detect.

SOCIAL VIOLENCE

The use of crime and force on the part of marginal groups seeking social equality has most often been viewed with alarm because of a cultural distaste for violence. Not all violence, of course, is regarded with such abhorrence. We support wars, an incredible annual automobile accident rate, and a high infant mortality. But, the criminal form of violence is intolerable. As has been observed, our fatal accident rate on the highway is four times higher than the annual murder rate—all because we value a form of transportation higher than human life. We are repulsed only by the more direct and messy form of murder. Social violence, moreover, is deplored mainly because it is disruptive to the smooth, and tranquil flow of social life. In short, violence is perceived as incidental rather than fundamental to the nature of society. Some observers view social violence as the likely outcome of any social structure that excludes some of its citizens from climbing the ladder of personal achievement. When all access is barred, violence may be the only remaining path, and in a peculiar way violence does afford equal opportunity. "In the world of violence, such attributes as race, socioeconomic position, age, and the like are irrelevant; personal worth is judged on the basis of qualities that are available to all who would cultivate them."

One important feature of violence is that it signals severe social dysfunction in the body politic. Violence catalyzes public opinion, and, despite the human suffering it causes, it eventually produces social change. This effect is greatly enhanced by the widespread dissemination of protest via the mass media. Upheaval in our society shapes our view of life, and a case can be made that an increasing number of us are ready for violent solutions to life's problems. Historically, social violence has found its finest hour in political and labor movements.

Some have concluded that American history has been bloodstained with labor violence. We have, in fact, a record of greater violence than does any other industrial nation. In most instances violence does not accompany a strike called by a recognized union; most often, it takes place in unorganized strikes that aim toward achieving recognition. Violence can occur, for example, when one group attempts to make a fundamental change in the conditions of employment and the other group (most often the employers) resists. When attempted changes are coupled with a serious grievance, violence is liable to result.

It is worth observing that the violence and destructiveness of the railroad riots and strikes of 1877 have never been equalled. When the Baltimore and Ohio railroad announced wage cuts in July 1877, widespread rioting followed. In these riots and in the 1886 railroad riots in Missouri, state and federal troops were employed to quell the disturbance. In the steel strikes of 1892, companies hired armed private police to manage the conflict. And, the 1894 strike of Pullman workers was nearly the most violent outburst of all times. More than a score of persons were killed and many more were injured. The coal strikes of the late 1890s and early 1900s led to armed clashes resulting in troop intervention. To this sordid list must be added the Rocky Mountain coal and metal miners' strike of the 1890s and early 1900s. This was a violent instance of assault and reprisal on both sides in which radical miners were simply "deported" from the area in violation of their civil rights. In each of these historical instances, a bloody war was waged against the birth of the unions. All the companies involved used professional strikebreakers and hastily deputized "guards."

The history of labor strife also includes municipal transportation strikes such as those in San Francisco in 1907, Cleveland in 1908, Philadelphia in 1910, and Buffalo in 1913. In Philadelphia, for example, it was reported that strikebreakers drove down a crowded thoroughfare at high speed shooting into the crowds of people on the sidewalk. The record goes on and on and involves almost every industry—lumber, copper, clothing, and so on. It was a time of bloody warfare between industrial barons and labor, but, following World War II, violence in labor disputes diminished as the National Labor Relations Board posed an alternative to the labor wars.

Political or ideological violence has been the handmaiden of extremism throughout American history. Both far right and far left have rejected the electoral and constitutional processes of democracy, choosing a clearer, swifter, more decisive alternative. Despite the spilling of much blood, however, both the extreme right and extreme left have failed. As one critic stated: "If violence is the refuge of unreason, then we must never be greatly surprised to find violent tendencies far out on those political extremities of the Left and the Right which have exchanged reason for passion and mystical faith."

Each century has had its political radicals who have disavowed violence except when necessary for self-defense. We forget too soon the anti-Catholic, anti-immigrant Native American Organization of the 1830s and 1840s or the Grand Council of the United States of North America (the Know-Nothings). As D. B. Davis writes:

148

This was not hate fringe; for when, in the election of 1854, the secret and violent order entered the open political arena (under the name of "the American party"), it elected governors in nine states and placed 104 of its members in the United States House of Representatives—then a body of 234. In 1856, former President Millard Fillmore, running as the Know-Nothing candidate, captured almost a million votes—about one-fifth of the total cast.

In the decade that was to follow, terrorist tactics moved south and the first Ku Klux Klan was founded. The "second Klan," active in the 1920s, had a membership of between four and five million. The peak of this radical movement probably occurred in 1940, when it joined the German-American Bund, at a meeting in New Jersey, and sang Hitler's marching songs. Racial violence rose to impressive proportions in the 1960s beginning with what has been called "Axe Handle Saturday" in Jacksonville, Florida, in August 1960. Since those days we have seen the birth of the Black Muslims and the Progressive Laborites. At the far right stand the John Birch Society and the Minutemen. This history of social violence underscores the observation made by Judd Marmor: "We rely on the sane people of the world to preserve it from barbarism, madness, destruction. And now it begins to dawn on us that it is precisely the *sane* ones who are the most dangerous ... who can without qualm and without nausea aim the missiles and press the buttons that will initiate the great festival of destruction that they, the *sane ones*, have prepared."

Perhaps we should be more optimistic about man's penchant for social aggression, but a more realistic conclusion would be W. Bloomberg's observation: "We mislead ourselves into a fool's errand if we ask how to eliminate violence from human affairs; we can only attempt to minimize the frequency, the duration, and the intensity of its manifestations, seeking constructive expression of our capacities for aggression. But if we try solely to suppress violence once it emerges, then we can be sure that it will appear frequently, be persistent, and reach great heights of destruction." It is not enough, socially, to be men of good will. We need, rather, to take a closer look at the nature of violence and the subcultures within our society that support and reward it.

SUBCULTURES OF VIOLENCE

Within any society only a few subcultural groups are predictably violent, while other subcultural groups are predictably nonviolent. Although every member of the species is capable of learning to be violent, this capacity seems especially noteworthy in the male, and among the males it is most evident in juveniles. The same may be said for other primate species—aggression is most typical of young adult males. Social worker H. W. Polsky has stated it most boldly: "Ultimate authority in the delinquent world rests upon tough boys dominating inferior boys by physical force.... Violence is a direct, uncomplicated, pervasive, and economical form of social control."

The use of violence in a youthful subculture is not viewed as improper, and the violent ones do not have to deal with feelings of guilt about their aggression. Violence, for them, is a life style, a useful way to resolve difficult problems. There is no conscious guilt because the victim of this youthful violence is usually a member of the same subculture and subscribes to the same beliefs. It is no accident that violence and aggression are used most frequently by "the immature, the disadvantaged, the dispossessed, the disorganized, the despairing, the depressed, and the deprived." It becomes natural for the person of this nature to use aggression in situations where he has had trouble in the past.

H. L. Nieburg, author of *The Behavioral Process*, has pointed out that the assertion of manhood by aggression against one's fellow man has its reasons and its uses. In a sense, violent aggression is a supremely human phenomenon and one to which the weak are always tempted since they lack other means to pit themselves against the strong. Violence—even when it fails—compels recognition, marking the aggressor's attempt to "do something," however futile or degrading. Nieburg maintains that blacks, more than any other group, have utilized violence. In turn, violence has produced action, radicalized some moderates, and crystalized the issues of civil rights and freedom.

If a distinctive subculture of violent persons exists, it is the population of citizens we confine in our jails. According to one writer, American prisons ought to be much more violent than they are—first, because American prisoners are violent people; and, second, because the roughest prisoners remain in jail because of fears that they will assault others if released. Because violence is the common language of the prisoners, no man can feel safe within prison walls. Yet, the fact is that measurable violence is small and the number of prisoners committing violence is smaller yet. Fewer than 1 in 100 men in prison commit violent acts. Paradoxically, in some ways, an individual may be safer from violence in prison than outside. In part this is true because almost every social force (privileges, early parole, and so on) is directed against the expression of violence. Prisons, moreover, are a kind of experiment in behavioral control of individual violence—even in an exceedingly violent subculture.

In the appraisal of violent behavior, one often overlooks the fact that violence even within a subculture is impulsive. It is not always a planned, purposeful activity. In the words of L. Berkowitz, author of several inquiries into the nature of aggression, neither is violence "the 'inevitable' result of internal drives or maladjustments. These things set the stage and help carry the action forward, but in many cases it is also important that there be a stimulus or immediate cue to trigger aggression."

of man and beast

Our long history of social and subcultural violence and the severity of modern violent upheavals have created a new level of anxiety and a new urgency in the quest for an explanation of human aggression. Recently, in desperation perhaps, we have turned to the animal kingdom in our search for the truth; there has been a small explosion of semi-scientific books arguing the position that man is an animal and animals are inherently aggressive. Accordingly, man is aggressive because of the instincts he inherits as a member of his species—instincts similar to those of other predators. The obvious conclusion is that man cannot be blamed for this violence since it is in his genes. No one in our society would need to feel responsible if human aggression were nothing but a fixed quality built into the species over the centuries. This simple view of human violence, however, is rejected by some of the most respected theorists of our time as a grossly erroneous view of man. Beginning with the romantic notions of the philosopher Rousseau, we have toyed with the idea that the human condition has been ruined by the influences of a crowded planet, a frantic pace of living, and the ceaseless clamor of industrial society. We have looked for hopeful signs in nature, but there is little probability that the anthill, beehive, or monkey colony has much to teach modern, interplanetary, atomic man.

It is true that other species usually manage to settle their disputes without killing one another and that bloodshed is rare. In this respect man is the only species that is a mass murderer and the only misfit in his own society. Territorial animals other than man, attack intruders once they have settled on a territory, but an animal still searching for a suitable territory withdraws when it meets an already established owner. Once you have taken possession of a territory, it is reasonable to drive off competitors; but when you are still hunting a territory, you are better off if you avoid established owners.

Aggression in Old World monkeys and apes is an adaptive mechanism that is an important factor in determining interindividual relations. Aggression is a frequent and highly rewarded part of intergroup relations when all the rules are mutually understood as a means to reducing fatal conflict. "When we humans observe fights among animals, we notice many similarities between animal aggression and human aggres-

151

sion. This leads us to wonder whether there are orderly principles to account for aggression throughout the animal kingdom." Nevertheless, I am convinced that we will learn little about the human condition by scrutinizing the animal kingdom. Studies of animals are relevant to the human condition only when applied to that very brief period in infancy when we are without the command of language. When we learn to speak, we leave our animal cousins behind and enter a universe no animal could begin to understand. When we learn to speak, we become a distinct species capable of understanding abstractions such as liberty, freedom, equality, brotherhood, and love. One must conclude that aggressive "instinct" is not an explanation of man's inhumanity to his fellow man; man is more than a vicious, snarling animal. The observation of J. Lukacs is appropriate. "This country is threatened by savagery, not violence: and this is not a play on words. The peoples of this world are governed by their characters rather than by their institutions; and there is a streak of savagery rather than violence in the American character."

A highly speculative and fanciful extension of the concept of instinctual aggression is popular writer Anthony Jay's view of the modern corporation man: he is a new version of the old-time hunter who goes out each day to stalk his prey, kill his game, and bring it back to camp. Corporate structures have their own status display, aggression, appeasement, comradeship, and tribal gatherings as, according to Jay, primitive man did. Corporate business life may be seen merely as a sophisticated version of tribal life in the jungle, if we strip away the grey flannel suit that disguises it. Jay's analysis, however, as other recent attempts, is a fanciful denial of responsibility for human aggression.

the development of violence

How is it possible to fashion an aggressive, hating, social monster? It is not easily achieved since our young seem to survive even the exceptionally bad child-rearing circumstances. Yet, if an aggressive personality is what we want, the means to that end are quite straightforward. It helps, of course, if the child is born poor, is one of many other children, crowded into too little space, and exposed to lying, cheating, stealing, and violent examples by adults. It also helps if the child is free to run the streets unsupervised, learning what is right and wrong in life from peers who are similarly trapped in an unrewarding, threatening life. If the child's real world is a panorama of nothing but constant danger, injury, insecurity, and ignorance, shaping him in the ways of violence will be easy. In such a ready-made environment, beatings, threats, scolding, and abuse to the child are unnecessary.

Hated children—who hate in return with equal intensity—learn simply that they must be patient until they are big enough, strong enough, or clever enough to fight society with more potent weapons. Even in an otherwise benign environment, parents can rear a violent social monster, simply by following the recipe. The first ingredient in the formula is to have no love for the child. Love is an element that can destroy the best of malicious intentions since love topples what hate constructs; love undermines rejection, softens the sting of anger, and dulls the edge of rage. Love forms a protective psychological cocoon that shelters us from the full impact of the blows of fate. The workings of love are invisible to the naked eye, but without love the child is an inanimate object that can be misused as anger dictates. The unloved child must twist life's arm to seize what is not freely forthcoming.

Shaping the child's view of the world is a second factor in rearing a hating social monster. By rewarding some responses and punishing others, the dimensions of personality can be shaped to taste. If a combined system of deliberate reward and punishment is established early enough, continued long enough, and matched with clear examples of aggressive responses to the world, the child will mature with a distorted vision of the benefits of violence. The helpless, dependent, uncomprehending child learns what he is taught, and he learns to do as people do—not as people say.

Convincing the child that violence is the only truth is a third way to form a violent individual. The child must be taught that his violent reactions and the hostile fashion in which he treats people are necessary, natural, reasonable, and correct responses to the realities of life. He must learn that violence is a preferred and desirable means to any accomplishment. He must learn that in a jungle only savages survive. In those rare instances when punishment is administered, it must be inappropriate and appear to be undeserved. Once the child is convinced that violence is an admired, rewarded, and rational response, he will begin to use violence to solve problems that he cannot otherwise handle.

A fourth way to ensure the rearing of a violent individual is to defend the child against the corrosion of education. Education takes advantage of the dependent nature of the growing child. It tries to inculcate peaceful values by teaching the child ways to become a cooperative member of the society, and it praises and rewards reasonable behavior. Education can even produce guilt, fear, anxiety, a sense of loss, alienation from others, and feelings of rejection in connection with violence. Since it is from these internal emotional experiences that the child's self-image and self-esteem are formed, you must armor him against the corrective influences that might make a decent citizen of him. This is not too difficult to do if he is taught, early in life, that education is a worthless pursuit.

These steps in child rearing are vital to the final shape of adult behavior, but they cannot be considered in isolation from the society to which the individual must adjust. In an organized, highly structured, stable society the "social animal" is peaceful and cooperative; in a society that is disorganized and in transition, the individual is capable of incredibly destructive, violent behavior. The child must learn to be dissatisfied with society and to reject, violently, the mechanisms it provides for change. This is a complicated recipe but the final violent stew is worth it—if this is what you have in mind. By all means, you can produce an aggressive personality, if you are willing to expend the time, effort, and energy it demands.

the aggressive person

The male of the species becomes warmongering and aggressive because he learns to gain pleasure and status from this social role. The female, as our society decrees, must find more subtle outlets for exactly the same feelings and impulses. Clearly, we encourage aggression and reward its appearance in males in a thousand ways, and the process begins in early childhood.

One explanation of the psychological structure of the aggressive personality is provided by the social psychologist Leonard Berkowitz, who assumes that aggressiveness is learned directly by experiences with the rewards and punishments of life. The aggressive person thus learns to have a "predisposition to be readily aroused" and becomes remarkably quick to respond to signals in the environment that trigger his anger. Given the "habit" of anger and an appropriate "stimulus," the aggressive personality will blow up frequently and violently.

When the cues or signals to aggression are not present, however, the aggressive person is very much like the rest of us—complaining and irritable, perhaps, but rational about nonprovocative, noncontroversial daily events. Since he is not exploding *all* the time, he sees himself as a calm, reasonable person—except on those few occasions when he is provoked beyond all human tolerance. If you ask him about his explosiveness, the aggressive person will undoubtedly state that most of the people in this world are too passive, spineless, and tolerant of injustice, incompetence, and insults from others. He might suggest that most of us *invite* mistreatment from others by compromising every confrontation and never standing up to resist or protest.

154

Since the aggressive person sees frustration in almost every event in life he will continuously be distressed, feeling threatened and anticipating that the future will be no different from the past. The tense nature of his daily encounters with his fellow man will also tend to underscore the need to be aggressive. When the expectation that things will always go wrong is coupled with low tolerance for frustrating events and an exceptional readiness to respond with anger, the aggressive personality expects trouble, searches for it, discovers it everywhere, and reacts in a predictably violent manner. Sensitized to frustration, ever ready to respond aggressively, and with few other available forms of response, he becomes the prototype of an aggressive personality and finds life a continuing hostile confrontation with others.

While it may not be perfectly accurate to say that we always kill the one we love, it is true that most of us have less to fear from crime in the streets than from violence in the home. This is why policemen commonly observe that responding to a call of "family trouble" is an exceptionally dangerous assignment. We know that most murdered victims have had a close relationship to their murderers and that death most often occurs on home ground. Murder rarely fits the stereotyped situation where an unsuspecting, helpless, passive victim is stalked by a cold, calculating killer. Most homicides are preceded by angry quarrels in which the victim plays an active part in bringing about his own death.

In 1969, one researcher studied 588 homicides in Philadelphia. Some of the conclusions of the study were (*a*) if you are under 16 years of age, your murderer will most likely be a parent or relative; (*b*) if you are a woman over 16, your murderer will most likely be a husband, lover, or relative; (*c*) women are more likely than men to kill their mates; (*d*) when a man is killed, the killer is most likely to be his wife; (*e*) spouse slayings are more violent than the average homicide; (*f*) the bedroom is the most murderous room in the house; (*g*) proportionately, more women are killed in bedrooms; (*h*) men are in greater danger of being killed in the kitchen.

We do not really kill the ones we love. Rather, we kill those emotionally closest to us—those close enough to destroy our self-esteem. Insult, humiliation, or coercion are powerful elicitors of hostility and probably the most important source of anger and aggressive drive in human beings. Laboratory studies of aggression and clinical studies of violent men consistently conclude that threats to our self-esteem render us impotent and diminish our status in our own eyes and in the eyes of others; sometimes the only way to restore our personal status and demonstrate power is to injure the provoking agent. The relationship between personal status and violence is especially exaggerated for males weaned on a warrior definition of the male image.

The ultimate forms of aggression are perpetrated by the male of the species. Males assault their fellow humans eight times more often than do females, and murder is seven times more often a masculine act. Negroes commit a higher absolute and disproportionately higher relative rate of fatal crimes. Violence in the South—by blacks or whites—is greater than it is in the North; and the rate of violence in the "inner city" of large metropolitan areas is uniformly high. Killing others is most frequent among members of lower socioeconomic classes, and particularly among the young—the years 20 to 39 being the most dangerous ages. This list of the "facts" of fatal encounter tells us very little, however, since any act—whether it be murder or not—is multiply determined and can only be understood as the result of forces both without and within the individual. In the case of murder, a single act is so dramatic that it obscures the very forces that led to it.

Contrary to popular belief, murderers may be the most docile, trustworthy, and least violent members of prison populations. Psychologist E. I. Megargee examined a criminal population by dividing them into two groups—those rated *extremely assaultive* (manslaughter, murder, mayhem, assault with a deadly weapon, and so on) and those described as *moderately assaultive* (beatings). In two other categories he placed those designated *nonviolent* (thieves, homosexuals) and *noncriminals* (ordinary men). Most of us would guess that the greatest degree of violence would issue from those who are most hostile and least self-controlled. Yet, Megargee concluded that assaultive criminals were less aggressive and more controlled than either the nonviolent criminals or the noncriminal population. Megaree suggested that assaultive persons come in two types—undercontrolled and chronically overcontrolled. Undercontrolled aggressive persons are those who are openly aggressive and possess relatively little self-control, but most often they express their hostility in mild or moderate fashion. In contrast, chronically overcontrolled human beings are those who have such strict control over their aggressive urges that they seldom explode. The explosion, when it comes, is violent and fatal.

Thus, marriage to an undercontrolled person might mean continuous strife and turmoil, but the amount of aggression released in any one of the frequent outbursts would not be excessive. Life with the chronically overcontrolled person would be peaceful and tranquil for many years; the history of man, however, carries the ominous bloodstain made by the quiet, uncomplaining husband who suddenly slaughters his wife in an unbelievably brutal fashion. These findings suggest that while murder is a highly visible measure of the violent individual, it need not reflect a lifelong pattern of assaultive behavior. Murder is often the desperate response of a normally unaggressive person who can no longer tolerate the pressures of life.

The study of aggression in man cannot be restricted to its appearance in a single individual. The nature of social and group aggression needs to be explored. Further, some extrapolation of our knowledge of aggression in the individual ought to be applied to the international leaders whose personal dispositions and aggressive response to frustrations may now prove fatal to us all. Aggression on an individual, national, or international scale remains a "person problem" that, in modern times, has assumed a new dimension of urgency. Aggression has ceased to be an academic, clinical, or professional problem—its comprehension has become a matter of life and death for all of us.

The flaw in the American attitude toward international violence is our unshakeable belief that we, as a nation, are not aggressive. Since we believe the urge to dominate others is bad, we tend to overreact and become excessively aggressive ourselves, if we feel other nations are aggressing against our interests. Our foreign policy is perceived by others as aggressive in the extreme; yet we deny the accuracy of this appraisal of ourselves, and we are easily angered by what we see as unwarranted violence by other countries. The international incidents which have triggered massive, violent reactions in us have been exceptionally trivial, in retrospect; but we are ready tomorrow to react in a similar fashion to any affront to our dignity. We would be outraged at the presence of foreign gunboats plying the waters of the Mississippi, but we cannot view our own presence in the inland rivers of other countries as provocative.

In our domestic politics, we deny power to those leaders up for election who openly and unabashedly seek power. This strange schizophrenia about power makes us vulnerable to bungled relations with other cultures. We may or may not be more aggressive than other nations, but we certainly seem to be less aware of our needs to assert ourselves and to dominate others. If we could admit we are an aggressive people, it would probably keep us from so much international adventuring.

death

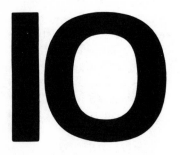

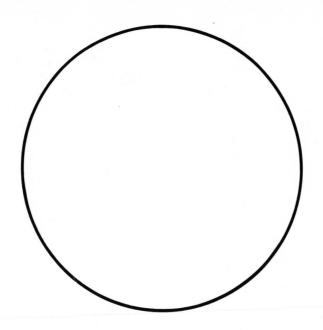

Two or more million of us die each year, but, by examining the literature, one would never suspect psychologists were aware of that fact. Like everyone else, psychologists observe the taboo in American society against speaking openly about death. We have almost managed to deny that death exists. The fear of death is no longer so much the terror of facing a final judgment as it is an anger that fate has somehow encroached on our right to life, liberty, and the pursuit of happiness. We try to cope with death by disguising it or pretending that it is not a fate each of us must one day face. We "exit," "cease," "expire," or "pass on"—but we rarely die. After death, our funerals are arranged more for the living than for the dead. Indeed, it is now a rare phenomenon for the average individual outside the medical and nursing professions to see a person die.

Doctors who see death every day may have been motivated to study medicine by their urge to find an answer to the riddle of their own certain death. A doctor can confront death trained, as few are, to stave off or delay collection of the universal debt of life. The idea of dying makes us anxious, and we seek in religion and philosophy some weapon with which to protect ourselves against this frightening end of consciousness. Death is inevitable, but psychologists have pretended this is not so. They have chosen to ignore this messy, painful, distressing, and disturbing aspect of existence.

Attitudes toward death evolve during the life cycle of each individual, and the end of life has different meanings at various periods of development. At about 4 or 5 years of age children know that life has an ending, but their principal concern is separating themselves from the parents upon whom they depend. The easiest solution to the problem of death is for the child to accept the prominant adult belief in a life after death—a life in which the child will be happily reunited with his loving parents. When the child becomes an adult and has children of his own, his concern about death rises above petty self-interest and is focused, rather, on what will happen to the wife and children if he dies. Later in life a new attitude emerges. "To the old person, death becomes a familiar. He has had much experience with it, has thought a good deal about it, and eventually expects the final visitor and may even await his call ... The elderly often tire of life and simply wish to drop out of the circle of the dance."

When you are old, life can become burdensome and death can appear as a relief from turmoil. For the aged, there may be contentment simply in knowing that descendants will carry the name or keep alive the spark of memory. For some individuals, tangible monuments to the work accomplished in their lifetime will remain. For the rest of us, immortality will be sought in our own way. Whatever the case, death is a constant part of the life of all of us.

Psychologically, death is what we make of it. It can be the gentle night or the great destroyer. In the words of one writer, death can reflect "surcease from pain and tribulation, reunion with one's family, loss of control, punishment, or loneliness. Developmental changes, cultural conditioning, religious orientation, personality characteristics, and level of threat, among others, contribute their shaping power." We must all look death directly in the eye, however, or we will always be victimized by the fear of it. Further, if we are to look directly at death, we must examine the process of aging that heralds its arrival.

yesterday we were younger

There really is no reason why all of us cannot live to be 150 years old—why we cannot penetrate the biological barrier between life and death. Yet, most of us will suffer some degenerative disease (cancer, a stroke, diabetes, or heart attack) that will usher us out of this life before we are fully prepared to go. In ancient days, men were prey to every order of deadly bacteria and virus; now that we have found cures to most fatal infections, four out of five of us will live long enough to die of some degenerative disease.

Researchers say it is becoming plausible for man to live 120 or 150 years. Heredity has in the past seemed to be the single key to a long life, but a few biologists now insist that they are on the threshhold of discovering how to prolong life through eliminating senility. One idea being pursued is that each individual has an innate amount of vitality that gets used up by repeated illnesses; in other word, the individual can weather only so much illness and stress before the erosion of sickness exhausts bodily life. Another theory assumes that every human being has a built-in "time clock" destined to run down at a rate determined by the environment and the way of one's life. Experimentation with rats, for example, has demonstrated that if the rat's food supply is sharply reduced to a bare minimum, the rat's life span is dramatically lengthened—even doubled in some cases. The solution to aging, then, would seem to be to slow down the clock and stretch time to its limits.

There is also a biochemical theory of aging that suggests fatal cell degeneration occurs when harmful chemicals build up in the 10 trillion cells of the body. For natural or accidental, man-made reasons, chemical units called "free radicals" may establish an unstable chemical balance that is fatal to the individual.

Living and dying is ultimately tied to the birth and death of bodily cells that form the cornerstone of human existence. The "error" theory of death maintains that, much like taking a picture of a photograph, printing the resulting negative, and then taking a picture of the new photograph, we may, in cellular life, reproduce successive copies of lower and lower quality until death eventuates. This theory is also labelled the "copy of a copy of a copy" theory—a process in which human bodies gradually weaken and wither away. Biologically oriented theories of this kind regularly ignore the psychological component of aging and refuse to credit evidence that variables such as work satisfaction and a positive attitude about life can be an effective predicator of the length of one's life.

Of current interest is the possibility that our cells die (and life perishes) for ecological reasons. That is to say, the air we breathe, the water we drink, and the food we eat poison us after a time and cause a fatal malfunctioning of the body. Other theorists are less gloomy about our poisonous environment; they feel that the poisons that kill us are the natural products of normal cell metabolism. Poisons accumulate, make us age, and finally kill us. Last, there is a "loss of control" theory which suggests that aging slows down all our nervous and chemical reactions until our growing "stiffness" or "rigidity" deprive us of the ability to bounce back when sick, injured, or emotionally distressed in a crisis.

It is impossible to determine which of these theoretical speculations contains more truth than error. And, perhaps, they are all equally true. All of us will grow older whatever our attempts to slow down the process. Some of us will display the ravages of time more visibly than others; some will seem ageless; and some will experience another full lifetime after most peers are dead and long buried. Those who perpetually appear young will take pride in their accomplishment, and others will feel envy.

Age reflects very little of what is important in man's relationships with his fellow men because, physiologically, we may be one age but, psychologically, we may have accumulated quite a different number of years. Perhaps all of us should reckon our real age in terms of flexibility, personality, and maturity rather than in terms of the years that have passed.

For centuries, older people have clung to the notion that scientific advances will run ahead of the aging process and save them from growing old. Recent comment on increasing longevity is not very encouraging, however. On the psychological side, we are exhorted to maintain a useful and satisfying role in society and keep a positive view of life, but this is in the end a rather vague guide to achieving longevity. On the physical side, we all have admired the strength and power of athletes and many of us have sweated hard and long to resemble them. But, being in excellent physical condition while young is no guarantee of a prolonged life. In one study of Harvard

162

athletes, major athletes (letter winners) tended to have the shortest lives; minor athletes (non–letter winners) had the longest; and nonathletes met death somewhere between the two. The differences in age at death were actually quite small, but clearly Tarzan would have about the same life expectancy as the rest of us.

Being old would be tolerable, if our culture were designed to accomodate the aged. Our cities, for example, develop and are redeveloped primarily for the benefit of the mobile, employed, high-consuming, younger citizens of the society. Modern cities tend to be efficient (shopping centers, medical centers, massive department stores) only to the young and mobile; they may, indeed be nightmares for the aged.

Compared with other civilizations we discard elderly citizens and effectively deny them a role in maintaining control over those who are younger. In preindustrial cultures, the aged were in an enviable position because they owned or controlled the property and resources upon which young people were dependent; their years of experience were vital to the continuation of the culture. Further, they were living links to the past and possessed rapport with the gods. Traditionally, they dominated the extended family of kinfolk all of whom clustered together in small, stable communities. The position of old persons has always been best when the productivity of the economy nears the ragged edge of starvation. The greater the poverty and struggle to survive, the relatively better off old people are, since every pair of helping hands becomes important. Yet, in some ancient cultures, the helpless elderly were abandoned to the elements to die—a somewhat crueler fate than our own retirement villages in California, Florida, or Arizona.

The cultural, economic, and social conditions of our modern era have given birth to what has been called "the elderly mystique." Despite a determined effort to think young, time takes its inevitable toll and the aging person begins to believe all the social myths about old people. When the aging male takes stock of himself, he becomes resigned to being a cultural discard. "As a worker, he has become a liability. His rigidity, his out-of-date training, his proneness to disabling illness, not to mention his irritability, lowered efficiency and arrogant manner, all militate against the likelihood of his being hired or promoted. Fussduddiness is his special quality. Besides, he is more than the pension plan ever bargained for. Moreover, there are younger people available for the vacant positions, and they are thought to need them more." The facts of aging are psychologically less important than the mystique that the elderly come to accept as true. These beliefs make the old-timer an active participant in his retirement from meaningful interaction in the culture, and in this way the aged contribute to their own cultural downfall.

the process of dying

It is abundantly clear to any aging observer that people today view death differently than in times past. Dying in a culture so mightily oriented to the needs of youth is no longer a matter of religious beliefs, values, or divine purpose; it is an accident, bad luck, fate, or a matter of poor judgment. Whatever the case, the responsibility for death has shifted away from God onto the person himself. Now, burials are quicker, and religious ceremonies are diminished.

We seem as much concerned about where and how we die as we do about the inevitability of death itself. We would prefer to leave this life in the privacy of home surrounded by friends and loved ones; yet, in all probability, most of us will die in the "dying places" we call hospitals. In this setting, we have little control over our way of death. Death has always been the enemy, but, in subtle ways, we are more conscious of it today than we have been for centuries.

A SENSE OF DOOM

Researchers studying death have reported that, when death approaches, only about 10 percent of the elderly will admit they fear it; another 30 percent will express mixed feelings; and the remainder will state that they are able to accept its inevitability. Despite these differing degrees of readiness to face the fact of dying, old wives' tales perpetuate the notion that subtle psychological changes signal when the end is coming. Chicago psychologist Morton Lieberman became interested in these changes when he observed that the chief nurse in a home for the aged seemed able to predict which residents would die several months before clear-cut physical changes were evident. She could not specify precisely how she knew but stated that these patients "seemed to act differently." Lieberman decided to explore this phenomenon with psychological measures; he concluded that indeed there were measurable, systematic psychological changes that occur many months before death, and these changes are not simply a response to physical illness. Persons who managed to recover even though they were seriously ill did not show the same psychological changes. Lieberman suggested that the psychological changes preceding death be viewed as the "individual's lessened ability to cope adequately with environmental demands, particularly because of a lowered ability to organize and to integrate stimuli in his environment." Lieberman went on to state that "Perhaps the aged individual, approaching his own death, experiences upheaval because of currently active disorganizing mental processes, rather than because he fears his approaching death."

The psychological withdrawal that is said to occur among the dying may be less a preoccupation with the self than it is a desperate

164

attempt to hold oneself together when experiencing chaos. The stages of emotional reaction to death and the process of dying have been described by Elisabeth Kübler-Ross. The first reaction is one of denial and isolation. ("No, not me. It cannot be true.") This reaction is shortly displaced by feelings of anger, rage, envy, and resentment. ("Why me?") These feelings are dispensed in all directions almost at random. Doctors, nurses, relatives, God—everyone—is blamed. This rage is to no avail, and the individual enters a third stage—bargaining. ("Maybe God will respond favorably if I am nice.") A fourth stage, when death can no longer be denied or bargained with, may be deep depression. This can be a form of preparatory grief in which the terminally ill patient begins the process of preparing himself for a final separation from the world.

The patient finally becomes neither depressed nor angry about what lies ahead, and he can face death with quiet resignation. He does not "give up" in despair, but he ceases any longer to battle against the inevitable. As Kübler-Ross notes, this is the time when the television gets turned off—it is a time of quiet, private moments. Each of these stages needs to be reacted to in unique ways, and the therapy of dying is a complex process.

SPEAKING OF DEATH

Americans do not speak much about death, and when they are hospitalized in anticipation of its arrival they discover that even doctors, nurses, and hospital personnel share this psychological avoidance of the topic. A credibility gap exists between what is practiced and what is preached in hospitals; professional persons are theoretically in favor of open communication about death yet regularly find good reasons to avoid actually talking about it. Once labelled a dying person, the patient becomes "different" from other patients, and people tend to avoid him. When he most needs help in dealing with his fears, the patient is left to resolve them on his own. Talking to a dying patient about his impending death is simply too devastating an experience for most persons and communication breaks down.

Once both the patient and the hospital staff know that the patient is dying, both parties may engage in a mutual pretense that the facts are otherwise. Because both parties participate willingly in this game, each follows the rule of not initiating conversations about death. A kind of silent bargain is struck between the patient and those who take care of him, so that the masquerade can ensure everyone's psychological comfort. Since the doctor and the nurse have the advantage of professional experience with this kind of game, they can act their part with greater skill than can the patient. In these instances, patient-doctor conversations focus pointedly on topics that are remote from death, and both pretend not to notice conversational slips that bring up the tabooed subject. This conspiracy of silence is aided and abetted by the medical-administrative design of hospitals which serves to keep information about the patient's condition "classified" and available to staff members only.

The brunt of caring for terminal patients falls on the nurses who must interact with the patient during the day. The doctor, knowing the case is terminal, may not visit the patient quite as often, giving his energy to patients who still have a chance to survive. The reactions of the nurses also reflect their awareness that there is no hope for the patient's survival. In the words of one observer, "So long as hope is real, and nurses feel they are working to save a life, they are apt to become intensely involved. High involvement is also likely when it seems especially tragic that the patient should die—he is young, has great promise, has an important job, has a devoted family dependent upon him. A gifted or beautiful patient has great appeal and the threat of death distresses nurses and drives them harder." When death is certain, however, nurses (without deliberately intending to) begin to delay responding to the patient's signals for care.

The ideal terminal patient is one who dies in a dignified manner, making it easier for everyone concerned. B. G. Glaser and A. L. Strauss, authors of an article called "Dying on Time," have described a model for such an ideal patient: he should try his best to maintain composure and cheerfulness as he faces the inevitable. He should not cut himself off from the world of the living but should remain a good family member and interact comfortably with other patients. When possible, he should contribute to the social life of the ward. He must not only cooperate with staff members but avoid distressing or embarrassing them. A patient who matches this model is respected for achieving an acceptable style of dying.

THE DYING

Dying in a hospital is not a simple matter. Decisions must be made about who lives and dies, how they will meet death, and where and when they will die. There is a priority to dying in which the lives of younger people have greater social value and are worth the time and effort invested in caring for them. Psychologist Richard Kalish stated, "as the result of age, race, sex, finances, and personality, decisions are made which affect who lives and who dies. These decisions are made by medical personnel, hospital ward personnel, other patients, relatives—just about everyone."

The who, how, when, and where of dying reflects the values and beliefs of our society. The patient is seldom the one to determine the details of his death, since he is not deemed competent to make such decisions. At some point in this social process, each of us ceases to own our life and our body. As Kalish asked, "When do you cease to have responsibility for what happens to your body or your thinking? Lack of responsibility for 'you' ceases before death if evidence can be given that 'you' are not capable of taking responsibility. Thus, 'you' may be medicated, sedated, tranquilized, operated upon, fed, bathed, and dressed without the prerogative of being an agent in the decision-making process." The dying have become a persecuted minority who are regularly deprived of their civil rights; but, no one cares.

Perhaps, as David Dempsey suggested in his article "Learning How to Die," we will finally take death seriously, stop treating it as a taboo subject, and learn to confront its approach. Despite evidence that the overwhelming majority of hospital patients want to know the nature and severity of their illnesses, hospital procedures together with professional attitudes prevent this from happening. Thus, the average American who is fatally ill will probably die without the dignity or tranquility that might make the passage more bearable. He is likely to die in a drug-induced stupor that destroys consciousness of his last moments on this earth. Dempsey noted that it is even harder to die today since the familiar signs of death may be contradicted by an electroencephalograph designed to detect the last few flickering brain waves.

> Few doctors today subscribe to the principle of mercy killing, but there are equally few who do not practice it. Sometimes treatment is simply discontinued. Less frequently, a patient will be allowed to make the decision himself, if he is conscious, with a bottle of sleeping pills left by the bedside. Apparently the most common solution is to turn off the life-support system. All of these are forms of "passive euthanasia." Nobody knows just how many hopeless patients die this way because nobody wants to talk about it, but it is the rare physician who at some time has not "pulled the plug." Or, more likely, who has not instructed the nurse to do it, for one of the moral dilemmas of "heroic" medicine is just who shall become the executioner when the time comes.

In New Haven, Connecticut, a corporation has been established to make living easier for the dying. Called Hospice, Inc., it is a home dedicated to making death more humane and meaningful. Hospice, Inc. was devised to counteract the fact that there is no place in the general hospital which is suitably equipped for dying. The Hospice attends to the wishes of the patient, letting him dictate important features of his life. It provides a sympathetic professional staff and invites family and friends to participate in making the patient comfortable. Terminally ill patients could choose the Hospice rather than the hospital for their final days.

the survivors grieve

Death destroys the social and personal balance of the survivors, and this tipping of the scales is greatest when the departed one made a significant contribution to the social order of the family. In ancient societies, infants and the newborn were most likely to perish; in our society the bulk of the dying are aged persons whose removal from the business of the society is hardly noted. Societies systematically invent ways to minimize the loss that is sustained in death by declaring whole classes of the dying as nonpersons. Primitive societies with high infant mortality, for example, may not recognize infants or children as full human beings until they reach a reasonable age. In much the same fashion, we devalue our aged and accord them a lesser role in society.

In primitive cultures the dead were gone, but they were hardly forgotten since it was believed that they could reappear as ghosts to haunt the living. Grieving among these primitive people was a brief event since the dead would soon be back to visit. As one writer suggested, a part of our rituals of grief and mourning for the departed may stem from the fact that the death "is more likely to remind survivors of the social and psychological debts they have incurred toward him [the departed]—debts that they may have been intending to pay in the coins of attention, affection, care, appreciation, or achievement. In modern societies the living use the funeral and sometimes a memorial to attempt to 'make up for' some of these debts that can no longer be paid in terms of the ordinary give and take of social life." This means that we moderns are liable to feel grief more intensely (but less frequently) than would members of an extended community in which all who die are mourned by all others and the closeness of personal relations is diffused among these many others. In primitive society, laughter, joy, and play can appear immediately after the funeral ritual is ended; in our society there is no specified time when the work of mourning officially comes to an end.

Grief and the process of mourning following death are the means by which each of us achieves emotional freedom from the memory of the relationship that has been severed. Grieving and mourning are uncomfortable tasks and persons who suffer serious maladjustment in the process may be those who resisted the expression of grief or could not mourn for lost loved ones. Grief and mourning inadequately dealt with at the time of death may return to plague survivors at a later date. The "anniversary reaction" has been described in which, on the anniversary of the death of a loved one, the survivor develops symptoms similar to those displayed by the deceased or experiences intense anxiety about the possibility of his own death. This may involve a delayed emotional reaction that occurs many years after the actual

168

loss or involve the appearance of an inappropriate degree of emotional upset at the death of someone only distantly connected to the individual.

There can be normal and neurotic grief following bereavement. One writer distinguished between the two by noting that neurotic grief tends generally to be excessive, disproportionate, protracted, associated with profound feelings of irrational despair and hopelessness, and involved with phobic feelings about one's own death. In addition, neurotic grievers may be unable to deal with their mixed feelings of love and hate toward the lost object or may feel that the decedent died on purpose as a way of rejecting or punishing the survivor. Neurotic grievers may maintain an irrational belief that somehow the death was their fault. They may, consequently, be less able to offer affection to others. They may begin to suffer from symptoms similar to those of the dead person, or they may undergo protracted apathy, heightened irritability, or aimless hyperactivity.

Grief and mourning are the inevitable consequences of being a human being. Grief occurs when something essential to one's emotional life has been lost. This loss could be compared to a wound, while the mourning process could be compared to the healing of that wound.

dust to dust

Every society must devise ways of dealing with the death of its members, providing for the expression of grief, disposing of the corpse, and making it possible for the mourners to return to their social tasks. In our society, however, death is also an occasion when much money changes hands. As one writer put it, "Elaborate floral arrangements, expensive coffins, and grave sites that will be given 'perpetual care' (at a price of course) make death one of the worst bargains that you or I will ever get in America."

The plain pine box for burial, the laying out of the dead by members of the family and close friends, and carrying of the coffin to the grave by hand were typical procedures in the funeral in America until the end of the nineteenth century. In the twentieth century, the business of dying became expensive. If the financial sacrifice of a funeral is severe enough, the monetary outlay can be a means of atoning for any real or fancied guilt that the survivors may feel. Paying an exorbitant price for a funeral also bolsters family pride by displaying to one and all the status the family enjoys in the society. Interestingly, there is a close correspondence between the cost of living and the cost of dying; as one rises, so does the other.

The more of us there are on this planet the greater becomes the annual death rate, and in some parts of the world the more crowded the cemeteries become. In Rio de Janeiro the problem has reportedly become particularly acute—each burial in the cemetery serving the southern half of the city entails the shifting of bodies buried earlier and the cost of a burial plot has risen astronomically. The solution proposed by one Brazilian architect is a 39-story skyscraper cemetery containing 21,000 tombs with an eventual capacity of 147,000 dead persons. The building, of course, will have a rooftop heliport for quick transport of bodies and an eight story garage for visitors. For those unable to afford such tombs, there will be a rental plan for five years. This represents a substantial "improvement" over the three-story, vertical mausoleum (capacity 9000 bodies) currently being constructed in Nashville, Tennessee.

Anthropologists have long maintained that a significant indicator of a society's norms or values is its burial rituals. If our culture were to be judged solely by how we dispose of our dead, we would not score very well; our funerary practices are as strange as any yet invented. Since our culture is addicted to viewing the dead, we do our best to make the corpse look as "normal" as possible. We pretty up death so that it seems to be an almost inviting state. As Jessica Mitford, the author of *The American Way of Death*, noted, we convert our dead into something resembling living dolls; the undertaker "has done everything in his power to make the funeral a real pleasure for everyone concerned. He and his team have given their all to score an upset victory over death."

If Robert Ettinger's theories are put into practice, however, the barbarism of present burial practices may be replaced with a new barbarism. In a book entitled *The Prospect of Immortality*, Ettinger proposes that at the time of death the individual can be given "cryogenic interment" rather than burial or cremation. Through the new science of cryonics, you would be frozen and kept in cold storage until the day—centuries from now—when scientists can safely thaw you out and restore you to a healthy life. If it works, man will have achieved the ultimate triumph of immortality. But with immortality would come a horrendous collection of barely imaginable social and psychological problems. Man has never quite managed to come to terms with death, and he is even less prepared to deal with perpetual life.

male and female

With the recent resurgence of women's liberation movements, the issues of being male or female in our society have regained much attention. The topic of gender, of course, is not a new one, but it has reappeared with a new impetus and promise for new significance in our lives. In the present chapter, we shall explore the social, psychological, and biological ramifications of being male or female.

of being male

Being born a male is not all fun and games. More males than females are born dead; twice as many male fetuses are miscarried as are female fetuses; and fewer males than females survive the first year of life. The male more often than does the female suffers injury at birth or displays congenital malformation. But for the male children who do manage to grow older, things do not get much better. Males more often than females die in accidents (the proportion rising as they grow older), and almost every possible defect plagues the male more than it does the female (autism, schizophrenia, epilepsy, limited vision, color blindness, brain injury, left-handedness, reading disability, hemophilia, speech problems and so on. The list is endless, including almost all the sensory and physical capacities human beings possess.

According to Patricia Sexton, author of *The Feminized Male*, the male is a pitiable creature indeed. He is not only feminized by life-long exposure to the social norms of women, but his attempt to assert his masculinity often results in gross personal and social pathology. Sexton reports that nearly 70 percent of the successful suicides are male; boys outnumber girls three to one in mental institutions for children; and boys are more likely to be labeled mentally retarded than girls. Boys also outnumber girl delinquents by five to one; they are 300 times more likely to join gangs and have always presented greater problems to the educational system. The special schools for problem children in New York—the "600" schools—are heavily populated with males, and more than two out of three students who fail one or more grades are boys. Males are implicated in 90 percent of the arrests for murder, negligent manslaughter, vandalism, weapon possession, drunkenness, assault, and sexual offenses. This sad account of what it means to be a male stands in shocking contrast to the glorified stories of man printed in the history books.

The image of man in history (faithfully or unfaithfully recorded by male historians) is heroic indeed. "In politics, in the arts, in religion, in philosophy, men's influence has been dominant for thousands of years. Power, learning, creativity—barring a few noteworthy exceptions—have been male prerogatives. Men have made the laws, the wars, and the epics. They have painted the pictures, hewn the statues,

174

constructed the universes of discourse; they have invented the machines, manipulated the markets, piled up and played with the millions."

Now and in the past, civilization has afforded richer opportunities for men than for women. Given equal native ability, men are encouraged and rewarded more than women since they are expected to compete in a race from which women often are barred. Achievement is the name of the game for men. Cattell's list of 1000 eminent persons in 1903 included only 32 women, and Lehman's 1953 compilation of 116 creative scientists who accomplished great things before 22 years of age referred to only three women. The male-female ratios of achievement did not vary significantly over this half century.

Man in history has been restless, mobile, and ever questing for new challenges and new tests of his worth. In America, the image was fashioned by the trapper, the hunter, the Indian fighter, and the cowboy—men who "did their thing," moved on, and seldom chained themselves to women and children. The frontier in pre-industrial America fostered the kind of male best suited to aggressive conquest, individual heroism, and willing isolation from the softening impact of feminine company. The male fought and died, tamed wild animals, developed the political state, governed, managed the land, provided for the weaker sex, and was free.

Then came the industrial revolution; men were compelled to abandon the pleasures of excitement and discovery for the security of routine work in which pleasing others became important. A century later, power and status had become the cultural game men played. Work, once highly individualized, became mechanical, and the enviable position of man was jeopardized. Unable to hew a home out of the wilderness single-handedly, they were nevertheless trapped by a wistful yearning for the good old days when the male was the provider, protector, and possessor. Now his sense of masculinity or manliness may only be experienced through the status he achieves or the material possessions he can accumulate. If status and material goods are not sufficiently reassuring, he may immerse himself in exotic and manly sports (Karate, scuba diving, deep sea fishing), devote his energy to playing games (disguised as exercises) with his colleagues, or rush home from his job to pour himself into the expensive and elaborate home workshop that makes him feel like a man again.

Goods, status, hobbies, and superficial interpersonal relations are hardly an adequate substitute for blood-stirring adventure and total independence where one is responsible only to oneself. The American male is having to deal with his feelings of being dethroned from a high social position. Confronted by an intense competition outside the home and pained by female discontent, the male faces a greater challenge to his maleness than ever before.

In this technological age, the male has the added burden of learning new skills, habits, attitudes, and values or being declared outmoded and obsolete. The older male may feel that while society allows his wife the knowledge of having completed the labor of raising children, his own work can never be called done. "All through American society, the male's behavior shows that he actually is experiencing a change which affects his traditional roles as father, lover, and provider. This change may be summed up in a single word: emasculation."

Whatever biological sex the newborn child may be blessed with, it must yet learn its gender role—it must learn what a female or male is. To know himself as a male, each man must achieve a sex-role identity—a set of beliefs about the match between his biological and psychological characteristics. He needs to acquire a concept of what, ideally, he ought to be. The education in sex-role identity begins early in life as children are taught to masculinize and feminize their environment; tigers, for example, though feline, are seen as masculine, while rabbits are seen as feminine bunnies.

To be male is to inhibit tendencies toward dependency, passivity, and conformity and to become suitably assertive and aggressive. Thus, the male must be active, strong, and powerful; almost every culture on this planet promotes these values in the male. This definition of maleness is perpetuated from generation to generation, the male child being expected to emulate the masculine father as masculinity is defined at that moment. "Like father, like son"—despite all the apparent exceptions we encounter—still remains the rule. Male parental norms "stress values such as courage, inner direction, certain forms of aggression, autonomy, master, technological skill, group solidarity, adventure, and a considerable amount of toughness in mind and body."

To achieve this sex-role identity, boys are disciplined to repress tender feelings; they may not cry and they must not do anything that will label them "sissy." They must fight when they would rather run away and compete destructively when they might prefer cooperative friendship. A study of kindergarten boys, for example, showed that more distinctive and appropriate sex-role behavior is demanded from the males than from females their age.

Boys see less of their fathers than girls see of their mothers and, therefore, find it harder to identify with the adult males. If the father is seen as a remote and punitive person, it becomes difficult for the son to choose him as a life model. The demand that one become a strong, decisive, courageous person who bears the burdens, protects the weak, and copes with difficulties is, indeed, overwhelming. It becomes especially difficult in families where there is seldom anyone

176

around to set such an example or assist in the process of learning. In primitive societies, it was easier for boys to gain confidence in their masculinity than it now is for male children in urban, industrial societies. In our society, the parental model is soon diluted by the male child's excursion into the outside world and by his encounters with his peer group. Through his friends, he will be exposed to a variety of new orientations to his sex role, and a particular social value will be assigned to the characteristics he has already acquired in imitation of his father. In adolescence, whether ready or not, he will be tested in terms of sexual interaction.

For Harvard psychologist J. Kagan there are two important six-year periods of sex-identity development. One occurs before puberty when peers teach the individual what the important sex-role characteristics ought to be, and one occurs in adolescence when the individual's sex-role identity either passes or fails the critical test of heterosexual adjustment. If the person fails this test, he need not decide between heterosexuality and homosexuality, but he may fall short of the cultural ideal of masculinity and be cast into the role of a feminine man. The accusation has been leveled at the American male that he is, if not emasculated, certainly feminized; he may not be homosexual but he lacks the robustness, vigor, and enthusiasm we attribute to the "ideal" heterosexual male. The opposite reaction may occur in the young male who is unable to be strong, unafraid, ready to risk death and injury, or be competent with females. An exaggerated, violent, masculine expression will appear—overtly or covertly—as long as society does not provide an acceptable alternate to this narrow definition of manhood."

The sociologist J. Toby has concluded that male biology is less likely to be the culprit in compulsive masculinity than is the nature of Western society. In some primitive socieities, the reverse is the case. Modern societies are more likely to include violence in the masculine ideal than are preliterate societies. In modern society, the bulk of early socialization is at the hands of mothers rather than males; the "compulsive masculinity" that emerges in some preadolescents and adolescents may be part of a necessary attempt of young males to free themselves from the bonds of female upbringing. Body-building, profanity, heterosexual conquest, and seemingly senseless violence may all reflect a need to reassure the self about possessing masculine characteristics in sufficient degree.

If we pursue this line of reasoning, we should predict that boys raised in households dominated by women will often behave violently, while boys with available and adequate father figures will be less so inclined. In much the same fashion, we could predict that boys who are slow to achieve masculine maturity will be more violent than those who mature relatively early. No one of these propositions can be confirmed conclusively, but existing scientific evidence is compatible with Toby's conclusions about developing maleness.

THE MALE AS LOVER

Sexually, the male has, for centuries, had it all his own way. He has enthusiastically constructed a lyric poetry, literature, and mythology which romanticizes and justifies his favored position. But, the contemporary male finds he has sexual responsibilities never demanded of his forefathers. Today he must cope with sexually liberated women; to be a man he must, at a bare minimum, be an adequate lover who both gains and gives sexual satisfaction. He can no longer use women without regard for their status as human beings, and he is not yet comfortable about being continually appraised by many females. Sexual adequacy or inadequacy, as defined by women, has formed a new dimension of the masculine definition, and concern about impotence haunts modern man as it never did before.

Sex plays a fundamentally different role in the life of the male and female. Sex, for the male, contributes more to his decision to marry and is a vital factor in his evaluation of satisfaction in his marriage. This is part of the context in which male sexuality occurs. Men are fascinated by the idea of sexual experience long before they actually encounter it, and they begin to masturbate long before girls do. (By age 15, 80 percent of boys surveyed, as compared with 20 percent of the girls surveyed, had begun to masturbate.) Sex, for men, is an odd mixture of fun and masculine status achieved through the conquest of women. In the words of one analyst: "It now seems clear that the basic difference in biology which causes differences in sexual behavior of males and females is that males' sexual responses are more easily conditionable than those of females. This means that each sexual experience of the male tends to affect his subsequent sexual behavior more than is the case for females."

Females, being less stimulated and conditioned by their environment, are less impelled to seek sexual stimulation actively. Their role teaches them to respond to the advances of the male. If this analysis is accurate, we must view the fact that males have historically initiated sexual encounters as a phenomenon which is based upon biological sexual differences. This male sexual responsiveness is primitive and urgent enough that the emotional involvement demanded by women is unnecessary. The male's sexuality often leads him to feign emotional involvement as one way of seducing his sexual partner. Indeed, if it is true that the male sexualizes human relationships while the female does not, we need look no further for the volatile compound that fuels the "war between the sexes" and prolongs the mutual misunderstanding of the sexes.

178

In actuality, the male devotes most of his psychic and physical energy to succeeding in the breadwinning role. Yet to be fully masculine, he must be sexually virile and attend fully to his partner, being able to make love freely and spontaneously. Not all males are capable of suddenly switching their energy from one activity to another, and the debilitating fatigue which males use as an excuse for marital abstinence may be mental more than it is physical.

Since the male defines himself primarily as a breadwinner, it is not surprising that his wife reacts accordingly, responding to him in a utilitarian way. The problem is that present-day working conditions are less rewarding and fulfilling than they were in the past. In a technological, bureaucratic society, searching for one's identity solely in work is dangerous, since the labor involved may lack the complexity and flexibility needed to service the whole man. The outcome may be a growing sense of powerlessness, meaninglessness, isolation, and self-estrangement which may, in turn, bring an early end to the role of male as lover.

An additional complication is that love (which males too often equate with sex) may become a commodity that is delivered only if he "behaves" and agrees to the conditions set by the female. "This puts the male in a weak and frustrating position in relation to the female, engenders hostilities in him toward her in the marital relationship, and further serves to flatten out and debase his conception of love. It is not to be wondered at that husband and wife only too often find each other inadequate; that women come to be regarded as cool and calculating monsters who devour their husbands, and their husbands come to be regarded as emasculated weaklings."

The plight of the male is further deepened by the details of the role prescribed for him by the society. Helen Hacker has listed such role prescriptions as (a) being patient, gentle, understanding, yet sturdy as an oak: (b) being a person on whom a wife can rely to make decisions but who leaves her free to make her own; (c) feeling a compulsion to succeed in gainful employment; and (d) being capable of evoking orgasm in his mate. This prescription may be filled effortlessly when one is young but becomes more difficult as the male ages.

THE AGING MALE

The male grows older, marries, and the prescription for his social role becomes even more stringent. He is expected to take the initiative in courtship and sex relations; he must support a wife who may, if she chooses, be self-indulgent and idle; he must keep up with community, national, and world affairs; serve in the armed forces, and generally show forbearance and strength come what may. This is no easy assignment if we recognize that, by nature, the male is no better equipped to meet such demands than is the female.

Although extensive research has been done on the young and the elderly man, relatively little has been devoted to the so-called middle years—a gray area that once began about age 45 but is now considered to begin around 40 or even 35. The masculine crisis may begin with a change in the amount of hormones secreted by the endocrine glands. These hormones affect not only the energy level but also the sleep patterns, weight, hair growth, coloration, and reproductive capacity of an individual. In the throes of the male climacteric, the individual may not know that something is happening inside his body to affect his emotions. He may only know that he is plagued with indecision, restlessness, boredom, and a "what's the use" outlook on life. Insofar as social class is concerned in the process, the blue-collar worker experiences similar changes, but he may be less likely than his more affluent middle-class counterpart to have the time or opportunity to dwell upon them morbidly.

Once a man has made a success of his career, a sense of panic and inadequacy may set in if he asks himself whether this is the sum of what he has struggled for. This is an unsettling time for men and women alike, and many marriages, unable to withstand the pressures of middle age, end in divorce. As one man put it: "I don't mind being a grandfather, but I can't stand being married to a grandmother." Dr. W. H. Masters and Virginia Johnson found that after 50 years of age, "the incidence of sexual inadequacy in the human male takes a sharp upturn." Even though doctors point out that physical conditions are the basis of only about 10 percent of male impotence, the fear of becoming impotent haunts many middle-aged men.

The present-day youth cult, with its emphasis on physical beauty, has further crippled the middle-aged man's ability to come to terms with an altered conception of masculinity. In a growing youth market that produces ever-younger corporate executives, the need for men in the business world to maintain a youthful image becomes essential. In reaction, perhaps, to this emphasis on youth, the American male clings to a nostalgic fondness for the good old days. As one man has expressed it:

> Those were the days, all right. A man was a man, and a woman was a woman and each of them knew what that meant. Father was the head of the family in the real sense of the term. Mother respected him for it and received all the gratifications she needed or wanted at home, doing her well-defined jobs. There were not many neurotic complaining women then. They loved to take care of their men, did everything to protect them. Man was strong, woman was feminine—and there was little loose talk about phony equality.

180

These may be comforting thoughts, but in reality it is a romantic myth, based on a fantasy and nourished by the masculine inability to comprehend the needs of the female of years past. The male must learn a new concept of masculinity and find a new meaning to manhood. As the male defines himself in terms that are less rough and tough and as the female becomes more adventurous and competent, it is possible both may become more civilized.

The male must learn to manage his life in a new way. He must learn to understand the attitudes, acts, and stereotypes of the female upon which his life is constructed, and he must learn to accept the woman as a human being first and as a female second. Further, he must become fully responsive, sensitive, and human in his relations with all others. Men have a choice. They can remain an embattled, sex at bay, or they can accommodate to the changing culture and share in its benefits. If they are lucky they may even learn a definition of masculinity that is not so corrosive of their psychological health.

of being female

Being born female is not nearly so bad as being male. The anthropologist Ashley Montagu contends that the female of the species is naturally superior to the male and has failed to make remarkable achievements only because she has been subjugated by the male. Female superiority is evidenced by the fact that they seem more resistant to disease; they live longer; they score higher on intelligence tests; they kill themselves less often; and they are better able to survive exposure, fatigue, pain, starvation, and shock. More importantly, for Montagu at least, females seem to be in possession of a superior humanity. This basic humanity is in opposition to the male's inclination to war, social destruction, pollution, and subjection of those physically and psychologically weaker than himself. Despite this catalogue of feminine superiorities, however, the image of the female has not fared well in history.

An ancient Sanskrit story maintains that when it came time for the creation of women, all the substantial materials had been exhausted on man and she had to be constructed of the less solid elements that remained. The Greek philosophers viewed woman as an evil or deficient object and Pythagoras wrote: "There is a good principle which has created order, light and man; and a bad principle which has created chaos, darkness and woman." And, just as Plato thanked the gods he was free (neither slave nor woman), Aristotle felt femininity amounted to the absence of certain qualities and suggested we regard the female nature as afflicted with a kind of natural defectiveness.

Similar examples can be drawn from early Semitic tradition. "One group of Bedouins says that women were created from the sins of the satans, another that she was manufactured from the tail of a monkey. From the South Slavs we get other details. In this case God absent-mindedly laid aside Adam's rib when He was performing the operation recorded in the Bible. A dog came along, snatched up the rib and ran off with it. God chased the thief but only succeeded in snatching off its tail. The best that could be done was to make a woman out of it."

If someone from another planet were to judge us solely by events recorded in the Old Testament they could only conclude that through-out history women begat nothing but male offspring. Ancient Jewish tribes treated a wife as a form of property, and in synagogues women were shunted aside to a special place while men daily gave thanks that they were Jew not Gentile, free not bond, and men not women. Moreover, had Eve not quested after knowledge, the human race would still be sitting pretty in Paradise.

As the centuries rolled on, woman's position did not improve much. Christianity supported monogamous marriage, defended women's right to inherit property, and tried to enforce a single moral standard on both sexes, but all this was coupled with a deep mistrust of the joys of the flesh. Women, as sexual beings, were considered dangerous. Everyone in the Middle Ages knew women were sexually insatiable and some lustful females were "known" to have consorted with the devil in their search for satisfaction. To St. Thomas, woman was simply a man gone awry—a form of life probably produced as a result of some weakness in the father's generative power.

In America, Puritanism elevated the male over the female; religi-ous symbolism was centered on a wrathful, punitive male god. Settling a wild, uncultivated country called for personal characteristics of brav-ery and physical strength, and these qualities were imprinted on his-tory as pioneers moved west from the eastern states. This imagery lingers in our literature and mass media, even though the man of strength, violence, and action has long ago disappeared. But, insofar as the female remains a nonmale, the culture reinvents reasons for subjugating women. Clearly, a thousand laws can be passed, but it will not make the slightest bit of difference if it does not become psychologically profitable for men to treat women as equals. Faced with the incredibly bad odds established by history, it seems that the revolution will have to be begun by women.

DEVELOPING FEMALENESS

Before being granted full membership in society, the female child must learn acceptable sexual attitudes, beliefs, and behaviors. The socialization of sexuality, however, poses complex problems. In part, these problems come from the discontinuity between the required nonsexual pattern of behavior in childhood and the necessity of the opposite pattern in adulthood. If the child acts in sexual ways before society deems it proper, or if the individual fails to display interest in heterosexuality at maturity, parents will become equally distraught. The socialization of sexuality begins early in life, but its success cannot be tested until some time in adolescence, when the dating and mating game begins.

Social sexual roles are clearly determined by the culture, even though anatomical and physiological differences are usually of some consequence in shaping specific roles. Thus, in most preliterate cultures, men gravitated toward work that requires muscular strength (warfare, metal working, hunting, mining, quarrying, boat building), and women tended to assume occupations centered on the home and children (basket making, gathering fruits and nuts, grinding grain, making pottery and clothes). Once these divisions of labor exist for a while, they get locked into tradition by taboo, ritual, superstition, prejudice, or other forms of social control.

Anatomical and physiological differences between men and women need not determine social and sexual roles, however. Both men and women may be passive, mild, gentle, and share the care of the children and other home duties. This is the case among the mountain-dwelling Arapesh, in which a division of labor between male and female is hardly recognizable. Among the Tchambuli people, however, distinct roles are assigned to each sex—but the Tchambuli woman is the aggressive, dominant member. The Tchambuli male fulfills what would be the role of the mother in our culture and is considered subordinate to and dependent upon his mate. This arrangement makes sense to the Tchambuli because, as they assert, females are clearly stronger than males. This role assignment is so complete that when the wife is about to give birth the husband enters confinement, is attended by midwives, and has sympathetic birth pangs symbolic of the event.

In our society training for maleness and femaleness begins earlier than most people might suspect. Parents begin to raise their children in accord with popular stereotypes from the very beginning. Girls are rewarded for being passive and dependent almost at once. In one study, mothers were already touching and speaking to 6-month-old girls more than they were to infant boys. When they reached 13 months, these girls were more reluctant than were the boys to leave their mothers; they returned more quickly and more frequently, and they remained closer to their mothers throughout the entire study session. When a physical barrier was placed between mother and child, the girls tended to cry and motion for help, while the boys made more active attempts to get around the barrier. One cannot measure precisely

183

the extent to which these apparent sex differences at 13 months can be attributed to the differences in the mothers' behavior at 6 months, but it is hard to believe that the two are unconnected. One author has described how this trend is continued.

> As children grow older, more explicit sex-role training is introduced. Boys are encouraged to take more of an interest in mathematics and science. Boys, not girls, are given chemistry sets and microscopes for Christmas. Moreover, all children quickly learn that mommy is proud to be a moron when it comes to mathematics and science, whereas daddy knows all about those things. When a young boy returns from school all excited over a biology class, he is almost certain to be encouraged to think of becoming a physician. A girl with similar enthusiasm is told that she might want to consider nurse's training later so she can have "an interesting job to fall back upon in case."

Through the socialization process, females are taught to look forward to the social roles society has designed for them. We train them to model themselves after the ideal image and to meet the expectations held for women as a group. Jo Freeman, author of the article, "Growing Up Girlish," states that, at the end of this socialization process, women felt they could be described as uncertain, anxious, nervous, hasty, careless, fearful, dull, childish, helpless, sorry, timid, clumsy, stupid, silly and domestic. On the more positive side women felt they were understanding, tender, sympathetic, pure, generous, affectionate, loving, moral, kind, grateful and patient. This is not a very favorable self-image, but it does correspond fairly well to the myths about what women are like. The image has some "nice" qualities, but they are not the ones normally required for the kinds of achievement to which society gives its highest rewards.

To counteract the inevitable sex-role stereotyping of growing girls, some modern-day parents are undertaking what is called nonsexist child rearing. The attempt is to treat each child as a total human being, without regard for the old stereotypes of what a boy or girl should or should not be. Considering the massive daily reinforcements that the culture heaps on boys and girls, one is not surprised to learn that the nonsexist experiments to date have produced traditionally masculine boys and feminine girls.

FINDING FULFILLMENT

Traditionally we have believed it is only through marriage and motherhood that a woman can find full satisfaction in life. This stereotype has been perpetuated by references to those single women who seem driven by neurotic needs that stem from some early lack in personal development. Some unmarried women are neurotic, of

184

course, but some of the married ones as well as some men are neurotic as well.

These attitudes about the single woman are being revised. Some women remain unmarried today, not because of a neurotic problem, but by choice or because there has been no opportunity. Being single no longer means, the absence of satisfaction or fulfillment in life. Yet, in a society which idolizes motherhood and feels the purpose and function of the female is to bear children, these "unhappy misfits" are often pitied as somehow not being real women. It is rare, for example, to uncover a male authority who suggests that a woman might find fulfillment without marriage and motherhood. And most men still believe that creative endeavors in women merely comprise some "additional" fulfillment.

When a female decides she has a perfect right to intellectual achievement, she has taken the first step on a long, arduous path in life. She soon learns that intellect is the male realm. As one woman writer has stated, "Thus consciously or unconsciously the girl equates intellectual achievement with loss of femininity. A bright woman is caught in a double bind. In testing and other achievement-oriented situations she worries not only about failure, but also about success. If she fails, she is not living up to her own standards of performance; if she succeeds she is not living up to societal expectations about the female role.... For women, then, the desire to achieve is often contaminated by the *motive to avoid success*." To compete means to take risks, and girls learn early in life to be less bold than boys. Sex differences in readiness for risk-taking appear quite distinctly between 9 and 11 years of age. When the time of choice does appear for the woman, it is often much too late for her to act effectively or with confidence.

The problem of prejudice against intellectual achievement in women is, unfortunately, not limited to male chauvinists. Philip Goldberg, researcher and author of "Are Women Prejudiced Against Women?", demonstrated this sad fact by asking female college students to rate a number of professional articles from each of six different fields. The articles were assembled in two sets of booklets: one set was attributed to a male author (John T. McKay), and the identical set was attributed to a female author (Joan T. McKay). After reading the articles, each student rated them for value, competence, persuasiveness, writing style, and the like. Goldberg found that the same article was given significantly lower ratings when it was thought to have been written by a female than when it was believed to have been written by a male. Goldberg fully expected this to be the result for articles representing fields dominated by men (law, city planning, and so forth), but he discovered that the female students also downgraded articles believed to have been written by females in the fields of dietetics and elementary education. In other words, these women rated male authors as better at everything. We have been led to believe that college educated women will be in the forefront of a breakthrough to greater freedom and fulfillment for women. Now it appears that, until educated women examine their own prejudices toward their sisters, the traditional role of women will be perpetuated.

According to one observer, the woman who is convinced that she can successfully combine marriage, a family, and a career may be the victim of a cruel hoax. Society holds out alternatives to the educated woman that are not really there. While she may be able to manage an undergraduate education, the graduate training needed for a desirable career is much more difficult with a husband and children to care for. As a married woman with children she is also expected to take second best in a career, since she must go where her husband's work takes her. In a very real sense, marriage is indeed a handicap in a woman's career.

One critic has pointed out that self-fulfillment for women is possible if they are sufficiently motivated to go and get it. ("She is free to choose, no one's standing in her way.") This argument overlooks the fact that a lifetime of socialization has given her far less than an equal chance to make a free decision. It is perfectly clear that there are no significant biological deterrents to such accomplishments. If this were the case, we would have to assume that women in the Soviet Union have unique hormones since they make up 75 percent of the Soviet physicians and about 35 percent of the engineers. The myth of the "joys" of homemaking was dispelled some years ago by Betty Friedan, but easy access to alternatives for fulfillment have not been provided. Some observers do not object to the homemaker role if freely chosen, but there are protests against the fact that the fate of the housewife is sealed almost at birth and is nearly perfectly predictable. One writer asks us to consider the following "predictability test": "When a boy is born, it is difficult to predict what he will be doing 25 years later. We cannot say whether he will be an artist or a doctor or a college professor because he will be permitted to develop and to fulfill his own unique identity, particularly if he is white and middle class. But if the newborn child is a girl, we can usually predict with confidence how she will be spending her time 25 years later. Her individuality doesn't have to be considered because it will be irrelevant."

THE AGING FEMALE

In a society in which child bearing and rearing are defined as the woman's primary life tasks, the aging female faces a host of new psychological problems, once the children are gone. Being a grandmother is not a full-time occupation any more. In 1890, the average woman lived only 12 years after her last child married, but with the longer life expectancy the average woman lives twice as long as this after her last child marries. Retirement for the woman arrives long before that of a man.

Rather than passively accept being put out to pasture, she may seek to recapture some fragment of her romantic and sexual self of years past. Inge Bell, author of "The Double Standard," summed up the situation nicely when she observed: "It is surely a truism of our culture that, except for a few kinky souls, the inevitable physical symptoms of aging make women sexually unattractive much earlier than men. The multimillion dollar cosmetics advertising industry is dedicated to creating a fear of aging in women, so that it may sell them its emollients of sheep's fat, turtle sweat and synthetic chemicals which claim, falsely, to stem the terrible tide." The fate of the male is less harsh since during his forties and fifties his attractiveness to others is likely to be defined in terms of his intelligence, accomplishments, or status in life. Thus, it is culturally acceptable for men to marry women as much as 20 years younger than they; but when a man chooses a wife who is more than four or five years his elder, there will be much sniggering gossip.

The female's aging problem becomes most evident as her hormone economy shifts over time. As the production of ovarian hormones decrease, estrogenic hormones are no longer available to keep her skin supple and wrinkle-free, and she begins to show her age. In a society oriented toward revering the young, the aging female who feels she must look young to be accepted attempts to erase the ravages of time by every means available. As one writer aptly put it, "The middle-aged woman who thickly masks her face with makeup, who submits to surgical breast lifting, who dyes her hair and corsets her body is as much a victim of socially instilled self-hatred as the black person who straightens his hair and applies bleaching cream to his skin." We no longer let women grow old gracefully. We have defined the female's social role in such a narrow manner that she cannot accept herself as a worthwhile person once her primary societal task of child-rearing has come to an end. In societies that respect the aged, wrinkles are badges of honor; in our culture, wrinkles signal the end of social usefulness.

the sexual revolution

When it was learned that William H. Masters and Virginia E. Johnson (now Mrs. Masters) of the Reproductive Biology Research Foundation in St. Louis were engaged in a scientific study of couples and individuals performing sexual acts, many people were shocked. The study reached far beyond that of Alfred C. Kinsey and his associates at the Indiana University Institute for Sex Research in which volunteers were interviewed about the details of their sex life. Surprisingly, the clinical observations of Masters and Johnson raised only a modest storm of public outrage. Some questions were asked about the morality of persons who would willingly participate in such studies, and objections were raised that wired, observed, clinical sex was mechanistic, dehumanization and repugnant on both moral and religious grounds. Nevertheless, Masters and Johnson's book, *Human Sexual Response*, became a best seller which, because of its heavy use of medical-technical language, was hardly read by anyone. This pioneering effort, however, provided the first direct scientific knowledge of the psychology of sexual response and led to the development of new methods of therapy for persons experiencing sexual difficulty.

In their experiments, Masters and Johnson reported on the sexual response of 382 women and 312 men ranging in age from 18 to 89. Most research volunteers came from the academic community connected to the medical center, but some were clinic patients who had sought help with their sexual lives. The study at first used prostitutes as subjects until it was learned there was a large, willing pool of volunteers in the community at large. There were, in fact, more volunteers than could be used in the study. Indeed, this sort of research seems feasible only when the temper of the times is suitable—when the subject matter ceases to be too sacred for exploration. This was, perhaps, the first victory of the sexual revolution in the laboratory.

sex and culture

Our use of the term *sexual revolution* stems from a comparison between the sexual practices and attitudes of today and those of the past. But, those who discuss the revolution seldom look beyond our cultural limits to examine the sexual life of those living in other social arrangements. To set the sexual revolution in its proper context, it is informative to look at anthropological studies in two other societies—one Polynesian and the other Irish.

Donald Marshall has reported on the culture of Mangaia, the southernmost of the Cook Islands located near the geographical center of Polynesia in the South Pacific. In Mangaia, sexual concern is reflected in the numerous labels they have for the sexual parts, coitus, and sexual activities and in their obsession with assessing the number of one's sexual partners and frequency of orgasm. This focus of social

190

interest, however, is not a matter of deeply anxious concern; it is a normal part of social life.

Social contact between the sexes in Mangaia is limited (by American standards) since copulation is always its predictable outcome—sex precedes the development of affectionate feelings. Boys and girls may play together until they are 3 to 4 years old, but after that they separate into sex-age groups that will define them socially for all the years to follow. This social division of the sexes is coupled with an emphasis on sensuality in dances and folk tales and a paradoxical prohibition about exposing the adult sexual organs. Young Mangaians may copulate at any age in the presence of as many as 15 other family members without anyone taking notice; everyone will seem to be looking in another direction. The male Mangaian, above all, values his ability to have many girls, to pleasure each of them timelessly, and to surpass those males who have previously enjoyed the same women. Parents encourage their daughters to have varied sexual experience in order to find the one male with whom she is most congenial. This is a society without evident homosexuality but one in which proof of husbandly virility is measured by the wife's pregnancy or excessive thinness presumably produced by her unusually active sexual life. Further, no man or woman among the Mangaians is so maimed, ugly, or poor as to be without a sexual partner—a remarkable fact in itself.

A startling contrast to the Mangaians is provided in J. C. Messenger's study entitled "The Lack of the Irish"; in this article Messenger describes an island in which misconceptions about sex and the absence of sexual knowledge has produced "the most sexually naïve of the world's societies, past or present." A society is described in which sex is never discussed in the home and sexual instruction is left to the trial-and-error learning that is supposed to occur when nature takes its course after marriage. Most of what can be termed "sophisticated" sexual activities are unknown to the Irish residents of this island. As Messenger observed: "Most girls on the island, when they reach puberty, are unprepared for the first menstrual flow and find the experience traumatic—especially when their mothers are unable to provide a satisfactory explanation. It is commonly believed that the menopause can induce insanity; in order to ward off this condition some women have retired from life in their mid-40s and in a few cases have confined themselves to bed until death years later."

On this island, sex is a sin and a duty women must endure because of the animal nature of the male. Female orgasm is unknown or considered a deviant sexual response. Sex is thought to be a debilitating experience for men, and male social interaction is limited to friendship with other males. The puritan tradition is so strong that a man is a "lad" until he is 40; and, of course, "lads" are not quite ready for

191

marriage. The contrast between these two societies' markedly different patterns of response to sexual stimulation tells us that there is little likelihood we will be able to agree in our society on a normal baseline for human sexuality and even less likelihood that we will be able to define, psychologically, what is good or bad sexually for human beings.

the changing patterns

The pattern of relations between the sexes has been changing for some time. In 1942, students in grades 6 through 12 were given a sociometric questionnaire regarding attitudes about sex; these responses were compared to responses to the same questionnaire in 1963. The results indicated that adolescents in 1963 expressed a much greater heterosexual interest than did the adolescents of 21 years previously. New norms for interaction between male and female preadolescent children were also evident in 1961. Surveys of sexual mores in the 1930s and the 1950s and 1960s indicated that in the 1930–1939 decade preadolescent girls were excluded from participation in masculine activities; contact between boys and girls in the thirties was restricted to socially approved events such as group games and dancing. The percentage of friendship choices extending across the sex barrier was nearly zero in the third and fourth grades and remained at a very low level until the children were eighth graders.

The times have changed, however. One study discovered that of the friendship choices of fourth, fifth, and sixth graders in a middle-class elementary school in a Southern urban community, nearly 52 percent of the fifth-graders and 38 percent of the sixth graders chose one or more friends of the opposite sex when given the opportunity to indicate whom they liked best of all the children they knew. Preadolescent boys and girls still prefer the companionship of their own sex, but an increasing number were able to feel positive about members of the opposite sex. A great majority of the children in each of the fourth, fifth, and sixth grades claimed to have a sweetheart and maintained that this feeling was reciprocated by their chosen object. For better or for worse boy-girl relationships began changing some years ago.

the slow revolution

For some social scientists, there appears to be a haunting similarity between difficulties in America today and those leading to the decline and fall of ancient Rome. As one writer suggested:

192

While the young men of both societies were busy defending the civilized world against barbarian hordes, the population at home was turning more completely to the diversions of the banquet and the bed. The harsh ascetic standards of the founding period were crumbling in favor of an opportunistic code in which the future and its obligations were gladly sacrificed to the pleasures of the moment. And among the sources of pleasure, none was pursued with greater intensity than those of a sexual nature. Both societies had their symbols of eroticism and their ardent spokesmen for the "new morality," as well as their outraged critics who denounced the decay of traditional values and practices. In short, the points of agreement between Rome in the first century A. D. and America in the twentieth century are striking and numerous.

In our society certain social classes have always lived by a different code of moral standards. What is different, however, is that a new portion of society has now apparently relaxed its sexual views. For literally thousands of years, in primitive as well as highly developed civilizations, the sexual double standard has predominated in the relationship between men and women. Human history records a variety of extraordinary devices and measures used by men to dominate and control the female's sexual behavior. Indeed, if a revolution exists, it is in the steady march of women toward sexual equality.

The double standard is tottering—if not yet fallen. A review of the literature published since the early 1920s reveals that it is at best a very slow but continuing revolution, which clearly began in the generation born in the decade 1900–1909—the generation that came of age sexually during or immediately after World War I. Since that time, women's attitudes in particular have changed from an orthodox concept of the double standard to a transitional view of the double standard—intercourse is acceptable for men under many conditions, but it is acceptable for women only when they are in love. This shift in attitude fits with the current refusal of some unmarried women to accept marriage as the proper dividing line between socially approved or disapproved sexual intimacy.

If Kinsey and his associates were to repeat their studies today they would probably find no more than a slight but steady increase in sexual trends already underway during the 1940s. As one writer has noted, sexual practices and attitudes for the young are more open than in the past and there is a consequent decline in the hypocrisy that shackled previous generations.

America's supposedly changing sex standards have been delineated in the studies of I. L. Reiss. He concludes that the popular observation that America is undergoing a sexual "revolution" is a myth. "The belief that our more permissive sexual code is a sign of a general breakdown of morality is also a myth. These two myths have arisen in part because we have so little reliable information

193

about American sexual behavior." Reiss has been one of the few behavioral scientists to make systematic investigations of racial as well as social class differences in sexual attitudes. His findings show that there are large variations between whites and blacks *of precisely the same class* in regard to premarital sexual permissiveness. "Among the poor, for instance, only 32 percent of white males approve of intercourse before marriage under some circumstances—compared with 70 percent of Negro males. The variation is even more dramatic among lower-class females; 5 percent of whites compared with 33 percent of Negroes. Generally, high school and college students of all classes were found to be more permissive than those in the adult sample. But even among students there were variations associated with race."

Thus, to speak of a sexual revolution we must take account of variations by social class and race. The classes and the races in America may operate from distinct and different cultural bases. Reiss also reports that feelings of guilt are no longer an adequate deterrent to sexual behavior. In his study, 87 percent of the women and 58 percent of the men said they had eventually come to accept sexual activities that once made them feel guilty. If a person continues to do what makes him guilty, the sense of guilt seems to diminish and variations in the forms of sexual behavior become the next step.

E. M. Brecher is one critic who refuses to accept the idea that we are undergoing a sexual revolution. He suggests, rather, that the current changes represent a process of gradual convalescence from the sexually debilitating disease of Victorianism. The stage of convalescence reached varies widely from individual to individual and from social group to social group. Among the young in our culture recovery seems to be proceeding at a more rapid rate, and, hopefully, most of us will one day be free of the Victorian taint that made sex sinful, shameful, and guilt-ridden.

For every yea-sayer, however, there seems to be a nay-sayer. H. Winthrop, for example, sees the new sexual freedom as an accelerating movement toward the horrors of a *Brave New World* rather than as a liberation from Puritan shackles. The mass media has artificially made the sexual revolution seem real, but it is actually a repackaging of the old into a new and fashionable form. Sex and related activities, says Winthrop, have become one popular way of demonstrating to others that one is socially and intellectually "liberated" from any hang ups. J. H. Gagnon is another critic who argues against the reality of the sexual revolution. His analysis suggests that the percentage of people engaging in premarital sexual activity has not changed over the last four decades. Gagnon states that only 5 to 7 percent of American women have intercourse with five or more men before they marry, and he regards these women as more exploited than liberated. Premarital intercourse happens for 70 percent of college men, for 80 percent of men with a high school education, and for 90 percent of males with an eighth grade education. It is difficult to see how there could be much of a revolution in the male sexual experience. One author, commenting on Gagnon's conclusions, believes that reports of increased percentages of sexual activity should be considered simply that—increased percentages, rather than a revolution.

The forces that resist recognition of the sexual revolution may draw their strength from what one author has labeled the "American Sexophobia." We live, according to this critic, in a sexually polarized society torn between license and restriction—between the Playboy bunny and Mary, Mother of God. What the males fear is not sex so much as it is the power that women might gain over them.

Modern sexual views are difficult for the older generation to accept, mainly because these changes are occuring in a context of events that is equally alien and bewildering to older persons. The simple facts of unchaperoned association between unmarried men and women and open acknowledgement of sexual matters suggest to the older generation that a serious decline in parental and religious authority has taken place. It is difficult for the elders to comprehend the degree to which the sexual moral code of the past was based on fears of pregnancy, disease, and social ostracism.

Spokesmen who favor a sexual revolution insist that a new morality is emerging in which the individual seeks to be himself regardless of interference by social rules and regulations. This humanist orientation accepts the proposition that human happiness is the goal of man and that guilt-free sexual enjoyment is a significant part of the good life.

the homosexual revolt

Freud contended that each of us is born with a psychological sexual duality, a capacity to express both male and female characteristics. Kinsey's finding that 37 percent of white American males have at least one homosexual experience in their lives set the stage for the homosexual revolution. A decade after Kinsey, the Wolfenden report issued in England by a parliamentary committee recommended that private, adult, consensual homosexual acts be made lawful. As never before, homosexuals have come out in the open, forming organizations and becoming active, militant lobbyists for an end to repressive legislation. Parades, protests, and picketing have become the order of the day for both male and female homosexuals. These demonstrations have had a marked effect on the nature and enforcement of existing laws, and heterosexual citizens have become more willing to abandon attempts to legislate human morality. But as one writer put it: "It would be facile and utterly misleading to imply that the American homosexual is on the threshold of victory in his battle for equality. It is still painfully true that every state but Illinois condemns the private, adult, consensual acts of homosexuals as criminal, that in seven states life imprisonment is a possible sentence for such acts, and that in thirty-five other states the maximum penalty is at least ten years."

Reform may well be on its way as part of the larger social liberation of sexual views, but there is little likelihood that homosexuality will achieve an equal social status with heterosexuality. Homosexuality flourished among the upper classes in ancient Greece, but then it filled the void that was created by a view that females were inferior articles of human property. The primary grievance of the new movement among homosexuals is the traditional medical and psychiatric view that the basis of the homosexual condition is a deep-rooted psychological disturbance. The gay liberation contends that homosexuality is normal at least for some human beings. The movement thinks there is no "cure" for its members' sexual proclivity and furthermore wants none. The movement also believes that if neuroses appear in gay individuals, they are created—not by perversion but by persecution.

the swinging scene

America is witness to a vigorous "swinging" scene and sexual freedom movement which euphemizes its activities with the label "co-marital sexual relations." The swinging scene is so commonplace it has lightly been suggested that "the family that swings together clings together." Group sex and partner exchange have only recently become topics in scientific literature, despite the fact that the exchange of sexual partners has been standard practice for hundreds of years in some other cultures. Wife-lending or wife-exchange in these societies, however, is only part of a larger pattern of mutual hospitality in which the sharing of women is one way of cementing the bonds of friendship or kinship. This recent wrinkle in the sexual activity of our society is not astonishing, though, since we have long known that human sexuality is completely malleable. None of our cherished sexual beliefs is a universal law of nature.

In 1957, an obscure men's magazine devoted to sensationalism and nude photos of well-endowed females published a short article on wife-swapping. This "first" unleashed a landslide of similar articles in competing magazines and produced an unexpected rush of letters from anonymous readers describing their own involvement in group sex. In short order, such magazines began to carry "help wanted" ads allegedly put there by mate-swappers seeking newer and lusher fields for sexual exploration. In the 1960s, this way of life assumed the label of "swinging."

The surfacing of this startling social development should have been a gold mine for behavioral scientists interested in the scientific study of sex. As one writer observed, "Here, for the first time in our culture, was a population ready and willing to have its sexual behavior observed in a natural setting rather than a laboratory. Here was an opportunity to make psychosexual and sociosexual field studies paralleling the Masters-Johnson physiological laboratory studies. Here at long last scientists could directly observe *how human beings behave after they have shed their inhibitions, repressions, and taboos.*" But, it never happened. This significant shift in social morality attracted the attention of an exceptionally few serious social scientists.

The little research that has been done indicates that the nature of the swinging scene shifts from city to city in different parts of the country. One also needs to make a distinction between "utopian" and "recreational" swingers. Utopian swingers believe they are building a better world by eliminating the evils of possessiveness, jealousy, and sexual exclusivity. Recreational swingers do it just for the fun of it. The extent of this group-sex enterprise is impossible to estimate accurately, but it has been calculated that, for example, there are at least 8000 organized swingers within the 200 mile area encompassing Chicago. In late 1970, there may have been, at most, 1 percent of the American population involved in swinging.

G. D. Bartell, author of *Group Sex*, collected data on 280 swinging couples in Middle America and concluded that these white, middle-class members of suburbia deviate from the norms of contemporary society only in their sexual practices. Since the swinging scene evokes in most of our minds salacious imagery of riotous, uninhibited sexuality, a sampling of some of Bartell's conclusions may dispel a few fantasies. The scene is less swing than one might imagine. For one, blacks are not welcome as sexual participants; male homosexual activity is exceptionally rare and nearly always disruptive to the swinging party. Nearly all women swingers engage in sexual activity with other women, and this is almost always a spectator sport for men. Swingers seem obsessively preoccupied with personal hygiene and showering seems to be a constant activity between sexual encounters. Swinging is inhibited by unspoken rules designed to limit emotional involvement among participants; for example, there can be intense sexual interaction provided there is only superficial human interaction. In sum, swingers are replaying the dating and mating games of their younger years, even though they vehemently insist that they represent the sexual avant-garde in America.

It is also abundantly apparent that "a rose is a rose" by whatever name. The fact is that swinging wives are bartered by husbands who seek access to a variety of female sexual partners. An illustration of this basic truth can be found in the swinger's code of ethics. If for one reason or another the male member of the couple leaves the party, his wife is welcome to remain; but, if the wife goes home, the male is no longer welcome in the festivities. The female is at a sexual premium, while the male is viewed by other participants as an exploiter—a user of others rather than one who is available to be used. He is, therefore, less suitable for the purposes of the orgy.

Swinging is a male game in which, unexpectedly, the female may be the winner. The male's sexual fantasies may be enflamed at the prospect of numerous willing and naked women, but he cannot quiet his secret doubts about carrying off a sexual performance that will bring both self-satisfaction and applause from onlookers. Bartell reports, for example, that fewer than 25 percent of the males are able to "turn on" regularly at large-scale swinging parties. The natural male anxiety about sexual prowess coupled with the ever-present hazard of personal, social, and professional disaster from public exposure make the male less than potent even when he finds himself in the midst of his secret fantasy of the best of all possible sexual worlds.

Charles and Rebecca Palson are anthropologists who studied the swinging scene as participant-observers. They have reported their observations on 136 swingers. Their study also indicates that swinging is initiated by the husband seeking sexual variety and accepted passively by the wife who wishes to please her spouse. The swinging itself is, for the woman, a continuation of her need to please men, rather than a search for personal pleasure. The Palsons also confirm the embarrassingly high rate of sexual impotence among males in this most free of all sexual situations, and they indicate that marital disharmony may appear among swingers who have been wed fewer than three years.

What can we conclude about this facet of the sexual revolution? Are swingers liberated from the constraints of middle-class society? Clearly, they are not. Is this to be the sexual wave of the future? Again, most probably not. It does seem evident that our past notions of appropriate sexual activity were probably too narrow and constricting for comfort, and new forms and patterns are about to emerge. Swingers seem to settle for the sexual second best. Their activity may satisfy some, and it may be necessary for others; but it cannot match the full experience achieved when sexuality is just one crucial part of a continuously deepening relationship between two persons who are emotionally committed to one another.

198

and then there were none

In the dark corridors of ancient history there may well have been a time when survival of the species made it necessary for woman to accept an unwanted pregnancy. Our population ecologists are now convinced that human survival depends on the limitation of pregnancies—wanted or not. Modern technology has made contraceptive methods widely available, but some form of birth control has been practiced throughout recorded history. Coitus interruptus (withdrawal) was alluded to in the Old Testament; Egyptians used crude methods to interfere with impregnation; and a variety of drugs, chemicals, oils, plants, and herbs have been used as contraceptives. When these methods failed, infanticide was practiced in some societies.

Concern about family planning in America was initially stimulated by the women's rights movement. Today, members of women's lib call for birth control as only one facet of a woman's right to control the use of her own body. Indeed, the age of contraception is at hand.

THE PILL

The impact of the contraceptive pill on the American way of life is made most evident by the fact that everyone knows what you are talking about when you mention "the pill". The steroid oral contraceptive called the pill was praised as the solution for mankind's (if not womankind's) sexual problems. But, it now appears to be a near miss in the history of contraception. Today's pill is incredibly effective, but it carries with it a host of unwanted, hazardous side effects. Oral contraceptives by stimulating the hormonal conditions that occur at pregnancy are designed to prevent the ovary from releasing eggs. When this happens, however, a number of bodily tissues and processes are altered or distorted in unpredictable and sometimes dangerous ways. The pill acts in two ways to contracept pregnancy. First it suppresses ovulation—if there are no eggs there will be nothing to be fertilized. Second, the hormones triggered by the pill stimulate the development of a thick secretion at the mouth of the womb that acts as a physical barrier to impregnation. But, no known medicine is perfectly safe, and the pill is no exception.

A newer birth control method focuses on treating the target organ itself, while bypassing the rest of the body when possible. An intrauterine contraceptive system (a soft, flexible, membrane-enclosed drug container) is inserted directly into the uterus; this device contains the drug progesterone which alters the thin layer of cells that lines the uterus (the endometrium) so that a newly fertilized egg cannot implant itself on the uterine wall. The drug container can be removed if pregnancy is desired. The benefit of this approach is that it eliminates

199

the necessity of drugging the whole body to achieve contraception.

Looking to the future; scientists speculate about the possibility of developing contraceptive devices such as birth control tampons, a drug-impregnated pellet implanted in the male to make him infertile, a morning-after pill that would nullify conception after the fact, or monthly injections to forestall pregnancy. Of this list of possibilities it appears that the morning-after pill is the most likely prospect. These pills, made of a synthetic estrogen, have been virtually 100 percent effective if taken within three days following intercourse. At the University of Michigan, for example, 1000 women have taken such pills since 1967, with neither adverse effects nor pregnancies. The pills, taken twice daily for five days, prevent the fertilized egg from implanting itself in the uterus.

The pill that is most familiar to us, however, has been praised to the skies by some theorists. Ashley Montagu, for example, says that "In its effects I believe that the pill ranks in importance with the discovery of fire, the development of the ability to make and employ tools, the evolution of hunting, the invention of agriculture, the development of urbanism, of scientific medicine, and the release and control of nuclear energy." Montagu feels that the consequences of the pill are likely to be manifold and may profoundly alter entire social systems of traditional beliefs, practices, and institutions. Birth control may humanize man by making him responsible for every instance of his reproductive behavior. People have sex for pleasure more often than they do for reproduction, and the pill allows us to make a clear distinction between the two kinds of activity. The pill has simply made sexual abstinence unnecessary for many. With the pill, the female no longer needs to resist the male's sexual advances on the grounds of risking pregnancy; this, in turn, should reduce the predatory and exploitative attitude of the male toward the female. The change in the female's attitude toward sex should find an echo in the male's attitude toward the female as a sex object. As far as the critics are concerned, pessimists declare that these measures will not become sufficiently widespread in time to counteract the burgeoning population explosion on this planet. Optimists insist that our children (or, certainly, the children of our children) will wonder what the pregnancy fuss was all about.

STERILIZATION

The surest method of contraception (and in the long run the cheapest) is sterilization. In the male, sterilization is accomplished by an operation called a vasectomy, which prevents the spermatozoa from making the journey into the female. The operation is a simple one which can be performed under local anesthesia; it is almost painless, takes only a few minutes, and the patient can go about his business the same day. In the female, sterilization is a somewhat more complicated operation, but the object is similarly to prevent the female reproductive cells (eggs) from traveling to a place where they may be fertilized by male sperm. The Fallopian tubes, down which the eggs pass, are "tied off" to withold the eggs. Surgically, however, these tubes are harder to reach than are the male tubes (vas deferens). In a different method of female sterilization a flexible instrument is introduced through the vagina and uterus into each of the Fallopian tubes, and the tubes are electrically "cauterized" ("welded" by heat). Scar tissue soon forms, and the tubes are sealed.

No adequate records are kept but it is estimated that something like two million Americans have been sterilized and that more than 100,000 men and women undergo voluntary sterilization each year. According to the attitudes of husbands and wives with regard to male vasectomy, 34 percent are reportedly satisfied and would recommend the procedure to others; 43 percent would qualify such recommendations; and 21 percent would not recommend it. There is little evidence that sterilization preserves marriages or improves sexual function; certainly, if the procedure is carried out only as a consequence of coercion, it can be the basis for conflict that finally dissolves the marriage.

The problem of sterilization has always been its finality; in most instances, it is not reversible, although modern technology holds promise that this may soon be the case. Sterilization for the male—despite medical disclaimers to the contrary—may be symbolically castrative. Only when this process is reliably reversible will it prove attractive to most males.

ABORTION

The existing abortion laws in our society are rapidly being altered, abandoned, and modified as one part of the sexual revolution. But, as one writer has regretfully noted, "In all the consideration of abortion there has been almost no consideration of women. She is regarded as nothing more than an encapsulating amniotic sac, and it is only the population explosion that has renewed interest in legalizing abortion."

Traditionally, abortion has been illegal even though in all societies it is the single most common form of birth control. The D and C operation (dilitation and curettage—scraping of the uterus) removes the fetus from the womb. This procedure, however, becomes more complicated if it takes place after 16 weeks of pregnancy. Statistically, an abortion, when done properly, is safer than carrying the child to full-term pregnancy. But, of course, when the abortion is performed illegally, the risk increases substantially.

Interestingly, abortion has been and is currently practiced in all societies, despite disapproval stemming from the Judeo-Christian ethic. Abortion was not made illegal until the nineteenth century, when it was banned on the basis of danger to the mother (as well it must have been before the awareness of sterile technique). Today, abortion is forbidden in most countries, unless the pregnancy endangers the life of the woman; in the same countries, the rate of illegal abortions continues to be high. The social issue that centers on abortion is the continuing conflict over the morality of "taking a life," even if it is in the fetal stage. But, attitudes on abortion are changing. Contraception remains the preferred solution, but legal abortion may become a necessary social device as we weigh the costs of bearing unwanted children in an overpopulated world.

The threat of overpopulation has led an increasing number of young people to question the morality of giving birth and thereby adding to the problem of overcrowding. Adoption agencies are receiving more and more applications from young couples who could have their own children but who have decided against it. If this willingness to adopt becomes a widespread attitude, it will certainly alter the basic value system of the white middle class. Tomorrow, a husband's virility or a wife's femininity may not depend upon the children they are able to bring into the world.

Before 1970, it was estimated that up to one million American women a year were undergoing illegal abortions. *Time* magazine reported that abortions, now legalized in many states, have provided operations for women mostly between the ages of 20 and 30 and mostly white and single. "Still, about half of the New York cases have involved married women. Hawaii authorities are now reporting requests from a growing number of older married mothers. The figures indicate that educated, middle-class women are better able, or more inclined, to take advantage of the liberalized laws. But blacks, whose birth rate is 50% higher than that of whites, have recently begun to follow suit in large numbers, particularly where abortion is made easy for the poor. In New York City, blacks now undergo one abortion for every three live births; whites, one for every five. Puerto Ricans, one for seven." One should realize that these pregnancies are not cases of rape, incest, or danger to the health of the mothers. They are simply unwanted pregnancies—even if unwanted after the fact, since all too often they result from taking no contraceptive steps in the first place.

women's liberation

The women's liberation movement has demanded an end to traditional definitions of maleness and femaleness and an end to the unequal distribution of privileges that favor the male. Radical lesbians, for example, demand freedom in their choice of sexual expression—most often, a choice between homosexuality and bisexuality, rather than a choice between homosexuality and heterosexuality. For these persons, our society seems to be obsessed with the relentless persecution of those who choose a sexual expression other than heterosexuality. Radical lesbians insist that, if lesbianism is caused by a hostility to men, then in a male-dominated society, lesbianism is a sign of health.

From the beginning of time, women have been relegated to the kitchen, bed, and church, and even so eminent a psychoanalyst as Bruno Bettelheim implied that women who seek careers as engineers or scientists truly prefer to be mothers and companions of men. Erik Erikson has also suggested that, because of their anatomy, women are destined to bear the offspring of their chosen male. And, Joseph Rheingold, author of *The Fear of Being a Woman,* has maintained that motherhood alone could produce feminine fulfillment.

Although the drive for liberation from male domination (and from the associated myths that have supported it) is a legitimate goal, the means of achieving it have most often provoked antagonism rather than sympathy. Irving Howe's review of Kate Millett's *Sexual Politics* underscores some of the limitations of women's theorizing about the relation between the sexes. Howe notes, for example, that no satisfactory explanation has been forthcoming with regard to the remarkable prevalence of male domination over the centuries in every form of society. The theorists of women's liberation are unwilling to grant that physical and biological differences between the sexes may once have determined a vital part of the sexual roles in society. Further, if male oppression has been so absolute for so many centuries, it seems there is little likelihood that the women's liberation movement will make more than a tiny dent in it.

In particular, Howe objects to Millett's feminist interpretation of the long history of male-female relationships. As Howe asks:

> The woman who worked sixteen hours a day in the Midland mines during the Industrial Revolution—was she really a "sexual object" up for "barter" to the "master group" (the wretched men who also worked sixteen hours a day in the same mines) quite in the same way as the bourgeois ladies of, say, Matisse's Paris? Does the "passivity" Miss Millett says patriarchal society induces in women characterize the American pioneer wife staking out a homestead in Oklahoma? Was the Jewish immigrant mother working in a sweatshop, often shoulder to shoulder with her equally exploited husband, "customarily deprived of any but the most trivial sources of dignity or self-respect"? Are the ladies of the Upper East Side of Manhattan simply "chattels" in the way the wives of California grape pickers are, and if so, are they "chattels" held by the same kinds of masters? Has the fact of being female been more important in the social history of most women than whether they were rich or poor, black or white, Christian or Jewish?

It requires some stretching of the imagination to consider a job on an assembly line as somehow superior to the labor of raising a family. The husband as well as the wife may be dehumanized and treated as a chattel by the surrounding society. Or, writing an endless succession of soap commercials in an ad agency may be substantially less creative than ministering to the developmental needs of children. If there is social exploitation, it may equally affect males and females in these times.

The primary problem for women's liberationists is summed up in Howe's analysis of the liberated woman's view of her unliberated sister. "She hates the perverse refusal of most women to recognize the magnitude of their humiliation, the shameful dependence they show in regard to (not very independent) men, the maddening pleasures they even take in cooking dinners for 'the master group' and wiping the noses of their snotty brats." Clearly, this is the problem posed for the revolution—the recruitment of support among the masses. The disconcerting but undeniable fact remains, however, that in a great many marriages and in a great many families the male-female relationship is one of mutual accommodation in which both parties feel free and neither senses that he or she is a prisoner.

The negative response to the feminist movement is described by Helen Lawrenson in her article, "The Feminine Mistake": "You might have to go back to the Children's Crusade in 1212 A.D. to find as unfortunate and fatuous an attempt at manipulated hysteria as the Women's Liberation movement ... a hair-raising emotional orgy of hatred as vicious as it is ludicrous, directed at love, marriage, children, the home, and encompassing en route, with wild catholicity, the penis, the Pill, false eyebrows, brassieres, Barbie dolls, Freud, Dr. Spock, the Old Left, the New Left, and detergent advertisements." To Lawrenson the aim seems to be the absolute subjugation of men rather than the liberation of women. For her, the liberationists are extremist freaks who respond to love as if it were a debilitating, counterrevolutionary illusion and who label men "superpig supremacists" or the "Hitler's in our homes."

One writer has suggested that we are undergoing a "revolution without ideology"—a loosening of male domination and the consequent freeing of the American female. But the pace of change has not been fast enough to match the rising expectations of some women. Robin Morgan, editor of *Sisterhood Is Powerful*, has described the pain experienced by women who are sensitive to male chauvanism: "Everything, from the verbal assault on the street, to a 'well-meant' sexist joke your husband tells, to the lower pay you get at work (for doing the same job a man would be paid more for), to television commercials, to rock-song lyrics, to the pink or blue blanket they put on your infant in the hospital nursery, to speeches by male 'revolutionaries' that reek of male supremacy—everything seems to barrage your aching brain, which has fewer and fewer protective defenses to screen such things out."

In addition, the average female must come to terms with the expectations her mate has for her. One observer has described the male fantasy of what a wife and woman should be: "Have to go on a business trip? She will pack your suitcase with clean clothes which she washed and ironed or sent to the cleaners (after picking them up off the floor where you dropped them). Want to talk? She will listen eagerly. Woman. She will look like a goddess at the crack of dawn and stand in the door as you leave for work, and be standing there waiting when you come home. Above all, she is an animal who will become a willing, anxious, sex-starved beast any day or night you wish."

BECOMING A LIBERATIONIST

It has been said that both figuratively and literally, men drive women crazy. Although this may sound like a modern sentiment, 60 years ago Alfred Adler described the social and cultural discrimination against women as a source of neurosis in both sexes. Today's femlibbers document this observation by examining sex differences in the statistics of mental illness: "Most female 'neuroses' are a result of societal demands and discrimination rather than the supposed mental illness of the individual. Therapists and husbands alike, however, persist in encouraging women to take the blame for their unhappiness—thus to be 'cured'."

According to the feminists, the symptoms women experience may not reflect mental illness so much as a natural reaction to the stress of being confined to a sex-role stereotype so narrow that it pinches psychologically. This female problem may spur the woman to reexamine the role society has cast her in and lead her to seek an alternative way of being. Anita Micossi, author of an article entitled "Conversion to Women's Lib," explored the basis upon which the women's lib movement gathered recruits, she reports that such women had fairly easy access to a variety of forms of self-expression and self-esteem. They were intelligent, educated, and upwardly mobile women who responded to parental encouragement for achievement, advanced schooling, and a career.

Once the seed of an alternative way of life is planted, it need only be nurtured by an awareness of the discrepancy between personal aspirations and potentials and the reality of life. Once the discrepancy is apparent, the feeling of being trapped, suffocated, and abused runs close behind. And, the most natural and visible target for this feeling is the male. As Sally Kempton stated in her article, "Cutting Loose," "A woman who is satisfied with her life is not likely to be drawn into the Women's Liberation movement; there must be advantages for her as a woman in a man's world. To be a feminist one must be to some degree maladjusted to that world, one must be, if you will, neurotic. And sometimes one must be antisexual, if only in reaction to masculine expectations."

The call of women's lib has not resonated in the ears of the white woman's black sisters. As one article stated, there is a vast difference between "the oppression of the black man and woman who are unemployed and the 'oppression' of the American white woman who is 'sick and tired' of *Playboy* fold-outs, of Christian Dior lowering hemlines or adding ruffles, or of Miss Clairol telling her that blonds have more fun. What does the black woman on welfare who has difficulty feeding her children have in common with the discontent of the suburban mother who has the luxury to protest washing the dishes on which her family's full meal was consumed?"

It should also be noted that the educated, intellectual, white, middle-class members of women's lib cannot believe that the 28 million women who watch soap operas on television are satisfied with their home-bound refuge from the working world. Having children is, for some, the perfect social excuse for being cared for by another rather than having to fend for one's self. No revolution can succeed if it fails to strike a responsive chord in the ranks of the oppressed masses. If the feminist revolution has the appearance of being designed primarily to gratify the needs and resolve the frustrations of an elite, well-educated, selfish minority it will not appeal to most women.

THE NATURE OF WOMEN'S LIB

Shulasmith F. Firestone, the author of *The Dialectic of Sex*, has analyzed the state of the women's liberation movement and divided it roughly into three major camps. Conservative feminists make up one camp. Organizations such as NOW (The National Organization of Women) are included in this group. NOW was founded in 1965 and is sometimes labelled the NAACP of the women's movement since it is populated by older professional women who have "made it" in careers in a male-dominated society. NOW opts to work with our social system rather than propose radical alterations of it. The second camp is composed of politicos or groups (leftist politically) that view women's liberation as a tangential aspect of a broader set of social issues. To them, women's lib is a useful tool to radicalize females and to organize them for the broader political struggle they see as inevitable. The politicos include some middle-of-the-roaders as well as some conservatives. The radical feminists make up the third major camp. Like the radical feminists of past eras, feminist issues are part of a larger revolution of the left. If the sexual revolution succeeds it will be one feature of a basic alteration of the social fabric at all levels. Radical feminist groups are extremists and are likely to produce most of the anti-sexual, anti-male hostility that men respond to negatively.

There is no question that the popular media has had a great deal of fun with women's lib. It has succeeded in selling us an image best portrayed by Norman Mailer: "A vision of thin college ladies with eyeglasses, no-nonsense features, mouths thin as bologna slicers, a babe in one arm, a hatchet in the other, gray eyes bright with balefire." The popular women's magazines have enthusiastically embraced the newsworthiness of the women's liberation movement, but this is not enough. A number of new publications devoted to the cause of women's lib has appeared on the current social scene. Some of the new efforts are do-it-ourselves in form and filled with radical, emotional, anti-male rhetoric featuring feminist history ("herstory").

The most extreme do-it-ourselves suggestion was that made by Valorie Solanis of SCUM (Society for Cutting Up Man). Since it is technically possible to reproduce without the aid of males and to produce only females, she favors beginning the process immediately. In her view, the male is a biological accident—the Y (male) gene being a deficient X (female) gene with an incomplete set of chromosomes. The male, in other words, is an incomplete female, a walking abortion, deficient even at the gene state.

On a more serious note, the members of women's lib have also formed consciousness-raising groups in which women can gather together to talk and be listened to, perhaps, for the first time. The groups are not so much designed as therapy sessions as they are intended to provide the kind of camaraderie that men have always had. The sharing of experiences and the escape from a sense of isolation have, however, proved to be therapeutic to the participants, and it has helped them become aware of the problem of oppression by the male. In addition to the consciousness raising groups, women's crisis centers have been established to organize community services and provide personal counseling for women. The intent is to create centers in which women feel responsible for other women—centers offering legal aid, emergency medical assistance for rape and assault cases, self-defense classes, and a place where women can go to talk without being "hassled by the male."

To traditionalists, it may seem that women's liberation goes too far in seeking to abolish the designations *Miss* and *Mrs.* and substitute *Ms.* as a universal form of address. It may seem trivial to men to disguise one's marital status, but this is a serious issue for women who feel they have been discriminated against long enough. Miss and Mrs. may be functional and revealing designations for the predatory male, but they are disgraceful to radical feminists seeking to achieve a state of equality in which individuals are treated as unique human beings rather than as one-half of a marital arrangement. A woman is a female, a person—she is not "just" a wife. The first all-female business phone directory, with its own yellow pages, is being compiled in New York. For economic as well as philosophic reasons the directory lists women workers and professionals and businesses owned or run by women. There are some fields where feminists feel that a woman, rather than a man, can best help other women; gynecologists and divorce lawyers are two examples.

Germaine Greer, author the *The Female Eunuch* and one of the least shrill of the radical feminists, insists that beneath the male-imposed, artificial femininity of passivity, dependence, noncompetitiveness, self-sacrifice, nonintellectualism, and sentimentality lies a true femaleness. Our social arrangement makes it easy for women to remain in an infantile state, playing a protected, coddled, menial role. Before long, the woman begins to believe the myth of romantic love, only later to discover that she is frustrated, irritable, and unfulfilled. Germaine Greer has been described as a feminist who likes men but sees women as castrated and forced into passivity by the male. She believes that sex need not be denied or abandoned to achieve a revolution. Sex, to her, should be the critical arena into which women redirect their energy in an effort to achieve a new status and a new relationship with men.

It is abundantly clear that the women's lib movement has captured the popular attention. Clinical psychologist J. Adelson has asked, however, whether the movement has in fact "captured the sympathy of women, and if so, which women, and how deeply, and for how long. Are we dealing with something which matters, or which only seems to matter? Do we have here one more of those items of sociological entertainment which the educated classes invent and consume so relentlessly?" Some are convinced that the ideas of the movement have had almost no impact outside the educated classes and that for the average citizen only the side-show aspects played up by the media have had any impact.

In Adelson's view, by and large the women of America do not care for women's lib. They are alienated by its aggressive reordering of life-long values and threatened by the suggestion that they might not be as free as they thought they were. They do not take to the ideas that they are passive victims of fear or that social indoctrination has forced them into a marriage that is slavery. In much the same manner, the average male citizen fails to recognize himself as a slobbering exploiter of women or as the rapist against whom the liberated female must learn to protect herself. Indeed, if the women's liberation movement continues to convey such images, its appeal will be confined to the white, educated, affluent few, and its impact will be limited to victories that are more symbolic than they are effectively real.

Adelson has sensed what many others have experienced from contact with ardent women's libbers—an uncomfortable feeling of being intellectually bludgeoned by someone who exhorts and lectures but who will not question any of the premises upon which her conclusions rest. As Adelson observes, "They so often seem to be suffused by an overweening sense of self. Behind the rhetoric, behind the talk of freedom and equality and oppression, one senses an injured narcissism, the feeling of having been deprived and cheated. There is so much talk of self—of self-fulfillment, self-realization, self-determination—and so little of one's devotion and responsibility to particular others—I don't mean mankind; I mean particular others. Perhaps this accounts for the strange absence of the child in so much of the literature of the movement. With so little felt to be available to and for the self, what can be left to offer another?"

The grouping of psychologically hurt women in the vanguard of the movement has been self-defeating because of the inability of these women to communicate with their sisters or meet negative reactions from their brothers. The suffragettes of the 1920s scored a critical success when they were "granted" the vote, but the movement lost its energy shortly thereafter. In much the same fashion, the ratification of a twenty-seventh amendment to the Constitution to guarantee psychologist C. Winick's analysis of the sexual revolution, we are abort the revolution.

sex and tomorrow

We have all witnessed an apparently radical cultural shift in the expression of sexuality and in the moral code regulating it. According to psychologist C. Winick's analysis of the sexual revolution, we are entering a "Beige Epoch"—a neuter age in which there will be unisex. Given names will cease to be gender-specific (Leslie, Robin, Tracy, Dana, Lynn, and so on); clothing and appearance will transcend previous sexual boundaries; masculine and feminine labels will no longer be applied to recreational pastimes (men hunt and women knit); and males and females will share labor in the home.

In the future, being a boy/girl, man/woman, husband/wife, or male/female—according to Marshall McLuhan and George Leonard —may only faintly resemble the experiences of the good old days. McLuhan and Leonard contend that the sexual patterns of the future may return to those of our tribal days when there was a free, playful, and not particularly significant activity. This would liberate the male from his present need to be a model of masculinity and release the female from pressures to emulate the *Playboy* center-fold.

If relationships between the sexes change markedly, the institution of marriage will also be changed to fit the new morality. It has always been the favorite indoor sport of prophets to predict that the institution of marriage will end in shambles; thus, John Watson, the father of modern behaviorism, was confident in 1925 that marriage would cease to exist by 1977. Marriage may well be transformed into a new and different shape in the years ahead, and it may also be true that only the young will adapt comfortably to its new form.

Multilateral or group marriage (in which a number of persons may band together as a family unit) may find favor with future generations. A few multilateral marriages have already been established. According to some participants, this form of marriage seems to be working at the moment and is designed to be a permanent union. However, the husbands and wives of tomorrow may require some readying for this new marital form. Robert Rimmer, author of *The Harrad Experiment*, has described an imaginary college with a curriculum suited for just such marriages. This fictional account of an educational and sexual utopia was widely read by young people during the late 1960s. Rimmer described an institution of higher learning in which computer-matched males and females were roommates; the roommates were free to choose whether to have sexual relations. Pregnancy was the equivalent of flunking out, and the expectant couple would be expelled from the dormitory and required to marry. Rimmer hoped to depict a sexually-oriented aristocracy of men and women in whom sexual inhibitions, repressions, and hate would be absent; he predicted that a goodly percentage of the student body would stick with monogamous marriage, while only an adventurous few would explore the advantages of informal group marriage. Unquestionably, if the forms of sex role and marriage change as drastically as this in the days ahead, we will all face a difficult adjustment to a new way of life. Moreover, we will probably respond at the outset as if new marital patterns were a form of social pathology to be cured rather than sanctioned.

marriage and
the family

All cultures on earth have some form of marriage and subsequent limitations on the sexual freedom of the married. From its inception marriage has been an exceedingly plastic arrangement, easily shaped by human and cultural needs; when societies in the past suffered an imbalance of men or women, marriage patterns whould shift to meet the problem. In subsistence or economically marginal societies, women are subjugated in marriage; when there is affluence, women are afforded the luxury of freedom. The notion of romantic love in marriage came into being in medieval times but was elevated to a societal ideal in Western culture only in the last hundred or so years. In most other cultures, a loving marriage might well be achieved over the years, but it rarely existed at the time the decision was made to wed. Whether a wedding is the outcome of a flaming romantic attachment between young lovers or an arranged, family-approved mating, the marriage itself may assume any one of a variety of styles over the years. Some of the less satisfactory possibilities shall be reviewed here.

One possibility is the *antagonistic marriage,* where husband and wife "slug it out" for years without fatally injuring one another. Their intense mutual antagonism is painful, but they may stay together because of mutual fear, exhaustion, need for revenge, or despair about the possibility of establishing any better relationship with someone else. A second possibility is the *friendly marriage.* The emotional content of the marriage may be meager, but husband and wife work diligently at getting along with each other in order not to jeopardize the social, sexual, and economic advantages marriage provides. They are, essentially, good roommates.

The *static marriage* is a third possibility. Both husband and wife may have anticipated a great deal more from the marital state, but their disappointment and doubt is suppressed or concealed in order not to rock the boat of routine companionship. If neither partner changes or grows very much and events in their lives do not intrude too insistently, the marriage may maintain this static and unexciting level until death does them part. The *cyclical marriage* is a fourth possibility, where the couple goes through life on an emotional roller coaster. Fearsome fights and acrid arguments alternate with periods of deep serenity and joy after making up. Over time, their love may grow and deepen, but the cost in personal pain and psychological vulnerability may be more than most are willing to pay. The *romantic marriage* is one last possibility, which might be the pattern least likely to survive the test of time. The sequence of a hasty and passionate courtship, poetic honeymoon, reality hangover, and disagreeable divorce is a frequent formula for broken marriages in America. These classifications do not make some marriages seem very appealing, but

214

the descriptions will probably do little to deter the young or alter the basis on which marital partners are selected.

The majority of young people today continue to marry persons who are very much like themselves; they tend to marry endogomously (within their own ethnic group) and to those with whom they are in daily contact. For the woman, marriage is still the key to upward mobility, since her social status is greatly determined by that of the male she weds. Thus, Catholic women achieve greater social status if they marry Protestant or Jewish males, and more Catholic women marry out of their faith than do Catholic men. In the same way, more Jewish men marry gentiles than do Jewish girls. For all our romantic illusions, status is still the name of the game for many, and "well-born" women are constantly in competition with their lower status, upwardly mobile sisters. The consequence of this competition is to produce a unique circumstance in our society—more high-status women remain spinsters, and more low-status males settle for bachelorhood. Moreover, in our culture, there is a marriage market in which both young and old men actively compete for young brides.

American women marry earlier than do most members of other industrialized societies, and almost all American women marry eventually. We are, as one writer has pointed out, a highly familistic society in which the unmarried woman or the childless wife are still social deviates. The most popular single age for marriage is 18 years old (one-fourth marry at this time), but, on the average, most women who marry are closer to 21 years of age. A recent shift in marriage statistics has occurred, and increasingly the young are shying away from making it legal. A growing percentage of the under-35 age group are now single, while the 35-and-over age group continues to marry at its former rate. Time will tell if the 20- to 24-year-old group is simply postponing marriage to a later date or planning not to marry at all.

Certainly the preliminaries to marriage have changed since the good old days. Even the game of courtship has been computerized. In our modern technological state, the young may register their needs, desires, preferences, and interests with a data bank that, in turn, identifies pairs who are deemed compatible by behavioral scientists. The handful of eligibles that the young person encounters in daily life can thus be augmented by a presumably vast inventory of possible marital candidates. Computers, of course, are no better than the information fed into them; but even this limited improvement may lead to marriage selections that are more rational than the haphazard accidents of fate which currently determine whom we will marry.

According to most reports, total wedded bliss is, indeed, difficult to achieve. In intensive interviews, for example, only 45 to 50 percent of the marital partners surveyed describe their marriage as successful.

The social structure of marital fidelity is equally a seldom-attained ideal. This does not mean that the unfaithful are always unhappy with monogamous life, but rather that sexual relations have been contaminated with a variety of other human needs. Sex, for one, has become an arena in which youthfulness, power, achievement, and acceptance can be tested.

Monogamy, for all its limitations, is liable to survive every assault that is made upon it. But even though monogamy will probably prevail, there is a growing feeling that not all marriages are made in heaven and consumated on earth. At least in our society, there is now an easy legal remedy for those marriages that drift onto the rocks of tormented interpersonal relationships; that remedy is, of course, the divorce court.

divorce

Come hell or high water, our society clings to the belief that marriage is sacred and divorce is blasphemy. Marriages are supposed to last for a lifetime since, in theory, wedded bliss is the natural state and divorce is a symptom of social decay. Times have changed, however, and the divorce rate has followed suit. In America in the 1890s there was one divorce for every 18 marriages; 15 years later the ratio fell to one divorce in 10 marriages. During the Roaring Twenties, the rate was one in seven, and just after World War II we had the highest rate in our history—one divorce for every 3.8 marriages. The rate has stabilized in the last 25 years at about one divorce for every four marriages, and it is evident that those who point to the "soaring" divorce rate as evidence of the imminent decay of our society are misreading the trend toward divorce that has stretched over at least 100 years. The divorce rate is not the same in all parts of our country. Western states have nearly four times the rate that Northeastern states have, but we cannot easily explain all the regional variations.

Shattered marriages most often have their end in the divorce court three years after the wedding. This fact is misleading, however, since the first year is the most difficult for marital adjustment, and divorce is usually the culmination of several years of growing incompatibility. The young marrieds have to learn to deal with the fact that the new spouse may, in reality, be quite different from one's premarital fantasy, and the natural tendency is to "talk out the problem." Contrary to what most of us might expect, however, the open, honest discussion of how one's husband or wife is failing to live up to expectations does little to adjust young marrieds to the issues that divide them. The art of open communication without hostility or pressure exerted on one another is not accomplished merely with good intentions.

216

When divorce becomes inevitable, the separation should be psychological as well as legal. Contrary to the advice given by most divorce manuals, we should cease making hypocritical attempts to have "friendly" divorces. Ex-partners are advised by some counselors to make a clean break and totally disentangle themselves from each other's lives in order to reorganize emotionally to love again. According to some, divorce has advantages if it "clears away the emotional smog smothering the whole family" and if it is an honest admission that adults cannot get along nor provide a model of a loving relationship for their children.

THE CHILDREN OF DIVORCE

An ancient myth persists that children can bring untold joy into family life and can even serve to steady a faltering marriage. The myth is exposed by the fact that more than one-half of divorcing couples have children and, further, that the proportion is rising. A more reasonable assumption is that children intensify existing conflict and subtly complicate its resolution. More than 6 million American children under 18 years of age have been touched directly by divorce; yet we know surprisingly little about the precise effect divorce and separation have on the young. One retrospective survey taken over a 13-year period furnishes some information. Judson T. Landis queried 3000 male and female college students and found that the children from broken homes start dating later than do children from happy marriages; they date fewer persons; and they date less frequently. The children of divorced parents apparently do not "play the field" as much, but they do go steady more often than do other children. Children from intact homes report more positive self-evaluations and a greater sense of confidence about their ability to relate to others.

Apparently, the degree of emotional shock the child undergoes is closely tied to the way he or she viewed the home before divorce takes place. If the child considered the home a happy one and the parents well-adjusted to one another, divorce comes as a shock, and his reaction to this misjudgment of reality may plague him for some time following the separation. Children who sensed a divorce was impending often experienced relief when the battle finally came to a head. These boys and girls were more secure and happy following the divorce, when the tension of marital strife was lifted from their lives. Nevertheless, divorce usually increased the emotional distance between father and child. Girls in particular grew much closer to their mothers.

Twice as many of the children from divorced or unhappy homes expressed doubts about the chances of having a successful marriage of their own. When patterns of marriage and divorce are traced over three generations, it does appear that divorce tends to run in the family; the children of divorced parents have more divorces themselves. One study on life stress and mental health revealed that the age of the child at the time of a parent's remarriage made little difference in the individual's adjustment if he came from the lower socioeconomic class. For the middle and upper classes, the earlier the remarriage of the parent, the better the child's eventual mental health rating. This study also found a high correlation between the mental health rating of the child and the child's opinion of how well he gets along with the stepparent.

Certainly, divorce may create special problems for any child. For one, conflict may be created in the child who is deeply attached to both parents; a second problem may be a continuing awareness of the parents' marital problem—the child may carry this with him for the rest of his life. Having to deal with the consequences of parents who could not agree on what constitutes the proper balance of freedom and restraint could be a third problem. The inevitable comparison of his life with the lives of children from normal homes is, of course, one more difficulty. A fifth possible problem is the development of emotionally disturbing attitudes toward one's parents, while the possibility of the transition from being a product of a broken home to being a stepchild is a sixth difficulty. Finally, there is the strain of shifting between households with different sets of standards.

J. Louise Despert, author of *Children of Divorce,* insists that the crucial factor in the psychological disturbances of children of divorce is the emotional estrangement between parents. She counsels divorced parents to work together for the welfare of their children, with each parent helping the child to have a positive image of the other parent. The temptation is great for parents to misuse the children as they battle one another for divorce. Parents, too, have problems, but in divorce the children may be the victims. One social institution, Parents Without Partners, was established in 1957 for the express purpose of bringing together divorced and bereaved parents. With the help of experts, parents can share their experiences and find new and more constructive approaches to the problems and children of divorce.

THE SECOND TIME AROUND

Statistically, divorce is no obstacle to remarriage. Rather, divorcees have a better chance of getting married than do those who have never married. More than three-fourths of all divorcing men will remarry, as will about two-thirds of all divorcing women. Thus, there are now approximately ten million marriages in which one or both partners have been married before. Eight million of these marriages involve children. Second marriages seem to succeed at a startling rate. Those who remarry are more likely to stay with their second venture than persons married only once. The new partners report they work harder at marriage, and perhaps they do so to avoid a repetition of the previous strife or to demonstrate to themselves (and the world) that they *are* capable of sustaining a relationship. Perhaps, secretly they want to show that they were blameless in the previous divorce.

The span of time between divorce and remarriage can be a trying one for the person who was formerly married. Long removed from the wear and tear of the dating game, they must learn the new conventions and find a graceful way to contact eligible prospects. Since it is traditional for the man to be the aggressor in courtship, the dating game is much more difficult for divorced women to play. One formerly married woman reported that she soon grew weary of explaining herself to each new man on the first date or two and she thought about making a resume for them. She would list her "college, major subject, degree, favorite composers, favorite books, how long married, reasons for breaking up, favorite foods, attitudes towards sports, religion and sex." The formerly married person is shocked to discover the extent to which the whole world seems designed to accommodate couples only.

At first the divorcee experiences a sense of liberation that may trigger a sudden wave of self-indulgence—a new wardrobe for the woman, a sporty new car for the male. This new feeling of freedom is real, of course, since the separated partners need no longer be concerned about the other's needs for the first time in many years. For a brief period of time, this may mean having meals when the mood dictates, eating caviar and peanut butter if the impulse strikes, or simply having as many drinks before dinner as one wishes. But this is a temporary phase. The divorced are great believers in marriage and will shortly yearn to return to the wedded state.

Marriage, divorce, and remarriage have a complex but intimate relationship to mental health. Studies comparing the mental health of the divorcee with that of the married person have found that, on the whole, the permanently divorced are afflicted with emotional problems more often than are those who have stayed married or have married again. Family life, for all its problems, seems to contribute to our mental health.

the family

It is fashionable nowadays to maintain that modern industrial and urban civilization has been achieved at the expense of our traditional family patterns. We were, in past times, all members of an extended family system; now we are trapped in the isolation of the parent-child nuclear family. For more than a quarter century, there has been a great public outcry about family breakdown and theorists have solemnly warned that unless we return to the domestic patterns of our grandparents the American family is doomed.

Some do not see it this way, maintaining that grandfather's bountiful farm was a myth and that in truth grandfather was most often poor and a marginally self-sufficient farmer whose children abandoned rural life as soon as they could. Some critics insist that today's nuclear family is not nearly so isolated from its relatives as the pessimists would lead us to believe. A survey in Detroit revealed that 67 percent of the families saw their relatives at least once a week, 20 percent several times a week, and only 13 percent several times a year or less.

Still, one marked change seems to have occurred between the families of today and yesterday—the father is no longer the absolute patriarch he was in our rural days. The endless expansion of the urban way of life, the decline in home-centered enterprise, the lessening of formal social and religious sanctions on behavior, the increasing freedom of women, the growing freedom of young people, and the rise of the social welfare state have all served to render the family best adapted to a rural life inefficient. So, instead of the companionship family with its intense concern for proper personality development in its members, we have a system by which to prepare family members to succeed in a bureaucratic society.

We still maintain some vestiges of the extended family. Mutual visiting, traditional holiday meals, and family rituals seem to have survived the invention of the nuclear family, even though family gatherings are more limited in size than they were in rural days when second, third, or even more distant cousins (shirt-tail relations) were included in festive occasions. Young married people have not abandoned ritual as much as they have modernized and modified it. They have rewritten the ritual form and altered the trimmings to invent new tradition; some young people, for instance, now compose their own wedding ceremonies. Holidays, particularly Thanksgiving and Christmas, are still times to enjoy the family and to be loved and loving. By the same token, these times of family togetherness can be the settings for emotional crises related to the family. Togetherness is not an unblemished joy even though we seem to have abandoned the practice of casting the "black sheep" out of the family circle.

Perhaps we can gain some perspective about modern family life if we look back to the family patterns of the Victorian Age. The Victorian family was a patriarchy that supported a double standard of sexual morality—marital fidelity was required of the wife but the husband was relatively free to pursue extramarital affairs with prostitutes or expensive mistresses. Victorians did not marry for love but for social convenience, and all marriages were "arranged." Divorce rarely occurred, but when it did happen it was at the pleasure of the husband since wives had no legal recourse for a husband's infidelity or brutality.

For both husband and wife, the family was a private place offering sanctuary from the harsh world outside. In this setting, parental responsibility to children was limited to clothing, feeding, and educating, and child care was not a critically important family activity. It is only in recent years that rearing children has become an obsession for parents. Seeing the child as a particularly vulnerable human being exposed to the enormous formative influence of the family is a very recent innovation. Our modern anxiety about character building in the family and our despair that we may have often gone astray are motivating reasons behind suggestions to abandon the nuclear family and seek a more productive alternative.

alternatives to the family

The nuclear family is not the only possible solution to the problem of raising a new generation of people who will become effective members of the community. Many societies do not consider our kind of mother-child relationship the only "natural" one and have established arrangements that minimally involve the biological mother. We believe it essential to mental health that the infant and young child experience a warm, intimate, and continuous relationship with the mother (or one person who consistently does the mothering).

In a communal system of child care the child routinely relates to many others from early in life, and when he is separated from his biological mother there is little anxiety since many other comfortable relationships are available. He can trust his environment and the people in it, and he learns acceptable social values without suffering emotional or personality disorders. Reports of studies comparing the psychosocial maturity of Austrian, Israeli, Polish, and Yugoslavian young people raised either at home or in group-care settings failed to reveal significant differences between them in psychosocial maturity. Some differences did exist (kibbutz-reared Israelis were judged to be more mature than Polish home-reared children), but the overall conclusion was that the group rearing of children is not necessarily destructive to the young. As we shall see, societies in which group care is provided for young children establish an institutionalized means for reinforcing group-learned role relationships. In this way, the society can be certain that the lessons taught the young will be useful in adult society.

THE KIBBUTZ

The kibbutz had its ideological roots in the Wandervogel (migratory bird) movement in Germany in the late 1800s; the young people of

221

that time revolted against the authoritarian standards of middle-class families and searched for a new way of life. The need to escape from the constraints of traditional family life coupled with the dream of an Israeli state in Palestine became an obsession with these young Jews. They were bent on forming a utopian society devoted to lofty ideals in a land that was once occupied by their spiritual ancestors. The cosmopolitan Jews of Europe were, however, poorly equipped for the rural, pioneering, agricultural life they had chosen; and, out of necessity, they designed the kibbutz to serve adult needs rather than those of children. The need to survive in a harsh land dictated the invention of a new social form, and, in time, it evolved into a philosophy of family life.

If the emigrants were to survive, a new Jew would be needed, and there were proposals among the first wave of settlers that marriage be banned for the first five years of the pioneering trials and tribulations. But, when the first child was born, new social policies had to be constructed to make both parents free for work in the fields. Children were assigned to communal care during their growing years, and a new familial pattern was formed. This invention was a startlingly radical move that rebelled against the double standard for men and women and abandoned the traditional structure of the Jewish family. In times past, wife and child had been subservient to the husband and father, and the traditional division of labor confined the woman to the home excluding her from community, social, cultural, and economic life.

More than any other, the Jewish religion had traditionally demeaned womanhood, segregated women from men, and viewed femininity as a curse rather than a virtue. The kibbutz venture offered women a way to freedom and equality if they were prepared to make the sacrifices needed to achieve this goal. Only childbirth remained an inescapable female assignment. In the kibbutz, husband and wife were treated as distinct individuals with independent jobs and roles in the communal society. Children lived apart from their parents and were attended by community members assigned to this task. Children slept, ate, and studied in special houses, and each age group led its own life with its unique social arrangements. In modern times, children meet their parents and siblings each day, spending afternoons and early evenings together. On Saturdays and holidays, children are with their parents most of the time, although they continue to have separate meals. Parents have little reason to thwart the child's wishes, so they can afford to be permissive, minimizing the authoritarian aspect of child-parent relationships.

For the kibbutz child, a sense of "we" and "they" emerges early in life. They support their group against others, exclude out-group members from play, and show concern when a member is absent.

They share objects in the children's house, and the child who shares is praised lavishly. "From the time they can walk, the children visit the various work-settings—the kitchen, fields, gardens, the garage, where they smell, touch, hear and taste the adult world, and equally important, see their parents at work—closing the gap, somewhat, between adult and child worlds."

What kind of young adult emerges from this pattern of communal child rearing? According to some observers, he is a healthy, intelligent, generous, somewhat shy but warm human being whose roots are in both his community and the larger Israeli society. Further, he seems free of emotional disturbance. When 17- and 18-year-old young people were questioned, most of them expressed satisfaction with communal living on the kibbutz. The girls, however, regretted not spending more time with their parents as children and expressed a desire to care for their own children more than their parents had cared for them. Another comprehensive study, however, reports that children born and reared in the kibbutz (Sabras) were shy, reserved, tended to maintain psychological distance, and seldom formed emotional attachments.

One researcher found that the kibbutz-raised child is also more rigidly concerned with taboos on premarital sexuality, is less ambitious and is less self-motivated since his orientation is primarily to the group; also, during the early years, infants in the kibbutz lag behind nonkibbutz children in development, but there are no residues of slower growth by 10 years of age. Finally, another observer has noted that adolescent life in the kibbutz seems too highly structured with too little time for individual activity or opportunity to develop interpersonal relationships. There seems too little time to be alone or time just to do nothing at all. In a world where one is constantly surrounded by peers, there seems to be too few places of retreat and solace—too little privacy.

As theorists try to relate the kibbutz experience to present-day America, there are recurring suggestions that communal child rearing might be the answer to our problems with poor children who are exposed to disruptive, broken families. The question is whether such group socialization could eliminate the psychological damage, resentment, and rebelliousness of our disadvantaged young? Probably not. Communal child rearing is no panacea, and these socialization practices are not likely to be transported intact to the American scene until we are prepared to overhaul drastically the goals of our society. It is folly to release children into an individualistic, competitive society after rearing them collectively and teaching them to value cooperation and responsibility for one's group over individual accomplishment. A child is certain to suffer painful and destructive conflicts if he is thrust unprepared into a society that stands opposed to all he has learned. The kibbutz may be free of the problems of delinquency, drugs, and alienation that plague our society, but this outcome is a part of the total life-style of the commune rather than a product of the specific patterns of child rearing. As Bruno Bettelheim stated: "The culturally deprived child—whether in city slums or impoverished rural areas—had best be reared in an environment different from his home, since his home life often makes him unfit for the world he must later enter. But can children be reared successfully away from their mothers, as kibbutz children? Prevalent feeling in the West seems to be that this is disastrous for the child."

It is also true that the kibbutz of the pioneering Israelis is not the kibbutz of today. The romantic image which many have of the kibbutz is one of spartan living, lush orange groves, and ennobling farm labor. If you visit the kibbutz today, you are as likely to find cosmopolitan tourist motels, factories for fruit and vegetable processing, manufacturing facilities for farm machinery, or irrigation equipment. The new enterprises include production of wood, furniture, metal, chemicals, sophisticated plastics, and electronics. One kibbutz, in fact, recently began producing Israel's first frozen TV dinners. More than half of the kibbutzim now have factories, and some have two, three, and four plants operating. The rugged life of the early 1900s can still be found, but only in the new communes begun in the occupied lands taken during the 1967 Arab-Israeli war.

THE COMMUNES

The isolated nuclear family is notoriously inefficient as an economic production unit, since it tends to keep females out of the labor market. When a society decides it must alter its level of productivity, one means to this end is to dispense with the nuclear family. "To a certain extent, this has been the policy of all Western societies at war and most systematically of the Hebrew kibbutz and the Chinese commune." In China the communal movement was established to destroy traditional loyalty to the *Tsu* (the patrilinear clan), substituting a new loyalty to the communist state. The commune successfully superseded the *Tsu* and took over many of its functions (helping the family with wedding or funeral arrangements, coping with financial emergencies, schooling, and so forth). In the community dining halls, the social and nutritional needs of the family were served. In both the Soviet Union and China, the economic revolution produced significant social change as it freed the woman from home drudgery and the care of small children.

In the Soviet Union, communal facilities for the rearing of children were initiated with the formation of the Soviet government, but in 1956 collective upbringing took a critical jump with the expansion

224

of nurseries and kindergartens and the introduction of boarding schools and "schools of the prolonged day." Soviet infants experience collective living early in life. They are placed in group playpens with six or eight children and later exposed to a regime of training. "Each child is on what a Western psychologist would view as a series of reinforcement schedules; that is, the upbringer spends a specified amount of time with him in stimulating and training sensory-motor functions."

From the beginning children are taught to share and to work and play cooperatively. When ready they are instructed to evaluate and criticize one another from the point of view of the good of the group. Before long, the task of discipline is turned over to the children themselves. Learning to become the New Soviet Man is made easier by the fact that the Russian child is confronted with far fewer conflicting or divergent views of the way adult life ought to be. While Soviet children will be more conforming than our own, they will also be less delinquent, less rebellious, and less anti-establishment. One writer reached this pessimistic conclusion when looking at the American and Russian societies: "If the current trend persists, if the institutions of our society continue to remove parents, other adults, and older youth from active participation in the lives of children, and if the resulting vacuum is filled by the age-segregated peer group, *we can anticipate increased alienation, indifference, antagonism, and violence on the part of the young generation in all segments of our society —middle-class children as well as the disadvantaged.*"

Soviet children, controlled by collective values and peer group standards, grow up to be polite, considerate, well-behaved adults. But some observers suggest the New Soviet Man is also docile, conformist, and without creative originality. As one observer stated: "I have often wondered why with such a wonderful upbringing, life and the people in the Soviet Union are so often gray and morose." This writer concludes that the Soviets have designed a pattern of child rearing geared to the requirements of both an authoritarian and industrial society. It is child rearing that produces adults who will fit smoothly and obediently into assigned social slots.

U. Bronfenbrenner, author of *Two Worlds of Childhood: U.S. and U.S.S.R.*, notes that American children are socialized mostly by their peers rather than by their parents. The critical difference is that American peer groups are sometimes in violent disagreement with the values, standards, and behavior approved by adults. If we continue to become an "age-segregated" society, peer influence will displace adult influence at an even greater rate, and many of us may not be pleased with the shape of New American Man. This dilemma reaches deep into the family structure and will contribute significantly to the American reaction to possible alternative forms of child rearing. For some of us, the collective form will only be palatable if it reinstates the lost virtues of discipline, authority, and obedience. The most successful American commune—the Hutterite Brethren—may represent a pattern of life that the general American society will be able to accept most readily.

THE HUTTERIAN BRETHREN

The Hutterian Brethren of Canada and the American Great Plains region is a singular example of a long-term, successful commune. These colonies have been in continuous existence since 1874 and are flourishing today in the midst of the larger alien society. This Christian communal sect numbers more than 18,000 souls organized in colonies of about 150 members who till farms approximately 16,000 acres in size. Since they believe it is sinful to marry outside the sect, all of the present descendants stem from the original 101 couples.

The Hutterian Brethren live an austere life (no radio or TV, uniform clothes, no personal property, few toys for the children, little inside plumbing, and so on) in a managed democracy where all positions are elective but where almost everyone gets elected at one time or another. When colonies get too large (population doubles about every 15 years), land is purchased and a new colony is formed. Both new and old colonies are kept under close surveillance to insure there is no laxity or self-indulgence. Since business expenditures over ten dollars must be approved by the farm manager, it is difficult to imagine much all-out luxuriating on the part of the colony members. "Cardinal principles of the Hutterites are pacifism, adult baptism, the communal ownership of all property, and simple living. Jewelry, art, and overstuffed chairs are regarded as sinful luxuries. Radio sets and the movies are taboo. Children are the only possessions to which there is no limit: the average completed family has more than ten."

This way of life may appear severe to most of us, but it seems to eliminate a great many of the social problems we in the "outside" civilization confront every day. The history of the Hutterites has no record of murder, arson, sex crime, severe physical assault, divorce, or family desertion. Members of the Hutterian Brethren do suffer emotional disorders and do have problems, but they seem comparatively free of the difficulties that haunt the outside world. The Hutterian Brethren live in an anti-materialistic, fundamental Christian brotherhood, which ensures its continuity with intense socialization practices. Hutterian children are trained from infancy to accept the social system and to suppress ambitions and material desires. At 3 years of age, children are removed from family care and put into nursery schools to learn the Hutterian way of life. Between birth and age 12, the children are almost completely insulated from contact with the outside world. At best, youngsters may catch a quick glimpse of the "other civilization" during brief trips to nearby small towns.

The Hutterians are rich, yet poor. They lead a personally austere but not poverty stricken existence, and their life offers a great many spiritual and emotional compensations, including a freedom from feeling alienated from the establishment. It is doubtful, however, that "the Hutterians can provide a model for the reconstruction of personal living in the affluent society. They are a very special and very isolated people. . . . We may learn from them that there is valid satisfaction in cooperative effort and some suppression of individual rights." After having separated themselves from the perils of modern society for more than 100 years, the Hutterians have found a satisfying way of life. It remains an open question whether their utopian vision will eventually be eroded by the civilization that surrounds them. Indeed, the fact that a Hutterite very rarely leaves the settlement should tell us something about the condition of our own society today.

marriage and the family of tomorrow

The psychologist John B. Watson prophesied in the 1920s that by 1977 marriage would no longer exist. By then, he believed, family standards would have broken down completely, and the automobile would have allowed our children to run out of control. In the 1930s, the sociologist Pitirim Sorokin prophesied that the rate of divorce and separation would increase until the difference between the married and unmarried would all but disappear; the home would become only an overnight resting place. In the 1940s, another sociologist concluded that the family was doomed unless we returned to the domestic style of our grandparents. These and other prophecies have no more credibility than do the current predictions of what the future will hold. But, the new views of tomorrow do tell us a great deal about the family condition of today.

Leo Davids, author of *North American Marriage: 1990*, tries to probe the form American marriage might take in the year 1990 and sees startling possibilities. He notes that we may see an end to the myth that parenthood is "fun" and substitute the more realistic attitude that it is a serious, trying, time-consuming task. Davids thinks procreation will eventually come under communal control; husband-wife roles will be equalized; and abortion and new forms of marriage will be commonplace. Persons unfit to be parents will be screened out (parent licensing); courtship will be computerized; marital options such as three- to five-year renewable contracts will be popular; and childless trial marriages will become common along with compound marriages. The right to bear children will be regulated, and fewer than a one-third of the married couples will be allowed to propagate. Even these will be permitted to have children only after suitable testing, qualification, and intensive parent training. In addition, male parents may be prohibited from accepting full-time employment during a child's growing years.

Increasingly, prophets speak of modifying the marriage contract so as to specify the rights and duties that partners will assume. The contract terms would become effective at the birth of children, and conditions defining the dissolution of the marriage and the division of property could be specified in advance. Under such a contract system, there might be a proliferation of triangular relationships. Preferred compositions of the triad would depend on the sexual inclinations of the members, but it is likely that the two female-one male combination will predominate since there is a growing shortage of eligible males in our society. These modern radical sentiments are, however, no more than an echo of past prophets who were convinced that marriage was a dying institution. In 1926, some prophets were insisting that marriage will have a relatively insignificant place in the future structure of society, since the state will assume the care of children, trained teachers and nurses taking the place of parents.

When social theorists examine the future prospects of the family, they toy with ideas such as child swapping in which parents will temporarily exchange problem children with other couples in the hope that someone else can get through to the child when they themselves clearly and painfully cannot. The trades may take any of a number of forms: straight two-way switches ("You take our boy, we'll take your girl"); one-way attempts to pair up a "bad" boy and a "good" boy; and what might be called back-and-forth ("We'll take them both for one school semester—you take them for another"). Experimentation with the family structure does not surprise Margaret Mead, however. "Whenever there is a period of upheaval in the world, somebody's going to do something to the family. If the family's being very rigorous and puritanical, you loosen it up. And if it's being very loose, you tighten it up. But you have to change it to really feel you're accomplishing something. If we go back into history we find over and over again, in moments of revolutionary change, that people start talking about family, and what they're doing to it, and what's wrong with it. They even predict it's going to disappear altogether. It is in fact the only institution we have that doesn't have a hope of disappearing."

The range of suggestions for altering the American family system is truly astonishing. There could be, for example, an end to marriage as a state-regulated institution; it could be replaced by a voluntary association in which those who so desire could have a state-certified marriage, but others would be free to try alternate forms such as polygamy, (one male-many females), polyandry (one female-many

228

males), or tribal marriage. Some might consider constructing an intimate network of three or four families which would band together to exchange intimacies, provide services for one another, and evolve new systems of values and attitudes. Perhaps, it would be useful if we were to have "third parents"—a male figure trained to serve the socializing needs of male children. Such alter-parents could help to overcome parental deficiencies in the families of tomorrow.

The possibilities of the combinations of family life are so enormous it has even been suggested that we need a new profession—that of marriage-inventor. Such a professional would catalogue new ways for men and women to cohabit and raise children so that no one would be at a loss for new forms to try when the old forms lost their lustre. Perhaps that is what the future holds for marriage and the family, but the probability is very low. Monogamy, for all its faults and limitations, will undoubtedly continue to be the wave of the future.

the quest
for identity

It would be patronizing to discuss youth's quest for identity, were it not for the fact that many middle-aged and older persons are still searching for answers and may never be able finally to proclaim "I know who, what, and why I am." In discussing the young, it is also important to underscore the statement H. Miller has made: "To generalize about contemporary American youth is to deny the only thing we really know about them: they are, like all human beings, infinitely complex and diverse in their behaviors. It is an exercise in ignorance, then, to draw a portraiture of an entire generation."

Not so long ago, the adolescent was viewed as a callow, flighty, mindless yearling, given to infatuations, wild enthusiasms, and transient moods. In recent years, two new images have appeared. One is the adolescent as visionary. "He is distinguished by a purity of moral vision which allows him to perceive or state the moral simplicity hidden by adult complication. In the way of prophets, he is also a Victim. He is betrayed, exploited, or neglected by the adult world." Another image is the adolescent as leather-jacketed, cruel, amoral victimizer of others. Neither of these images is much more than a cultural stereotype, but each indicates the peculiarly intense reactions that the adolescent evokes in American thought and feelings. Nevertheless, when the adolescent is stereotyped and labeled by adults, he begins to conform to that label.

the generation gap

Conflict between the young and their elders today is different from that of the past. In the encounters of previous eras, the young fought impatiently for the right of entry into the system—to be free to do as their seniors did. This kind of struggle still exists, of course, but it takes the form of who should be in the driver's seat and when a change of drivers should take place. The new form of age-antagonism is much more profound since some of the young "feel as if they were locked in the back of a vehicle that had been built to corrupt specifications, was unsafe at any speed, and was being driven by a middle-aged drunk. They don't want to drive; they don't even want to go where the car is going, and they sometimes distrust the examiners too much even to be willing to apply for a license. What they want is to get out while they are still alive; if they succeed in that, they will try to camp where they happen to be, hoping to make it if they can stay together and leave ambition and the Great Society to us."

In *The Greening of America*, Charles A. Reich asserted: "Young people see clearly a society that is unjust to its poor, its minorities, is run for the benefit of the privileged few, lacks its proclaimed democracy and liberty, is ugly and artificial, destroys the environment and the self. Old People shunted into institutional homes, streets made hideous with commercialism, the competitiveness and sterility of suburban living, the loneliness and anomie of cities, the ruin to nature of bulldozers and pollution, servile conformity, and the artificial quality of plastic lives in plastic homes." This statement of despair sums up America for many of the young and establishes the need to find a personal identity that will produce a different world.

The threat that the young present to those of the establishment generation is evident. By dropping out, the young reject the whole fabric of society and remove themselves from contact with those who would socialize them into the life patterns of their parents. A vitally important group of the young has threatened the established generation by total rejection. The elders, needless to say, have not accepted such drastic criticism easily or gracefully.

THE ANCIENT GAP

The generation gap has an extended history in America. One writer has described it succinctly:

> To the stuffy, inhibited, puritanical parents of the 1920s, the gin-swizzling, rowdy, belligerent, sexually-promiscuous adolescent was a shameful enigma. That was indeed a "Lost Generation" which could be found in illegal speakeasys or in the indelible pages of F. Scott Fitzgerald. Nor was the serious-minded, socially-conscious adolescent of the 30s any less of a mystery to his adult contemporaries. The fact that he denounced capitalistic society from corner soapboxes, crusaded on picket lines and wrote inflammatory poetry was a bitter thorn in the side of his depression-plagued, morally-repressed and rigidly conformist parent. In the 40s, the alumni of the firebrand, rebellious "Lost Generation"—now paunchy and middleaged—despairingly found that they had spewn forth a generation of spineless, "adjust" jelly fish who worshipped security above ambition; silence above protest.

The young of the 1950s were called the silent generation, but by the late 1960s and 1970s a new dimension was added to the generation conflict.

The generation gap is even more ancient, of course. Hieroglyphics in Egyptian tombs relate the unwillingness of the younger generation of that time to respect the wisdom of their elders or to honor and obey the established laws of the society. Indeed, this "new" crisis is a timeless one. Ours is not the first society in which the young have proclaimed that old methods have failed. Perhaps, the time has come to bestow the right of problem solving on the young. The cry of communication failure between the generations is equally dated,

233

but it is reasonable to suggest that no amount of information exchange between the young and the old can really close a gap caused by viewing the same phenomenon from diametrically opposed vantage points. Perhaps, it is the fate of the young always to push for change while their elders are defending the status quo. The cultures of these two generations never have spoken one another's language.

Margaret Mead has analyzed the generation gap by making a distinction among three different kinds of culture. One is the *post-figurative,* in which children learn primarily from their forebears: the *cofigurative* is where both children and adults learn from their peers; and *prefigurative* is where adults also learn from their children. In postfigurative cultures change is slow enough that grandparents look to their own past lives as a guide to the future of the children; the past of the adults is a model for the future of each new generation. In a cofigurative society old and young alike assume that it is "natural" for each new generation to differ from that of preceding generations; but elders are still in power since they set the style and define the limits of the behavior of the young. The young change but look to their elders for final approval rather than to their peers. Present-day society is tending toward the prefigurative culture. "Today, suddenly, because all the peoples of the world are part of one electronically based, intercommunicating network, young people everywhere share a kind of experience that none of the elders ever have had or will have." For the first time in history the generation gap is world-wide, and no previous generation has ever known, experienced, and witnessed such rapid changes.

THE GAP TODAY

Mead agrees there is a generation gap today, but she maintains it has nothing to do with parents and children. Rather, the gap is between all the people born and brought up after World War II and all those who were born before it. If you happen to be a parent who was born and brought up before World War II, and you happen to have children at this moment, you are on one side of the generation gap and they are on the other.

Some of those on the far side of the gap came to the defense of the new generation and tried to bridge the distance by subscribing to the new beliefs as an improvement over the values of past times. One enthusiast felt that, of the generation pushing toward 50, only the supremely healthy could have as many honest moments as those who are now under 30; this critic believed that those under 30 represent the first American generation that has been free to form its own morality, while rejecting a prefashioned code handed down from their elders. Some of the older generation believe that "it is quite right the young should talk about us as hypocrites, since we are." Such critics welcome the generation gap since without it our society would become static and each generation would be exactly like the last.

Some observers believe that we are witnessing more than the usual developmental-generational conflict between parents and their adolescent children. It is seen as a full-scale clash of cultural patterns in which the young value being able to express their emotions, while elders value achievement, goal-directedness, rationality, and individual responsibility. The older generation does not value feelings or sensory experiences for their own sake, the quest for intimacy, or self-exploration. Neither have the members of the establishment cried out for greater communication with the young.

As young people persist in their quest for identity, misunderstandings arise among the elders who witness it. Perhaps, the generational gap is best conveyed in the complaint of the father who stated: "I survived the Great Depression, World War II, three economic recessions, and a heart attack. Now my 18-year-old kid sneers and tells me I don't know what life is all about!"

The young do complain they cannot "relate" to or establish open, spontaneous communication with their elders. Some young people believe the only meaningful contacts with others are the spontaneous ones, but this "dogma of spontaneity" can also be used as an excuse for irresponsibility. An example would be dismissing relationships if they have to be worked at or dismissing as neurotic possessiveness a partner's demands for responsibility. In much the same fashion, doing your own thing can be a me-first-you-second declaration and a rationalization for ignoring the needs of the partner. "Another syndrome characterizing the way youth avoid intimacy is shared love, or what we call *spreading it thin*. The best example is the girl, commonly a member of hip communities or a commune, who takes on the role of Earth Mother. She loves and cares for everyone; and because she does not refuse anyone, she is responsible to no one in particular."

The young accurately diagnose the hypocrisy and shallowness of many adult interpersonal relationships but have yet to devise a better formula.

As stated, great discord arises between the generations because of young people's apparent lack of deep commitment to adult values and roles. Since adults feel that young people do not share their values and cultural expectations, a sense of alienation results. This alienation works both ways. From the young people's point of view, the grownups are offering a dissatisfying adult pattern of life. If young people do not trust the adult world and view it as cold, mechanical, and emotionally meaningless, then they must search for an alternative."

Many adults are unhappy with the rebellious image of the adolescent, even though they acknowledge that the young of today may have more knowledge, cultural advantages, and sophistication than did previous generations. Many adults simply are not convinced that the "new species" is an improvement over how they remember themselves at that age. Apparently, someone must be blamed and guilt for the condition of the young is most often laid at the door of permissive child rearing. As psychologist Elizabeth Hurlock observed: "If, as a small child, the adolescent of today wanted to explore, he was permitted to do so regardless of whether or not he broke some of his parents' choicest possessions or turned the parents' hair prematurely gray for fear that he would hurt or kill himself. He was permitted to say what popped into his mind, regardless of whether what he said hurt peoples' feelings or deflated their egos. Permissiveness, once established, is hard to change, especially if parents believe it is "good for the child" even though hard for them to take."

The next most pervasive explanations lay the blame on our permissive legal system or on progressive education. ("Pupils run the schools and teachers and principals cater to the children's whims.") Sigmund Freud and Dr. Benjamin Spock have been blamed as the authors of permissiveness just as affluence has been denounced as a poisonous influence on child rearing. Indeed, the list of culprits is endless. Elizabeth Hurlock is one of the more outspoken of the disenchanted adults. Her descriptions of the new species of American young people are in unflattering terms, to say the least. According to Hurlock, the young are driven by a compulsion to follow the herd; they fear being original or different and are frighteningly conformist. As a corollary to this compulsion, the young are preoccupied with status symbols that will identify them as accepted members of a worthwhile peer group. Further, they are irresponsible about anything that requires effort or interferes with their search for pleasure; and they are anti-intellectual, despite the fact that increasing numbers of them attend college.

Understandably, the young are not understood by the older generation. Their new values are hedonistic and self-seeking. According to Hurlock, they are disrespectful of age and experience, and they disregard age-old rules and laws. They have become the first affluent generation of juvenile delinquents. Finally, they have an unrealistic level of aspiration for cultural change and improvement. After this lengthy damnation of the young, Hurlock concludes that this generation is not likely to become superior adults. As she notes, the young are not happy now and there is little reason to anticipate they will be happier later in life—with or without drugs.

The problems of a distinctive youth culture are not limited to the United States. British psychologist B. Sugarman indicates that in Britain similar values and norms operate to set youth apart as a subculture. In our society, there seem to be two distinct subcultures—middle-class pupils who are bound for college, and lower-class youths who begrudgingly remain in school or drop out to join the work world. Sugarman has suggested one reason for intense anti-school feelings among British young people—especially among dropouts—may be that the extra-curricular activities of British schools are severely limited.

June Bingham, writer of the article "The Intelligent Square's Guide to Hippieland," suggests that there are helpful rules of thumb for members of the establishment who wish to deal rationally with the gap of values between the young and old. For one, members of the older generation must abandon feelings of guilt and despair, since such feelings are inappropriate, counterproductive, and useless emotions. They must rely on experience to teach the young basic lessons no parent can communicate. Older people must learn the difference between affection (given unquestioningly) and approval (which must be earned). You can love a child who misbehaves, even though you do not condone his misbehavior. Finally, older people must learn to provide a living model of tolerance and understanding and be patient about the time it takes for the young to progress to another stage.

Patience and tolerance are necessary since, as one observer has pointed out, the hippie dream is a regression—a fantasy of return to the tribal life of the American Indian or to the satisfying life of a closely knit extended family where adults and children live together more intimately and humanely. A cohesive, emotionally close, basic human unit is thought to be a more natural state than the present family structure. This fallacy of romantic regression ignores the fact that bureaucracy, with all its faults, provides security. It was invented as a reaction to the arbitrary and inhumane practices that passed for management science in the early days of the industrial revolution.

GENERATION GAP—NO!

The whole notion of a new form of generation gap is, according to clinical psychologist Joseph Adelson, no more than "pop" sociology —a false idea whose time has come. Like every false idea, it carries just enough truth to make its promotion believable. Adelson insists that the difference between generations does not come from the actual fact of greater sexual freedom, the difference in generational politics, widespread alienation, or the marijuana culture. Rather, the gap comes from the fact that the young and old mutually agree there is a significant difference between them.

If scientific evidence rather than the popular media were examined, Adelson believes that no extensive degree of alienation would be found between parents and their children. One study of 12- to 18-year-old youngsters from all regions and social classes concluded that few signs of serious parent-child conflict exist. Further, the adolescent was not seen as a prisoner of the opinion of peers, except in trivial matters such as clothing, hair style, musical taste, and the like. There is, simply, much less arbitrary parental authority and much less open rebellion than is popularly supposed.

Adelson observes that to identify the young with liberal or radical tendencies makes sense only when one focuses on the elite university campus. American youth as a whole has a quite different complexion. Thus, the analysis of the 1968 presidential election by the University of Michigan's Survey Research Center (based on 1600 interviews with a representative sample of voters) revealed that voters under 30 years of age were over-represented in the George Wallace constituency both in the North and the South. The young who worked in factories were evidently appalled at an apparent collapse of patriotism and respect for law and order. In a democracy, the game shifts to "one man one vote"; and it was in this arena that the silent majority of young persons found a way to express themselves and swamped the views of their college-educated, liberal peers. Adelson points out that over the stretch of years about 75 percent of the young have voted the same party as their parents. Further, Adelson contends, that for the most part the "rebellious" student is not rebelling against the politics learned at home. Radical activists are children of radical or liberal parents who—overtly or tacitly—sympathize with what their children are doing.

Despite radical tendencies in our society, about 80 percent of the young tend to be traditionalist in their values, and there is as great a gap between different factions of the young as there is between young people and their elders. The fact is, no one really knows how deeply the generational division runs, how rapidly change is taking place, or in which segments of the population the change is truly significant. We do not truly know how much is fact and how much is popular rhetoric. The revolution may exist only in the minds of those who wish it to be true. According to Adelson, whatever generational revolution does exist may be considered as no more than an attempt of the young to claim credit for a movement that began years before their birth and only now is peaking in a visible fashion.

If there is a generational gap at all, it is clearly confined to the urban members of the upper middle class—it does not include blacks, poor people, the children of laborers, or young people from rural settings. Certainly, the generation gap we read about is not a division between all young people and old people but between the wealthy and secure and the old. Questioning the system is a luxury which only those who have no more need for success and financial stability can afford. It is not an issue for those who must face the daily reality of trying to succeed or just get by. We may be exaggerating the impact this select group of protestors will have on the direction of our society in the years ahead—especially since no one has bothered to seek the opinions of working or lower middle-class young people.

Despite their large numbers, 18- to 24-year-old blue-collar men and women are the forgotten people of the 1970s. One hope, however, is the proposed Labor Department study to explore this level of social life and return it to the consciousness of national policy makers. It is difficult for most of us to keep in mind that 70 percent of the young people between 18 and 24 are not in school and that they, too, may have feelings of being crushed into institutional molds that they do not fit. The community colleges may service them in an antiquated fashion and the unions may be preoccupied with issues better fitted to a culture of 20 years ago. Whatever the actual case may be, it is flagrantly short-sighted to maintain that this is a group of young people who are free of all tensions, doubts, or unsatisfied needs. Indeed, this could be the next group to explode against the status quo.

In the opinion of R. A. Kalish, a California psychologist interested in gerontology, the generation gap is neither new nor limited to a division between youth and the middle-aged establishment. Lack of understanding or communication between generations is just as likely to occur between a 70-year-old man and his 42-year-old son. "If their conflict is not as widely publicized as that between the latter and his 20-year-old son, it is probably because the conflict is less dramatic and less intense, rather than because of fewer differences in basic values."

It is instructive to consider some of the details of the gap Kalish describes between a 42-year-old man and his 70-year-old father. The father would have been born at the turn of the century; he would have grown up without telephones, TV, movies, automobiles, running water, electricity, social security, or income taxes. When he was about 30 years old, the Great Depression left him penniless and unemployed with a family to feed. Surviving at a near subsistence level for a number of years, he made a considerable sacrifice to send his son to the university to get the education. This aging father cannot comprehend the disruption and discontent in a society that was once stable and predictable; "progress," for him, is too rapid and bewildering. As a consequence, he has retreated and severed contact with much of the world.

His 42-year-old son remembers being poor when he was young and recalls being taught the value of getting an education and working hard to succeed. He followed this dictum scrupulously, moved steadily up the economic ladder, and has been able to give his children all the "advantages" he never had. As Kalish points out, the son's children will now have grown up in times that are distinctly different from those of their father or their grandfather; this third generation may or may not hold similar views about hard work, productivity, material gain, or achievement.

Oddly enough the young and the very old find themselves in the same boat. The very old are not productive; they have little income; and they are dependent on others. They, like the young, live in an age-segregated society of persons their own age, and they have little voice in the decision-making apparatus. If the young are alienated from society, so are the very old for whom there is also no meaningful place. Thus, it is clear there are gaps and gaps—some within and some between generations. The anti-society gap that most concerns us is neither new nor is it representative of most of the young. The mass media have magnified the gap by scrutinizing and publicizing its every dimension, but the percentage of truly dissident persons remains quite small.

the roots of protest

The vision of social scientists is not always unobscured. In 1964, certain sociologists declared that the existence of a rebellious youth subculture was a myth, and they denied that youth and adults were in serious conflict over their respective value systems. Then, of course, came the storm of student protest and rebelliousness. To place current events in their proper historical perspective, it should be mentioned that the revolutionary cry of "power to the people" was first heard in Russia in the 1800s when children of nobility were arrested for protesting the status quo. In the United States, few give note to the Oberlin Peace Society formed by students in 1843, the protest marches at Princeton in 1859, or the strike against war by the National Student League in 1934. In May 1915, the Collegiate Anti-Militarism League polled 37 colleges and revealed that 63,000 students were against introducing military training into the curriculum while 17,000 favored such a move. Thus, modern student protest has an ancient history. New forms of protest must work with what is, and they most often recombine old elements to make the new.

Hair length is an example. Hair length became the "now" badge of youthful revolt, but few of the bearded, long-tressed young were aware of the timelessness of this way of expressing disagreement. Fads and fashions have shifted whimsically over the centuries, and men have risked death and damnation over the length of their hair. Indeed, hair, virility, and war have long been inseparable. Alexander the Great had his army cleanshaven in order to foil the enemy in battle, while among the North American Indians it was a point of honor to allow one chivalrous lock of hair to grow so as to assist the victor in taking a scalp. In days long past, England was divided politically into short-haired Roundheads and curly-haired Cavaliers; the Puritan's associated long hair with vice and iniquity. In short,

240

hair length has long signaled one's political and religious persuasion.

Religious outrage about long hair reached such an extreme during the eleventh century that those with flowing tresses could be excommunicated and denied the benefits of prayer when dead. The Bishop of Worcester was among the most fanatic; he carried a pocket knife; and, when long-haired supplicants knelt before him, he would cut off a handful of long hair, throw it in their faces, and launch into a harangue, raving that long hair made one destined for hell. Beards, moustaches, and long hair have been taxed as well as forbidden. In August 1838, for example, the King of Bavaria forbade all civilians to wear moustaches under the threat of arrest.

Thus, the great hair issue of the 1960s and 1970s has a rich precedent in historical, religious, and political conflict. As a symbol of belief, as a statement of position, and as a declaration of differences, hair length has always been an easy, highly visible act of public defiance. The next best pattern of protest is to alter one's style of life, making it clearly in opposition to established norms. The Hippie New Morality, for example, contradicts the "straight" way of life, but it too has had its precedents.

Bennet Berger, author of "Hippie Morality—More Old Than New," spent months in the San Francisco Bay Area asking hippies what the New Morality was all about. He concluded that there is not much, if any, of the New Morality around. As Berger pointed out, the basic principles of hippiedom were laid down 40 years ago by the Bohemians of the 1920s. The Bohemian Doctrine espoused the principle that society was systematically crushing the spirit of the young and that salvation could be achieved only through a new, free generation. Today's "do your own thing" ethic had its counterpart 40 years ago in the philosophy of self-realization through self-expression. Even then, paganism was advocated, and the body was treated as a shrine in which love-making was the ritual form of prayer. Living for the moment, total freedom from inhibition, female equality, drug usage, and incessant movement from scene to scene are not new ideas; elaborated with flowers, beads, bells, and costumes, they are recent expressions of an ancient idea.

STUDENT DISSENT

The sheer number of college-aged youth makes that group worthy of comment—aside from the fact that America deems them important and eulogizes them as the leaders of tomorrow. From about 1960 to 1968, the war babies came of age, and the 18- to 24-age group increased by 43 percent. Thus, with five and a half million students in college, if only 2 percent dissent about some social issue, we are still talking about 100,000 young citizens who object to the way our society is being conducted—enough people to give any revolutionary a sense of power.

Student dissent is the dominant mood in America, if one were to believe everything given out by the mass media. For all the publicity accorded it, overt dissent was spectacular only in the elite universities of America. In most instances, even when rioting occurred, it consisted of 5 percent activists and 95 percent onlookers living out the adage "riots are fun." Kenneth Kenston, author of *The Uncommitted: Alienated Youth in American Society*, contends that student dissenters fall along a continuum stretching between activists at one end and culturally alienated students at the other. The activists take a stand and are found in the middle of demonstrations, protesting the injustice they feel is being done to others less fortunate than themselves. The activists work within the American system to improve it as they feel it should be improved. The culturally alienated are strictly opposed to the "establishment" or the "system" but are so pessimistic politically that they do not become directly involved. Dropping out, for them, is the only sensible option. "Whereas the protesting student is likely to accept the basic political and social values of his parents, the alienated student almost always rejects his parents' values. In particular, he is likely to see his father as a man who has 'sold out' to the pressures for success and status in American society; he is determined to avoid the fate that overtook his father."

J. Revel has looked at the campus upheaval in a longer time perspective and concluded that it is one part of a larger revolution. This larger revolution involves "a radically new approach to moral values; the black revolt; the feminist attack on masculine domination, the rejection by young people of exclusively economic and technical social goals; the general adoption of non-coercive methods in education; the acceptance of the guilt for poverty; the growing demand for equality; the rejection of an authoritarian culture in favor of a critical and diversified culture that is basically new, rather than adopted from the old cultural stockpile; the rejection both of the spread of American power abroad and of foreign policy; and a determination that the natural environment is more important than commercial profit."

Laudable as these issues may be, Revel is not optimistic about the meaningfulness of student revolt. Among the complaints of student revolutionaries is that much of the research and scholarship conducted in universities is irrelevant since it has little direct and immediate application to daily human life. With a seemingly anti-intellectual, foreshortened vision, student activists have attacked academe's concentration on pure, basic research and demanded universities address themselves exclusively to the social issues the students see as most urgent today.

242

Even those who are sympathetic to present-day youth and to the current social scene are prone to label and categorize. R. E. Kavanaugh, for example, refers to malevolent dreamers and the kept generation in his article "The Grim Generation." *Malevolent dreamers* are, for Kavanaugh, activists, leftists, radicals, and anarchists whose goal is to overthrow the authority of all our institutions whatever the consequences. In contrast, most students are members of the *kept generation*; they are moderate, have good reputations, are preoccupied with grades, are not involved in extracurricular events, and are not really cynical about life. The *benevolent dreamers* are students who have managed the identity crisis and now devote themselves to active revision of the culture; they tutor in the inner city, raise money to educate minority youth, lead campus governments, edit newspapers, and form action committees to get things done.

It is the "hippy" who hopes to find himself and discover meaning and sanity in his experience with American life that poses the problem. He probably loves others no more than do most of us and provides little other than simplistic answers to life. Nevertheless, he has managed to create a horizontal gap between students of the far left and their middle-of-the-road peers.

To some observers, the problem of student unrest can be traced to the exceptional prolongation of adolescence in industrialized cultures. Adolescence is no longer a briefly awkward transitional stage between child and man but a segment of life that may last, psychologically, for as long as 15 years. In this artificial interim, it is not surprising that the young develop their own cultural style replete with its own goals, values, traditions, and sources of motivation and satisfaction. Because of the enormous numbers of the young who are now concentrated in universities, this situation has become critical in the last decade. For some students, the university has become a home territory that comfortably fills a decade of their life, whether they are in school or not.

MIDDLE AMERICA REACTS

Though some are distressed by the new adolescent man who pursues questions of "identity" while living in upper middle-class university ghettos, others are outraged by the flourishing "now" scene. Max Rafferty is one such outraged observer who states that conservatives believe student activism is a conspiracy designed to tear down the society: "As for the Black Students Union, the Panthers, the Muslims, and their ilk, everyone who has really paid any attention to these groups puts them in exactly the same category as the Mafia in modern times and the infamous Molly Maguires of my own Irish ancestors prior to the turn of the last century. They thrive on terror, they fatten upon fear, and they live by threats and intimidation. I regard them with the same mingling of reprobation and contempt which before their advent I reserved for the Ku Klux Klan, a racist gang which they resemble more than somewhat, incidentally."

Tough talk, perhaps, but it probably echoes the suspicious sentiment of many "middle Americans" bewildered by the leftist orientation of the student population. Giving power to the students is seen as somewhat akin to letting convicts run the prisons, the mentally ill manage the asylums, or the patients govern the hospital. Rafferty's appraisal of student rebels is equally unflattering. "Many of the unwashed and hairy rioters, exuding a visible aura of unwashed disinhibition and looking remarkably like so many unmade beds, are present-day counterparts of the old English remittance man. Their families can no longer stand to have them around, so they get monthly allowances on condition that they stay as far away from home as possible."

Like Rafferty, the columnist Jenkin Lloyd Jones is an outspoken critic of the counterculture and some of the members of the newer generation. To Jones, it is a culture in which any young person can become a full-fledged member simply by (a) donning the uniform (jeans, long hair, a peace necklace, and an Indian headband); (b) learning a dozen or so slogans and clichés (contempt for the establishment, the university, the Puritan ethic); and (c) crediting oneself with all the virtues (honest, open, and no "game playing").

The late Philip Wylie also looked askance at this generation and suggested that anyone who believes in "doing his own thing" is a potential monster. "It is often the slogan of the absolutely selfish and to use it that way is to be what one does, a thing.... I have observed many own-thing doers, and noted them as parasitical freeloaders, dependent on their scorned elders, irresponsible for ideas or acts, intellectual quacks and minimal artists of life." Only on a desert island, perhaps, could "doing your own thing" not have an effect on a community of people.

Suppose we accept the premise that society is imperfect and badly in need of repair. Then, every young adult must feel a sense of responsibility about choosing a personal strategy to deal with it. J. Fischer has calculated that there are only four basic alternatives open to young people. One alternative would be to drop out. This is an ancient strategem for those who find the world too complex or cruel. You can drop out by using drugs or alcohol or simply by not participating. Dropping out, however, can become a parasitic way of life in which the larger society is used but no responsibility is assumed with regard to it. A second alternative is to flee. You can run to a new way of life in an attempt to romanticize the simpler

244

pastoral existence; you can occupy the land from which so many farmers are fleeing every year.

Planning a revolution is a third alternative. If you have no patience with the tedium of the democratic process, you can plan a revolution in which everything will be changed for the better. If you succeed, the critical problem will be how to keep the new establishment from becoming a carbon copy of the old one. The fourth alternative is, of course, to try to change the world gradually. This is the least glamorous solution to impatient, idealistic young people. Yet, over the long reach of history, this is the only effective way—even if the victories are unspectacular and leave a lot to be done by the generations that follow.

Revolutionaries look with justifiable contempt upon the path of gradualism since it often proves to be the approach through which conservative ingenuity can forestall change. Some young people see our current condition as a life-or-death situation, and they know that one does not sedately walk out of the way when about to be run over by a truck. If there is no crisis, then the impatience and aggressiveness of activists is inappropriate; but if a crisis exists then they are showing an exceptional degree of restraint. Whatever the case, when militant leaders go too far, conservative members of the society funnel their anxiety, discomfort, and resentment onto particular individuals, while completely rejecting the changes those individuals are championing. In his article "Cultures in Collision," P. E. Slater states clearly: "The old culture will not simply fall of its own weight. It is not rotten but wildly malfunctioning, not weak and failing but strong and demented, not a sick old horse but a healthy runaway. It no longer performs its fundamental task of satisfying the needs of its adherents, but it still performs the task of feeding and perpetuating itself. Nor do the young have the knowledge and skill successfully to dismantle it. If the matter is left to the collision of generational change it seems to me inevitable that a radical-right revolution will occur as a last-ditch effort to stave off change." As psychoanalyst and author Rollo May has indicated, it is unfortunate that the adolescent student rebellion was defined so narrowly by knowing only what the revolution was against rather than what it was for. Strategically, such an approach puts the student in the awkward position of having to wait for those in power to react to demands for change before next moves can be planned.

One upshot of the stirrings on campus is psychiatrist Seymour Halleck's observation that a new kind of patient is seeking therapeutic help on the college campus today. This patient is not the social activist or the hippy but the stylist—a person whose life is dominated by dissent, the immediacy of his needs and experiences, and the search for relevance. The stylist complains that life is boring and meaningless, but he cannot define the nature of his personal dissatisfaction with existence. In Halleck's view, "the stylist lives one day at a time and while he wishes to experience everything that can be experienced, he experiences nothing in depth. One week he is 'into poetry,' the next week 'into Marcuse,' the third week 'into painting.' The poem or painting is never completed; the books are never read beyond the first chapter."

It is the very "nowness" of the stylist's life that eliminates any depth of relationship that is necessary to deal with personal problems. For the stylist, boredom slips easily into despair or deep depression, since his personality is empty of meaningful content. When the future is uncertain and the past inadequate, only the now makes sense—but the now is gone tomorrow leaving only emptiness.

THE FAMILY OF PROTEST

Taking a psychoanalytic view of the relations between generations, L. Feuer argues that the sons are attacking the authority of their fathers. In their irrational rebellion, the sons become alienated from their fathers and all the fathers stand for. Feuer contends that guilt over their intent to rebel leads the sons into self-defeating actions, self-destruction, and failure. Further, student protests are oriented symbolically toward destruction of the father and elimination of paternal authority.

Other theorists feel that the student protest movement is the result of children living out the *ideals* of their fathers. The sons are *like* their fathers only more so. If the fathers are liberal politically (but tend to preach more than they practice), the sons have become liberal or radical practitioners as well as preacher. This is hardly generational conflict. Young people, according to this view, cannot be explained and understood simply as a generation in revolt. For most of them, this is not an effort to break free of the constricting, tradition-oriented, or obsolete values of parents. The parents of student protestors share with their offspring an unusual divergence from conventional religious, political, and social attitudes. Most activists come from special kinds of middle- and upper middle-class families in which both parents are highly educated, the father is a professional, and the mother may also have a career. Both parents and children tend to be political liberals, and it is agreed that their parents have been permissive and democratic in their upbringing.

Researchers have differentiated between two expressions of alienation in family relationships. Activists were raised by educated, upper middle-class parents who were interested in national politics. Alienated youth show a marked degree of estrangement from their

246

families, when compared to the activists. In short, the data suggest that the extent to which a young person believes he is supported by his parents is a basic determinant of whether he will actively confront social problems or passively retreat into an alienated subculture.

An absence of family conflict over the student's liberal, activist participation is reported in two other studies. In one study, it was found that, from a sample of Washington peace demonstrators, 50 percent reported parental approval of their activity. Similar family support was discovered in a study of demonstrators who were arrested at the 1968 Democratic National Convention; 48 percent of the demonstrators indicated that both parents approved of their behavior, and 59 percent reported that at least one parent approved. The studies confirm the report that liberal student activists come from affluent families where the father has a high status occupation and where both parents have high educational attainment, hold liberal political beliefs, and are politically active. Of course, as we shall see in the subsequent discussion, protest, political involvement, and dropping out did not prove to be the answer for all young people.

the jesus trip

The young, the alienated, and the susceptible have traditionally formed the vanguard of every new religious movement. Further, each of these "discoveries" of God is an emotional experience more than it is an intellectual experience. Today, there is a mind-boggling variety of religious forms including spiritualism, Zen Buddhism, and pentecostalism, as well as drug-induced religious experiences. In particular, the appearance of variant forms of Eastern religious outlooks reflects a turn-about from the rise in traditional church attendance during the 1940s and 1950s. The sharp decline in church attendance occurred when the religious impulse—particularly in the young —began to find an outlet in social and political activism.

The recent rise in religious fervor has followed an unpredictable path, leading us into a tangle of bewildering religions and quasi-religions rooted in Asian thought. Traditional Christian beliefs emphasized social activism and the need to earn salvation from the eternal fires of hell. In contrast, much of Eastern religious thought suggests that God is reached primarily through self-knowledge and awareness of one's inner experience. Such beliefs allow the disciple to turn away from the urgency of social problems and seek tranquility within himself.

The 1969 edition of *The Yearbook of American Churches* lists 79 established religions in the United States—*established* meaning those which have no fewer than 50,000 members. Below the 50,000 mark, the various churches may well be numbered in the thousands. It has been said that in Los Angeles one could change religions every day of the year, since some of these religions exist for only a few months. Indeed the California religious scene among the young has its own special flavor: "Standing in front of the Berkeley campus at noontime, one can see a group of 'Buddhist monks' go dancing by in long yellow robes, their feet bare, their heads shaved—all natives of Oregon or Arizona. Meanwhile, a group of Christian hippies tries to drown out the Buddhists' drums by shouting the name of Jesus, and a 'naturist pantheist' sells fruits and vegetables grown without fertilizer."

Despite the importance of religious events in the lives of many human beings, psychologists have not displayed much curiosity about the experience of sudden religious conversion. No notable work has been written since the 1920s when William James wrote *The Varieties of Religious Experience*, and little has been done since to explore the mystical state. Psychologist W. H. Clark, who teaches in a theological college, is one writer who has reported on the mystical experience. According to Clark, it is "a perception of unity, accompanied also by a sense of timelessness, of holiness, and by the feeling that one has directly encountered ultimate reality accompanied by a sense of great peace. It would be easy for the psychologist to pass off this strange state of ecstasy as just another aberration, were it not for the wholesome changes of personality that often follow it." Some of the Jesus People relate that their experience closely resembles Clark's description of a mystical conversion.

The tenets of belief among the Jesus People are fairly immediate and direct: the Bible is taken literally; miracles can really happen; and God so loved the world that He gave it His only begotten son. To these people, Jesus is a martyr to the cause of peace and brotherhood, a fellow rebel, and a living God with whom they can and must establish an intense personal relationship. The Ten Commandments are strictly subscribed to, and Jesus, like a wondrous father figure, bears an authority, love, and understanding important to the young.

Among social scientists, there has been a rush to explain the meaning of the Jesus phenomenon, but these first attempts do little more than skip along the surface without penetrating very deeply. Nonetheless this first ripple of social comment portends a wave that will engulf us if such fundamentalist religious persuasion proves to be more than a fad. For better or for worse, Jesus has become the newest heavy trip for young, white, middle-class suburbanites. Jane Howard calls them "the Groovy Christians" who bewilder the older generation with enthusiastic declarations of Christian love. Parents, in their turn, are not sure whether they should be enchanted or appalled. After

248

peace marches, long hair, meditation, drugs, and macrobiotic diets, the Jesus bag—to parents—is only one more evidence of the fadishness of the young.

One of the current sects—the Children of God—has caused much concern among the public, and some parents have asked whether their children are being hypnotized, brainwashed, or robotized by their peers or religious leaders. For some parents this is the only plausible way to account for the immersion of their offspring in the Jesus People cult.

Many of the members of the Children of God sect are alienated young who have been rejected by society and have traveled the path of drugs and disorder. The rules of communal life in their Christian Houses are consequently considered strict. Communal rules permit no smoking, drinking, or dating within the group, and the new member may be required to memorize 300 Bible verses in the first two months of residence. Drugs are out, and there may be bedtime curfews and assigned chores. Still the Children of God colonies claim they lose only 15 percent of their converts, as compared to the 50 percent that most Jesus People organizations lose.

Related to the Jesus People phenomenon is a Catholic Pentecostal movement. When members are moved by the spirit of Jesus, they may "speak in tongues" (glossolalia, prayer in the form of a babbling nonlanguage). This movement has been criticized by church elders for proclaiming absolute truth and for fostering an obsessive, narrow, rigid vision of religion as the literal enactment of the Bible.

Inevitably, this movement adapted the modern media to its evangelistic purposes. Unlike the traditional dignified approach of established religions, the movement has spawned Jesus T-shirts, a Jesus-People watch (with smiling white or black Jesus), Jesus bumper stickers, posters, buttons, a Jesus cheer, and a Jesus signal (raised arm, fist closed, with index finger pointing up to heaven). Rock albums ("Jesus Christ Superstar") and an off-Broadway play, *Godspell* (Gospel discording to St. Matthew), have appeared, and there is a Jesus press of more than 50 newspapers across the county.

Does the Jesus movement of Street Christians signal a religious revival in America and a coming way of life that will absorb the energies of future young generations? It is unlikely. The demands of involvement, sacrifice, and the total abandonment of a previous way of life are simply too much for most people. Converts to fundamentalist Christianity are frequently drawn from the ranks of young people who have "bottomed out" emotionally after their involvement with the drugged, unattached, self-indulgent, aimless hippie scene. And, perhaps, finding Jesus can be a way of atonement for the guilt some young people feel when considering the lives they have led.

Radical departures from conventional forms of social life can only appeal to a large portion of any age group if it strikes a highly responsive emotional chord. Apparently, the Jesus People have not struck a responsive chord in most of the young. In their quest for identity, the young have too many other alternatives to explore in life. The evangelist Billy Graham has aptly described the promise offered by the Jesus Generation: "As a child of God, you need never suffer spiritual defeat. Your days of defeat are over. From now on, you will want to live every minute to its fullest. Certainly, you will welcome each day as another twenty-four hours to devote to Christ. Every new day will be filled with opportunities to serve others. You will spend many moments with God, and you will know that your sins are forgiven and that you are on the way to heaven." To the young who are unable to get life all together this formula assures instant and total meaning for every waking minute on earth and for eternity.

A careful study of the Jesus Generation made by R. L. Adams and R. J. Fox divides the new wave of revivalist religion into two clear groups. One group is made up of so-called "Jesus-boppers"—teen-agers attracted to the action and excitement of rock concerts followed by an invitation to accept Jesus. The second element is a more intense group of young adults who are opting out of the drug culture and beginning to re-enter the larger cultural setting where a work ethic and adult values prevail. Adams and Fox feel the Jesus trip is tailor-made for adolescents. "Not only does commitment to Jesus preserve childhood morality with its absolutistic definitions of right and wrong, but it also provides an ideology based on personal, internal and, for the most part, unexplainable experience rather than on critical, rational or realistic analysis. Indeed, the ideology is unchallengeable and thereby not available for analysis by the uninitiated. The Jesus trip also provides adolescents with the necessary peers, rituals, creeds and programs—brothers, baptisms, speaking in tongues and a source for the ideology, the Bible. Approval and affirmation by peers are guaranteed within the movement."

These researchers conclude that the Jesus trip is a step backward from maturity, since—like drugs—it is being used as a way of avoiding the anxieties that are a natural part of the identity crisis. Young people use up their energy in a display of religious fervor, trying to substitute a packaged, pre-arranged identity for the hard labor of evolving an individuality that is distinctly one's own. Adams and Fox indicated: "In normal development the new dimensions of identity are added to the previously established identity, modifying it to some degree; some parts of one's previous identity will be discarded, submerged or eradicated by new behavior. Instead of progressing toward adult ethics, the Jesus person clutches tenaciously to childhood morality, with its simplistic black-and-white, right-and-wrong judgments. Rather than developing behavior oriented towards reality, he flies into ideational, ideological abstractions to numb his awareness of his newly arisen needs." For some of the young Christians this experience will be a transient event in life, and the quest for identity will continue along some yet unknown future path.

the waning rebellion

At the height of campus rebellion in the late 1960s, the public lashed back at the protestors in an effort to counteract the actions of an extreme few who were occupying buildings, disrupting the course of education, taking hostages, and destroying the university's physical plant. The shootings of students at Kent State by the National Guard and the bombing of university buildings on other campuses so shocked the student combatants that the path of violence was abandoned. One writer has expressed the sentiment among most observers: "The great youth trip, that heady, sometimes breathtaking, sometimes frightening, roller-coaster ride that careened through the late years of the nineteen-sixties and plunged headlong into this decade, is slowing down and may be almost over."

Another writer has graphically described the circumstances that signalled the decline and fall of San Francisco's Haight-Ashbury: "Haight Street acquired in the space of a few months so carnival and Dantesque an atmosphere as to defy description. Hippies, tourists, drug peddlers, Hell's Angels, drunks, speed freaks (people high on Methedrine), panhandlers, pamphleteers, street musicians, crackpot evangelists, photographers, TV camera crews, reporters (domestic and foreign), researchers, ambulatory schizophrenics, and hawkers of the underground press ... jostled, put-on, and taunted one another through a din worthy of the Tower of Babel." Countless people still live their own versions of the old Haight-Ashbury dream, but the movement lost its energy and had nowhere to go. The movement came together as a community of young people reacting to the isolated, barren lives of their parents. They banded together in political collectives, urban crash pads, and rural communes; and, for a while, it seemed a revolution. The seed of conflict in the hippy culture was the tug-of-war between individualism and collectivism. On this question, the new culture talked out both sides of its mouth—one moment pitting ideals of cooperation and community against old-culture competitiveness, the next moment espousing the individualism of the old culture with exhortations to "do your own thing."

It is tempting to generalize glibly about all the so-called hippie subculture. Not all are flower children; not all are intelligent; not all are visionary; and not all are mentally healthy. "Some are mentally ill or not very bright; some are merely uninformed and seduced by the gross simplifications and absolute certainties that seem to result from even a rare use of LSD or a heavy use of marijuana. Mental hospitals throughout the United States report a startling drop in admissions of the two kinds of schizophrenics whose symptoms are similar to those of someone on an LSD trip; the young, inappropriately laughing hebephrenics and frozenly posturing catatonics have gone to live among the hippies who tolerate them, thus discouraging their seeking psychiatric treatment."

In a poll of 2000 college seniors, one researcher concluded that today's students are idealistic and more socially aware than previous generations. Their idealism often consists of contempt for the hypocrisy of the older generation, rather than being a total rejection of existing institutions. The altruistic ideals of the young are less often acted upon than talked about, however. Seven in ten, for example, believe their generation is going to make a better world; yet only 13 percent of them believe they can create a society free of prejudice. It is apparent that the young have yet to manage an integrated value system.

The generation whose only heroes were themselves has moved from self-worship and a sense of power to a sense of resignation about producing meaningful institutional change. The establishment has become less an ogre and radical violence has been replaced by greater patience, tolerance, and a subdued willingness to take a longer look at life. Anarchy and apocalypse no longer seem to be just around the corner. The colleges have gone silent; the high schools have followed them; and attendance at football games has risen again.

As the Vietnam war winds down and the country wallows in recession, the impact seems to have touched students. This is not a return to the apathetic fifties. It is exhaustion following the agitated sixties. As concerns the quest for identity, "It is an admirable search, but alas it is a misguided one. Youth perpetuate the error of their parents; they emphasize the object and not the subject, they measure their freedom by a minima of external constraints rather than a maxima of internal possibilities. It is to the great lesson of mankind that they should attend, involvement brings liberation; commitment *is* freedom."

psychology
and utopia

The theologian Paul Tillich stated: "It is the negative in existence which makes the idea of utopia necessary." For many of us, the idea of utopia evokes visions of a mysterious, imaginary paradise located on some uncharted island in the far seas. Utopia has always been a beautiful, but impractical, dream of social perfection in which mankind is finally free of pollution, prejudice, oppressive taxes, restrictive laws, criminal behavior, grueling labor, ignorance, hatred, and all other social irritants.

The literal meaning of utopia is *nowhere,* and utopian thought is simply man's attempt to examine the world about him and dream about how it might be better. Every member of the human race is a secret utopian, but the fantasies of most of us remain just that—splendid, half-conscious dreams that are crowded from our minds by the ever-present urgencies of the daily world. Yet, these idle dreams can fashion the future, shape society, and make the difference between a fulfilling life or a life of drudgery and frustration. "Utopia, therefore, differs from mere proposals of or exhortations to a certain religious, ethical, economic, political, social, or 'cultural' way of life or from theories or explanations of human society; it presents an ideal type of society as if it actually existed in order to serve as a model or reference group to guide and stimulate change toward what is thought to be perfection." Although social analyst Rene Dubos called utopias the "dreams of reason," he was fully aware of the psychological problems all utopias encounter. As he said of utopian experiments in the past: "Dreams of human harmony were soon dispelled in the heat of human conflicts and rivalries under practical conditions. Utopias invariably bring out the traits of human nature—and there are many obvious ones—that stand in the way of unselfish and stable relationships." Dubos perceived a simple and immediate psychological truth when he concluded that modern utopias must be kinetic and experimental rather than static and rigid as were the utopias of past ages. Utopias need to be hopeful stages rather than permanent states; they must encourage a form of change in which the social condition continuously modifies itself as it responds to changing conditions.

At this juncture, psychology and the utopian dream come together. Psychology, if it is to be relevant to man's personal and social existence, must be a practical mixture of art and science, useful to those who are searching for a better way of life. The idea of utopia can be a testing ground for the worth of psychological insights, discoveries, and conclusions. To wring some practical sense out of psychology—to make its facts, theories, methods, and principles essential components of a vision of our future life—we need to learn a great deal more about the nature of man. Utopia is always a highly personal concept, and one man's utopia may be another man's social nightmare. Before we can glibly decide what is good or bad for our fellow man, before we set the rules about how he ought to lead his life, and even before we assemble enthusiastic friends and rush back to nature to begin our alternative society, we must examine utopian thought over the ages.

ancient utopian thought

The herdsman Amos of Israel lived in the eighth century B.C. in a time when there was prosperity for the few and exceptional oppression and poverty for the many. Amos publicly railed against the misery perpetuated by that age and, to a few listeners, described a utopia in which the poor would literally inherit the earth. As the Old Testament records it, Amos had a vision of a golden age in which brotherhood and justice would prevail. Amos' call to utopia was echoed in the words of the prophet Hosea a quarter of a century later and appeared again in the words of Isaiah during the years 740 to 700 B.C.

Isaiah denounced those who worshipped through burnt offerings, silver, and gold. Like the prophets before him, Isaiah predicted that the Israelites of that day would perish, leaving only a handful of survivors to build a nation in which men would no longer learn war. Characteristic of the utopianism of that age, Isaiah prophesied a glowing future—a time of peace, serenity, health, security, and rejoicing. Even "the desert would blossom like a rose."

The Old Testament offers a lush variety of utopian ideas and ideals. Jeremiah described a promised land where young and old would rejoice together. Ezekiel dreamt of an age in which property would be evenly distributed among all; and the little-known visionary Deutro-Isiah described a millennium in which honest toil would get its proper reward and the gift of eternal life would be granted every man. From 200 B.C. to 150 A.D. the pessimistic writers of apocalyptic visions predicted utopia would follow only after an awesome cosmic cataclysm; the angry God would destroy all evil leaders and reward righteous persons with an ideal existence. In other distant centuries, social prophets and religious leaders have vaguely sketched dramatic visions of heaven on earth, giving hope to their oppressed brethren. The poor, downtrodden, enslaved masses have populated the earth throughout history and the promise of utopia has often been the hope that kept them alive. Utopian ideas have flourished whenever social misery becomes intolerable.

Plato (427–347 B.C.), for example, reacted against the tyranny, corruption, and war that surrounded him and abandoned hope for the governing institutions of ancient Athens. Since outspoken criticism of one's society was exceptionally unhealthy in those days (Socrates had been executed in 399 B.C. for voicing similar sentiments). Plato disguised his dissent by constructing a make-believe Republic that just "happened" to be totally different from the Athens of his day. In Plato's ideal city-state, everyone's needs were cared for, but no one could be described as wealthy: an equitable distribution of worldly goods was designed to strike a balance between the idleness encouraged by wealth and the bitterness produced by deprivation. The state was populated by three classes of citizens: artisans, warriors, and a ruling class called the guardians.

The guardian class was to be selected from among the most intelligent, able, just, and powerful 50-year-olds in the society; these leaders were to divide their time between studying philosophy and governing the people. Being a guardian was no easy life. These prospective rulers were educated in the art of temperance, goodness, and nobility from early life, and, much like modern times, persons deficient in the ability to learn science were drafted into the warrior ranks at age 20. The "draft" was the first hurdle in educational selection. At age 30, the student guardians were sorted into rough categories of "more" or "less" promising. The most able stayed in the Graduate Schools of the Republic, while the less able were dropped out and assigned to routine political positions. At 35, the educational survivors were allowed to begin an apprenticeship in governing the Republic. Only at age 50, however, were guardians considered properly prepared to assume full responsibility for the lives of others. The social and personal patterns of life demanded of the guardians were remarkable indeed. They owned no private property, ate together in common dining halls, were forbidden to handle gold and silver, were conditioned not to eat from vessels made of precious metals, and could not enter a house that possessed such corruptive objects. In addition, marriage was communal, with wives and children shared as a single family unit.

The Republic is a fascinating utopia; but it is hardly perfect by present standards. The happy citizen of the Republic had to tolerate censorship of fiction, a ban on innovations, regulation of marriage by the state, communal child rearing, selective breeding of citizens, and being ruled by the elders. Women were declared equal, but, even then, men were more equal than women. Further, all citizens were required to adjust to the social rank for which nature had suited them. The Republic represents a state best described as autocratic communism—or a dictatorship of philosophers. Opportunities to gain influence in the society were barricaded early in life for most citizens, since education was restricted for the "inferior" classes. A great deal of reliance was placed, however, on a hoped-for incorruptibility of the ruling class. As one critic pointed out, Plato was incapable of comprehending the problems of "a utopia with steel mills and ten-cent stores"; in short, the thoughts of this ancient Greek have little relevance to the critical problems of today.

from plato to more

Two thousand years elapsed between the visions of Plato and the political utopia described by Sir Thomas More (1478–1535). During those intervening years, some of the energy of futuristic and utopian thinking was diverted into a romantic nostalgia for the mythical golden ages of times past. Roman writers, for example, extolled the superiority of ages more ancient than their own—ages when life was thought to be less complex and when purity and justice were said to exist in more bounteous measure. In this imaginary time and place, the Romans assumed there was a primitive tribal existence "closer to nature" and superior to the patterns of civilized life. This sentiment is still found in modern times, and some young citizens are even now abandoning the present "civilization" in order to return to the supposed purity and truth of Mother Earth.

In the centuries following the decline and fall of Rome, the cost of utopian thinking was, at times, life itself. A firey religious reformer named Savonarola (1452–1498), for example, attempted to reform his native city of Florence after the citizens had driven out the corrupt Medici family. Through Savonarola's spiritual leadership a form of theocracy was established—a utopia in which men would be ruled by direct intervention of divine powers. For a while the citizens of Florence were enthusiastic about this form of governance, and there was a marked increase in morality and proper public behavior. But, Savonarola's claim of divine inspiration coupled with his acrid criticism of Pope Alexander VI earned for him excommunication, trial and conviction by an ecclesiastical court, and, at the age of 46, death by hanging.

Thus, the centuries between Plato and Sir Thomas More were not devoid of utopian thought; More, however, coined the word *utopia* and managed to reach the popular imagination. His book was translated into every known language and was printed in 300 editions over the years. Surprisingly, More was clearly a part of the establishment of his day (lawyer, arbitrator, Lord Chancellor of England, religious scholar); yet, he revolted against the excesses and injustices that surrounded him. His design was a communistic version of a model society—a kind of communism he thought would have been favored by the fathers of the early Christian church. Emulating Plato, More created a mythical place as a subtle attack on the evils of English society.

Although the intent of the work was serious, it was written tongue in cheek by a man who was reputed to be a great lover of jokes. Thus, for example, the name of More's hero Raphael *Hytholdaeus* means, in English, Ralph Nonsense. Indeed, More's utopia included social arrangements that seem a little odd in modern times. For one, his utopia practiced euthanasia (painless death for the aged or those suffering from incurable diseases). They observed a six hour work day, divorce by mutual consent, and a ritual that required wives to kneel before their husbands each month to ask forgiveness for supposed transgressions. Premarital intercourse was punished by life-long celibacy, and engaged couples were required to inspect each other for defects (while naked) before marriage. The death penalty was used for repeated adultery, and slavery was the punishment for crime. There was communal ownership of property; and, every 10 years communal houses were changed by lottery. All babies were breast fed; taverns were abolished; and priests were elected by the community. These ideas seem startlingly modern, despite the fact that they were written down nearly 500 years ago. Unfortunately, Thomas More died for his political, social, and religious convictions.

Probably the next greatest utopian was the philosopher and scientist Francis Bacon (1561–1626). Bacon, like More, was Lord Chancellor of England, but he fared much worse even than More. He was, in fact, convicted of a number of crimes in 1621, and these departures from grace were deemed so reprehensible that he was fined 40,000 pounds and sentenced to life imprisonment. His concept of utopia, *New Atlantis*, was written during his imprisonment. Bacon selected an imaginary island as the locus of his utopia and described a society dominated by scientists dedicated to the bettering of human life. This was the first "scientific" utopia—a society in which the welfare of the citizens rested upon the whims of a select group of 12 super scientists. Bacon's account of utopia was written 100 years after Thomas More; beyond this significant treatise, however, the seventeenth century was not notable for its contributions to visionary thought.

twentieth-century utopias

The dawning of the twentieth century brought with it a host of new utopian thinkers—theorists concerned with prophecy, science fiction writers playing with unexplored universes, and negative utopians who dreamed nightmares. Futuristic, utopian, and escapist thought once more became an integral part of the human reaction to an imperfect society.

Modern utopias differ from those of the near and ancient past in one clear respect—today's utopias are markedly more psychological in form. As one observer noted: "While eighteenth- and early nineteenth-century utopian thinking still fitted in neatly with physical science in the shape of the smooth-flowing Newtonian world-machine ... in the latter part of the nineteenth century two scientific hypotheses about the nature of man appeared to raise almost insurmountable barriers to the prolongation of the utopian dream: the discoveries of Darwin and of Freud. Both were shattering to those men of the nineteenth century who had had visions of a peaceful, orderly, progressive world form which antagonism and aggression were virtually banished and where man's creativity would flower forever." Darwin and Freud cast a pessimistic shadow across utopian thought, and visionaries were forced to probe ways in which man might evolve on a psychosocial rather than on a physical level, if he is to conquer the killer animal hidden within him.

BRAVE NEW WORLD

In 1932, Aldous Huxley wrote a savage, witty, frightening account of one possible world of tomorrow. The book was prophetic and undoubtedly has greater relevance to the present generation than it did to the generation in the 1930s. Indeed, in modern times, *Brave New World* is a fantasy that has become increasingly difficult to distinguish from reality.

Huxley imagined a streamlined Eden where advances were made not so much in the natural sciences as in "the application to human beings of the results of future research in biology, physiology, and psychology." As Huxley stated: "It is only by means of the sciences of life that the quality of life can be radically changed." In 1946, nearly 15 years after writing *Brave New World*, Huxley concluded that it was even more likely that tomorrow will bring "vast government-sponsored enquiries into what the politicians and the participating scientists will call 'the problem of happiness'—in other words, the problem of making people love their servitude." It will require a revolution in the human mind to accomplish this, but Huxley suggests that with the aid of drugs and a fully developed science of human differences such a "utopia" will be possible.

What would life be like if you lived in Huxley's Brave New World? To begin with, you would be decanted or hatched rather than born, and you might be exposed to "Bokanovsky's Process" in which a single fertilized human egg is made to proliferate into as many as 96 identical human beings. While in your embryonic state, you would be bottled and predestined to a specific social role that would fulfill current needs of the society. Suppose, for example, that the society had an acute shortage of sewer cleaners. You would be fashioned into a lower-caste Epsilon by being deprived of oxygen at a crucial point in embryonic life. With your subhuman intelligence, you would then be happy laboring in the sewage systems of the new society's cities.

After birth, you might be conditioned to love country sports but to hate the countryside; thus, you would "consume" transportation to get to the country and quickly return to the city where you feel you belong. Formal learning would be effortless since the bulk of it would be accomplished through "hypnopedia"—learning while you sleep. As you grow older, life would hold even greater charms. Your attractive Malthusian belt, for example, would contain contraceptives and the ever-present grams of Soma. Soma—a drug with all the advantages of Christianity and alcohol but with none of the drawbacks—is a cornerstone in the foundation of the Brave New World. It has effects which are euphoric, narcotic, and pleasantly hallucinogenic—the perfect drug for a new society. For further entertainment, evenings could be idled away at the "feelies"—movies in which the sensuality portrayed on the screen is realistically experienced by the audience.

In this Brave New World old age no longer poses a problem, since blood transfusions from the young and artificial metabolic stimulation makes everyone feel young until about 60 years of age. Males and females all remain desirably "pneumatic" throughout life, since they are both expected and required to participate in an enthusiastic, promiscuous sex life. The Brave New World is an artificially inseminated, decanted, conditioned, drugged society in which no man's chemistry is his own.

Huxley's utopia has just one flaw—at its geographical edge is a reservation occupied by savages born of primitive mothers who have indulged in abhorrent natural insemination. These savages—primeval, superstitious, and incorrigible—are viewed as an undesirable refuse heap of malcontents and misfits incapable of comprehending the many advantages of a Brave New World. Disturbingly, the beliefs, values, and attitudes of these savages very much resemble those of our present-day society. To these savages, the Brave New World is a Lunatic New World in which human sentiment and behavior had been distorted and warped beyond recognition.

Nearly three decades after publishing *Brave New World*, Huxley reappraised modern society even less optimistically. "The prophesies made in 1931 are coming true much sooner than I thought they would," said Huxley. In his 1958 revisit to Brave New World, Huxley was concerned most deeply about overpopulation of the planet. In his novel, he had solved the people problem, but, looking ahead, he was not certain there would be time for modern society to escape death by overcrowding. Huxley also was disturbed by the thought that the generations ahead might be subjected to a "slavery of the mind"; this might result as societies get more complex and must of necessity be "over organized" to be efficient. Huxley felt we might find it easier to place power in the hands of fewer and fewer persons than to contend with the nagging problems of society ourselves. The invention of a scientific dictatorship that could never be overthrown is what Huxley feared most. As he stated: "Men and women will grow up to love their servitude and will never dream of revolution."

ISLAND

Old utopians such as Aldous Huxley don't die—they just fade away to a mythical South Seas island. Huxley's next attempt at paradise had the advantage of isolation. As he had one of his characters say, "So long as it remains out of touch with the rest of the world, an ideal society can be a viable society." The imaginary island Pala was the setting for a host of social innovations—contraceptives paid for by the government and delivered by the postman at the beginning of each month, the right of children to migrate to the houses of relatives when Home Sweet Home became oppressive, sexual freedom at a tender age, early detection and remedy of physically and psychologically unfit citizens, work and career assignment according to constitutional body type, widespread therapeutic use of hypnosis, a mingling of education and play, and the MAC (Mutual Adoption Club) designed to broaden the individual's emotional attachments to other beings. Each of these innovations was designed to produce adults who were adapted to a society free of neurosis, poverty, hatred, and war. As the final touch to the perfect society, the residents of Pala chewed Moksha—a psychedelic drug that produced beautiful visions and total contentment. The story, unfortunately, does not end happily. In the name of progress Pala is subverted from within, invaded from without, and transformed into a military dictatorship that will assume full membership among the ranks of the other "civilized" societies of the planet.

1984

Some modern utopians have written dystopias—downbeat versions of society at its very worst. Probably no utopian vision has so captured the modern imagination as that described in George Orwell's 1984. Orwell's fantasy is a "negative utopia"—less a drama of what ought to be than a nightmare of what life might become. Written in 1948 (transposed by Orwell to read 1984), this novel presents a world of Thought Police, continuous warfare, full women's liberation (the anti-sex league), and brainwashing; through mind-control each tortured citizen is led to the conclusion that he really loves Big Brother who controls the society.

As Erich Fromm commented, Orwell's message "is that of near despair about the future of man, and the warning is that unless the course of history changes, men all over the world will lose their most human qualities, will become soulless automatons, and will not even be aware of it." In Fromm's words, the psychological question asked by Orwell is: "Can human nature be changed in such a way that man will forget his longing for freedom, for dignity, for integrity, for love—that is to say, can man forget that he is human?"

If you lived in Orwell's 1984, your existence would be dominated by giant telescreens that would monitor you continuously and that could not be turned off. Your every move could be tracked by police helicopters which could dart anywhere, even to spy through your uncovered windows. Standard English would be replaced by a new language called "Newspeak"; the words themselves would fashion your thought by making it impossible for you to conceive of certain ideas. You would learn to believe the slogans of the Party: "War Is Peace; Freedom Is Slavery; Ignorance Is Strength." You would participate enthusiastically in public ceremonies such as the Hate Week, directed at the current enemies of society.

If you were a woman living in 1984, you might wear a scarlet sash signifying that you are chaste and anti-sex. If you were a child of 1984, you would be encouraged to join the Spies and have the priceless opportunity of becoming a cultural hero by denouncing your parents to the Thought Police for making unpatriotic remarks. All public information would be controlled by the Party and would continuously be subject to correction. Past statements by governmental leaders, for example, would be altered so as to square with present facts; former leaders currently in disfavor would be eliminated from history by becoming unpersons; and yesterday's enemy would conveniently and convincingly be portrayed as today's ally.

Scientific research in 1984 would be pursued by scientists who were a unique combination of "psychologists and inquisitors." They would study "with extraordinary minuteness the meaning of facial expressions, gestures, and tones of voices, and testing the truth-producing effects of drugs, shock therapy, hypnosis, and physical torture." In the world of 1984, there would be no private life, and it would be dangerous to let your thoughts wander freely, since the slightest change in facial expression (a facecrime) could be a punishable offense. Each regulation and social rule in 1984 would be calculated to create a belief, attitude, mood, frame of mind, or pattern of behavior that would ensure a docile citizenry and uninterrupted power for the Party. It would be a utopia in which all the citizens were happy (they love Big Brother); and potential dropouts, deviants, or criminals would be rehabilitated (brainwashed) to make them happy once again. It is also a utopian vision of how psychology could be used to imprison man rather than free him. Orwell designed this negative utopia to match the known psychological principles of nearly

25 years ago. Yet, the prophecy of 1984 rings true today, and the methods of controlling human beings have subtly moved from fantasy to frightening reality.

WALDEN TWO

A special niche must be reserved in utopian history for psychologist B. F. Skinner's *Walden Two* (1948). For 15 years after its publication, there was little public notice or reaction. Then, in the 1960s, the novel rode on the crest of a new wave of interest in utopian thought. At that late date, its message was received by a generation of young people, two decades removed from the time of its creation. Skinner chose America as the site of his utopia, and he populated it with persons who sensed that something was wrong with the existing society. The idea of a Walden Two community offered the young an alternative—a way to "start all over again the right way." This was to be a society in which human problems could be resolved through a scientific technology of human conduct—the forerunner of modern behavioristic psychology, which has become so much a part of present-day living. Further, it was to be a community free of the deadly "institutional" feeling so common to most utopias.

Daily labor was to be rewarded with labor-credits rather than with money. Since all goods and services were to be shared, only four hours of work would be required of each citizen each day. Babies were to be raised in climate-controlled Skinner boxes until they completed their first year of growth, and then they would be moved to group quarters with the one- to three-year-olds. They would be taught freedom from envy, jealousy, and other annoying emotions; joy and love would be the curriculum. From an early age, the "high-voltage excitement" of hate, fear, rage, and anger would be eliminated. Child training would involve behavioral engineering in which "opposite emotions" were practiced. For example, children would be taught self-control by having to stand patiently for five minutes before "steaming bowls of soup," even when they were extremely hungry. When five minutes elapsed, a coin would be flipped and the "heads" would be allowed to sit down to eat, while the "tails" practiced five more minutes of self-control. This and related exercises would form the basis of ethical training for children. Reward would be the keynote, and punishment would be outlawed.

Education would continue throughout the life span. The techniques of learning and thinking, rather than subject matter, would be taught. The children of Walden Two would learn but seldom be taught. Since they would enter the labor market at an early age, much of childhood learning would be practical, on-the-job training. Going to college would have no meaning in a community dedicated to a continuous educational experience for everyone at every age.

Women would marry young and bear children early; and sex would become a natural, pleasurable, honorable, and admired activity. Women would be finished with child-bearing at age 22 or 23 and then, still young in mind and body, they would be free to become involved in a personally fulfilling adult life. The classic form of the family would disappear in Walden Two, since there would be separate rooms for husband and wife. Simple friendship between the sexes would be encouraged; trial marriage would be sanctioned; easy divorce would be provided; and children would be raised by the community rather than by the parent pair.

Walden Two, like the utopias of the past, was designed to allow people to live happily within a social structure, while maintaining the maximum possible degree of individual freedom. But the degree of social consensus portrayed in Skinner's novel may not be very realistic. As one writer insisted, "Universal consensus means, by implication, absence of structurally generated conflict. In fact, many builders of utopias go to considerable lengths to convince their audience that in their societies conflict about values or institutional arrangements is either impossible or simply unnecessary. Utopias are perfect—be it perfectly agreeable or perfectly disagreeable—and consequently there is nothing to quarrel about. Strikes and revolutions are as conspicuously absent from utopian societies as are parliaments in which organized groups advance their conflicting claims for power." It will become the task of social scientists to assess both the possibility and probability that such forms of society can really exist and prosper.

psychology and today's utopias

All of us live in a utopia of sorts. To be sure it is a fairly old utopia, begun in 1776 and designed by this country's Founding Fathers; but it is a utopian plan for society nevertheless. It will be granted that ours is an imperfect society and that the personal lives of many are filled with fear, anxiety, insecurity, hardship, disappointment, and resentment. A distressing sign of the spreading disaffection with the utopia called America is the growing number of citizens who drop out, abandon the values and beliefs of our society, and search for utopian visions more suitable to their own states of mind. These latter-day social dissidents search for a new sense of purpose, meaning, togetherness, honesty, and intimacy and strive for the feeling of one-ness that comes from a return to life's basic values. Admittedly, the experimental utopias of today are populated by a small minority of the members of our society; but it is a young, educated, bright, crea-tive minority—a minority whose potential contribution cannot be casually discarded without a second thought.

266

Little remains stable in this world and the feelings, attitudes, and tastes of man shift with the times. Utopias of any sort are patterned by the times that spawn them and last about as long. Rene Dubos stated: "The responses of the human mind cannot help being modified by changes in environment; however well organized society may be, these changes are inevitable, and their effects are to a large extent unpredictable. Even the dogs most carefully prepared by Pavlov lost their conditioning when their environment was suddenly altered. Konrad Lorenz has shown that 'imprinting,' the behavior pattern acquired by birds early in life, can also be removed."

It seems apparent that psychology has new responsibilities to assume in the years ahead and that it must concern itself with the whole man rather than with those fragmentary parts of him that can conveniently be studied in the safe confines of the laboratory. We need to study the joys and sadnesses of man in society and look at his utopian dreams of how life might be improved. It is true that the psychology of man remains complicated and only partly understood. Social scientists know too little of the interplay of the biological, cultural, social, and individual forces that impinge upon man. We know too little about the impact of experiences at various times in man's life, too little about how he adjusts, and too little about how to repair him when he is psychologically crippled or emotionally distorted by his encounter with life.

Since its inception, psychology has dealt primarily with the internal psychic life of the individual. Psychologists find themselves on alien soil when they are expected to answer questions about how man ought to live in community with other human beings. In *Walden Two*, B. F. Skinner made a first attempt at applying psychology to the whole man. It is a significant comment on the primitive state of psychological knowledge that no comparable visions have been written by theorists of psychoanalytic, humanistic, or other psychological persuasions. If psychology is to make the necessary transition from the laboratory to real life, concern with utopian thought might be a most appropriate path to follow.

alternative
societies:
the communes

Visions of a better way of life are always most vivid among the young. Today, however, a wider range of the socially disaffected have become active in constructing a counter culture rooted in communal life. These modern-day communards have withdrawn from the larger society to search in new ways for an honesty, intimacy, and sense of togetherness that gives meaning and purpose to life. As stated by one observer, today's communes are "started by political radicals, return-to-the-land-homesteaders, intellectuals, pacificists, hippies and drop-outs, ex-drug addicts, behavioral psychologists following B. F. Skinner's *Walden Two*, humanistic psychologists interested in environments for self-actualization, Quakers in South America, ex-monks in New Hampshire, and Hasidic Jews in Boston." All such efforts seek what mankind has always longed for—tranquility and joy in living. Before appraising the psychological impact of this new movement, we need to recall that during the 1700s and 1800s America was swept by a similar wave of communal endeavors. In nineteenth century America nearly 100,000 men, women, and children in more than 100 communities experimented with alternative social arrangements for living. Some of these communities lasted a few months; others survived as long as 100 years. "From first to last, as was inevitable in a movement that tested the validity of almost every belief and almost every convention, there was a large number of cranks and a high proportion of fanatics."

At the beginning of the eighteenth century, a group of German Pietists led by Magister Johannes Kelpius sailed to America to build a tabernacle in the wilderness. Believing that the second coming of Christ was imminent, the brethren mounted telescopes on the roof of the tabernacle and watched the skies for a sign that the time was near. As the Millennium took longer and longer to come about, these nightly vigils grew wearisome, and even ardent believers began to drift away from the commune. Kelpius himself moved into a cave and devoted himself to astrological occultism. Eventually, he started to believe that the American Indians were one of the lost tribes of Israel and that he was destined to be immortal. Kelpius died at the age of 35, and the brotherhood was finally dissolved in 1748. Such bizarre group philosophies were the exception rather than the rule in the American experience of communal life. Nonetheless, a review of America's first attempts at alternative societies will be useful here, since many of the lessons that were learned then can still be applied to the current sentiment about "returning to the land."

american utopias of years past

The early immigrants who departed for the American wilderness were undoubtedly a more adventurous breed than those who remained safely behind in Europe. This psychological receptivity to a new way of life was, for some, coupled with an intellectual heritage of utopian thought that had been evolving over most of Europe since the early 1800s.

At the time of the French Revolution, a number of social philosophers (Voltaire, Rousseau, Saint-Simon, Fourier) were concerned about the need to alter existing social institutions and redistribute private property. Among the utopians of that revolutionary century, probably the thinking of Charles Fourier (1772–1827) had the greatest impact on American communal life. Fourier was an activist and socialist whose imaginings sound rather odd today. He had visions of lions pulling carriages and whales pulling vessels across oceans, but the fundamental tenet of his thought was a peaceful society based on the love of one person for another. Fourier's ideas were exported to America in 1840, and 34 experimental utopias were established in this country in an effort to make his vision a reality. All of the attempts failed (as did Fourier's own experimental society), but an important intellectual contribution was made to the history of social organization.

While France was in the midst of a political and social revolution, England was suffering the growing pains of a massive industrial revolution. As historians have noted, the industrial revolution produced pernicious child labor, misery, unemployment, and starvation for the workers, at the same moment that it spawned a host of radical, utopian thinkers. One such thinker was Robert Owen. Swayed by socialistic-utopian ideas, Owen made drastic and progressive changes in labor conditions in his mill in Scotland. He sold goods to workers at cost, provided decent housing and education for their children, and promoted workers according to their personal conduct. Owen believed that modern machinery could produce enough wealth to wipe out poverty, if a modified form of communism could be established. He envisioned villages (from 500 to 2000 persons) that would grow, prosper, and unite with other villages until the entire planet would be one world village.

Others scoffed at his ideas, but Owen bought 30,000 acres of land in Harmony, Indiana to form an experimental community that would demonstrate the practicality of his plans. This enterprise failed in fewer than three years, and Owen returned to England to devote himself to a scheme for merging the English trade unions and cooperatives into a single political, social, and economic force. This scheme also failed to find a responsive audience. Despite these failures to achieve reform in his own time, Robert Owen is viewed as the theoretical father of modern British socialism.

The Pilgrims and the Puritans are the utopians best known to most of us, since the story of their search for a new life is a part of our cultural folklore. It is less widely known that nineteenth century America was an exceptionally fertile ground for utopian thought. The editor Horace Greeley, for example, became a popular champion of the emancipation of labor and the moving spirit behind a national association that included Emerson, Thoreau, and Hawthorne. The community that evolved from this group was the Brook Farm experiment conducted at West Roxbury, Massachusetts. Brook Farm provided free education and medical care to its members and established the unheard of maximum workday of only ten hours. In 1846, six years after its birth, the experiment failed.

The early American experiments with alternative societies were every bit as deviant and daring as their present-day counterparts. One way to capture the flavor of these early communes is to compare them on the basis of a single dimension; since modern America is still struggling to resolve the complicated issue of proper relations between the sexes, perhaps this is an appropriate single thread to follow.

The first true sex liberationists in our society were the nineteenth century Shakers and the Oneidans, who abandoned classic prescriptions for male-female relations and dared to define their role in new and unique ways. To anticipate somewhat, we shall see that women, who have never fared well in the long history of male-dominated civilization, did not do much better in the utopian social experiments in America.

THE SHAKERS

Mother Ann Lee, the illiterate daughter of an English blacksmith, joined the United Society of Believers as a consequence of her heavy burden of guilt about the early deaths of her four children. To Ann Lee, sexual desire seemed to be the source of her mental anguish, and one way to expiate her sins was to devote herself to the revivalist movement of James and Jane Wardley. This Quaker revivalist sect adhered to the belief that Christ's second coming would be in the form of a woman; Ann Lee, after reporting visions of a visit with Christ, was hailed as the Christ incarnate. In 1774, she founded a community, and by the time of the Civil War nearly 6000 people were living in Shaker settlements. Outsiders derided the Shakers' (or Shaking Quakers) emotional, gyrating form of worship and persecuted them for deviating from the "normal" way of life.

The Shaker creed included public confession of one's sins, celibacy, communal property, and withdrawal from the world. To the Shakers, God was bisexual; lust was the basis of all sin; the women were considered more sinful than men (Eve and the apple). Celibacy (for those who could manage it) was the path by which the spirit could conquer the flesh and prepare one for the coming millennium. The Shaker society was exceptionally strict about sexual congress. Contact of any sort between males and females was scrupulously limited; the sexes were segregated to such an extent that third persons were used to relay messages between men and women. The rules of relations between the sexes were severe: private union was forbidden, togetherness was to be brief, businesslike, and connected to duty. Touching one another, working together, giving presents, passing on the stairs, or mingling of any sort was strictly forbidden.

In addition to maintaining an austere appearance, women were expected to work at a trade and take care of housekeeping chores. In all, it was a separate—but unequal—arrangement. Shaker females were relatively freer than were women in the outside community, but their absolute freedom was minimal when compared to present-day standards.

THE ONEIDA COMMUNITY

The Oneida Community of Perfectionists was not as populous or well-known as were the Shakers, but they were even more controversial. John Humphrey Noyes, the leader of the group, was swept up in the religious fervor of the early nineteenth century and advocated the notion that the second coming of Christ had taken place long ago in 70 A.D. Noyes reasoned that man had already been redeemed from sin and no longer needed to be repentant. When he expounded this doctrine publicly, he was declared a heretic by the leaders of the traditional church. Faced with excommunication, he formed a communal society in which each convert not only relinquished all claim to property but abandoned "selfish" possessiveness of other persons.

Noyes and his band of followers established a system of "complex" marriage in which any member of the group could freely cohabit with any other. Any person could refuse an undesired sexual request, and females as well as males could take the initiative sexually. The young, at puberty, were indoctrinated in the ways of Oneidan sex practices and practical experience was provided by older members of the opposite sex. Young boys were paired with post-menopausal women to learn the self-control necessary to avoid unwanted pregnancies. When children were born, they were raised communally.

When the local townspeople heard of the nearby "free love" community, Noyes and his group were soon run out of town. The Oneida Community moved to New York State, struggled successfully, and enlarged the scope of its activities to include manufacturing and spoonmaking. But, the surrounding American society continued to harass the Oneidans, and they were eventually forced to abandon the practices of free love and joint marriage. Community ownership of property disappeared shortly thereafter, and, in 1881, the community formally came to an end.

It is abundantly apparent that what is currently called the sexual revolution is less unique and spectacular than most of us suppose. Women members of the Oneidan Community had to forego exclusive ties with men, other women, or with children since each person was to love all others equally. The collapse of the early attempts at communal life has been attributed to a variety of causes: too little advance preparation, too little capital, too little screening of the motives of the members, too little experience with the agricultural basis of community effort, too little preparation for conflict between personality and principle, too little readiness for the mismatch of reality and idealism, and too little recognition of the difficulties inherent in any social experiment surrounded by a larger, alien society.

today's communes

In 1966, there were approximately 100 "intentional communities" in the United States, founded and populated by religious fundamentalists, utopian socialists, and conscientious objectors. Today, as an outgrowth of the hippie movement, there are about 3000 communes, one-third of which are located in rural settings. According to Charles Reich, a total American Utopia has all but arrived; its insignia is evident everywhere in the dress, language, and gestures of young people. There is even a romantic and exotic quality in the names chosen for modern communes—Word of God, Family of Mystic Arts, Yellow Submarine, Magic Forest, Hog Farm, Himalayan Academy, City of Light, Greenfeel, or Drop City.

All of us have become superficially familiar with the nature of the communal movement since its more bizarre forms have been reported in the Sunday supplements of every major American newspaper. Establishment clothing manufacturers are mass producing "hippie clothes" (complete with phony patches) that imitate real-life communal dress, and television commercials have inundated us with communal newspeak. We have all been "wowed," "groovied," "heavied," and "right on'd" to death!

No two communes are exactly alike. Some are anarchistic way stations for drug-freaks who are running from purpose rather than searching for meaning in life. Some are "scientific communities based on information and approaches drawn from the behavioral sciences —Walden Two being one example. Other communes are radical, religious, or political communities seriously dedicated to a totally new

274

way of life; and some are sexually revolutionary in doctrine. Each pattern of communal life poses distinct and unique problems of group association, and each must brace itself for the probable consequences of seeking perfection in imperfect human beings. We cannot judge the success of failure of any commune solely in terms of its survival. Living in a commune may be a temporary, transient episode in an individual's life span; yet it may also be a vital educational experience, a crucial human encounter that raises the individual from a previously pointless existence.

The communal movement represents one of the most idealistic persuasions that the young have taken to heart in many decades. D. Fairfield visited communes across America and accurately described the basic ideals which the utopians have in common. According to Fairfield, these young people are choosing and creating an environment that reflects their own needs and the needs of others. They are interested in homemade food, individualized clothing, natural surroundings, and whole-person education. They want to return to the essentials of life through learning what one's needs really are, abandoning a dependence on material things and relocating a lost spiritual base. Getting back to the land is a way to combat alienation from the Earth, while freeing oneself from pollution and the concrete jungles of the cities.

Getting back to other human beings is another goal of the young utopians. They wish to eliminate the separateness, isolation, and loneliness fostered by modern society, and return to human cooperation. They are also involved in a search for the self—finding out who you are, what your potential is, and how to grow and develop as a sensitive human being. According to Fairfield, setting a social example is another important ideal, since it is believed that people learn by what others do, rather than by what they say. Further, these present-day utopians believe that destroying society is not an answer to the critical issues of the times. The avowed purposes of communal life can only be admired; but, in practice, we shall see that has often proved to be an imperfect Eden.

COMMUNES—THE WORD

The young are fascinated by the idea of communal living mainly because it is a great thing to do, and their elders are fascinated because they fear this very attractiveness of an alternative way of life might turn their children on. In response to both sets of needs, the communards and those who watch the communards have begun to write and publish.

The passionate literature of the young communards describes a unique version of the good life. One reviewer who reported on several recent works noted: "Their image of the good life is one of friends as family always gathered round, possessing and consuming as little as they need rather than as much as they can be induced to want; the communal household set amidst green fields and hills and valleys—a household always full of people putting out good vibes, brothers and sisters living harmoniously with nature, spending their time together working, playing, eating, drinking, smoking, loving, rapping, hanging out."

This amounts to a romanticized, idealized perspective on life with juvenile overtones. It is a sheltered society in which the young never assume significant or meaningful roles in the conduct of human affairs which reach beyond the gratifications of the immediate self. If time and development could be halted, such utopias would probably work; but it seems no society can mature if it is devoted solely to a search for identity among its members. From the current accounts of utopian experiments, it is painfully apparent that no magical solution has been found for the disturbing personal problems that inevitably accompany any human effort to live together. This becomes peculiarly bothersome when you find that living in a commune still depends upon the larger society for its very existence. Money from home, federal food stamps, and the hypocrisy of theft, commercial hucksterism, and exploitation of others are the poisonous roots of a very tender vine.

THE EVILS OF EDEN

One problem of the communal movement is posed by its psychological composition. As Philip Slater noted in his book *The Pursuit of Loneliness*, young people ironically form communes that create the same narrow, age-graded, class-homogeneous society in which the young themselves were formed and from which they fled in desperation. Any community which subtracts old people, children, white- and blue-collar workers, and all variety of both eccentric and conventional human types is no community at all—it is only a truncated social deformity that calls itself by another name.

The new dropouts are certainly idealistic, but they are also too naive and too cerebral to create a stable community. "Intellectuals" are not prize material from which to construct a stable community; they have a weakness for theorizing, a fondness for argument, and are prone to get lost in a jungle of verbiage. When the intellectual glibly pontificates about the nature of goodness, truth, and beauty, the cow goes unmilked and the hay crop rots in the rain. In some cases, even close-knit groups of radical intellectuals who have attained a unique mutal understanding have not managed the acid test of achieving stability in communal life.

276

Time is inexorable and children eventually grow up. The sociologist Bennett M. Berger and his research team are observing children in 36 California communes. From what has been reported thus far, one can predict that these children will certainly be an unpredictable breed of adults. In contrast to the traditional view, communards tend to treat children as human beings first and as children second. They are human beings worthy of love and respect but not necessarily worthy of continuous attention or total parental absorption. Since children are seen as having distinct personalities all their own, rearing the child is not a task for which the communard parent accepts credit or blame when the outcome is good or bad, happy or sad. Such an attitude may in some respects be a refreshing change from the tendency of a few traditional parents to "raise the children to please the neighbors."

The people we call "hippies" reject conventional definitions of an ideal adult. After all, they themselves have turned away from the models that society offers to seek new ways of finding the mature self. If they can teach their children the way of wonder, love, innocence, passion, and spontaneity, they may have reached their parental goal. Berger is concerned not only with observing the children but also with interviewing their parents and grandparents. Through this perspective of three generations, Berger will explore the possibility that the young "hippie" parents are simply "acting out" the basic values of their own parents, while preparing their offspring to go an additional step beyond past values.

The children of the communes are part of a family unit that typically consists of mother and child, with the father absent. The departed father is a "deserter" only in the classic sense of the term. The parents most often have agreed upon a philosophy of life in which man and woman stay together only as long as they can maintain a wholesome, creative, reciprocal affection. As they say: "When the vibes become bad, dull, or routine, it's time to split." If the male feels his first responsibility is to himself, then separation becomes a logical and natural event in the course of the parental "love" relationship. Perhaps, other commune males furnish fathering to all the communal children, thus replacing the personal attention of the biological father. Whatever the case, the communal movement is clearly engaged in a radical social experiment involving a new and innovative approach to producing a new species of adult.

BACK TO THE LAND

In one observer's experience, the typical life cycle of a commune involves a gathering of like-minded friends, a temporary experiment in cooperative living in an urban setting, transition to the countryside, breakup in one or two years, and then resettlement in a new location by a nucleus of those who are most committed. The notion of a return to the nurturing land fascinates white middle-class, urban born and bred young people, primarily because such a life diverges so greatly from everything they have ever known. Dissatisfied with urban life, they declare concrete, glass, and stainless steel the cause of their unhappiness.

When rural communes are formed, the initial attempts to "figure out farming" sometimes border on the ludicrous. I was appalled, for example, to witness two city-bred communards discuss for 20 minutes the proper method of mounting a rip-saw blade on a motor; the lumber was needed to construct housing before the first snows of winter. High idealism in the absence of technical know-how is expressed in the homily that "poets abound, but plumbers are scarce" in communal life. Farm labor is, at best, a hard, exhausting, unending—and boring—enterprise that demands more than a careful study of the Whole Earth Catalogue. Perhaps, young utopians contemplating a return to nature might be well advised to "kidnap an old farmer." For most of the young, true autonomy is not possible in their new way of life, since they have a continuing dependence on the larger social and are not prepared to make it on their own. The popular communal sentiment insists (or hopes) that straight America will collapse because of its inherent hypocrisy and corruptness. If this prediction were to come true, however, the existing communes would topple with the larger society, and the dream would be shattered. Mother Nature can be a harsh and implacable foe—one not easily subdued by the wistful dreams of the young and inexperienced.

THE RIPOFF

Some members of the new communal endeavor have severely compromised existing morality and euphemized their actions by describing theft as no more than a "revolutionary ripoff." By defining the larger society as evil, they justify their parasitic existence and reserve for themselves the right to steal. The difficulty is, of course, that the ripoff mentality is not a one-way street marked "the people versus the rest of society." The "ripoff"—in which one human being exploits another—is as ancient as time itself and has been a prime reason for the failure of the free stores, crash pads, co-ops, and other people-oriented endeavors of recent years. The free-loader, the bad check artist, and the one who uses others have always abandoned every revolutionary philosophy when the gratification of their personal pleasure is threatened.

278

The ripoff is most frequent and oppressive in those widely publicized communal efforts that gain national prominence. One deliberately anonymous commune gives this advice to those intent on launching a new communal effort: "Publicity is the death of a community. If you last for two years, you will find you have dozens of visitors a week, often coming in such crowds as to make you feel like an animal on display.... It would probably be a good idea to refrain from giving yourselves a name. You will be harder to talk about without a handle."

One problem lies in the variety of human beings who seek out this way of life. There are "wanderer-freaks" who move restlessly across the national landscape seeking easy answers to serious internal problems. There are the weekend and vacation pseudohippies who seek a "cool" experience before returning to the comfort and security of their affluent homes; and there are the aging hippies who hope to find for themselves the freedom of anarchistic communal life. Each may regard group living as the key to unresolved psychological problems, but the commune cannot be a second family in which young people can grow up all over again. It is difficult enough for most of us to manage a one-to-one relationship; it is improbable that more than two people can live together happily; and it may be impossible for more than three people to live together at all, unless they are very mature and very tolerant of the failings of others. Unfortunately, a great many members of the youth culture live with the delusion that they are beautiful people, when in reality they are sorry mirror images of their "square" parents. Still, the myth persists that anyone with long hair who shouts "off the pig" is a beautiful person. When the inevitably painful human conflicts of communal life develop, arbitration of hostilities is unlikely, since the issues may quickly be transformed into endless political dialogue. Abstract semantic conflicts obfuscate the real human problems that arise when people try to live together in harmony.

communal advice

Even when the communal movement is appraised with a sympathetic eye, one must concede there is a substantial risk that the idea will not match the reality. Fairfield, for example, feels he has learned a number of lessons in the last few years of involvement in American utopias. He concludes that the great utopian dream is meaningless if it is no more than an exercise to impress oneself and others that you are "current" or "with it." Dreams of an alternative way of life can, in fact, make the dreamer painfully miserable if the contrast with daily life is too extreme. Fairfield is convinced that experiencing a superior reality is not accomplished simply by massively altering the environment or people who surround you. It occurs when you grow as a person and growing involves exceptional psychological discomfort and risk taking. A better world demands better people, finding them takes time. It begins with the self and cannot be achieved by fruitlessly roaming the world in search for the "good" people unless you have first carefully examined the potential of the people around you.

There is hope that meaningful communal life can emerge from dedicated involvement with group psychological encounter techniques. This is, despite the conviction of the young, far from a new technique. As R. M. Kanter points out:

> Successful 19th-Century communities used a variety of group techniques, including confession, self-criticism, and mutual-criticism sessions, to solidify the group and deal with deviance and discontent before they became disruptive. The individual could bare his soul to the group, express his weaknesses, failings, doubts, problems, inner secrets. Disagreements between members could be discussed openly. These T-group-like sessions also showed that the content of each person's inner world was important to the community. . . . Possibly because they developed such strong group ties, successful 19th-Century groups stayed together in the face of outside persecution, financial shakiness, and natural disasters. Unsuccessful utopias of the past, on the other hand, did not tend to build these kinds of group relations.

The primary drawback to encounter, T-group, or group confessional techniques is that their effectiveness is limited by the training and experience of the leaders. A communal confessional group is particularly susceptible to erosion by unproductive, self-centered ego trips among its members. Instances in which Messianic leaders "play God" and try to instruct their followers in a unique view of life are equally misdirected.

The single reliable fact of communal living is that religious communities have survived much longer than have secular ones. The systematic, ideological regularity provided by religious belief seems to be the cement that can hold groups together. Robert Hine analyzed communal living in the Golden State and concluded: "The average life of religious colonies in California has been over twenty years, while that of secular colonies has been well under ten. Most analysts of utopian experiments ... have observed this discrepancy between the life spans of the sectarian and secular and, therefore, have concluded that religious fervor is one of the ingredients requisite to colony longevity."

Modern communes don't have a formal religious heritage from

which to draw strength or find purpose, but many of them are experimenting with new and mutant combinations of belief systems by borrowing bits and pieces from Christian communion, Indian lore, Buddhist mysticism, and drug-related occult and visionary experiences. Such original compilations of fragments of other bodies of thought are too new for social scientists to determine if exposure to time and the elements will weather and strengthen them or erode and destroy them.

It is impossible to reach conclusions about the modern communal movement before it has had its due time to succeed or fail. But, if history teaches us anything, it is that for most of the seekers of an alternative society, communal living will prove not to be the answer. It takes a special kind of person to survive the rigors of group living and it is reasonable to conclude that alternative ways of life are best begun and most probably achieved by dealing here and now with life's problems. Solutions will not be found in some exotic setting in a fabled elsewhere.

Whether the communal movement makes it or goes under, history may record that it was a much needed attempt at revolution. As Fairfield suggested: "Outer space is now the province of the scientists and the bureaucrats; inner space, the province of mind-expanding drugs, rock music and religion. Interpersonal space is the province of the commune movement."

encounter groups

In an article entitled "The Age of Encounter, " Eleanor Hoover has summed it up neatly: "If anyone exists who does not yet know that we are well into the throes of the Age of Encounter, he simply has not been listening." Hoover reports that more than six million people have by now participated in one or another kind of encounter experience; these persons include "lawyers, policemen, clergymen, housewives, addicts, businessmen, teachers, doctors—everyone." This sudden spate of group feeling has not escaped the notice of those who react emotionally, and sometimes violently, to the threat of change. As Hoover mentions: "The Birch Society has a serious campaign going against encounters as hand-maiden to sex education, the breakdown of the family and Communist brainwashing. Even professionals who admit to some of the positive aspects of encounters have called them a kind of fascism of the emotions that tyrannically imposes the will of the group on the individual." The very emotionality of the subject makes it an area which social scientists should take note of.

A quarter of a century ago, Kurt Lewin, the founder of Group Dynamica, and his colleagues at the Massachusetts Institute of Technology promoted the notion that training in human relations skills is vital to modern society. With their guidance, the first *T-groups* ("T" for "training") were held in Bethel, Maine, in 1947. In the initial groups, the participants were instructed to observe their interactions with others and to notice what was happening in the group process itself. It was hoped that as members of a group they would learn to understand their personal manner of functioning and become aware of their impact on others. The Bethel idea evolved into the now famous National Training Laboratories; at first, this enterprise focused on groups drawn from industry, but it was later expanded to include a variety of participants.

Another branch of the group movement was formed at about the same time by Carl Rogers and his associates. They assumed the task of designing a brief but intensive training course to prepare professionals to become effective personal counselors for G.I.'s returning from World War II. They abandoned the idea of traditional classroom lectures and experimented instead with intensive group experiences where trainees met with each other for several hours every day. The aim was for the trainees to understand themselves better and to become aware of personal attitudes that might be inappropriate in this new counseling relationship with veterans. The success of this effort, in terms of the meaningful experiences it provided the trainees, led to its continuing development and exploration in the years that followed.

In Carl Rogers' work with groups, the interaction is primarily verbal rather than sensory or physical. His groups are directed to

284

find their own guide lines for the experiences that they will share. When the "official" leader clearly indicates that he will not take responsibility for directing the group, they must succeed or fail on their own. Often, there is an initial period of hesitation, awkward silence, confusion, and frustration. The group then expresses mixed feelings about the nondirective process and may lash out against one another or against the group nonleader. This is usually followed by a spontaneous process of divulging personal revelations which, in turn, produces a working basis from which the group can organize itself.

The ideas of Rogers and Lewin caught the popular imagination, and the T-group has now become a way of life for some and a personal panacea for many others. As one writer states:

> The housewife who finds little intimacy in her relationship with her husband, the salesman who finds little that is fulfilling in his work, the student who remains puzzled by the empty promises of his university, all come flocking to the T-group seeking a sense of belonging and a momentary closeness to other human beings. Some come to experience a sense of potency and power, for at least they can hope to be effective in their group even if they cannot alter the course of history or change the direction of their nation. In a real sense, then, the T-group movement is like a new religion for these persons.

H. M. Ruitenbeek, author of *The New Group Therapies*, interprets modern enthusiasm for the encounter group experience in social and cultural terms. Ruitenbeek states that the very fact that we structure our personal needs in the form of encounter groups, traditional group therapy, nude therapy, or marathons indicates that people have lost the ability to find the satisfaction of all their needs in a spontaneous and nonstructured manner. The group idea is not new, of course. Members of communities have always felt the need to group together to exchange ideas or discuss problems. Today, however, this need is no longer being met through the ordinary channels of society, and we have been forced to establish artificial forms of human interaction. "It is as if in the field of psychology and in the nation the historical pendulum has swung away from concern with and for the individual to an obsessive pursuit and promotion of the group." New methods, techniques, and innovations are continuously being introduced to the encounter movement, and this element of novelty has an appeal to those who live by the dictum, "new is better."

Fewer than 20 years ago, group therapy was regarded as the dumping ground for untreatable patients. Yet, in a survey covering more than 200 practicing psychotherapists in New York City, it was found that nearly all of them were currently involved in some form of group therapy, and more patients than ever before were asking for the group experience. Since man defines himself through his social affiliations and since with urbanization and greatly enhanced mobility these affiliations have become increasingly more tenuous, psychotherapy has evolved into a discernibly new and different form.

the varieties of group encounter

Today's newest encounter group is often ancient history in an exceptionally brief time span. The following, then, can only be a sample of the various forms taken by the human potential movement in its recent history. The human potential movement has been described as a form of reeducation in which one learns to recognize, experience, and control one's emotions. The possibilities include: sensory awareness, expressive movement, environmental awareness, social-emotional expression, aesthetic appreciation, intellectual problem solving, creativity, ethical values, social sensitivity, social competence, endurance, and mystical experience. Carl Rogers has said it best: "In the rich, wild, new tapestry that is the intensive group experience one looks in vain for reliable or familiar designs. If such exist, we remain a good stout distance from discerning them. . . . It is a potent new cultural development, an exciting social invention, a truly grass roots movement that has grown out of personal, organizational and social need."

Centers such as Esalen have been established to foster human growth via experimental and experiential workshops, devoted primarily to exploration of the senses and feelings of man. These centers are communities which offer a collection of encounter experiences; the participant may choose exercises in body awareness (getting in touch with one's body) or sensory awareness (experiencing all one's basic perceptual and sensory events).

Even these famous centers have aged and lost some of their exotic charm, however. The late Fritz Perls, in his autobiography *In and Out of the Garbage Pail*, felt that the trend in group therapy should be to move away from group meetings to establish Gestalt kibbutzes.

> I now consider the piecemeal group meetings and workshops to be out-of-date. The marathon meetings are too forced. I propose now to conduct the following experiment. In the kibbutz, the split between seminarians and staff has to be abolished. All the work has to be done by the people coming to the kibbutz. Permanent staff: 1) the caretaker and developer, someone who has a background in building, etc. 2) the therapist. The main accent is on developing a community spirit and maturation. There will be a turnover every month of ten leaving and

ten arriving. There will be organic and vegetable farming and a craft shop for making simple furniture.

Perls tried to unite the idea of utopia with the concept of personal growth and development, but the experiment has not developed very far.

BIOENERGETICS

Classical psychoanalytic technique imposed one very definite taboo—patient and analyst may not touch each other. Bioenergetics reverses this formula by emphasizing bodily contact; and physical encounter is believed to be the way to liberate our bodies from the irrational, rigid controls we have imposed on them. This orientation to the body is aimed "at the creation of a new man—sensuous, immediate, playful—whose prime vocation will be enjoyment, not labor, and whose best work will be very much like play. Thus they [new group therapists] define the task of therapy as awakening the senses and returning erotic awareness to the total body.... Their goal is greater wonder and sensitivity rather than more rationality and control. 'Lose your mind and come to your senses,' said Fritz Perls."

People may be physically as well as emotionally uptight, since the body reflects the mind's psychological involvements and problems. If the mind-body interaction is a two-way street, it follows that changing the way the body moves or reacts will alter psychological hang-ups. The tone of one's voice, one's posture, facial expression, movement, and breathing may all be avenues to developing a strong mind in a tension-free, uninhibited, expressive body.

In their pursuit of a full awareness of the body, therapists have revived ancient oriental disciplines (Yoga, Zen awareness). They have reexplored the therapeutic features of drama and dance and have devised a new theory and technique of structural integration called *rolfing*. Rolfing starts with the assumption that one's attitudes and feelings are visible in posture and other patterns of bodily movement. Personality, in other words, is reflected in the musculature of the body. "The rolf practitioner uses fingers, elbow, clenched fist or open hand to exert the necessary kind and amount of force. And on occasion the tortured client is called upon to cooperate in the manipulative process by moving, stretching, or providing muscular resistance." This technique attempts (often painfully) to correct the "structural integration" of muscles and ligaments of the body; the aim is to free the body for maximal functioning at a minimal level of energy output. Blending the methods of the masseur and the chiropractor, the therapist twists, pushes, pulls, and pummels the body into a new relationship of parts and corrects the bad habits accumulated during childhood.

287

The emotional release provided by this physical working-over is felt to be superior to that achieved through verbal psychotherapy.

A psychodrama is a kind of improvised play in which the therapist is director and the group members are players. The play is acted out on a stage with the details of dialogue improvised as one's mood and emotions dictate. By acting in a variety of roles in the same play, participants are able to experience the emotions of each protagonist and gain insight into the complexity of every emotional exchange between people. Thus, for example, the patient might play the mother, then the father, and then the son in a family argument in order to sense how each person would feel. The Moreno Institute in New York is one place where such psychodramas have been conducted nightly for a substantial number of years.

In the guided fantasy movement (another approach related to psychodrama), the therapist or group leader steers a "daydreamer" through a public reverie to reveal that part of the self which is not usually made public or available to conscious inspection. Wishes, fears, dreams, and ambitions are made conscious and, with constructive help from an observing group, are dealt with in ways that are adjustive and creative rather than self-defeating.

MARATHON

These group encounters may employ any of a variety of techniques to achieve a forced emotional breakthrough in a brief but intense experience. The marathon has been described, disparagingly, as a boon for intelligent, well-educated neurotics who are barely able to manage their lives even with the help of tranquilizers and sleeping pills. Marathon groupers have also been described as persons who must experience some breakthrough in an immediate crisis if life is to continue to make sense. Since 1963, marathon groups have been designed to cut through usual psychological defenses hopefully to bring about permanent changes in one's response to the problems of living.

The method is straightforward and involves its own ten commandments. Everyone stays until the end; only the therapist is allowed to take naps; physical assault is forbidden but brutal frankness may be encouraged; no alcohol or drugs are allowed; openness and intimacy are the watch words; and behavior in the group itself (not prestige and status in the outside world) is the only matter of importance. When one person leaves his seat, somebody else may take it in order to keep the group constantly changing. Different marathons have different rules, of course, but each set of regulations is designed to keep personal contact intense and prolonged, beyond the capacity of most persons to "keep up a good front." The continuous, unremitting exposure to others focusing on the self is the force that is calculated to bring about change.

NUDE THERAPY

Nude therapy is a frontal assault on our habit of wrapping ourselves in deceptive clothing to keep from revealing the inner self to others. Although the element of nudity has titillated the public imagination, discarding one's clothing is often only one of many ways to sensory experience in such encounters. For example, in one of the groups run by Paul Bindrim, an early leader among psychologists in encounter, participants were told to bring with them things they enjoyed smelling, touching, tasting, and hearing. This would provide stimuli for the sensory saturation intended to induce a peak sensory and emotional experience.

The meaning of nudity to the individual has always varied with the culture and the era; as it happens, we are today modest about bodily areas of absolutely no concern to other societies now and in past ages. The human body and our feelings about it, however, are critical aspects of our view of the self and the world. "Our body images grow out of our subjective experiences with our bodies and how we organize these experiences. Basically, body image is our idea of how our own bodies appear to others. Often this image does not agree with the images of us that others hold: muscle builders may harbor weak body images, yet appear the epitome of virile masculinity."

The nude marathon involves 20 or more hours of uninterrupted, intimate, intensive human interaction. The very intensity of the experience pressures the participants to take off their social masks as well as their clothes and start communicating openly without playing games. In theory, the nude marathon group "moves from mistrust to trust, from polite acceptance to genuine critique, from peeping-Tomism to participation, from dependency to autonomy, from autocracy to democracy. During this trial by intimacy, one's roles, masks and pretenses tend to peel away layer by layer, revealing a more authentic self." Participants report a sense of pleasure in their new freedom to look at the bodies of others and to be looked at in return. This relief from guilty concern about one's body is said to bring greater group closeness. As one writer states:

> Many members reported a sense of going out, a traveling through and beyond the boundaries of ordinary experience and an approach to something variously called "God," "warm, white light," "birth," "the beauty of the whole thing," "the stream of the universe," "a white nirvana," and so on. These experiences seemed to have a lasting effect on the

post-marathon attitudes and behavior of many of the participants. An increased sense of inner worth, a sense of having completed a crucial psychic or spiritual cycle, helped some to a better understanding of their marriage partners.

THE GAMES OF ENCOUNTER

Each leader seems to have developed his own repertoire of games to be played in the group—hand-wrestling, bouncing in a blanket, touching, or group groping. For some leaders, verbal interactions are the key method—telling about oneself, describing the most distressful or shameful thing in one's life, or telling a secret never revealed before. For others, the techniques or "games" of encounter are designed to translate feelings into experience by dramatizing emotions that usually go unexpressed or unrealized. A few of these techniques can be reviewed here.

In "the blind walk," one person plays blind, deaf, or dumb, while his partner leads him on a journey using only body signals for communication. The partners then switch roles, each exploring how it feels to depend upon the other and to be unable to communicate through normal channels. In "the hold down," the group members render an individual helpless by forcibly pinning him to the ground. Feelings of powerlessness are dramatized for analysis by the group. "Breaking-in and breaking-out" is a technique whereby participants form a circle with arms locked; one person tries to enter or depart using a reasonable amount of force to do so. This game allows the social outcast or inhibited person to feel the emotions that go with an assertive or aggressive relationship to a social group.

"Falling" is an exercise in basic trust. One person falls backward with eyes closed, trusting his partner to catch him and prevent injury. A variation is falling from a height into the arms of a group of catchers. In the "group grope," all members close their eyes and feel one another in order to get acquainted and loosen inhibitions that might stand in the way of openly expressing one's emotions. In "eye to eye," without speaking, group participants violate the usual social rules by staring intently into one another's eyes, thereby confronting one another directly. The "do-it-yourself" encounter program of sensitivity training is designed for couples to use in the privacy of their own home in order to "enrich their marriage." It consists of long-playing records, lesson plans, and workbooks containing exercises that are designed to help couples express powerful feelings they may have withheld from one another.

For all the diversity of methods and techniques used, most sensitivity and encounter groups share a series of broad, general aims. For one, they aim at bringing people closer together psychologically and emotionally; the intended results are joy in living and loss of the feeling of aloneness and meaninglessness. Second, encounter groups try to open up previously sealed off areas of thought to permit deeper feelings toward others as well as a sense of personal freedom. A third aim is to increase one's sensitivity to the feelings and emotional reactions of others, thereby improving human communication and understanding. A fourth aim is to develop trust and openness in relating to others; promoting conditions that will allow this new learning to carry over to relationships outside the group is an additional goal.

These are admirable goals, but there is more than a little disagreement about the methods which should be used to achieve them. One observer suggested that some of the techniques of group therapy make use of inadequacy as a vehicle for hastening change—an example would be groups where one person is singled out and criticized openly by the rest of the participants. When the victim is exposed to such critical assault and stripped of his usual methods of warding off criticism, his practiced skills, justifications, or rationalizations for behavior may no longer work; the outcome can be a painful confrontation with one's inner sense of inadequacy. Creating targets can be tolerable, if it is sanctioned by all group members and each participant knows that he will eventually have his turn at being the victim. If the pain of realizing one's shortcomings can lead to new and healthier patterns of response, then group theorists believe it is worth the price.

reactions to the new groups

An outspoken critic of the human growth and encounter movement, William Blanchard, suggests that "ecstasy without agony is baloney." Blanchard insists growth centers have become pawns that are manipulated in a race for prestige.

> Growth centers compete with one another to sign up leaders with the most prestige and to billboard the most impressive-sounding seminar titles. There is a rush to invent new and different awareness-enhancing techniques. . . . William Schutz at Esalen began with a rather modest promise of "Joy" and followed it with "More Joy." Herbert Otto . . . introduced "Peak Joy." . . . Then the Elysium Institute at Los Angeles countered with "Cosmic Joy" and "Advanced Cosmic Joy," for which the "Awakening Seminar" is a prerequisite. Any day now we can anticipate a program on Super Advanced Cosmic Joy. Like the makers of Tide, Bold and Ivory soap, the seminarists are always improving their product.

The actual fact that such peak experiences of joy and heightened awareness are quite infrequent in human life is not a deterrent to the human-potential hucksters. They peddle this ultimate human experience as if it were a common commodity available to any and every enthusiastic participant. For Blanchard, at least, there are risks in thinking that great rewards come easily.

In the Puritan tradition, M. P. McNair has suggested that too much emphasis on human relations encourages people to feel sorry for themselves or makes it easier for them to abandon responsibility. To McNair, the cult of human relations is nothing but sloppy sentimentalism whereby the individual's psychological background is used as an excuse for failing to abide by social norms as do the rest of us. Others have reported on the critics of the human relations movement: "They say that the sensitivity training movement is 'spreading like a cancer through every state in the Union,' cajoling the innocent to 'pay for the privilege of being helped to feel like worms' and calculated to hasten 'the breakdown of all inhibitions, moral and physical.' The movement's aim, they say, it to 'turn people into manipulated zombies'." This somewhat sensationalized statement is only one of many accusations that have been leveled at America's new groupiness. Jane Howard, author of *Please Touch*, has listed some of the charges: it is said that groups are run by corrupt, mediocre charlatans; groups invade privacy by coercing the participants; groups foster sexual promiscuity; and groups do psychological damage. The group movement has been accused of evolving a ridiculous jargon, while its members have been labeled as anti-intellectual. The answer to these charges is simply that all of the accusations are true of some groups; not one is true of every group; and some are true of some of the groups some of the time. As one observer noted, sensitivity training is a human venture that arouses intense emotions in its participants, critics, and defenders; it is difficult to discuss the movement with any appreciable degree of detachment.

THE PROFESSIONALS

The professionals who are critical of the encounter movement say that a cult is spreading—a cult that preaches sensitivity, humanism, and openness while cloaking itself in an aura of pseudo-psychotherapy. Encounter groups operating in churches, public schools, universities, prisons, and corporations may be led by persons who have no professional credentials or training; their only qualification may be personal participation in other groups. Since encounter group members include a wide spectrum of persons, there may be a danger for those who need psychotherapy but do not realize it until a breakdown is experienced following group contact. Those who need help less acutely may feel somewhat better after the group encounter and therefore resist seeking expert assistance until problems are at a critical level.

Of course, some encounter leaders are trained psychotherapists who became disillusioned with one-to-one psychotherapy and believe some new means of growth is necessary for the times. Nevertheless, many of the new group therapists do not meet professional standards for clinical practice but are motivated by an urge to help people. For the latter kind of leader, charisma is a credential that assures success and a devoted following. These homemade therapists who defy tradition and ignore the conventions of therapy are the greatest distress to practitioners who have been through a long training and who insist some standards of therapeutic skill and insight must be maintained.

Charisma is beautiful when it emanates from extensive knowledge and penetrating insight; it can be ugly when it is no more than an ego trip. Human predators who rely upon a veneer of charm and awareness while feeding on the distress of others are not unknown in the encounter movement. The trained therapist who has wrestled with the difficult task of making proper appraisals is understandably distressed by the ease with which some of the new group leaders make final pronouncements about "other people's hang-ups."

Almost every form of psychological therapy operates on the fundamental premise that any lasting psychological change must affect the way an individual handles his fears and his unconscious problems. A man who usually avoids competition, for example, may break out of a circle in an encounter group and experience his feelings about competition. This will not lead him to change his behavior, however, if his avoidance of competition is rooted in the basic fear that he will be destroyed if he loses. Encounter groups ignore the Freudian notion of a timeless unconscious that is a repository of such fears, fantasies, and experiences stretching back to childhood. Indeed, it is difficult to believe that human psychology can be reduced to the one-dimensional stature some group therapists ascribe to it. Further, there is no evidence that the new groups can be a replacement for individual therapy. Psychological insight is not achieved easily or quickly, and any insight is only the beginning of a long process of application in a variety of situations. The new group therapies do not prepare the participants for this critical step in personal maturation. Feeling exhilaration and joy after having discovered something new and exciting is a worthwhile experience, but these are particularly fragile emotions that quickly dissipate once the members of the supportive group have dispersed.

It is also possible that this is professional sour grapes. Perhaps, the rapid growth of group therapy is occurring because individual psychotherapy by and large has not been effective with the new breed of patients. As one writer noted, they are "vague in their complaints about themselves and others, although they verbalize rather well; there is an air of discontent about them, a general malcontent with the way things are, they have little to fall back upon, their childhood memories are not necessarily traumatic or even very bad, but there is not too much they feel good about. They do function pretty well in their jobs and in the world at large, but they lack the touch of intimacy and warmth, which are the ingredients for plain happiness and satisfaction."

AFTER THE GROUP IS OVER

Traditional therapists and social commentators have naturally viewed the rapid expansion of the human potential movement with alarm. Psychiatrically oriented psychotherapists have had a firm hold on individual therapy for half a century, and it is distressing to them to lose this monopoly on human adjustment and happiness. The traditionalists are most bothered by the fact that the encounter groups have recently left the psychological laboratories to move into the outside world, and they have taken this bold step before calculating the cost of such a venture in human terms.

Traditionalists feel that the need for uniform standards of trainer development and preparation is obvious, if the public is to be able to discriminate between good and bad group theory and practice. They claim that this American movement was, at first, a learning experience with therapeutic side effects; it has now become a therapeutic experience with learning side effects. Most trainers are thought to be ethical, but the field of group therapy offers fertile soil for the growth of new and noxious therapeutic weeds.

Members of the therapeutic establishment insist that encounter groups have not yet perfected a fool-proof method. One investigation discovered that the casualty rate from group encounters may be as high as 10 percent—a casualty, in this instance, being a person who as a result of the group experience suffered "continued and persistent psychological distress." In this same investigation, the members of groups were better judges of possible psychological damage than were the group leaders. A prime variable in persistent psychological distress among group members proved to be the style of the group leader; among the 18 groups studied, 16 psychological casualties were traced to just four leaders.

These problem-producing leaders were described as aggressive stimulators who were intrusive, challenging, and antagonistic in their encounters. They were charismatic persons (in an authoritarian manner) who led high-risk groups in which an individual member could expect to bear the brunt of personal confrontation with the dynamic leader. In low-risk groups, leaders tended to be more loving and to create an accepting, trusting environment. It is important to note that the encounter group casualties originally came to the group

294

in an attempt to remedy a damaged self-concept. Seeking salvation, they may have been particularly vulnerable to a forceful leader who demanded more than the group members could possibly be expected to deliver. Casualties may also result from a peculiar meshing of unrealistic expectations among the members and a particular personality of the leader. They are casualties nevertheless and must be added into the balance when the assets and liabilities of the new group approach are tallied.

After a comprehensive review of the research literature, two investigators have concluded that evidence of the ability of T-groups to induce behavioral changes "back home" is convincing—but quite limited. The "research" is often no more than individual testimonials. As Carl Rogers reports, for example, in follow-up studies involving 481 persons three to six months after encounter-group experience, only two felt that the experience had been damaging or had changed their behavior in unacceptable ways. A moderate number felt the experience had made no perceptible change in their behavior; an additional small number felt their behavior had changed only temporarily; and the overwhelming majority felt the group had given them a deeply meaningful experience that continued to make a positive difference in their behavior. Other investigators have reported that, six months after participation in 24-hour marathon groups, students stated that the experience was a highly positive one that produced a greater awareness of inner feelings, increased openness and spontaneity, more honesty, greater trust in others, more self-confidence, and so on.

Different uses of the group method and appraisal of results have also been reported. One group of therapists attempted to relieve the rising friction between urban police forces and members of the black community, by conducting T-groups for 1400 policemen and an equal number of community members in Houston, Texas. It is hard to tell whether the project worked, but the Mayor's office did report a 70 percent drop in citizen complaints about police behavior for the seven-month period following the beginning of the program. There is a public consensus that it did indeed work, but 18 hours worth of discussion in each T-group could hardly be expected to perform miracles in long-term human relations.

We will not be able to predict alterations in real-life response, until we are able to state exactly how, and to what degree, each individual can be expected to change through T-group training; in other words, we will have to know the kinds of group experience in which change might be expected to occur or the kinds of persons most susceptible to change. Certainly, sensible theorists do not suggest that any method will affect all persons equally or be as effective in one "home situation" as another. We need to know which part of the process has an effect, what the nature of the effect is, and in which life situation the effect will be felt. T-groups need to be compared with other ways of influencing human beings. Before we can draw conclusions, we need to know the exact nature of the experience of the individual and the nature of his interaction with the group. We also need to explore the structure of T-groups, the time period, the setting, and the participants.

AND TOMORROW

Some observers believe that in the years ahead encounter groups and other techniques of the human potential movement will penetrate every aspect of our culture. Universities will give credit for growth experiences; businesses will use group techniques to improve decision making; and married couples, aware that marriage eventually becomes relatively lifeless, will form small groups with other couples to exchange views and to revitalize the marital relationship. According to some thinkers, the critical question for tomorrow may be the success with which the human potential movement can influence the massive governmental bureaucracy; the object would be to render it less exploitative and paternalistic and more concerned with the inner experience of individuals searching for the good life. Other prophets predict that in the decade ahead encounter leaders will require some form of certification; legal and ethical standards will be controlled and leaders will be licensed by the state. If the human potential movement proves to be more than a temporary fancy in social life, these will undoubtedly be accurate prophecies.

Until the encounter movement sorts itself out, there are some reasonable cautions one should observe—especially since the demand for group experience has grown at a rate that greatly exceeds the supply of trained, professional leaders. A group experience led and managed by an untrained person may provide a disastrous path to personal goals. E. L. Shostrum, in an article entitled "Group Therapy: Let the Buyer Beware," lists a series of "nevers" with regard to selecting a group experience. First, one should never respond to a newspaper ad for group experiences; second, never participate in a group of fewer than six persons; third, never join a group on impulse or as a fling; and, fourth, never join a group with close associates. Fifth, one should never be overimpressed by fancy settings or surroundings, and, sixth, never stay with a group that has a theoretical ax to grind. Finally, never participate in a group that does not have professional connections or credentials.

Group encounters do bring joy and that will remain the prime attraction. The professionals of tomorrow will feel more comfortable, however, when they know more about how this joy comes about, which after all will be all the better for spreading it to more people.

296

behavior control

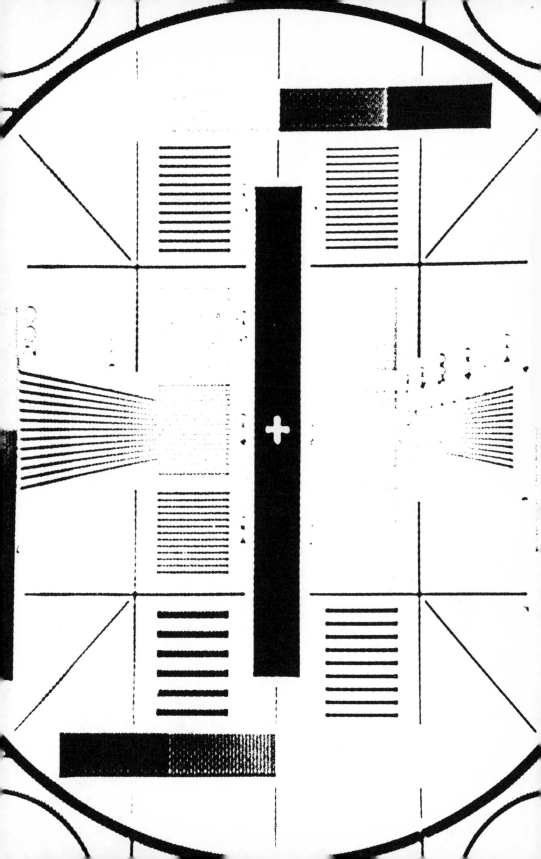

As other writers have also observed, John Watson's dynamism and his way with people took him to the forefront of American psychology when, in the years surrounding World War I, he founded behaviorism. John Watson also had a way with words. One of his much quoted statements is of particular interest:

> Give me a dozen healthy infants, well formed, and my own specified world to bring them up in and I'll guarantee to take any one at random and train him to become any type of specialist I might select—doctor, lawyer, artist, merchant-chief, and, yes, even beggerman and thief, regardless of his talents, penchants, tendencies, abilities, vocations, and race of his ancestors.

It was from this challenging statement, yet humble laboratory beginnings, that the social and psychological issue of behavior control was born in the modern world.

In itself, behavior control, or the ability to get others to do what you wish them to do, has been practiced throughout time. But in the past, obedience has been accomplished most often by force or some mixture of persuasion and education. Our modern anxiety is that much more precise and reliable means have been evolved to control people's actions, thoughts, and emotions. Moreover, as one observer stated, such control may come, "not by the will of tyrants but by the invitation of all of us, for we have been schooled to readiness for all these things and will demand their benign use regardless of their potential risk. The capacity for control will continuously grow, evolving from benevolence."

As long as there was open, unashamed tyranny, there was little need for subtlety in methods of coercing others. In ancient days, life was cheap and human freedom was a utopian dream rather than a functioning reality. As times changed, so did the methods of manipulating man. Physical means of influence gave way to a sophisticated set of psychological techniques by which to direct behavior. The least subtle of these psychological techniques is fear of punishment. The difficulty with the use of fear to control behavior is that it can only be administered after disobedient behavior has taken place. Consequently, it is an inefficient, time-consuming means of behavior control. Nonetheless, the fear of being deprived or punished has long been used to coerce people, since there are more ways to frighten people than to hurt them. Fear, moreover, can be enormously exaggerated in fantasy and can last a lifetime. As P. London suggested in his work, *Behavior Control*: "The host of fearsome possibilities includes not only the threat of every kind of physical punishment but the excrutiating mental pain of grief and shame as well, with their endless variants of embarrassment, loss of status, bereavement, and loneliness."

Carl Rogers, for one, despairs of the direction mankind seems to be taking. He notes that we have acquired the ability to shape the judgments that group members will make; we can predict who in the society will be delinquent; we know how to produce hallucinations and other abnormal reactions; and we can destroy a man's concept of himself and disintegrate his personality structure. If we can destroy man's self-confidence, making him dependent on others, then we can control exactly what he will or will not do.

We have known for many years that as social animals we can be influenced by the views and opinions of other members of the group, and we have learned that personality differences greatly determine the degree to which each of us can maintain independence from others. In experiments carried out by the researcher S. Crutchfield, for example, it was found that one-third of the responses in a group could be swayed by the majority opinion—even when that opinion was false. A few persons were swayed by the majority opinion on almost every item, but others were hardly influenced at all. When Crutchfield analyzed the personality characteristics of the members of these groups, he found that those who were swayed by the majority opinion were defensive, tended to put up a good front, had little understanding of themselves, were rigid, moralistic, and deeply respectful of authority. They were also somewhat anxious, guilty, suggestible, unable to tolerate ambiguity, lacking in self-confidence, vacillating, and easily confused under stress. The persons who resisted group pressure were, in contrast, active, effective, persuasive leaders in whom others felt confidence. They had confidence in themselves; they were nondefensive, expressive, unconventional, and adventurous.

Knowing that our opinions can be swayed and modified by subtle pressures from the group should—in theory—make it easy for us to resist such outside influences and agree only when we have thoughtfully chosen to do so. As we will soon see, this is hardly the case.

obedience

If there is a single study of behavioral control that has fascinated modern scientists, it is S. Milgram's work on obedience. Milgram was intrigued by the submissive, obedient manner in which millions of Jews in Nazi Germany walked passively to their own slaughter; he was also intrigued by the "obedience to orders" that allowed so many Germans to cooperate willingly in the mass genocide. Every society exacts a certain amount of obedience to social rules, but when this readiness to obey serves inhumane ends, it becomes worthy of psychological study. As Milgram recounts, from 1933 to 1945, "Gas chambers were built, death camps were guarded, daily quotas of corpses were produced with the same efficiency as the manufacture of appliances. These inhumane policies may have originated in the mind of a single person, but they could only be carried out on a massive scale if a very large number of persons obeyed orders."

William L. Shirer's book *The Rise and Fall of the Third Reich* describes the fatal experiments conducted by Dr. Sigmund Rascher on involuntary human guinea pigs. Rascher's investigations into the effects on human beings of sudden decompression at high altitudes or of freezing at subzero temperatures required the assistance of a great many persons, including medical doctors. At the infamous Dachau concentration camp, hundreds of prisoners were used for experiments in which they were left naked in the snow overnight or dumped into a tank of ice water until death intervened. The revulsive nature of such experiments was matched in horror only by the casual fashion with which other scientists greeted this inhuman misuse of science. In October 1942, in Nuremberg, 95 German scientists examined the results of these death experiments and not one protest was voiced. In all, 400 freezing experiments were performed on 300 helpless prisoners—undoubtedly the 400 most shameful pages in the history of science.

Milgram designed an experiment to study the nature of such destructive obedience. In his experiments, a subject was ordered to administer electric shocks to a victim. The victim was really a trained confederate who only pretended to receive the shock. The "shock machine" was marked with voltage levels ranging from 15 to 450 volts and labeled on a continuum from "Slight Shock" to "Danger: Severe Shock." The 40 subjects were told that the experiment was designed to study the effects of punishment on memory, and they were instructed to administer increasingly severe shocks to the "victim." Twenty-six of the 40 subjects obeyed the experimental commands completely and administered the most severe shocks possible. All of the subjects administered shocks up to the "Intense Shock" range, despite the victim's protests.

Given these findings, it is less difficult to understand how German concentration camps and medical experiments could have existed. If the situation justifies or sanctions obedience, men apparently will obey even when the behavior is hurtful to others. When the setting is appropriate, behavioral control can occur simply by instruction. This, however, is only one of many ways in which man may dominate his fellow man.

302

sensory deprivation

We take pride in having a firm grip on consciousness, in knowing who we are, and in being able to differentiate between fantasy and reality. Psychological researchers in recent decades, however, have suggested that each of us maintains no more than a finger-tip hold on that which makes us uniquely human. Our sense of self, our identity, and our ability to resist external pressure may only be as strong as the flimsy web of stimulation that surrounds our senses every waking moment. If we are deprived of this sensory stimulation, our grasp of reality may disintegrate, despite heroic efforts to resist.

Much confusion arises about the precise meaning of the term *sensory deprivation*, as is evident in the broad range of terms researchers and theorists have used. Researchers have referred to "sensory deprivation," "isolation," "perceptual isolation," "reduced sensory input," "interference with reality contact," and "deafferentation." This diversity of terms signifies both the complex quality of the area and our ignorance of the details of what is actually occurring. Since input from the environment can be reduced by cutting down on sensory stimulation, reducing the patterning of sensory stimuli—or simply by making the sensory environment monotonous—experimenters are certain to reach different conclusions about the critical feature of the environment or about what needs to be removed to achieve a state of sensory deprivation.

In Canada, three McGill University researchers confined subjects for several days and nights in a small, soundproofed room. Then subjects wore frosted goggles; their ears were covered by a sponge-rubber pillow containing speakers; and their hands and forearms were covered with cylinders. The outcome of this initial experiment was startling. The subjects shortly began to hallucinate; their ability to think clearly deteriorated; they were unable to concentrate; and a significant loss appeared in their performance on an intelligence test. Later experiments demonstrated that as little as one or two hours of sensory deprivation was enough to induce such hallucinations. These and a host of experiments that followed made it clear that patterns of sensory stimulation are a vital part of the individual's psychological life, and we are quickly disorganized mentally when our normal range of sensory input is diminished.

Typical of recent experiments is the work of J. H. Mendelson and his colleagues. Each of the 12 men who took part in the experiment was asked to lie on his back in a tank-type respirator (iron lung). The motor of the respirator ran constantly, producing a steady hum that drowned out other sounds in the room. The vents of the respirator were left open so that the experimental subject breathed for himself while in the tank, but his arms and legs were restrained by long cylinders. In this position he could see no part of his body—only the front of the tank, the blank white walls, and the ceiling of the room were visible. The experiment was scheduled to last 36 hours unless the subject asked to end it sooner. At the end of the experiment, each subject was interviewed about himself and about his feelings, fantasies, preoccupations, and experiences of time and space orientation during the experiment.

The research subjects used in most such perceptual isolation experiments have been drawn predominant from universities or other institutional settings; thus, it is sensible to assume that these persons are accustomed to urban living and its high level of stimulation and activity. It has been suspected for some time that disturbances of perception, cognition, and emotion more often take place when the experience of perceptual isolation is radically different from one's everyday level of stimulation. Thus, three investigators selected a group of young men reared on isolated, rural farms and matched them with a group of men brought up in an urban center. The experiment was conducted in Norway where it was possible to find subjects whose daily life was decidedly not stimulating—in other words, little contact with others, geographic isolation, long Norwegian winters, and so on. The experimental procedure consisted of having each subject lie quietly for five hours, with his eyes open, in a sound-insulated room in which light and noise levels were kept constant.

As the researchers predicted, the country boys (social isolated) displayed fewer and less intense disturbances in response to such isolation than did their urban counterparts. Those accustomed to isolation as a way of life did not "see moving figures or scenes," nor did they "hear voices or music." In contrast, the urban young men experienced hallucinatory body sensations and perceptual distortions (walls moving, colors changing intensity, objects changing size, and the like). During the experiment the social isolates thought about everyday experiences—such as the work they planned to do on the farm—while the young urban men found it impossible to concentrate or think coherently about anything. They, in fact, spent their time in an assortment of fantasies, daydreams, and confused reveries.

Psychological affects similar to those produced in experiments with sensory deprivation can be induced simply by using what psychologists call a *ganzfeld*. In the *ganzfeld*, the subject sits surrounded by a uniformly whitewashed visual field. Unable to find a spot on which to focus, experimental subjects soon feel as if they are swimming in a fog; they report dizziness, loss of coordination, fatigue, and, at times, hallucinations. Obviously, it takes very little alteration of our environment to loosen the controls over our psychological capacities. Scattered reports have suggested that, under conditions of sensory deprivation, our attitudes, beliefs, opinions, and convictions can be altered to suit the experimenter. If continued research verifies this possibility, we may have entered a whole new era of behavior control.

brainwashing

Some years ago E. Hunter coined the term *brainwashing* as a loose translation of the Chinese term for a "cleansing of the mind"—the process by which one is reeducated and old beliefs are replaced by the new. "Thought reform" programs for intellectuals were conducted in institutions known as "revolutionary colleges" just after the communist takeover of China. Observers of this phenomenon described it as *"an induced religious conversion, as well as a coercive form of psychotherapy,"* or as a "coercive persuasion" to control men's minds.

When men publicly confess their previous errors of dogma, doctrine, and belief, the usual public response is to assume they have been drugged or exposed to special psychological methods of producing conforming behavior. But, as investigators have demonstrated, it requires much less than that to shake a man's belief in the principles he has long lived by. Brainwashing first became a household word in 1953 during the Korean war, when we learned that some Americans had collaborated with the Chinese Communists, and that 21 "turncoats" refused repatriation to the United States. This number of men should seem miniscule when compared with the great many prisoners captured in that war, but our citizenry nevertheless found it incredible to acknowledge that loyal Americans could voluntarily turn their backs on democratic society. Thus, the concept of brainwashing was invented to comfort us, since it smacked of coercion and torture and allowed us to keep faith in the American way.

It was not long before behavioral scientists began to explore the issue of "brainwashing." Most of what we know of the process stems from interviews with the American prisoners who were repatriated from Chinese prisons after the great prisoner exchange of 1953. Civilians released from Chinese prisons were also studied. The Chinese did not torture their prisoners but used more sophisticated psychological mechanisms to achieve their ends—repetition being one example. They patiently repeated charges against the prisoners and demands for confessions over and over and over and over again, to erode the prisoner's resistance. The demands for confessions were paced, beginning with innocuous trivial points, until the habit of responding was established. Then the Chinese moved to more important commitments. Prisoners were not allowed to remain passive while this was taking place; they were required to respond in written or verbal form, and they had to copy statements, engage in group discussions, make public confessions, or participate in public self-criticism. When correct responses were made, reward immediately followed; incorrect responses were met with punishment, deprivation, or threat. For the prisoner, living in the prison camp became a tricky problem in survival. If he could solve the problem, he lived; if he failed to find the answer, he died. For the Chinese, this was a justifiable program of reform and rehabilitation of international criminals.

Conversion to communist thought reportedly involved three steps: unfreezing, changing, and refreezing. Thus, the individual must be induced to have doubts about the ideology he has previously subscribed to; he must then be helped to see the merits of a new philosophy; and, finally this new position must be consolidated and regarded as congenial. In all, "brainwashing" works—but not very well and not for many persons. In psychological terms, there seems to be a definite formula for producing conformity to a new set of beliefs and behaviors.

> Manage to arouse a need or needs that are important to the individual or the group. Offer a goal which is appropriate to the need or needs. Make sure that Conformity is instrumental to the achievement of the goal and that the goal is as large and as certain as possible.... Do everything possible to see that the individual has little or no confidence in his own position. Do everything possible to make the norm which you set appear highly valued and attractive. Set it at a level not too far initially from the starting point of the individual or group, and move it gradually toward the behavior you wish to produce. Be absolutely certain you know what you want and that you are willing to pay an enormous price in human quality, for whether the individual or the group is aware of it or not, the result will be CONFORMITY.

This theoretical prescription has a very practical application in political matters: "If you can isolate an individual from his normal contacts with others, remove him from the usual social supports for the attitudes he holds, you have him one step on the road toward adopting the position you advocate. Every dictator worth his salt quickly seeks to take absolute control of the communications media in his society; if he can isolate the entire society and feed his own message into it he has already won much of the battle over most of the people."

From a variety of clinical reports, it seems apparent that in American prisons we reconstruct some of the conditions of brainwashing when we place prisoners in solitary confinement ("the hole") for extended periods of time. Prisoners so confined may be driven to tense pacing of the cell, yelling, and noisemaking until they exhaust themselves and regress to a withdrawn, dissociated state. The prisoner escapes into inner fantasies, detaches himself from his surroundings, and must be roused to reenter the world of reality.

When an individual feels he is no longer able to influence or control his life situation, it may affect his chances for survival. One investigator reviewed the consequences of isolation from fellow human beings and noted that most shipwrecked sailors die within three days even though they are capable of surviving hunger, thirst, and exposure for much longer periods. The assumption has always been that these marooned men simply give up hope and perish. Bettelheim has confirmed the idea that the hope of rescue makes the difference in survival; he has noted that a feeling of helplessness among concentration camp prisoners in Germany signalled the probable end of their lives—not at the hands of prison guards—but simply by "turning their face to the wall" and ceasing to exist.

Brainwashing or similar situations are not merely ancient history. Brainwashing is a continuing part of the modern involvement with behavior control. Dr. James McConnell, for example, has stated: "Somehow we've got to learn how to *force* people to love one another, to *force* them to want to behave properly. I speak of psychological force." Pursuing this line of thought, McConnell insists that there are only two means of educating people psychologically—reward them for doing the right thing, or punish them for doing the wrong thing. Thus, McConnell recommends positive brainwashing for criminals and foresees the day when the worst criminal can be converted "into a decent, respectable citizen in a matter of a few months—or perhaps even less time than that." The remedy, however, is drastic. McConnell's final statement may be prophetic; as he stated: "Today's behavioral psychologists are the architects and engineers of the Brave New World." Let us hope that brainwashing will not be revived in the search for methods of behavior control. On second thought, however, even brainwashing might be better than electrical shock to those who cannot behave.

esb

Behavior control by electrical stimulation of the brain (ESB) is the newest wrinkle in the scientific world. When exceedingly fine wire electrodes are inserted into specific areas of the animal or human brain, messages can be sent to the brain (in the form of electric shock) and predictable behavior can be obtained. Perhaps the most dramatic demonstration of this form of behavior control was a famed "bullfight" conducted by the physiologist Joe Delgado. After implanting electrodes in a bull's brain, Delgado used a remote signal transmitter to stop the bull dead in its tracks. When the bull charged Delgado in the ring, he pushed a button sending an electric shock to the bull's brain; when this happened, the bull lost interest in the charge and abruptly stopped.

A host of other behavioral consequences have been produced with ESB in lower animals. Rats, cats, and monkeys have had their behavior patterns turned on and off like a light switch. "Brain stimulation has been used to make animals docile or savage, alert or lethargic, dominant or submissive, and obese or emaciated. With brain stimulation rats have been known to press a lever up to 7000 times an hour to get an intercranial electric jolt; female animals have undertaken male sexual behavior (one female rat tried to mount her male partner unsuccessfully for eight weeks!); and male animals have developed an unquenchable sexual appetite (copulating with their partners as long as stimulation continued)."

Electrodes have been implanted in the human brain and have revealed not only that such pleasure centers exist in man but also that in certain parts of the surface of man's brain electrical stimulation can reproduce memories. One investigator described this phenomenon "as though a wire recorder, or strip of cinematographic film with sound track, had been set in motion within the brain. The sights and sounds, and the thoughts, of a former day pass through the man's mind again." There is a difference, however, between the reactions of human beings and the reactions of animals to electrical brain stimulation. While the lower animals respond in a rigid, limited way, man is still able to control some of his actions and to interpret and modify his response to electric shock. He does not become an electrified automaton.

Arthur C. Clarke suggested that one day artificial memories could be fed into the brain by electrical means. Indeed, it is a small stretch of the imagination to envision people in the future wearing self-stimulating electrodes. These electrodes might "render the wearer sexually potent at any time; . . . put him to sleep or keep him awake, according to his need; . . . curb his appetite if he wanted to lose weight; . . . relieve him of pain; . . . give him courage when he was fearful; or render him tranquil when he was enraged." As our technological capacities advance, the ability to control behavior by electrical means may break through existing limits, but human behavior control in the near future is liable to spring from much more prosaic roots.

the ethics of control

Social scientists and members of the society at large must now decide upon the ethical issue of manipulating the behavior of others. Social scientists have recently begun to debate vigorously about the propriety of managing the lives of others. Those scientists who are against any form of behavior control have occupied an existentialist-humanistic position; according to this position, it is immoral to control another person's behavior, principally because control is dehumanizing. Whenever an individual is deprived of his right to make choices, he becomes a thing, a unit, a number—and not a person. Human beings should not be coerced to comply with the wishes of another, nor should they be seduced into agreeing to this coercion for their own good. Ideally, they should be free to decide for themselves how life should be lived.

In his book, *Beyond Freedom and Dignity*, B. F. Skinner argues the opposite point of view; Skinner contends that man must finally surrender his individual rights in order to accomplish a drastic redesign of his culture. To Skinner, this redesign is essential to man's survival; thus, he proposes an all-pervasive institutional system of behavioral controls, designed to reinforce altruistic behavior and eliminate undesirable or selfish behavior. In Skinner's world, man will stop polluting, over-populating, rioting, and making war—not because he has learned that the results will be disastrous—but because he has been conditioned to do whatever serves the best interests of the group.

From this behavioral scientist's viewpoint, control is not an issue since all human actions follow laws, rules, and patterns and are, in that sense, controlled. Behavior control techniques merely replace the so-called normal influence of nature and society, which may include parents, teachers, and TV programs. Man responds in consistent ways to his environment. The question is, however: should man be controlled by the erratic forces of nature or by man himself? The "man" who would control others may be one of a number of technical specialists such as therapists, priests, police, or teachers.

These messages may be startling to some, but they are not really surprising to those who have read Skinner's *Walden Two* or followed the development of his thought over the last several decades. In 1955, for example, Skinner spoke of freedom and the control of men; at that time, he stated that behavior technology ought to aim at making men happy, informed, skillful, well-behaved, and productive. Even then Skinner was convinced that democracy would not be the final form of government which man was likely to evolve. Then, as now, he felt our Western culture might die and be replaced, perhaps by the more disciplined cultures of the Soviet Union or China. If that happens, Western man will lose the only form of immortality he can hope for—the survival of his way of life.

The question for Skinner is whether we will rely on accidents in our cultural evolution or whether we will design and construct an environment suitable for the man of tomorrow. Skinner contends that our behavior today is already controlled in a multitude of ways over which we have no control, and it will take a conscious effort to replace these. As Skinner insists, we immunize ourselves against disease and do not rely on the vagaries of accidental immunization; so, too, we must immunize ourselves against externally applied control by others.

The field of psychotherapy has seen many direct applications of the principles of behavior control. In the words of one writer, psychotherapy differs from brainwashing, however, primarily in the patient's implied consent to this kind of manipulation.

BEHAVIOR THERAPY

Behavioral modification and *behavioral therapy* have become fighting words among present-day theorists of different persuasions; *behaviorism*, however, is a term which is easily a quarter of a century old. In 1949, P. Fuller reported attempts to teach a "vegetable human organism" a simple response. The hospitalized 18-year-old patient could not walk or talk; he lay flat on his back in bed and was unable even to chew his food. Fuller began by depriving the patient of food for 15 hours, and then, whenever he raised his right arm, a sugar-milk solution was administered orally by syringe. Even in this remarkably deteriorated conditon, the patient began to raise his right arm to be rewarded with food. In a recent case in England, A. Goorney used behavior modification to cure a 37-year-old man of compulsive gambling. The treatment required the administration of 675 electric shocks to the patient's upper arms during nine days of therapy; but the outcome a year later seemed worth it, since the patient's 13-year gambling habit had disappeared and his life seemed to be on the upgrade.

Behavior therapy is a group of treatment techniques based on theories of learning, which have as a goal the modification of problem behaviors rather than the achievement of complicated personality change. The different techniques employed may include modeling, operant conditioning, or complex "social system" approaches, plus counterconditioning, reciprocal inhibition, positive reconditioning, and experimental extinction. When the efforts of behavior therapists are observed by therapists of other persuasions, the conclusions are not always positive. Four researchers who observed behavioral therapists at work concluded that there has been an undesired broadening of the kinds of cases behavioral therapists are asked to treat and this fact has produced some strain as well as a decreased rate of "cures."

These researchers reported that patients were subjected to more than a little indoctrination, teaching, and exhortation in attempts to enhance patient motivation and provide a rationale for treatment. The observers also noted that there were more appointments per week

310

and that treatment was extending as long as a year, despite the increased frequency with which the patient was being seen.

An even more significant comment on the evolution of behavior therapy is the subtle alteration in the claims which enthusiasts have made over the years. The percentage of cures has steadily declined from 90 percent, to 80 percent, to 70 percent, and it looks like the future holds an even more realistic appraisal of this method's effectiveness. The critics of behavioral therapy insist it is dangerous to proceed recklessly with a form of therapy that may be based on faulty assumptions and an oversimplified theory. British psychologist H. J. Eysenck's reply to such charges is representative of the conflict that exists in the field today: "Take a group of heroin addicts, knowing that if they cannot be cured, they will be dead within five years. Knowing that nothing else is likely to work, should we refrain from administering aversion therapy, which seems to work, because we do not know all the complexities of human misery?"

Some commentators see the growth of behavior therapy as an indicator of the direction our social processes and cultural developments are taking. According to one critic, "Behaviorism has nothing at its core that prevents its practitioners from becoming behavior controllers at the service of whatever groups happen to have power in the society. If this sounds too extreme another point seems inescapable: Behavior therapy is one of the therapeutic approaches most inclined to confuse mental health with conformity to social standards." Indeed, if the lessons of behavior therapy are eventually applied to social groups such as states or nations, we may all live in a controlled tomorrow.

A CONTROLLED TOMORROW

In their book *Requiem for Democracy*, L. M. Andrews and M. Karlins look to the end of the road of behavior control. What they see is a "psytocracy, a society where all things, including people 'things,' are subject to careful and precise technical manipulation. In order to secure the success of long-range social planning, individual variability is restricted to predictable and manageable channels. A psytocracy is a form of tyranny, but not in the classical sense of the word. The slaves and the masters are indistinguishable. Each person is so conditioned to social norms and values that he eagerly performs whatever the social machine demands." In such a system we would have to be passive, surrender autonomy to the society as a whole, and be happy choosing among various programmed alternative patterns of how to live. This is a vision of man "hapless, helpless, hopeless," and estranged and dehumanized to the point of alienation—a familiar vision of the apocalypse. When man becomes uncertain and lost, when he loses touch with his soul and is faced with a crumbling religion, he may seek to salvage what little dignity remains by handing control of his life to those whom he feels are wiser. In this instance "those who are wiser" might be computers free from human error and able to become the new electronic deity. There does seem some hope, however. "If each man sees himself as nothing more than a simple reflex organism—a dim, flickering light in the universal pinball machine—then a psytocracy is inevitable. If, however, the potential of modern man has been underestimated—if he has the potential to be free—then there is hope."

In fairness we must underscore the positive outcomes of man's control over behavior. It was recently suggested, for example, that it might be possible to develop a peace pill. Kenneth Clark, president of the American Psychological Association, dropped a bombshell at an APA convention when he suggested this startling cure for international aggression—chemical behavioral control. Sensing that the survival or extinction of human civilization has come to rest in the infirm hands of a few planetary leaders, Clark called for an imperative new world that will include psychotechnical medication to curb aggressive behavior and channel the energy of personal power drives into constructive paths. This course of action is not intended to produce a nation of drugged robots. Rather, it is designed to enhance the positive qualities of our culture in an affirmative and humane fashion and end the trial-and-error approach to social policy. For Clark, the behavioral sciences have become the critical force for human survival. As long as man owns nuclear weapons the planet is not safe, and all of us are at the mercy of the psychology of a few leaders. The problem is that wars are regularly initiated by seemingly rational men who believe they are protecting mankind's welfare rather than contributing to its destruction. Nonetheless, a peace pill is a far-fetched possibility.

The trouble with using psychopharmacologic agents to control the mind is that they are not at all reliable. Some drugs may produce startling improvements that seem to be complete remissions from symptoms in some persons. However, there is usually a larger proportion of patients in whom only a little change in the desired direction is produced, and there is always an additional group of patients (as many as 20 or 30 percent) who are unchanged or made worse. We simply cannot predict which patients will respond in which ways. Thus, a peace pill is a fantasy used to underscore the critical need for controlling the leaders of the human race in the interests of the welfare of all the citizens of the world. Even though we may never find a pill, we must search for some way to control some parts of human behavior.

The debate between the humanists and the behaviorists, which has become increasingly more vigorous, was begun by Carl Rogers and B. F. Skinner. In 1956, the humanist Rogers and the behaviorist Skinner outlined distinct courses which the users of psychological knowledge might follow. Skinner stated: "What is needed is a new conception of human behavior which is compatible with the implications of a scientific analysis. All men control and are controlled. The question of government in the broadest possible sense is not how freedom is to be preserved but what kinds of control are to be used and to what ends." In rebuttal, Rogers suggested: "If this line of reasoning is correct, it appears that some form of *Walden Two* or of *1984* (and at a deep philosophic level they seem indistinguishable) is coming. The fact that it would surely arrive piecemeal, rather than all at once, does not greatly change the fundamental issues. In any event, as Skinner has indicated in his writings, we would then look back upon the concepts of human freedom, the capacity for choice, the responsibility for choice, and the worth of the human individual as historical curiosities which once existed by cultural accident as values in a prescientific civilization."

In this memorable intellectual exchange the broad lines of ethical discussion were drawn, but the urgency of the issues has become increasingly evident as psychological scientific knowhow brings us closer to the moment when man can fully control his fellow man. As the issue of behavior control ceases to become an academic problem and invades the daily life of each of us, choices must be made. The choices available now and tomorrow were beautifully delineated by Carl Rogers.

> We can choose to use our growing knowledge to enslave people in ways never dreamed of before, depersonalizing them, controlling them by means so carefully selected that they will perhaps never be aware of their loss of personhood. We can choose to utilize our scientific knowledge to make men happy, well-behaved, and productive.... Or at the other end of the spectrum of choice we can choose to use the behavioral sciences in ways which will free, not control; which will bring about constructive variability, not conformity; which will develop creativity, not contentment; which will facilitate each person in his self-directed process of becoming; which will aid individuals, groups, and even the concept of science to become self-transcending in freshly adaptive ways of meeting life and its problems.

Amen.

the quality of life

In the last quarter century, America has achieved an incredible degree of dynamic change and material growth. We take for granted a standard of living that would have been considered utopian 25 years ago, and from a nation of 142 million persons in 1946 we have become more than 207 million and may well number in excess of 300 million by the year 2000. While our population was increasing by 46 percent, productivity jumped 138 percent; as a consequence, more of everything is available today. We are better paid, better fed, better housed, and better supplied with the niceties and luxuries of life than ever before in history.

We have made materialistic history. Our buying power has increased 77 percent; 100 percent more of us own houses; and almost all of the homes with electricity have a TV set. Forty percent of us, in fact, are the proud possessors of both a color and a noncolor set. The list of readily available appliances is endless—refrigerators, washing machines, clothes dryers, home freezers, air conditioners, toasters, infra-red ovens, trash mashers, and automatic garage door openers. But, our love affair with the automobile is truly spectacular. Twenty-five years ago fewer than half of the American families owned a car; today the figure is about 80 percent. We make more, spend more, and save more than we did in 1946. We carry more life, hospitalization, and accident insurance and enjoy greater social security than ever before.

In the last 25 years, life has changed most distinctly in two areas—education and leisure. We have increased the numbers of college goers by 304 percent and raised the number who receive advanced degrees by more than a 1000 percent. We have lengthened by nearly 200 percent the number of weeks of vacation we take every year, and, as a consequence, visits to our national parks have increased by nearly 1000 percent. In the jet age, travel abroad has expanded unbelievably, and we regard as commonplace today what the citizen of 1946 would surely have deemed the ultimate in affluence and luxury.

These changes in the American way of life have had a price, however, and it is likely the cost will escalate even more in the years ahead. If the average working time is reduced in the future, we will have to learn to fill the void with other activities. We may decide to devote more time to narcissistic, self-centered activities such as plastic surgery, physical culture, or even cosmetic psychiatry, since the image we project to others may become unduly important. We may indulge in a frantic pursuit of forms of self-development guaranteed to make us unique in an increasingly conforming world.

Despite the apparent freedom leisure time will afford us, we may experience an even greater sense of helplessness in our attempts to establish a meaningful, personal relationship to government or industry. If the national bueaucracy expands proportionately, social power will be concentrated in the hands of fewer and fewer people, and much of our leisure may be devoted to coping with the distant social apparatus that insists on governing us.

the symptoms of social discord

For the very young the quality of life is viewed against the backdrop of a brief past and a largely unknown future. For their elders, the quality of life is judged by comparing the present with the past and with bygone hopes for what life might become. Judged from any perspective, we are experiencing widespread doubts that our present direction holds even a modest promise of fulfilling our needs. The evidence points to a disturbing conclusion: as a nation we are richer; as a people we are unhappy. Before long our teen-agers will become the young married, and, despite their denials, most of them will adapt to the competitive, materialistic culture as comfortably as did the generations before them. Everyone agrees material objects do not bring happiness, but we have yet to reach the saturation point of consumption.

Erich Fromm, who has seen a specter in our midst, made a chilling prediction of what may happen to American society: "It is a new specter: a completely mechanized society, devoted to maximal material output and consumption, directed by computers; and in this social process, man himself is being transformed into a part of the total machine, well fed and entertained, yet passive, unalive, and with little feeling. With the victory of the new society, individualism and privacy will have disappeared; feelings toward others will be engineered by psychological conditioning and other devices, or drugs." Fromm's view of the potential quality of American life may be excessively pessimistic, but we cannot disregard the substantial increase in the symptoms of severe discord in our social life.

OUR PARANOID SOCIETY

The suspiciousness, hypersensitivity to criticism, hostility, or feelings of persecution that are typical of paranoid persons may have become the norm for our society. To the psychotherapist, paranoia is a delusional way of thinking—a view of life that allows the individual to rid himself of intolerable personal impulses by unconsciously attributing them to other persons, thus denying their existence within him. Most of us, for example, react in a paranoid fashion if we are exposed to exceptional tension or unusual personal catastrophe. That is, we become suspicious, misinterpret the motives and intentions of others, become hostile, and react aggressively or violently to imagined dangers. The suspicious person not only mistrusts the motives of others,

317

but he also actively tries to confirm his perceptions of the true state of affairs. He will devote himself to assembling incontrovertible proof of the plot which he believes a mysterious "they" have launched against him. The characteristics of paranoid persons would be of no concern to us here if those so afflicted were committed to institutions to be cared for. The problem is that many paranoid personalities are at large in the community reacting to the fancied plots of an imagined foe.

One may reasonably argue that the level of "normal" social paranoia has increased in response to the stresses and strains fostered by our modern society. Thus, the college students of today are less trustful of the establishment and its social institutions than at any time in the past. A report on the views of incoming freshmen at Peabody University from 1954 to 1968 reveals a significant decline in trust over these years. Trust (the extent to which people are seen as moral, honest, or reliable) diminished in relation to the establishment (national and international politics, the judiciary, the mass media) and in relation to the general society (the hypocrisy, self-seeking, and competitive character of people). Certainly, the young are more suspicious, hostile, aggressive, and mistrusting of the motives of their elders than were other generations, and these are the young people who will inherit the earth.

The disenchantment of the young is probably the most damning indictment of the quality of life today. As one critic observed: "The young pursue life-styles that mock tradition in dress, sex, manners and morals. More profoundly, perhaps, the young are pointing to gross inadequacies in the American dream of justice, equality and opportunity and to the dark side of the national history. Many of the young are thoroughly pessimistic, even cynical, about the future ... social conflict and the drive for change are generating culture shock. It is unlikely that the American ethos as we know it will survive intact." Indeed, young people's concern about justice and happiness has made us reconsider the path America has been blindly following.

THE ARCHITECTURE OF FEAR

When America was a land of vast, unexplored frontiers, an endless wilderness was open to those who found life oppressive. Today, the frontiers have vanished but the typically American impulse to "cut and run" when life becomes difficult remains with us. The problem is that there are fewer places to run to.

Even in our Promised Land—the Golden State of California—nearly one-third of the residents insist they would rather live somewhere else. This restless disillusion is made all the more poignant when we consider that an estimated 1.5 million persons have migrated to California since 1963 in search of a better life. Now half of these persons are convinced that the joys of life are to be found elsewhere. The 30-year-old California dream was crushed by its own weight, when 20 million happiness seekers crowded together, each hoping the other knew the answer to the meaning of life.

Today, the number of Americans migrating to other countries is on the increase. An estimated 40,000 persons leave our shores each year with no plans to return. More than half of them go to Canada, which now welcomes twice as many emigrants from the United States as it did ten years ago; the others move principally to Israel, Australia, and Britain. Moreover, those abandoning the American dream are not the disaffected young. Today's expatriates are in their twenties or thirties, and they are professionals or highly skilled technicians.

More and more of us run away each year, and those who stay behind have developed a "stockade mentality." The most starkly visible evidence of decline in the quality of American life is to be found in the inner city. You can see it everywhere; steel gates have replaced doors; Plexiglas barriers have replaced the open counter; concrete walls appear everywhere. It is a world of fences, guards, alarms, and barricades. Our central business districts empty quickly at nightfall, and we run to the suburbs leaving the elderly and the poor behind as hostages of the inner city. We have evolved an architecture of fear in which apartment buildings are fortified compounds, and the "extras" offered by developers are trespass-proof or vandalism-proof apartment complexes. One "dream" development offered an encircling wire mesh fence, two entrances flanked by guardhouses, ID cards for residents, and a private minibus to bring children to a regular school bus stop at the front entrance. As far back as 1961, Jane Jacobs suggested that residences in the major cities of America would resemble pioneer life in a stockaded village where sentries were posted along the walls and armed guards accompanied by patrol dogs prevented interlopers from straying into the compound. Having our fences patrolled makes us prisoners, but we seem willing to pay this price so we can control our environment and predict the kinds of human interactions we will have each day.

It is bad enough that we are the victims of a growing "stockade mentality." Within the stockade all is not well. In our society of high-rise apartments, we have become a community of strangers. We seldom know our neighbors; no one is willing to get involved; and no one of us can count on help in a moment of crisis. This unique impersonality spawned by the urban situation has produced a monotonous series of accounts of murder and assault—witnessed by many yet interfered with by none. We have learned the art of ignoring the plight of our fellow man, and we lend assistance only when a very particular set of conditions exists.

In March 1964, for example, Kitty Genovese was brutally attacked as she returned home from work late at night. Although at least 38 of her neighbors heard her frantic cries for help, none came to her assistance. No one even bothered to call the police during Miss Genovese's futile half-hour battle for her life. This incident prompted a good deal of discussion about man's indifference to his fellow man, and one theme running through the commentaries was the growing sense of alienation in contemporary urban life. The result of this alienation is a heightened feeling of estrangement from other people and a reluctance to accept ideals whereby we feel that we are our brother's keeper.

People use many reasons to justify their reluctance to help in emergencies. Research shows that many of us simply do not want to become involved. Further, we are more inclined to deny the reality of an emergency when we have a direct personal responsibility for taking action than when someone else has this responsibility. We tend to "adjust" our understanding of what is happening in order to justify our nonaction.

The conditions that make us decide to help others in distress are researchable and can be specified. One researcher, H. A. Tilker, contrived a situation in which an observer watched while a "teacher" appeared to apply severe electric shock to a "learner" strapped in an electric chair. The observers were given feedback by the learner/victim, ranging from verbal protests to visual proof of the victim's seemingly painful contortions. The observers were assigned several degrees of responsibility for the conduct of the experiment—no responsibility, ambiguous responsibility, or total responsibility. Tilker concluded: "If a person is forced to 'get involved' or 'feel responsible' for the safety and well-being of another, and is receiving maximum feedback from that person regarding his condition, then he will be most likely to react in a socially responsible manner and attempt to alter the course of events."

Our national problem is that we have evolved a social way of life in which these psychological conditions seldom exist. And, we have paid a high price. Few of us feel as safe on the streets today as we did even 10 or 20 years ago. While our fears undoubtedly outrun the actual danger, it is evident that as a people we have become alienated from one another.

alienation

The labels attached to the condition of alienation are legion: estrangement, disaffection, anomie, withdrawal, disengagement, separation, noninvolvement, apathy, indifference, and neutralism. All of these terms suggest a sense of loss and a sense that the gaps between men are growing ever greater. Whatever the gains of our technological age, whatever the recorded decrease in suffering and want, whatever the increase in opportunities and freedoms, many Americans are left with an inarticulate sense of unrelatedness and detachment from the larger society. Seldom has there been such great confusion about what is valid or good, and there have never been so many who question the official visions of the future. For those who look closely and critically, disintegration, decay, and despair are the prevailing images of our culture.

A good part of Western man's anxiety may come from the conflict between his ability to achieve and his own powerlessness to cope with his own inventions. Modern man is threatened by the tools he himself invented in efforts to make life liveable. His sense of optimism, hope, and certainty have been rudely shoved aside by pessimism, despair, and uncertainty. There was an age, not so long ago, when man "believed in himself and the work of his hands, had faith in the powers of reason and science, trusted his gods, and conceived his own capacity for growth as endless and his widening horizons limitless. Bold in his desires for freedom, equality, social justice and brotherhood, he imagined that ignorance alone stood in the way of these desires. But tumult and violence have unseated these traditional beliefs and values. Knowledge has spread, but it has not abolished war, or fear; nor has it made all men brothers. Instead, men find themselves more isolated, anxious and uneasy than ever."

In short, many of us suffer from alienation—a condition which involves a sense of loneliness, personal isolation, a confusion of values and beliefs, apathy, powerlessness, rootlessness, meaninglessness, despair, and loss of a sense of self. We are experiencing *anomie*—a label the sociologist Emile Durkheim attached to normlessness, or a condition wherein the rules of social conduct have collapsed and become meaningless for the individual. The anomic person has abandoned the goal of being an "integrated" man freely and productively involved in society and its groups. This is not the first time in history alienation and anomie have been so widespread. The history of mankind is filled with eras in which dehumanization, alienation from nature, a sense of being lost in time, and a feeling of being distant from the gods have been central aspects of living in community.

The experience of alienation or anomie may have an impact on children much earlier than anyone suspects. Recent surveys of children in grades three through eight reveal that, even at this tender age, only 45 percent believe the President always tells the truth about the Vietnamese war. Fewer than 31 percent believe he is doing the right thing in foreign policy. The question is: What will be the long-range outcome of this skepticism among our children? Perhaps, these youngsters will avoid the sharp and painful disenchantment experienced by their older brothers and sisters in the 1960s. Certainly, the attitudes of today's children toward our political leaders will be reflected in the quality of American life tomorrow; perhaps, a new dimension will be added to the current estrangement, alienation, and social anomie. A waning faith in government is not limited to the young, of course. Cynicism among adults also may have reached epidemic proportions; nearly half the persons interviewed during the 1970 elections felt our government is run primarily to serve the interests of the few rather than the many. Further, several polls showed that people feel America, as a society, is on the wrong track and steadily losing ground.

Dehumanization is an even more discouraging dimension to alienation. Feeling psychologically something less than a complete human being can be an exceptionally effective defense against the onslaught of painful or overwhelming emotions. This mental stance permits one to view others as nonhuman, inanimate objects whose suffering does not substract much from a belief in the brotherhood of man. Once dehumanized—as well as alienated from others—we can become unresponsive witnesses of the mass destruction of others. Observers contend that such maladaptive dehumanization includes not only an inability to be horrified at man's inhumanity to his fellowman but also an increased emotional distance from other human beings. Dehumanization also means a diminished sense of personal responsibility for the consequences of one's actions, an obsessive involvement with bureaucratic problems to the detriment of human needs, an inability to oppose dominant group attitudes or pressures, and feelings of personal helplessness and estrangement.

P. E. Slater, author of *The Pursuit of Loneliness*, has listed some of the many human desires that tend to be deeply frustrated by American cultural patterns. One is the desire for *community*. This is the wish to live in trust and fraternal cooperation with one's fellows in a total and visible collective entity. Second, there is desire for *engagement*, or the wish to come directly to grips with social and interpersonal problems. Third, there is the desire for *dependence*, or the wish to share responsibility for the control of one's impulses and the direction of one's life.

In part these frustrations have been spawned by an incredible technology which by its very efficiency has separated us from one another. It has given us separate rooms, our own television, a personal car, and little personal contentment. We have taken a giant step back from immediate experience with others, and we suffer accordingly. Slater also noted that, in times past, "The poor were visible and all around. Psychosis was not a strange phenomenon in a textbook but a familiar neighbor or village character. The aged were in every house. Everyone had seen animals slaughtered and knew what they were eating when they ate them; illness and death were a part of everyone's immediate experience."

This is no longer so, and we are left with uneasy feelings about what has been subtracted from life. We really do not think much about one another, but we feel empty when confronting the possibility that we will all become Nowhere Men trying to escape to outer space or retreat into a fantasy of the "good old days." In his description of the quality of American life, A. Etzioni commented on the absence of channels for expressing frustrations, grievances, and personal needs. Only in this century, he observed, have we witnessed so spectacular an increase in the number of public demonstrators drawn from the "ranks of previously respectable" social groups—teachers, social workers, doctors, policemen, firemen, and nurses. Although each of us has the right to vote, organize, and join groups, these moves do not seem to make our social system truly responsive to our needs. For Etzioni, the human condition in American society "is like being caught in an invisible nylon net. He [the American man] is often unable to identify the sources of his frustrations. He frequently has a sense of guilt because had he not played along it would have been impossible to sustain the system and he would not have ended up being manipulated. His resentment against being caught is in part a resentment against himself for allowing himself to be taken."

If alienation is the modern sickness, there must be some antidote—some remedy for the American malaise. A few generations ago, it was different; there was once an age of belonging, but the dream died. We once felt we could control life through the management of our internal forces; now we feel we are manipulated by external events and fear that we have become faceless members of a lonely crowd. There is, however, according to M. Seeman, a way to cope with the great conglomerate we call the metropolis. We can acquire some sense of self-reliance and power by belonging to powerful organizations that collectively exert control over our occupational destiny; in that way we can fight personal alienation from the society. As Seeman suggested, learning to belong to social units larger and more powerful than the individual may be the antidote to modern alienation. What we cannot attain alone may still be ours if we learn to relate to others within the organizations that society has invented to counteract personal anomie. Seeman's advice is somewhat like a counsel of despair, however, since he asks each of us to submit meekly to the very social structure that has made us feel like strangers in our own land.

the death of privacy

The diminishing quality of the American way of life is reflected in a growing awareness that we live in a Goldfish Age. The details of our private lives have increasingly become matters of business and governmental concern. This cannot be compared, however, to life in a small town on the American frontier where everyone knew everyone else's business—but hardly anyone cared. Now, we are in transition to an electronic way of life that promises to alter our existence. Our children may shortly be assigned birth numbers that will stay with them throughout life, and we may be the first culture to become a "Dossier Society." As A. R. Miller tells us in his book, *The Assault on Privacy*: "The dossier society's genesis dates back several decades to the federal government's entry into the taxation and social welfare spheres. Since then, greater and greater quantities of information have been elicited from individual citizens and recorded.... Add to this the enormous quantities of investigatory information generated by the loyalty-security programs that were an inevitable by-product of the nation's emergence as a dominant world power."

Although we have always thought of ourselves as rugged individualists, in no other society is so much counting, measuring, interrogation, testing, and record keeping the order of the day. Furthermore, we accept this state of affairs passively. Sadly, we can look forward to more, rather than less, of the same. It seems certain the government will intrude even further into our private affairs as the national bureaucracy becomes bigger and more remote from daily life. Indeed, it will become increasingly difficult to remember that ours is a government of, by, and for the people.

This has also become an age of sophisticated social technology. We are now able to store as many as 3200 alphabetic characters on one square inch of magnetic tape; we can record the equivalent of a 300-page book on each American citizen and store that mass of information in a one-story building about 100 feet square. Computer hardware has evolved through several "generations" of development and each generational change has invented faster, more compact, and more complex technology to record the details of our lives. Since about 60 percent of the world's computers are located in America, our society may have the doubtful privilege of being the first nation in history to accumulate fully detailed computer dossiers on each citizen. When those closest to computer development venture a guess about the advances yet to come, it reads like science fiction rather than fact. Miller has suggested that eventually it may be possible to store the medical records of every citizen in a space the size of a cold capsule, while the tax records of the nation may be fitted into one file cabinet. Researchers are now exploring even more exotic media, such as laser beams, chemical solutions, and photographic materials for the storage of information.

It is astonishing how most of us will willingly furnish reams of personal information to strangers who will record it for uses that are not even clear to us. Apparently, we adjust to this invasion of our privacy, just as we have adjusted to TV cameras that watch our every move in department stores or to bank cameras that mutely record our financial dealings. A coming innovation in observation has been reported in Mount Vernon, New York, where television cameras (equipped with zoom lenses for close ups) maintain a 24-hour surveillance of the town's main street. The cameras are remote controlled from police headquarters and use light amplification scanning tubes developed by the military to convey bright pictures even in the dark.

The fourth amendment to the Constitution proclaims the inalienable right of the people to be secure in their persons, houses, papers and effects. But, no one in 1776 anticipated the computer age. We are without a suitable historical precedent to define the proper relationship between computer technology and legal standards of privacy and confidentiality. We have no guidelines that will define the rights and obligations of those who gather and store information; nor do we have any guides to delimit the necessary and permissible areas of inquiry, set standards for the accuracy of data gathered, provide safeguards on the confidentiality of information, or delineate the right of access each of us should have to the information gathered on ourselves. We may need to invent a new system of penalties and sanctions against those who treat data irresponsibly; and we may also need to design procedures to correct or delete erronious information about ourselves. Further, a Psychology of Privacy is needed, since we can no longer predict what psychological effect the growing loss of privacy will have on our personal well-being. The mindless computer has become a convenient scapegoat for many of us—an inanimate, non-retaliatory pile of machinery that silently absorbs an undeserved blame for irritations that have no other reasonable target. Secretly, however, each of us knows that the trouble is not in our computers, but in ourselves.

social science and american life

The quality of each individual life in our society is basically an issue of social mental health. As a nation, we excel at gathering indices of our Gross National Product, but we lack an equivalent system of social accounting. The length of our life does not measure the quality of living, any more than a census of the populations in our mental institutions provides an adequate guide to the nature of the emotional disturbances among us. As one critic observed, extended longevity does not mean that people are free of anxiety and depression. Living in better housing does not mean that we feel safer on the streets of our neighborhoods; and extended schooling does not guarantee that we will feel more self-fulfilled or less alienated.

This same critic has urged us to design a series of psychological indicators that will generate information about the frustrations, attitudes, satisfactions, values, and aspirations of the members of our society. We must have reliable indicators of our shifting mood, the closeness of individual and group attachments, and the severity of the hostility between persons and groups. "One gets the impression these days that our nation is being torn into pieces—young against old, blacks against whites, students against hard hats, hawks against doves, even recently women against men. How much of this is rhetoric and how much is real?"

An additional index which is sorely needed for these times is a measure of the state of alienation. Since an increasing proportion of our population seems to have turned away from the basic political and social values of past generations, we need to find a new consensus to regain the lost sense of community. When social values are no longer shared in society the degree and kind of social pathology increases accordingly; indeed, the symptoms of social pathology in these times are distressingly apparent.

The shifting mood of America has led to speculation that we are undergoing a revolution of personal attitudes and values—a revolution in living. One story has been used to illustrate. Two thousand years ago, men with long hair and a strange garb preached brotherly love. The called themselves Christians and they were thrown to the lions. Today the young men with long hair and a strange garb are preaching brotherly love and are being thrown to the Christians. It is not just the young Americans, however, who are raising questions about the condition of society. We have all reached the point of asking what kind of country America is going to become. There will be no easy wedding of social scientists and those who make the national policy that governs our daily life. In part, this is true because we choose to be governed by persons who claim to have graduated from the school of hard knocks. Such political personalities believe they have a personal social science file accumulated the hard way and in contact with Real People. And, to them, this file seems more practical than any information which could be manufactured by ivory tower social scientists.

The paradox is that we have yet to evolve an effective profession of social engineers who can plan, forecast, and provide feedback about social development. Psychology, in particular, has contributed very little to the solution of our social problems. We have not been blind or indifferent to these issues, but we are always too late, too impractical,

326

or simply wrong in our suggested solutions. Our society has always made—and continues to make—policy on a trial-and-error basis. In a time of accumulating crises, this simply is not enough. If social scientists are to cope effectively with the changing society they must take to heart the advice of Jerome Wiesner in his article, "The Need for Social Engineering." First, Wiesner suggests we must develop better long-range predictive capabilities; second, we must create much more sensitive feedback mechanisms to monitor and accurately report changes in our physical, social, economic, and psychological environment. Third, we must instrument small social experiments that will reduce our national policy errors to manageable little ones. Fourth, we need to conduct a varied series of experiments to maximize the rate at which our society can examine alternative social policies; and, finally, we must master the means of effectively informing the American public of the outcome of our labors in their behalf.

If we were to follow Wiesner's advice, we would concentrate our social scientific energies on developing a set of social indicators that would delineate the state of education, health, safety, and personal happiness. Health indicators would address themselves to the issues of life expectancy and physical health throughout life. Equally important would be reliable indicators of the social mobility of those trapped in poverty or bound hand and foot by discrimination. In this age of ecological concern, we must also find some measure of the quality of the physical and psychosocial surroundings in which life is lived. Pollution and privacy ought to be primary concerns. In much the same fashion, we need regular readings on the inequitable distribution of poverty and affluence, on public safety, and on political persuasions. Beyond this, we need to assess the nature of the delicate balance we maintain between individualism and a sense of community; we should be able to assess the balance between human satisfaction and dissatisfaction with life.

We need to measure these critical factors in human existence so as to arrive at root causes and sensible remedies. We also need to develop a human value index that assesses the impact of products and inventions on human life. Thus, the success of medicine would not be determined solely by the number of hours life can be prolonged but in terms of the degree to which human beings feel healthy while alive. In the same way, we must evaluate public housing programs, not according to the number of human beings housed, but according to the joy they take in their surroundings. The methodology of the social sciences is still embarrassingly inexact. Nonetheless, it offers greater hope than did all the pseudoscientific systems that preceded it. Before a massive system of total control is instituted as the only solution to social problems, we need for once to try a democracy that is based on something other than trial-and-error.

psychology
tomorrow

20

The psychologist G. A. Miller has asked the pertinent question about tomorrow: "Is there something that a person trained in the methods and theories of contemporary scientific psychology can do to reduce or alleviate the never decreasing burden of troubles that our children will inherit by the year 2000?" Speculating about the nature of psychology in the future is an ultimate foolishness but a foolishness too tempting to resist—even though history regularly makes liars of most self-appointed prophets. How many of us, for example, could have predicted the birth of the hippie movement, the upsurge of drug usage among the young in the late 1960s, or the spread of utopian communes by a tidal wave of alienated and disaffected members of our society? In 1959, would you have predicted that a graven female image, the Barbie doll, would be purchased by more than 100 million persons, have a fan club of one million members, and get 400 letters a week from persons seeking advice about life? Serious psychological prophecy usually deals with matters somewhat more weighty than the exaggerated physical proportions of Barbie dolls. But, the perils of prediction are many, since so many of the most visible trends in modern social life contribute only briefly to the course of human affairs. However seriously each fad or fashion may be viewed, one must keep in mind that fads, by their nature, represent no more than an initial, simplistic response to complex social issues.

the perils of prophecy

The perils of psychological prophecy are painfully evident to the unfortunate few who have made predictions but have lived long enough to witness their hits and misses. In 1964, the psychologist W. G. Bennis made just such an adventurous series of predictions at the beginning of an important era he has called "our spastic times." As Bennis was sadly to lament five years later:

> Perhaps only a Homer or Herodotus, or a first-rate folk-rock composer could capture the tumult and tragedy of the five years since that paper was written and measure their impact on our lives. The bitter agony of Vietnam, the convulsive stirrings of black America, the assassinations, the bloody streets of Chicago have all left their marks. What appears is a panorama that goes in and out of focus as it is transmitted through the mass media and as it is expressed through the new, less familiar media, the strikes, injunctions, disruptions, bombings, occupations, the heart attacks of the old, and the heartaches of the young.

Bennis' prophecy of the future of our society coincided with the appearance of a new species of young people. This was to be a generation of *militants* (victimized and infantilized with no way out but to mutilate and destroy the system); *apocalyptics* ("This sad society

330

will burn to the ground"); *regressors* ("Only the past was decent, orderly, humane, and civilized"); *retreators* (drugged, withdrawn, seeking instant Nirvana, and hoping reality will go away); *historians* ("It was always like this; it is a passing phase"); *technocrats* ("The future is to be embraced lovingly whatever it may be"); and *liberal-democratic reformers* ("Man is ultimately perfectible, science will solve these societal problems, and human irrationality will cease to exist"). Despite the painful complexity of these times, Bennis remains convinced that "The importance of inventing relevant futures and directions is never more crucial than in a revolutionary period, exactly and paradoxically at the point in time when the radical transition blurs the shape and direction of the present."

We have no choice about living in the world of tomorrow, but we do have a choice of how we will react as we migrate in time. We can assume the passive attitude of an audience watching a Greek tragedy, letting the play drift inexorably toward its blood-stained conclusion without raising a finger; or, as one concerned critic stated: "We can behave like utopians, to a greater or lesser degree, and propose measures that will better the fate of mankind and hopefully better mankind itself."

Prophecy may be perilous, but is is more promising than hiding one's head in the sand hoping tomorrow will never come. At least we have some rough guidelines to direct us in a dangerous game. A best guess, for example, is that there will be little noticeable genetic change in our species in the next half century. We *are* changing genetically, of course, but at such a slow rate that none of us will live long enough to be aware of it. Such predictions, therefore, are fairly nonproductive; if we are to penetrate the fog that obscures our future, we must speculate about technological and social alterations of soceity. We must consider changes that will involve a different distribution of existing goods and privileges (education for everyone, freedom from poverty, the right to health); we must consider structural changes in society (rearranged political institutions, reshaped religions, new media for communications); and we must consider the alteration of the relations between this nation and the rest of the world. (It is unlikely that we have fought our last war, for example.) Three-quarters of those who are now living will usher in the year 2000, but we may be forced to share the future with seven billion other persons. Obviously, if the human race is to survive, we must become more sophisticated psychologically. The question is whether life tomorrow will be worth the price of admission.

the psychotechnology of tomorrow

It is easy to predict that the hardware, machinery, and technology we are accustomed to will get bigger, more efficient, more complex, and more sophisticated. One of our strongest myths is that unsolved technical problems will inevitably be dissolved by our determined scientists. Further, each new technological advance is uncritically assumed to make life immeasurably better. Technological prediction is not as simple and direct as we might suppose, however, since it has two primary weaknesses: technological extrapolations tend to be too optimistic ("we will be living in capsules on Mars by 1975"); and it tends to ignore the negative spin-off of positive scientific efforts (the hundreds of thousands killed at Hiroshima and Nagasaki, guided anti-missile missiles, overpopulation, pollution, poverty, and social disorder and rebellion). According to one author, America is already "becoming a 'technetronic' society: a society that is shaped culturally, psychologically, socially, and economically by the impact of technology and electronics, particularly computers and communications."

It has become impossible to disentangle the mass of technological innovation from the fragile quality of human psychological life. In their book *The Year 2000*, H. Kahn and A. J. Wiener, for example, assembled a speculative list of 100 technical innovations likely to appear between now and the year 2000. These innovations may, indeed, be technical, but even a casual inspection of the items indicates how man and science have become inextricably entwined. Suppose, each of the following possibilities became tomorrow's reality: dreams programmed to individual taste; chemical methods of improving memory and learning; human hibernation for extended periods of time; free choice of the sex of unborn children; optional cosmetological alteration (freedom of choice of skin color, physique, features); instant relaxation and sleep with no side effects; chemical management of most mental illness and senility; near abolition of hereditary and congential defects; a variety of safe drugs to control fatigue, mood, personality, and fantasies; the postponement of aging combined with limited rejuvenation of the old; efficient and reliable methods to control behavior; and effective appetite and weight control.

This dream of a magical psychotechnological culture may lead us meekly into what Allen Schick has labeled "the cybernetic state." In this state, a society of experts and systems engineers are appointed to control public and private life in ways yet undreamed of—in ways that may leave us free only to obey. Not many of us are ready to live in a culture that automatically programs, monitors, adjusts, and distributes human resources, rewards, and reinforcements from cradle to grave. And, few of us may find life joyous in an Automatic Society devoted exclusively to "behavior instrumentation."

Most of us would find no comfort in the idea that we may be required to undergo bio-feedback training to learn how to control our brain waves so as to fit into the new society. The bio-feedback

332

prophets such as D. M. Rorvik nevertheless suggest that self-induced brain-wave control will allow us to monitor inner space, unlock the next step in human evolution, and achieve such feats as athletic performance on a purely mental level, self-instigated diagnosis and preventive medical action, management of muscle tensions, or control of heart beat and blood pressure. In the more speculative and distant future bio-feedback training might also produce: the abolition of mental hospitals via programmed treatment of emotional disorders; control over aging and the unnecessary death of cells; enhancement of creative capacities; art, light shows, and music composed of brain waves; and personal control of anxiety, fear, and joy. The questions remain: Will man and his bio-feedback machine be the combination that propels homo sapiens into undreamed realms of achievement, or will these predictions prove to be the figment of an overactive scientific imagination?

Whatever our technological future, one observer has proposed that we will need a number of social-technological inventions in a complex, crowded, psychotechnological society. We will need, for instance, electronic rehabilitation systems to monitor our citizens in their natural social environment; these systems would alert authorities when persons were in need of emergency medical care or psychiatric attention. We will also need automated public opinion sampling; response terminals using telephone lines would register instant views on current public issues. Two-way public television is a third needed social-technological invention; monitors would be used between hospital patients and the outside world, prisoners and relatives, or elderly persons and friends.

In short, tomorrow's society may need a wide array of behavioral prostheses to help it function: "simple communication tools, miniaturized behavior recording devices, partially automated prompting or reinforcing apparatus, and portable multisensory aids" are a few examples. Thus far, we have adjusted comfortably to contact lenses, hearing aids, artificial organs, and heart pacemakers; but we can expect future psychotechnology to contribute both good and bad to the quality of life in the years ahead. For the most part, we will not be able to resist the siren call of these predictable technological advances. After all, in an ecological age, trash-mashers seem logical; and further we unfortunately seem unable to break the equation of "new equals better."

The irresistible lure of technology was most appropriately intimated by J. R. Platt: "To be warm and full and free, these are our first needs ... but what dissolves and remolds societies unaware is that we also want, like children, to have sweet smells, music, pictures, entertainment, bright lights, and powerful servants. We want to make magic, to run like the wind and to fly like the birds and to talk across miles and to be as beautiful as gods and to know how everything works." In other words, we seem to be too self-indulgent to resist the sensual joys of psychotechnology. Consider, for example, our cultural response to the simple but pervasive credit card. That little piece of plastic allows us to borrow at will against a promise of future proper behavior (bill paying) in order to enjoy today what we cannot afford until tomorrow. We have openly welcomed this technical innovation and subtly transformed our society into a new and different shape.

If we are to be swept up into the whirlpool of technology, then psychological survival can best be assured by the intervention of a counterpsychotechnology. We are admittedly at the "fumbling age" of behavioral technology, but the electronic innovative age in the behavioral sciences lies just around the corner.

the children of 1984*

The future seems alien and threatening primarily because it is coming at an accelerated rate which bewilders those of us who are adapted to slower movements. We are seldom aware of the inevitable hardening of our perceptions as we age, and we all suffer from being imprisoned in the perceptions of our own childhood. In this sense, the future acts to undo the past by making it unrecognizable. The future has no recognizable objects placed in a familiar order, and this is always frightening.

We forget that our children are maturing in the midst of talk about doomsday machines which will destroy planetary life, discussions on neutron bombs which destroy people but leave buildings intact, or speculations on battlefields in outer space or poisonous chemicals in our water supply. What is bizarre to us will become commonplace to our children. Our young people are not startled by the fact that men can for the first time not only kill his fellowman but also invisibly change his genetic structure. Indeed, our children have already begun the process of absorbing a culture that we are desperately trying to "adjust to" and "compensate for." Our young children will be very different from ourselves, and they will show unmistakable signs of a psychological evolution that will be alien to the older generation. Like the conservative Neanderthal Man who could not comprehend the advances of Cro-Magnon Man, the next generations may be better suited to a social climate that seems abhorent to the older generation. The future is properly reserved exclusively for the young, since only

*Adapted from E. B. McNeil, *Human Socialization* (Belmont, Calif.: Brooks/Cole Publishing Co., 1969), pp. 249–251. With permission.

they are free from the fears of the past and have the courage and optimism to face the future without flinching.

The negative side of the expanding foundation of human culture is certain to alter the psychological nature of our children. Raised in the shadow of world destruction, they will need a psychological toughness that exceeds our own considerably. They will acquire it, and they will survive. Those who grow to maturity in near darkness seem to find light enough.

It is tempting to recoil in horror at what seems to be the psychologically dehumanizing directions of the future. But this reaction can occur only if we suffer from a very short memory. If we recall the horrors of our own and past eras—the concentration camps, the extermination ovens, the Depression, the Inquisition, the Children's Crusades, the Roman arena, wars, plagues, and starvation—we can only marvel at the capacity of the human species to survive against seemingly impossible odds.

Referring to the nightmarish world of 1984 has become so commonplace that familiarity seems to have bred a kind of numb resignation in the face of an inevitable fate. What we must realize is that 1984 will not emerge suddenly or full-grown in a cataclysm of political thunder and lightning. The roots of 1984 are being nurtured now in the fertile soil of our children's minds. Children perceive the real world—not the polite façade that we often try to present to them. For our children, 1984 will not seem noticeably different from 1983 because year by year they will have moved imperceptibly to wholehearted acceptance of the way things are. For our children, 1984 will hold fewer terrors and will seem less alien.

psychology in the year 2000

One of the elder statesmen of psychology, Gardner Murphy, speculated that in the years ahead psychologists will learn a great deal more about the psychophysics of bodily experience as well as conscious thought and behavior. Concomitant with this development will be an increase in man's ability to "scan" internal physiological happenings, to decode the blurred messages of the body, and to manipulate and control them. The exploration of man's inner space will delve deeper into the unconscious and make it a proper territory for experimental psychologists as well as therapists.

Our emotions, impulses, and moods will become subjects for renewed exploration as man learns to control his brain waves and his organs and to turn physiological systems on and off as he desires. Hopefully, he will learn to interpret, categorize, label, and define a host of physical and psychological experiences only dimly perceived

335

in the past. At the far limits of speculation, Murphy suggested that extrasensory and parapsychological experiences may also become less mysterious to us all. Psychologists may study the biological and genetic cornerstones of human behavior with the same vigor previously invested in studying the peculiar social arrangements man has invented.

PSYCHOLOGISTS AND PSYCHOCIVILIZATION

The prophets of the past were without the necessary knowledge of how society hangs together, how its bits and pieces are related to one another, which elements are susceptible to change, and which are not. According to Kahn and Wiener, what is needed now is a systematic awareness of the "nature of social systems: their boundaries, the interplay of values, motivation, and resources, the levels of social organization, and the constraints of custom and privilege on change. If there is a decisive difference between the future studies that are now under way and those of the past, it consists in a growing sophistication about methodology and an effort to define the boundaries ... of social systems that come into contact with each other." If our probes into the world of tomorrow are to give us clear views, it may be the methods and systems of psychology will make the difference. American psychologists constitute 92 percent of the psychological personnel in the world, and it is their contribution to the events of the next 30 years that must achieve a workable world order if there is to be a future psychology.

One version of the future of psychological man is that of J. M. R. Delgado, who sees us living in a Psychocivilized Society—a society that will be dedicated to direct and calculated interference with the fate of man. We must, according to Delgado, find a way to treat the underlying problems that, in recent generations, have produced "an anxious search for freedom and personal identity, an attempt to escape from the faceless mass of a technological society, and a rebellion against traditional morality, ethical principles, and ideological clichés."

> In this challenge to established values, sensory stimulation has grown louder, men's hair longer, skirts shorter, and rebellion has become the goal—to be free from family, teachers, and society; to let the mind float, searching for the depth of the self, perhaps with psychedelic aids, perceiving a stream of uninhibited messages and dreams; to live a natural life without the artificial pressures of schedules and obligations; to have free speech, free expression, artistic creativity without established rules, and a multiperception of feelings flooding the senses.

To counteract such social aims, Delgado recommends a socially calculated program of *psychogenesis* early in each individual's life.

It would be a program using all our physiological, psychological, and psychiatric knowledge to form and shape the child's personality. Psychogenetic principles would be taught to parents and educators and made an integral part of each child's waking hours. Behavioral controls to one degree or another have been exercized on new generations throughout human history; a variety of such methods are in wide use at the present time; and Delgado is certain that they will expand enormously in the times ahead. It is no longer a question whether human behavior should or should not be controlled. The only question is what kinds of control are desirable and to what degree they should be exercised—who will be controlled, what type of control will be used, who will institute control, and to what end will control be imposed?

In the psychocivilization we will all be well behaved (as that term is defined by the needs of the time). Psychology tomorrow, according to Delgado, may be devoted to gathering information and insight into the mechanisms of the brain; researchers will want to know which mechanisms make men behave and misbehave, which give us pleasure and suffering, and which promote love and hate. Delgado contends that the times are ripe for the use of chemical and physical agents. Human neurophysiological activity could be altered by psychoactive drugs, direct electrical manipulation of the brain, and behavioral control through positive and negative social reinforcement.

BEYOND FREEDOM AND DIGNITY

If B. F. Skinner has his way, tomorrow's psychologists will be very busy engineering a drastic redesign of the entire society. In his book *Beyond Freedom and Dignity*, Skinner develops the fictional theme of *Walden Two* into a startling formula whereby individual freedom is replaced by a system of psychological controls over man's behavior and his culture. In Skinner's behaviorally regulated, managed society, we will no longer make war, riot, pollute, or overpopulate—not because we will have matured enough to understand the disastrous consequences of such actions, but because we will have been conditioned to want only that which best serves the greater interests of society. Believing, as Skinner does, that behavior can be shaped and maintained by carefully designed schedules of positive reinforcement (reward), it will require an incredible number of psychological technicians to install such an all-pervasive system of behavioral controls.

The prospect of a coalition between the Delgado and Skinner forces is frightening to consider, even if it promises full employment for generations of psychologists yet unborn. A society totally managed and controlled by social scientists is not the only alternative for psychology tomorrow. There is an equally vigorous humanistic move-

337

ment whose disciples contend that every person in the world is a completely original and unique individual whose task in life is to achieve fulfillment of his personal potential as a human being.

Unlike behaviorists, who view man as an essentially passive object that can be governed through the proper manipulation of external and internal stimuli, humanists believe positive social change can result from man's potential for growth and maturity on a rational rather than mechanistically conditioned level. The humanistic position is closer to the beliefs most of us hold about ourselves in particular and about human nature in general.

If a humanistic philosophy prevails in the years ahead, the psychologists of tomorrow will be fully engrossed in the task of helping each member of society be the kind of human being he is uniquely capable of becoming. Only in this way, say the humanists, can man evolve psychologically to a point where he can rationally and emphatically make decisions for the good of all mankind. A society of carefully and systematically conditioned citizens will be incapable of the spontaneity and creativity necessary to progress to a better future. Psychological battles continue to surge back and forth, and the outcome is still doubtful. In whatever fashion the struggle is resolved, however, psychology will come of age in the next few decades and will be a crucial part of our future.

THE NEW CHALLENGES

Psychology tomorrow must meet a series of challenges never present in past eras. Outer space, for example, has become a psychological problem, and psychologists will be needed to select those men and women most suited for interplanetary voyages. Psychologists will have to assess the limits of these voyagers' capabilities, design how best to prepare them for a hostile environment, and deal with the psychological effects of excursioning in the universe. The invasion of space will be man's most complicated psychological undertaking because, however long they rehearse, human beings can only simulate and speculatively approximate the conditions of existing on alien planets or in the cold reaches of outer space. On a level closer to home, one observer has predicted:

> By the end of this century the citizens of the more developed countries will live predominantly in cities—hence almost surrounded by man-made environment. Confronting nature could be to them what facing the elements was to our forefathers: meeting the unknown and not necessarily liking it ... eating artificial food, speedily commuting from one corner of the country to work in another, in continual visual contact with their employer, government, or family, consulting their annual

338

calendars to establish on which day it will rain or shine, our descendants will be shaped almost entirely by what they themselves create and control.

In much the same vein, another observer has predicted that by 1980, 75 percent of us in America will be living in metropolitan areas. If this prediction comes true, the messages intercepted from Martian spacecrafts might claim that human beings are not only too violent and uncivilized to possess the hydrogen bomb but are also too violent and uncivilized to dwell so closely together in the humanoid clusters called cities. The list of the possible forms that society might take in the future is as endless as imagination itself. Nonetheless, psychology will most certainly be a vital part of the fabric of any society yet to come.

bibliography

chapter 1—parascience

Allport, G. W., & Vernon, P. E. *Studies in expressive movement.* New York: Macmillan, 1933.

Anthony, D. S. Graphology. In N. L. Farberow (Ed.), *Taboo topics.* New York: Atherton Press, 1963. Pp. 64–79.

Anthony, D. S. Is graphology valid? *Psychology Today,* August 1967.

Bakan, D. Is phrenology foolish? *Psychology Today,* May 1968.

Buckner, H. T. Flying saucers are for people. *Trans-Action,* May/June 1966.

Castenada, C. *The teachings of Don Juan: A Yaqui way of knowledge.* New York: Ballantine Books, 1968.

Chambertin, Ilya. *Astro-analysis.* New York: Lancer Books, 1970.

Cheiro. *Palmistry for all.* New York: Arc Books, 1969.

Gardner, M. *Fads and fallacies in the name of science.* New York: Dover Publications, 1952.

Gibson, B., & Gibson, Litzka R. *The complete illustrated book of the psychic sciences.* New York: Pocket Books, 1968.

Hyman, R. *The nature of psychological inquiry.* Englewood Cliffs, N. J.: Prentice-Hall, 1964.

Kaufmann, H. *Introduction to the study of human behavior.* Philadelphia: Saunders, 1968.

Koch, S. Psychology cannot be a coherent science. *Psychology Today,* September 1969.

Kursh, H. Don't Get trapped by a psychoquack. *Today's Health,* March 1964.

Malinowski, B. *Magic, science, and religion.* Glencoe, Ill.: Free Press, 1948.

McNeil, E. B., & Blum, G. S. Handwriting and psychosexual dimensions of personality. *Journal of Projective Techniques,* 1952, **16**, 476–484.

Metzner, R. *Maps of consciousness.* New York: Collier Books, 1971.

Stagner, R. The gullibility of personnel managers. *Personnel Psychology,* 1958, **11**, 347–352.

Stevens, S. S. The market for miracles. *Contemporary Psychology,* 1967, **12**, 1–3.

Swanson, G. E. *The birth of the gods.* Ann Arbor, Mich.: University of Michigan Press, 1960.

Ulrich, R. E., Stachnik, T. J., & Stainton, N. R. Student acceptance of generalized personality interpretations. *Psychological Reports,* 1963, **13**, 831–834.

chapter 2—parapsychology

Barry, J. General and comparative study of the psychokinetic effect on a fungus culture. *Journal of Parapsychology*, 1968, **32**, 237–243.

Crumbaugh, J. C. A scientific critique of parapsychology. In G. Schmeidler (Ed.), *Extrasensory perception*. New York: Atherton Press, 1969. Pp. 58–72.

Girden, E. A review of psychokinesis. *Psychiatric Bulletin*, 1962, **59**, 353–388.

Hall, M. H. A conversation with J. B. Rhine. *Psychology Today*, March 1969.

Hilgard, E. R., Atkinson, R. C., & Atkinson, R. L. *Introduction to psychology*. (5th ed.) New York: Harcourt Brace Jovanovich, 1971.

Jonas, A. D., & Klein, D. F. The logic of ESP. *American Journal of Psychiatry*, 1970, **126**, 1173–1177.

Martin, E. (Ed.) *Test your ESP*. New York: New American Library, 1970.

McConnell, R. A. ESP and credibility in science. *American Psychologist*, 1969, **24**, 531–538.

Morris, R. L. Psi and animal behavior: a survey. *Journal of the American Society for Psychical Research*, 1970, **64**, 242–261.

Moss, T., Chang, A. F., & Levitt, M. Long-distance ESP: a controlled study. *Journal of Abnormal Psychology*, 1970, **76**, 288–294.

Murphy, G. *The challenge of psychical research*. New York: Harper, 1961.

Murphy, G. Parapsychology. In N. L. Faberow (Ed.), *Taboo topics*. New York: Atherton Press, 1963. Pp. 56–63.

Murphy, G. Parapsychology. New neighbor or unwelcome guest. In *Readings in psychology today*. Del Mar, Calif.: CRM, 1968. Pp. 43–46.

Rhine, J. B. Evidence of precognition in the covariation of salience ratios. *Journal of Parapsychology*. 1942, **6**, 111–143.

Rhine, J. B. *Parapsychology today*. New York: Citadel Press, 1968.

Rhine, J. B., & Pratt, J. G. *Parapsychology: Frontier science of the mind*. Springfield, Ill.: Charles C. Thomas, 1957.

Rhine, L. F. *Hidden channels of the mind*. New York: William Sloane, 1961.

Rhine, L. F. *ESP in life and lab*. New York: Macmillan, 1967.

Schmeidler, G. R. The influence of belief and disbelief in ESP upon individual scoring level. *Journal of Experimental Psychology*, 1946, **36**, 271–276.

Schmeidler, G. R. (Ed.) *Extrasensory perception*. New York: Atherton Press, 1969.

Schmeidler, G. R. High ESP scores after a swami's brief instruction in meditation and breathing. *Journal of the American Society for Psychical Research*, 1970, **64** (1), 100–103.

Schmeidler, G. R., & McConnell, R. A. *ESP and personality patterns*. New Haven, Conn.: Yale University Press, 1958.

Soal, S. G., & Bateman, F. *Modern experiments in telepathy*. New Haven, Conn.: Yale University Press, 1954.

Stanford, R. G. Extrasensory effects upon "memory." *Journal of the American Society for Psychical Research*, 1970, **64**, 161–186.

Stevenson, I. The uncomfortable facts about extrasensory perception. In R. V. Guthrie (Ed.), *Psychology in the world today*. Reading, Mass.: Addison-Wesley, 1968. Pp. 145–154.

Stevenson, I. Precognition of disasters. *Journal of the American Society for Psychical Research*, 1970, **64**, 187–210.

Ullman, M., & Krippner, S. ESP in the night. *Psychology Today,* June, 1970.

Warner, L. A second survey of psychological opinion on ESP. *Journal of Parapsychology,* 1952, **16,** 284–295.

chapter 3—hypnosis

Arnold, M. Nature of hypnosis. Paper presented at meeting of the American Psychological Association, Cincinnati, Ohio, 1959.

Barber, T. X. Antisocial and criminal acts induced by "hypnosis." *Archives of General Psychiatry,* 1961, **5,** 301–312.

Barber, T. X. Experimental evidence for a theory of hypnotic behavior II. Experimental controls in hypnotic age-regression. *International Journal of Clinical and Experimental Hypnosis,* 1961, **9,** 181–193.

Barber, T. X. Experimental controls and the phenomena of "hypnosis": A critique of hypnotic research methodology. *Journal of Nervous Mental Disorders,* 1962, **134,** 493–505.

Barber, T. X. *Hypnosis: A scientific approach.* New York: Van Nostrand Reinhold, 1969.

Barber, T. X. Who believes in hypnosis? *Psychology Today,* July 1970.

Barber, T. X. *LSD, marihuana, yoga and hypnosis.* Chicago: Aldine, 1970.

Barber, T. X., & Deeley, D.C. Experimental evidence for a theory of hypnotic behavior: "Hypnotic color-blindness" without "hypnosis." *International Journal of Clinical and Experimental Hypnosis,* 1961, **9,** 79–86.

Brownfain, J. Hypnodiagnosis. In J. E. Gordon (Ed.), *Handbook of clinical and experimental hypnosis.* New York: Macmillan, 1967. Pp. 203–237.

Casler, L. Death as a psychosomatic condition: Prolegomena to a longitudinal study. *Psychological Reports,* 1970, **27,** 953–954.

Erickson, M. H. An experimental investigation of the anti-social use of hypnosis. *Psychiatry,* 1939, **2,** 391.

Gardiner, W. L. *Psychology: A study of a search.* Belmont, Calif.: Brooks/Cole, 1970.

Gebbard, J. W. Hypnotic age-regression: A review. *American Journal of Clinical Hypnosis,* 1961, **3,** 139–168.

Gill, M. M., & Brenman, M. *Hypnosis and related states: Psychoanalytic studies in regression.* New York: International University Press, 1959.

Gormley, W. J. *Medical hypnosis: Historical introduction to its morality in the light of papal, theological and medical teaching.* Washington, D.C.: Catholic University Press, 1961.

Hilgard, E. R. *Hypnotic susceptibility.* New York: Harcourt, Brace & World, 1965.

Hilgard, E. R., Atkinson, R. L., & Atkinson, R. *Introduction to psychology* (5th ed.) New York: Harcourt Brace Jovanovich, 1971.

Hilgard, E. R., & Tart, C. T. Responsiveness to suggestions following waking and imagination instructions and following induction of hypnosis. *Journal of Abnormal Psychology,* 1966, **71,** 196–208

Hull, C. L. *Hypnosis and suggestibility.* New York: Appleton-Century, 1933.

Kroger, S. *Childbirth with hypnosis.* New York: Doubleday, 1961.

London, P. Subject characteristics in hypnosis research. Part I. A survey of experience, interest, and opinion. *International Journal of Clinical and Experimental Hypnosis,* 1961, **9**, 151–161.

London, P. The induction of hypnosis. In J. E. Gordon, (Ed.), *Handbook of clinical and experimental hypnosis.* New York: Macmillan, 1967. Pp. 44–79.

Marcuse, F. L. Animal hypnosis and psychology. In M. V. Kline (Ed.), *Hypnodynamic psychology.* New York: Julian, 1955.

Marcuse, F. L. *Hypnosis: Fact and fiction.* Baltimore: Penguin, 1959.

McNeil, E. B., & Sparer, P. The use of phonograph records for the induction of hypnosis. *Journal of Abnormal and Social Psychology,* 1948, **43**, 546–547.

Meeker, W. B., & Barber, T. X. Toward an explanation of stage hypnosis. *Journal of Abnormal Psychology,* 1971, **77**, 61–70.

Moss, C. Brief crisis-oriented hypnotherapy. In J. E. Gordon (Ed.), *Handbook of clinical and experimental hypnosis.* New York: Macmillan, 1967. Pp. 238–259.

Munn, N. L., Fernald, L. D., Jr., & Fernald, P. S. *Introduction to psychology.* Boston: Houghton Mifflin, 1969.

Orne, M. T. The potential uses of hypnosis in interrogation. In A. D. Biderman & H. Zimmer (Eds.), *The Manipulation of human behavior.* New York: Wiley, 1961.

Orne, M. T., & Evans, F. J. Social control in the psychological experiment. Antisocial behavior and hypnosis. *Journal of Personality and Social Psychology,* 1965, **1**, 189–190.

Pattie, F. A. A brief history of hypnotism. In J. E. Gordon (Ed.), *Handbook of clinical and experimental hypnosis.* New York: Macmillan 1967. Pp. 10–43.

Ratner, S. C. Comparative aspects of hypnosis. In J. F. Gordon (Ed.), *Handbook of clinical and experimental hypnosis.* New York: Macmillan, 1967. Pp. 550–587.

Reiff, R., & Scheerer, M. *Memory and hypnotic age regression.* New York: International University Press, 1959.

Reiter, P. J. *Antisocial or criminal acts and hypnosis: A case study.* Springfield, Ill.: Charles C. Thomas, 1958.

Rosenhan, D. On the social psychology of hypnosis research. In J. E. Gordon (Ed.), *Handbook of clinical and experimental hypnosis.* New York: Macmillan, 1967. Pp. 481–510.

Sanders, R. S., Jr., & Reyher, J. Sensory deprivation and the enhancement of hypnotic susceptibility. *Journal of Abnormal and Social Psychology,* 1969, **74**, 375–381.

Sarbin, T. R., and Andersen, M. L. Role-theoretical analysis of hypnotic behavior. In J. E. Gordon (Ed.), *Handbook of clinical and experimental hypnosis.* New York: Macmillan, 1967. Pp. 319–344.

Sutcliffe, J. P. "Credulous" and "skeptical" view of hypnotic behavior. *International Journal of Clinical and Experimental Hypnosis,* 1960, **8**, 73–102.

Sutcliffe, J. P. "Credulous" and "skeptical" views of hypnotic phenomena: Experiments on esthesia, hallucination and delusion. *Journal of Abnormal and Social Psychology,* 1961, **62**, 189–200.

Tart, C. T. *Altered states of consciousness.* New York: Wiley, 1969.

Watkins, J. G. Anti-social compulsions induced under hypnotic trance. *Journal of Abnormal and Social Psychology,* 1947, **24,** 108-119.

Watkins, J. G. Hypnosis. In N. L. Farberow (Ed.), *Taboo topics.* New York: Atherton Press, 1963.

Weitzenhoffer, A. M. *Hypnotism: An objective study in suggestibility.* New York: Wiley, 1953.

West, L. J. Psychophysiology of hypnosis. *Journal of the American Medical Association,* 1960, **172,** 672–675.

White, R. W. *The abnormal personality* (3rd Ed.) New York: Ronald Press, 1964.

Young, P. C. Antisocial uses of hypnosis. In L. M. LeCron (Ed.), *Experimental Hypnosis.* New York: Macmillan, 1958. Pp. 376–409.

chapter 4—education

Allen, D. W. The seven deadly myths of education and how they mangle the young. *Psychology Today,* March 1971.

Ausubel, D. P. Some misconceptions regarding mental health functions and practices in the school. *Psychology and the Schools,* 1965, **2,** 99–105.

Bard, B. Why dropout campaigns fail. *Saturday Review,* September 17, 1966.

Bernstein, E. What does a Summerhill old school tie look like? *Psychology Today,* October 1968.

Combs, A. W. Fostering self-direction. *Educational Leadership,* 1966, **23,** 373–376.

Dinkmeyer, D., & Dreikurs, R. *Encouraging children to learn: The encouragement process.* Englewood Cliffs, N.J.: Prentice-Hall, Inc., 1963.

Fader, D. *The naked children.* New York: Macmillan, 1971.

Farson, R. E. Emotional barriers to education. *Psychology Today,* October 1967.

Friedenberg, E. Z. *The vanishing adolescent.* New York: Dell, 1959.

Gartner, A., Kohler, Mary C., & Riessman, F. *Children teach children: Learning by teaching.* New York: Harper & Row, 1971.

Goodlad, J. I. The schools vs. education. *Saturday Review,* April 19, 1969.

Goodman, P. *Compulsory mis-education.* New York: Horizon Press, 1964.

Green, R. L. After school integration— what? Problems in social learning. *Personnel and Guidance Journal,* 1966, **45,** 704–710.

Greene, M. F., & Ryan, O. *The Schoolchildren, Growing Up in the Slums.* New York: New American Library, 1967.

Gross, R., & Gross, B. (Eds.) *Radical school reform.* New York: Simon & Schuster, 1969.

Hechinger, F. M. Open schools: They can be a bit too open. *The New York Times,* September 26, 1971.

Henry, J. Vulnerability in education. *Teachers College Record,* 1966, **48,** 135–145.

Herndon, J. *The way it spozed to be.* New York: Bantam Books, 1965.

Herndon, J. *How to survive in your native land.* New York: Simon & Schuster, 1971.

Holt, J. *The underachieving school.* New York: Dell, 1969.

Illich, I. D. *Celebration of awareness: A call for institutional revolution.* New York: Doubleday, 1970.

Illich, I. D. *Deschooling society.* New York: Harper & Row, 1970.

Jackson, P. W. Alienation in the classroom. *Psychology in the Schools,* 1965, **2,** 299–308.

Jackson, P. W. The student's world. *The Elementary School Journal,* April 1966, 345–357.

Keniston, K., & Lerner, M. The unholy alliance against the campus. *The New York Times Magazine,* November 8, 1970.

Koerner, J. *The miseducation of american teachers.* Boston: Houghton Mifflin, 1963.

Kohl, H. *36 children.* New York: New American Library, 1967.

Kohl, H. *The open classroom. A practical guide to a new way of teaching.* New York: Vintage Books, 1969.

Kozol, J. *Death at an early age.* New York: Houghton Mifflin, 1967.

Little, J. K. The occupation of non-college youth. *American Educational Research Journal,* 1967, **4,** 147–153.

Mackler, B. Win. *Psychology Today,* April 1971.

McNeil, E. B. Analysis of an ailing monster: School organization. In E. M. Bower and W. G. Hollister (Eds.), *Behavioral science frontiers of education.* New York: Wiley, 1967, Pp. 235–256.

Neill, A. S. *Summerhill–A radical approach to child rearing.* New York: Hart, 1960.

Oettinger, A. G., with Sema Marks. *Run, computer, run. The mythology of educational innovation.* New York: Collier Books, 1969.

Postman, N., & Weingartner, C. *Teaching as a subversive activity.* New York: Delacorte Press, 1969.

Postman, N., & Weingartner, C. *The soft revolution,* New York: Dell, 1971.

Pressman, H. Schools to beat the system. *Psychology Today,* March 1969.

Reimer, E. *School is dead. Alternatives in education: An indictment of the system and a strategy of revolution.* Garden City, N. Y.: Doubleday, 1971.

Sava, S. G. When learning comes easy. *Saturday Review,* November 16, 1968.

Schwebel, M. *Who can be educated?* New York: Grove Press, 1968.

Schwitzgebel, R. L. A belt from big brother. *Psychology Today,* April 1969.

Sexton, Patricia. *Education and income.* New York: Viking Press, 1961.

Silberman, C. E. *Crisis in the classroom.* New York: Random House, 1970.

Warner, W. L., Havighurst, R. J., and Loeb, M. B. *Who shall be educated? The challenge of unequal opportunities.* New York: Harper, 1944.

Wilkerson, D. A. Compensatory education? In S. Chess and A. Thomas (Eds.), *Annual progress in child psychiatry and child development.* New York: Brunner/Mazel, 1969. Pp. 308–318.

chapter 5—drugs

Barron, S. P., Lowinger, P., & Ebner, E. A clinical examination of chronic LSD use in the community. *Comprehensive Psychiatry,* 1970, **11,** 69–79.

Berg, R. H. Why Americans hide behind a chemical curtain. *Look,* August 8, 1967.

Blum, R., *et al. Utopiates.* New York: Atherton Press, 1964.

Blum, R. Drug pushers: A collective portrait. *Trans-Action,* July/August 1971.

Bozzeti, L., Goldsmith, S., & Ungerleider, J. T. The great banana hoax. *American Journal of Psychiatry.* 1967, **124,** 678–679.

Cohen, S. *The drug dilemma.* New York: McGraw-Hill, 1969.

Cohen, S. Pot, acid, and speed. In R. E. Horman and A. M. Fox (Eds.), *Drug awareness.* New York: Discus Books, 1970. Pp. 44–55.

DeFleur, L. B. & Garrett, G. R. Dimensions of marijuana usage in a land-grant university. *Journal of Consulting Psychology,* 1970, **17,** 468–476.

Evans, W. O. Mind-altering drugs and the future. *The Futurist,* June 1971.

Farber, L. H. Ours is the addicted society. *The New York Times Magazine,* December 11, 1966.

Farnsworth, D. L., and Oliver, H. K. The drug problem among people. *Rhode Island Medical Journal,* 1968, **51,** 179–192.

Fisher, D. D. LSD for science and kicks. In M. O. Hyde (Ed.), *Mind drugs.* New York: McGraw-Hill, 1968. Pp. 66–80.

Fort, J. The semantics and logic of the drug scene. In R. E. Horman & A. M. Fox (Eds.), *Drug awareness.* New York: Discus Books, 1970. Pp. 87–98.

Freedmen, D. X. On the use and abuse of LSD. In R. E. Horman & A. M. Fox (Eds.), *Drug awareness.* New York: Discus Books, 1970. Pp. 270–311.

German, J. Human chromosomal breakage. *Journal of Pediatrics,* 1968, **72,** 440–442.

Giordano, H. L. The prevention of drug abuse. *Humanist,* March-April 1968, 20–23

Goplerud, C. P., & Miller, G. H. Drugs in pregnancy. *Journal of the Iowa Medical Society,* 1968, **58,** 706–707.

Grinspoon, L. *Marihuana reconsidered.* Cambridge, Mass.: Harvard University Press, 1971.

Gustaitis, R. *Turning on.* New York: New American Library, 1969.

Hager, D. L., Verner, A. M., & Steward, C. S. Patterns of adolescent drug use in middle America. *Journal of Counseling Psychology,* 1971, **18,** 292–297.

Hayman, M. The myth of social drinking. *American Journal of Psychiatry,* 1967, **124,** 39–48.

Hogan, R., Mankin, D., Conway, J., & Fox, S. Personality correlates of undergraduate marijuana use. *Journal of Consulting and Clinical Psychology,* 1970, **35,** 58–63.

Johnson, R. D. Medico-social aspects of marijuana. In R. E. Horman & A. M. Fox (Eds.), *Drug awareness.* New York: Discus Books, 1970. Pp. 369–392.

Katz, M. M. What this country needs is a safe five-cent intoxicant. *Psychology Today,* February 1971.

Keniston, K. Drug use and student values. In R. E. Horman & A. M. Fox (Eds.), *Drug awareness.* New York: Discus Books, 1970. Pp. 112–128.

Klee, G. D. Drugs and American youth—A psychiatrist looks at the psychedelic generation. In R. E. Horman & A. M. Fox (Eds.), *Drug awareness.* New York: Discus Books, 1970. Pp. 99–111.

Kupperstein, L. R., & Susman, R. M. A bibliography on the inhalation of glue fumes and other toxic vapors—A substance abuse practice among adolescents. *International Journal of Addictions,* 1968, **3,** 177–197.

Lipinski, E., & Lipinski, B. G. Motivational factors in psychedelic drug use by male college students. In R. E. Horman & A. M. Fox (Eds.), *Drug awareness.* New York: Discus Books, 1970. Pp. 129–138.

Louria, D. *Nightmare drugs.* New York: Pocket Books, 1966.

Lucas, A. R. Drug treatment for the troubled child. *Michigan Mental Health Research Bulletin,* Winter, 1971, **5,** 5–22.

Ludwig, A. M. Altered states of consciousness. *Archives of General Psychiatry,* 1966, **15,** 225–234.

McGlothlin, W. H. Cannabis: A reference. In D. Solomon (Ed.), *The marijuana papers.* Indianapolis, Ind.: Bobbs-Merrill, 1966. Pp. 401–415.

McGlothlin, W. H., & Arnold, D. O. LSD revisited: A ten-year follow-up of medical LSD use. *Archives of General Psychiatry,* 1971, **24,** 35–49.

McNeil, E. B. *Human socialization.* Belmont, Calif.: Brooks/Cole, 1969.

Nabokov, P. The peyote road. *The New York Times Magazine,* March 9, 1969.

Nielson, J., Frederick, U., & Tsuboi, T. Chromosome abnormalities and psychotropic drugs. *Nature,* 1968, **218,** 488–489.

Nowlis, H. H. Student drug use. In F. F. Korten, S. W. Cook, & J. I. Lacey (Eds.), *Psychology and the problems of society.* Washington, D.C.: American Psychological Association, 1970. Pp. 408–419.

Rogers, J. M. Drug abuse—Just what the doctor ordered. *Psychology Today,* September 1971.

Rosenthal, M. P. Legal controls on mind- and mood-altering drugs. *Journal of Social Issues,* 1971, **27,** 53–72.

Seidenberg, R. Drug advertising and perception of mental illness. *Mental Hygiene,* 1971, **55,** 21–31.

Simmons, J. L., & Winograd, B. *It's happening: A portrait of the youth scene today.* Santa Barbara, Calif.: Marc-Laird Publications, 1966.

Simon, W., & Gagnon, J. H. Children of the drug age. *Saturday Review,* September 21, 1968.

Skakkabaek, N. E., Philip, J., & Rafaelson, O. LSD in mice: Abnormalities in mitotic chromosomes. *Science,* 1968, **160,** 1246–1248.

Smart, R. G., & Jones, D. Illicit LSD users; Their personality characteristics and psychopathology. *Journal of Abnormal Psychology,* 1970, **75,** 288–292.

Snyder, S. H. Work with marijuana: I. Effects. *Psychology Today,* May 1971.

Stafford, P. G., & Golightly, B. H. *LSD the problem-solving psychedelic.* New York: Award Books, 1967.

Strauss, R., & Bacon, S. D. *Drinking in college.* New Haven, Conn.: Yale University Press, 1953.

Suchman, E. A. The "hang-loose" ethics and the spirit of drug use. *Journal of Health and Social Behavior,* 1968, **9,** 146–155.

Szasz, T. S. The ethics of addiction. *Harper's Magazine,* April 1972.

Ungerleider, J. T., Fisher, D. D., Fuller, M., & Caldwell, A. The "bad trip"—The etiology of the adverse LSD reaction. *American Journal of Psychiatry,* 1968, **124,** 1483–1490.

Ungerleider, J. T., and Fisher, D. The problems of LSD-25 and emotional disorder. In R. E. Horman & A. M. Fox (Eds.), *Drug awareness.* New York: Discus Books, 1970. Pp. 312–329.

348

Weil, A. T., Zinberg, N. E., & Nelsen, J. M. Clinical and psychological effects of marijuana in man. *Science,* 1968, **162,** 1234–1242.

Zinberg, N. E., & Weil, A. T. A scientific report—The effects of marijuana on human beings. *The New York Times Magazine,* May 11, 1969.

chapter 6—race

Abrahams, R. D. *Positively black.* Englewood Cliffs, N. J.: Prentice-Hall, 1970.

Armstrong, C. P., & Gregor, A. J. Integrated schools and Negro character development: Some considerations of the possible effects. *Psychiatry,* 1964, **27,** 69–72.

Ascoli, M. Of black and white. *The Reporter,* March 21, 1968.

Baldwin, J. *Notes of a native son.* Boston: Beacon Press, 1955.

Baughman, E. E. *Black americans.* New York: Academic Press, 1971.

Bereiter, C. The future of individual differences. *Harvard Educational Review,* 1969, **39,** 310–318.

Billingsley, A. Black families and white social science. *Journal of Social Issues,* 1970, **26,** 127-142.

Brannon, R. C. Gimme that old time racism. *Psychology Today,* April 1970.

Brazziel, W. F. A letter from the South. *Harvard Educational Review,* 1969, **39,** 348–356.

Brotz, H. *The black Jews of Harlem.* New York: Free Press, 1964.

Calnek, M. Racial factors in the countertransference: The black therapist and the black client. *American Journal of Orthopsychiatry,* 1970, **40,** 39–46.

Carmichael, S., & Hamilton, C. V. *Black power, the politics of liberation in america.* New York: Random House, 1967.

Centers, R. An effective classroom demonstration of stereotypes. *Journal of Social Psychology,* 1951, **34,** 41–46.

Cronbach, L. J. Heredity, environment, and educational policy. *Harvard Educational Review, 1969,* **39,** 338–347.

Crow, J. F. Genetic theories and influences: Comments on the value of diversity. *Harvard Educational Review,* 1969, **39,** 301–309.

Daniels, R., & Kitano, H. L. *American racism—Exploration of the nature of prejudice.* Englewood Cliffs, N. J.: Prentice-Hall, 1970.

Delany, L. T. Racism and strategies for change. *Psychology Today,* August 1969.

DeVos, G., & Wagatsuma, H. *Japan's invisible race.* Berkeley, Calif.: University of California Press, 1966.

Eisenberg, L. Racism, the family, and society: A crisis in values. In S. Chess and A. Thomas (Eds.), *Annual progress in child psychiatry and child development.* New York: Brunner/Mazel, 1969. Pp. 252–264.

Elkind, D. Piagetian and psychometric conceptions of intelligence. *Harvard Educational Review,* 1969, **39,** 319–337.

Fried, H. A four letter word that hurts. *Saturday Review,* October 1965.

Gilbert, G. M. Stereotype persistence and change among college students. *Journal of Abnormal and Social Psychology,* 1951, **46,** 245–254.

349

Gregory, D., with Lipsyte, R. *Nigger: An autobiography.* New York: Pocket Books, 1965.

Grier, W. H., & Cobbs, P. M. *Black rage.* New York: Basic Books, 1968.

Griffin, J. H. *Black like me.* New York: New American Library, 1961.

Hernton, C. C. *Sex and racism in America.* New York: Grove Press, 1965.

Hunt, J. McV. Has compensatory education failed? Has it been attempted? *Harvard Educational Review,* 1969, **39**, 278–300.

Hyman, H. H., & Sheatsley, P. B. Attitudes toward desegregation. *Scientific American,* December 1956, **195**, 35–39.

Hyman, H. H., & Sheatsley, P. B. Attitudes toward desegregation. *Scientific American,* July 1964, **211**, 16–23.

Jensen, A. R. How much can we boost I.Q. and scholastic achievement? *Harvard Educational Review,* 1969, **39**, 1–123.

Kagan, J. S. Inadequate evidence and illogical conclusions. *Harvard Educational Review,* 1969, **39**, 274–277.

Karlins, M., Coffman, T. L., & Walters, G. On the fading of social stereotypes. *Journal of Personality and Social Psychology,* 1969, **13**, 1–16.

Katz, D., & Braly, K. W. Racial stereotypes of one hundred college students. *Journal of Abnormal and Social Psychology,* 1933, **28**, 280–290.

Killian, L. M. *The Impossible Revolution.* New York: Random House, 1968.

King, M. L., Jr. The role of the behavioral scientist in the civil rights movement. *American Psychologist,* 1968, **23**, 180–186.

Klineberg, O. Negro-white differences in intelligence test performance. *American Psychologist,* 1963, **18**, 198–203.

Klineberg, O. Black and white in international perspective. *American Psychologist,* 1971, **26**, 119–128.

Kovel, J. *White racism:—a psychohistory.* New York: Pantheon Books, 1970.

Lawrie, J. W. Making it—the hardest way. *Psychology Today,* November 1969.

Leinwand, G. (Gen. Ed.) *The Negro in the city.* New York: Washington Square Press, 1968.

Lomax, L. E. *The Negro revolt.* New York: New American Library, 1964.

Mayer, T. F. The position and progress of black America: Some pertinent statistics. In H. Gadlin & B. E. Garskof (Eds.), *The uptight society: A book of readings.* Belmont, Calif.: Brooks/Cole, 1970. Pp. 102–116.

Montagu, A. *The direction of human development.* New York: Harper, 1955.

Montagu, A. *Man's most dangerous myth: The fallacy of race* (4th rev. ed.). Cleveland, Ohio: World, 1964.

Myrdal, G. *An American dilemma.* New York: Harper, 1944.

Pettigrew, T. F. Negro American personality: Why isn't more known? *Journal of Social Issues,* 1964, **20**, 4–23.

Pettigrew, T. F. Racially separate or together? *Journal of Social Issues,* 1969, **25**, 43–69.

Pettigrew, T. F. *Racially separate or together?* New York: McGraw-Hill, 1971.

Pinkney, A. *Black Americans.* Englewood Cliffs, N. J.: Prentice-Hall, 1969.

Poussaint, A. F. A Negro psychiatrist explains the Negro psyche, *New York Times Magazine,* August 20, 1967.

Report of the U. S. National Advisory Commission on Civil Disorders. Washington, D.C.: U.S. Government Printing Office, March 1, 1968.

Thomas, C. W. Psychologists, psychology, and the black community. In *Psychology and the problems of society.* Washington, D.C.: American Psychological Association, 1970. Pp. 259–267.

Wilcox, R. (Ed.) *The psychological consequences of being a black American.* New York: Wiley, 1971.

Wilhelm, S. M., & Powell, E. H. Who needs the Negro? *Trans-Action*, September/October 1964.

Willie, C. V., & Levy, J. D. Black is lonely. *Psychology Today*, March 1972.

Wright, R. *Black boy.* New York: Harper, 1945.

chapter 7—poverty

Allen, V. L. Theoretical issues in poverty research. *Journal of Social Issues*, 1970, **26**, 149–167.

Black, M. H. Characteristics of the culturally disadvantaged child. *The Reading Teacher*, March 1965, 465–470.

Bluestone, B. Lower income workers and marginal industries. In L. A. Ferman, J. L. Kornbluh, & A. Haber (Eds.), *Poverty in America.* Ann Arbor, Mich.: University of Michigan Press, 1971. Pp. 273–302.

Caplan, N. The new ghetto man: A review of recent empirical studies. *Journal of Social Issues*, 1970, **26**, 59–73.

Chess, S. Disadvantages of "the disadvantaged child." *American Journal of Orthopsychiatry*, 1969, **39**, 4–6.

Clapp, R. F. Spanish Americans of the Southwest. In L. A. Ferman, J. L. Kornbluh, & A. Haber (Eds.), *Poverty in America.* Ann Arbor, Mich.: University of Michigan Press, 1971. Pp. 198–217.

Clark, M. Patterns of aging among the elderly poor of the inner city. *Gerontologist*, 1971 (1), 58–66.

Coles, R. & Brenner, J. American youth in a social struggle (II): The Appalachian volunteers. *American Journal of Orthopsychiatry*, 1968, **38**, Pp. 31–46.

Davis, A. *Social class influences upon learning.* Cambridge, Mass.: Harvard University Press. 1948.

Frost, J. L., & Hawkes, G. R. (Eds.) *The disadvantaged child.* Boston: Houghton-Mifflin, 1966.

Haggstrom, W. C. The power of the poor. In L. A. Ferman, J. L. Kornbluh, & A. Haber (Eds.), *Poverty in america.* Ann Arbor, Mich.: University of Michigan Press, 1971.

Harrington, M. *The other America.* Baltimore, Md.: Penguin Books, 1962.

Hill, H. Racial ghettos: The crisis of American cities. In L. A. Ferman, J. L. Kornbluh, & A. Haber (Eds.), *Poverty in America.* Ann Arbor, Mich.: University of Michigan Press, 1971. Pp. 141–152.

Hurley, L. *Poverty and mental retardation: A casual relationship.* New York: Vintage Books, 1969.

Krogman, J. Cultural deprivation and child development. *High Points*, 1956, p. 38.

Leinwand, G. (Ed.) *Poverty and the poor.* New York: Washington Square Press, 1968.

Lewis, O. The culture of poverty. *Scientific American,* 1966, **215,** 19–25.
Miller, S. M. Poverty research in the seventies. *Journal of Social Issues,* 1970, **26,** 169–173.
Miller, W. B. Lower class culture as a generating milieu of gang delinquency. *Journal of Social Issues,* 1958, **14,** 5–19.
Ornati, O. Poverty in America. In L. A. Ferman, J. L. Kornbluh, & A. Haber (Eds.), *Poverty in America.* Ann Arbor, Mich.: University of Michigan Press, 1971. Pp. 24–39.
Pearl, A. The poverty of psychology—an indictment. In V. L. Allen (Ed.), *Psychological factors in poverty.* Chicago: Markham, 1970. Pp. 348–364.
Piven, F. F., & Cloward, R. A. The relief of welfare. *Trans-Action,* May 1971.
Rainwater, L. The problem of lower class culture. *Journal of Social Issues,* 1970, **26,** 133–148.
Rainwater, L., & Yancey, W. L. *The Moynihan report and the politics of controversy.* Cambridge, Mass.: M.I.T. Press, 1967.
Report of the President's Commission on Rural Poverty. The rural poor: Education, health and housing. In L. A. Ferman, J. L. Kornbluh, & A. Haber (Eds.), *Poverty in America.* Ann Arbor, Mich.: University of Michigan Press, 1971. Pp. 383–393.
Riessman, F. *The culturally deprived child.* New York: Harper & Row, 1962.
Rodman, H. Family and social pathology in the ghetto. In S. Chess & A. Thomas (Eds.), *Annual progress in child psychiatry and child development.* New York: Brunner/Mazel, 1969. Pp. 292–307.
Rosenthal, R., & Jacobson, L. F. Teacher expectations for the disadvantaged. In *Contemporary psychology.* The Scientific American, 1968, 448–452.
Schorr, A. L. The family cycle and income development. In L. A. Ferman, J. L. Kornbluh, & A. Haber (Eds.), *Poverty in America.* Ann Arbor, Mich.: University of Michigan Press, 1971. Pp. 39–61.
Schulz, D. A. *Coming up black. Patterns of ghetto organization.* Englewood Cliffs, N. J.: Prentice-Hall, 1969.
Schrag, P. Appalachia: Again the forgotten land. *Saturday Review,* January 27, 1968.
Scrimshaw, N. S., & Gordon, J. E. (Eds.) *Malnutrition, learning, and behavior.* Cambridge, Mass.: M.I.T. Press, 1968.
Sexton, T. *Education and income.* New York: Viking Press, 1961.
Sheppard, H. L. The poverty of aging. In L. A. Ferman, J. L. Kornbluh, & A. Haber (Eds.), *Poverty in America.* Ann Arbor, Mich.: University of Michigan Press, 1971. Pp. 176–189.
Taba, H. Cultural deprivation as a factor in school learning. *Merill-Palmer Quarterly of Behavior and Development,* 1964, **10,** 147–159.
Taylor, W. L. *Hanging together.* New York: Simon & Schuster, 1971.
Winick, M. Malnutrition and brain development. *Journal of Pediatrics,* 1969, **74,** 667–669.

chapter 8—ecology

Adams, Ruth. *Say no.* Emmons, Pa.: Rodale Press, Inc.
Auerbach, A. M. The alternate-people plan. In J. R. Landis (Ed.), *Current perspectives on social problems.* Belmont, Calif.: Wadsworth, 1966. Pp. 220–225.

Barker, R. G., & Wright, H. P. *Midwest and its children.* Evanston, Ill.: Row, Peterson, 1954.

Barker, R. G. Ecology and motivation. In M. R. Jones (Ed.), *Nebraska symposium on motivation.* Lincoln, Neb.: University of Nebraska Press, 1960. Pp. 1–49.

Barker, R. G. (Ed.) *The stream of behavior.* New York: Appleton-Century-Crofts, 1963.

Bartz, W. R. While psychologists doze on. *American Psychologist,* 1970, **25,** 500–503.

Berg, I. A. Cultural trends and the task of psychology. *American Psychologist,* 1965, **20,** 203–207.

Berke, J., & Wilson, V. *Watch out for the weather.* New York: Viking Press, 1951.

Calhoun, J. B. Population density and social pathology. *Scientific American,* 1962, **206,** 139–146.

Chase, S. *The most probable world.* New York: Harper & Row, 1968.

Commoner, B. *Science and survival.* New York: Viking Press, 1963.

Commoner, B. *The closing circle.* New York: Knopf, 1971.

Crain, R. L., Katz, E., & Rosenthal, D. B. *The politics of community conflict: The fluoridation decision.* Indianapolis, Ind.: Bobbs-Merril, 1969.

DeMott, B. *Supergrow.* New York: Dutton, 1969.

Dolan, E. G. *T.A.N.S.T.A.A.F.L. (There ain't no such thing as a free lunch): The economic strategy for environmental crisis.* New York: Holt, Rinehart and Winston, 1971.

Dublin, C. I. *Suicide.* New York: Ronald Press, 1963.

Dubos, R. *Man adapting.* New Haven, Conn.: Yale University Press, 1965.

Dubos, R. Man adapting: His limitations and potentialities. In W. R. Ewald (Ed.), *Environment for man.* Bloomington, Ind.: Indiana University Press, 1967, Pp. 11–26.

Dubos, R. We can't buy our way out. *Psychology Today,* March 1970.

Dubos, R. Man overadapting. *Psychology Today,* February 1971.

Ehrlich, P. R., & Ehrlich, A. H. *Population resources environment.* San Francisco: W. H. Freeman, 1970.

Ehrlich, P. R., & Harriman, R. L. *How to be a survivor: A plan to save spaceship earth.* New York: Ballentine, 1971.

Eiseley, L. *The immense journey.* New York: Random House, 1946.

Esposito, J. C. *Vanishing air.* New York: Grossman, 1970.

Ewald, W. R. (Ed.) *Environment for man: The next fifty years.* Bloomington, Ind.: Indiana University Press, 1967.

Fawcett, J. T. *Psychology and population.* New York: Population Council, 1970.

Festinger, L., Schacter, S., & Back, K. *Social pressures in informal groups: A study of human factors in housing.* New York: Harper & Row, 1970.

Frank, J. D. Galloping technology, a new social disease. *Journal of Social Issues,* 1966, **22,** 1–14.

Freedman, J. L. A positive view of population density. *Psychology Today,* September 1971.

Friedman, H., Becker, R. O., & Bachman, C. H. Geomagnetic parameters and psychiatric hospital admissions. *Nature,* 1963, **200,** 626–628.

353

Goldman, M. I. The convergence of environmental disruption. *Science*, 1970, **170**, 37–42.

Goodall, K. Litterbags and dimes for litterbugs. *Psychology Today*, December 1971.

Graham, F. *Since silent spring*. Boston: Houghton Mifflin, 1970.

Hall, E. T. *The hidden dimension*. Garden City, N. Y.: Anchor Books, 1969.

Howard, J. T. Some thoughts on the future. In W. R. Ewald (Ed.), *Environment for man*. Bloomington, Ind.: Indiana University Press, 1967. Pp. 275–278.

Huxley, A. *The politics of ecology: The question of survival*. Santa Barbara, Calif.: Center for the Study of Democratic Institutions, 1964.

Kahn, H., & Wiener, A. J. *The year 2000*. New York: Macmillan, 1967.

Krutch, J. W. A naturalist looks at overpopulation. In F. Osborn (Ed.), *Our Crowded Planet*. New York: Doubleday & Company, 1962.

Landers, R. R. *Man's place in the dybosphere*. Englewood Cliffs, N. J.: Prentice-Hall, 1966.

Looft, W. K. The psychology of more. *American Psychologist*, 1971, **21**, 561–565.

Marx, W. *The frail ocean*. New York: Ballentine Books, 1967.

Mead, M. Towards more vivid utopias. In G. Koteb (Ed.), *Utopia*. New York: Atherton Press, 1971. Pp. 41–55.

Michelson, W. M. *Man and his urban environment: A sociological approach*. Reading, Mass.: Addison-Wesley, 1970.

Milgram. S. The experience of living in cities. *Science*, 1970, **167**, 1461–1468.

Miller, G. A. Psychology as a means of promoting human welfare. *American Psychologist*, 1969, **24**, 1063–1075.

Neuhans, R. *In defense of people. Ecology and the seduction of radicalism*. New York: Macmillan, 1971.

Price, D. K. Purists and politicians. *Science*, 1969, **163**, 25–31.

Proshansky, H. M., Ittelson, W. H., & Rivlin, G. G. (Eds.) *Environmental psychology*. New York: Holt, Rinehart and Winston, 1970.

Rohles, F. H. Environmental psychology: A bucket of worms. *Psychology Today*, June 1967.

Safdie, M. K. Habitat '67. In W. R. Ewald (Ed.), *Environment for man*. Bloomington, Ind.: Indiana University Press, 1967. Pp. 253–259.

Schwartz, D. C. On the ecology of political violence: "The long hot summer as a hypothesis." *American Behavioral Scientist*, 1968, **11**, 24–28.

Sears, P. B. Utopia and the living landscape. In F. E. Manuel (Ed.), *Utopias and utopian thought*. Boston: Houghton Mifflin, 1966. Pp. 137–149.

Sechrest, L., & Wallace, J. *Psychology and human problems*. Columbus, Ohio: Charles E. Merrill, 1967.

Sommer, R. *Personal space: The behavioral basis of design*. Englewood Cliffs, N. J.: Prentice-Hall, 1969.

Theodorson, G. A. *Studies in human ecology*. New York: Harper & Row, 1961.

Udall, S. L. *1976, agenda for tomorrow*. New York: Harcourt, Brace & World, 1968.

Wagar, J. A. Growth versus the quality of life. *Science*, 1970, **168**, 1179–1184.

White, L. The historical roots of our ecologic crisis. In G. DeBell (Ed.), *The environmental handbook*. New York: Ballentine Books, 1970. Pp. 12–26.

Winkel, G. H. The nervous affair between behavior scientists. *Psychology Today*, March 1970.

Wohlwill, J. F. The discipline of environmental psychology. *American Psychologist*, 1970, **25**, 303–312.

Wolfgang, M. E. *Patterns in criminal homicide*. Philadelphia: University of Pennsylvania, 1958.

Wright, H., & Barker, R. Psychological ecology and the problem of psychosocial development. *Child Development*, 1949, **20**, 131–143.

Zimbardo, P. G. The human choice: Individuation, reason, and order versus deindividuation, impulse, and chaos. In *Nebraska symposium on motivation*. Lincoln, Neb.: University of Nebraska Press, 1969. Pp. 237–307.

chapter 9—violence

Beattie, R. H., & Kenney, J. P. Aggressive crimes. In M. E. Wolfgang (Ed.), Patterns of violence. *The Annals*, 1966, **364**, 73–85.

Berkowitz, L. *Aggression: A social psychological analysis*. New York: McGraw-Hill, 1962.

Berkowitz, L. Impulse, aggression and the gun. *Psychology Today*, September 1968.

Bettelheim. B. Violence: A neglected mode of behavior. In M. E. Wolfgang (Ed.), Patterns of violence. *The Annals*, *1966*, **364**, 50–59.

Bloomberg, W., Jr. American violence in perspective. In T. Rose (Ed.), *Violence in America*. New York: Vintage Books, 1969. Pp. 359–371.

Boelkins, R. C., & Heiser, J. F. Biological bases of aggression. In D. N. Daniels, M. F. Gilula, and F. M. Ochberg (Eds.), *Violence and the struggle for existence*. Boston: Little, Brown, 1970. Pp. 15–52.

Buss, A. H. *The psychology of aggression*. New York: Wiley, 1961.

Cloward, R. A., & Ohlin, L. E. *Delinquency and opportunity*, Glencoe, Ill.: Free Press, 1960.

Cohen, M. *Reason and the law*. New York: Collier Books, 1961.

Conrad, J. P. Violence in prison. In M. E. Wolfgang (Ed.), Patterns of violence. *The Annals*, 1966, **364**, 113–119.

Coser, L. A. Some social functions of violence. In M. E. Wolfgang (Ed.), Patterns of violence. *The Annals*, 1966, **364**, 8–18.

Daniels, D. N., Gilula, M. F., & Ochberg, F. M. (Eds.) *Violence and the struggle for existence*. Boston: Little, Brown, 1970.

Davis, D. B. Violence in American literature. In M. E. Wolfgang (Ed.), Patterns of violence. *The Annals*, 1966, **364**, 28–36.

Feshbach, S. Dynamics and morality of violence and aggression: Some psychological considerations. *American Psychologist*, 1971, **26**, 281–292.

Forster, A. Violence on the fanatical left and right. In M. E. Wolfgang (Ed.), Patterns of violence. *The Annals*. 1966, **364**, 141–148.

ISR Newsletter. Violence worries Americans: Men in study often justify severe police action to quell disorder. Spring, 1971.

Jay, A. *Corporation man*. New York: Random House, 1971.

Lukacs, J. America's malady is not violence but savagery. In T. Rose (Ed.), *Violence in America*. New York: Vintage Books, 1969. Pp. 349–358.

Marmor, J. Some psychosocial aspects of contemporary urban violence. In T. Rose (Ed.), *Violence in America*. New York: Vintage Books, 1969. Pp. 338–348.

McNeil, E. B. Psychology and aggression. *The Journal of Conflict Resolution*, 1959, **3**, 195–294.

McNeil, E. B. Violence and human development. In M. E. Wolfgang (Ed.), Patterns of violence. *The Annals*, 1966, **364**, 149–157.

McNeil, E. B. Violence today. *Pastoral Psychology*, 1971, **22**, 21–30.

Megargee, E. I. Assault with intent to kill. *Trans-Action*, 1965, **2**, 26–31.

Nieburg, H. L. *The behavioral process*. New York: St. Martin's Press, 1969.

Polsky, H. W. *Cottage six*. New York: Russell Sage Foundation, 1962.

Richardson, L. F. *Statistics of deadly quarrels*. Pittsburgh, Pa.: Boxwood, 1969.

Rose, T. (Ed.) *Violence in America*. New York: Vintage Books, 1969.

Rubenstein, R. E. *Rebels in Eden–Mass political violence in the United States*. Boston: Little, Brown, 1970.

Schur, E. M. *Our criminal society*. Englewood Cliffs, N. J.: Prentice-Hall, 1969.

Schmeck, H. M. Depths of brain probed for sources of violence. *The New York Times*, December 27, 1970.

Siegel, A. E. Violence and aggression are not inevitable. In *Confrontation*. Glenview, Ill.: Scott, Foresman, 1970. Pp. 196–199.

Stewart, T. D. Fossil evidence of human violence. *Trans-Action*, 1969, **6**, 48–53.

Taft, P. Violence in American labor disputes. In M. E. Wolfgang (Ed.), Patterns of violence. *The Annals*, 1966, **364**, 127–140.

Tinbergen, N. On War and peace in animals and man. *Science*, June 28, 1968. Pp. 1411–1416.

Toch, H. H. *Violent men*. Chicago: Aldine, 1969.

Warshaw, R. *The immediate experience*. Garden City, N.Y.: Doubleday, 1962.

Washburn, S. L., & Hamburg, D. A. Aggressive behavior in Old World monkeys and apes. In *Confrontation*. Glenview, Ill.: Scott, Foresman, 1970. Pp. 160–168.

Wolfgang, M. E., Violence and human behavior. In F. F. Korten, S. W. Cook, & J. I. Lacey (Eds.), *Psychology and the problems of society*. Washington, D. C.: American Psychological Association, 1970. Pp. 309–326.

chapter 10—death

Birren, J. E. The abuse of the urban aged. *Psychology Today*, March 1970.

Blauner, R. Death and the social structure. In B. L. Neugarten (Ed.), *Middle age and aging*. Chicago: University of Chicago Press, 1968. Pp. 531–540.

Bowers, M., Jackson, E. N., Knight, J. A., & LeShan, L. *Counseling the dying*. New York: Thomas Nelson, 1964.

Dempsey, D. Learning how to die. *The New York Times Magazine*, November 14, 1971.

Eissler, K. R. *The psychiatrist and the dying patient*. New York: International Universities Press, 1955.

Engel, G. L. *Psychological development in health and disease.* Philadelphia: Saunders, 1962.

Ettinger, R. C. W. *The prospect of immortality.* New York: MacFadden-Bartell, 1964.

Evans, I. M., & Smith, P. A. *Psychology for a changing world.* New York: Wiley, 1970.

Feifel, H. Death. In. N. L. Farberow (Ed.), *Taboo topics.* New York: Atherton Press, 1963. Pp. 8–21.

Feifel, H. Attitudes toward death: A psychological perspective. *Journal of Consulting and Clinical Psychology,* 1969, **33**, 242–295.

Frazer, G. *The fear of the dead in primitive religion.* London: Macmillan, 1933.

Fulton, R. *The sacred and the secular: Attitudes of the American public toward death.* Milwaukee, Wis.: Fulfin, 1963.

Fulton, R. *Death and identity.* New York: Wiley, 1965.

Fulton, R., & Geis, G. Death and social values. *Indian Journal of Social Research,* 1962, **3**, 7–14.

Glaser, B. G., & Strauss, A. L. The dying patient and his social loss. *American Journal of Nursing,* 1964, **64**, 119–121.

Glaser, B. G., & Strauss, A. L. Dying on time. *Trans-Action,* May-June, 1965, **2**, 27–31.

Goody, J. *Death, property and the ancestors.* Stanford, Calif.: Stanford University Press, 1962.

Hertz, R. The collective representation of death. In *Death and the right hand.* Translated by Rodney and Claudia Needham. Aberdeen, Scotland: Cohen and West, 1960.

Hilgard, J., and Newman, M. F. Anniversaries in mental illness, *Psychiatry,* 1959, **22**, 113–121.

Hinton, J. *Dying.* Baltimore, Md.: Penguin Books, 1967.

Jeffers, F. C., Nichols, C. R., & Eisdorfer, C. Attitudes of older persons toward death: A preliminary study. *Journal of Gerontology,* 1961, **16**, 53–56.

Kalish, R. A. The aged and the dying process: The inevitable decisions. *The Journal of Social Issues,* 1965, **21**, 87–96.

Kalish, R. A. Social distance and the dying. *Community Mental Health Journal,* 1966, **2**, 152–155.

Kasper, A. M. The doctor and death. In H. Feifel (Ed.), *The meaning of death.* New York: McGraw-Hill, 1959.

Kastenbaum, R. The reluctant therapist. In R. Kastenbaum (Ed.), *New thoughts on old age.* New York: Springer, 1964. Pp. 139–148.

Kram, C., & Caldwell, J. M. The dying patient. *Psychosomatics,* 1969, **10**, 293–295.

Kubler-Ross, E. *On death and dying.* New York: Macmillan, 1969.

Lidz, T. *The person.* New York: Basic Books, 1968.

Lieberman, M. A. Psychological correlates of impending death: Some preliminary observations. In B. L. Neugarten (Ed.), *Middle age and aging.* Chicago: University of Chicago Press, 1968. Pp. 509–519.

Lindemann, E. Symptomatology and management of acute grief. *American Journal of Psychiatry,* 1944, **101**, 141–148.

McNeil, E. B. *Human socialization.* Belmont, Calif.: Brooks/Cole, 1969.

Mitford, J. *The American way of death*. New York: Simon & Schuster, 1963.

Montagu, A. *The humanization of man*. New York: Grove Press, 1962.

Palmore, E. Predicting longevity: A follow-up controlling for age. *Gerontologist*, 1969, **9**, 247–250.

Pfeiffer, E. *Disordered behavior*. London: Oxford University Press, 1968.

Pine, V. R., & Phillips, D. L. The cost of dying: A sociological analysis of funeral expenditures. *Social Problems*, 1970, **17**, 405–417.

Polednak, A. P., & Damon, A. College athletics, longevity, and cause of death. *Human Biology*, 1970, **42**, 28–46.

Roberts, J. L., Kimsey, L. R., Logan, D. L., & Shaw, G. How aged in nursing homes view dying and death. *Geriatrics*, 1970, **25**, 115–119.

Rosenfelt, R. H. The elderly mystique. *The Journal of Social Issues*, 1965, **21**, 37–43.

Rosow, I. And then we were old. *Trans-Action*. January/February 1965.

Schneidman, E. S. The enemy. *Psychology Today*, August 1970.

Still, J. W. Why can't we live forever? *Better Homes and Gardens*, August 1958.

Time. Raising the dead. November 1971.

Wahl, C. W. The differential diagnosis of normal and neurotic grief following bereavement. *Psychosomatics*, 1970, **11**, 104–106.

Wallace, J. *Psychology: A social science*. Philadelphia: Saunders, 1971.

chapter 11—male and female

Baker, L. G. Sex, society, and the single woman. In L. A. Kirkendall & R. N. Whitehurst (Eds.), *The new sexual revolution*. New York: Donald W. Brown, 1971. Pp. 115–130.

Barry, H., III, Bacon, M. K., & Child, I. L. A cross-cultural survey of some sex differences in socialization. *Journal of Abnormal and Social Psychology*, 1957, **55**, 327-332.

Bell, Inge P. The double standard. *Trans-Action*, November-December 1970, 75–80.

Bem, D. J., with Sandra L. Bem. *Beliefs, attitudes, and human affairs*. Belmont, Calif.: Brooks/Cole, 1970.

Blauner, R. *Alienation and freedom*. Chicago: University of Chicago Press, 1964.

Bloustein, E. J. Man's work goes from sun to sun but woman's work is never done. *Psychology Today*, March 1968.

Brenton, M. *The American male*. New York: Coward-MCcann, 1966.

Frankel, C. The third great revolution of mankind. *The New York Times Magazine*, February 9, 1958.

Freeman, J. Growing up girlish. *Trans-Action*, November-December 1970.

Friedan, B. *The feminine mystique*. New York: Dell, 1964.

Gilman, R. Where did it all go wrong? *Life*, August 31, 1971.

Goldberg, P. Are women prejudiced against women? *Trans-Action*, April 1968.

Goldberg, S., & Lewis, M. Play behavior in the year-old infant: early sex differences. *Child Development*, 1969, **40**, 21–31.

Hacker, H. M. The new burdens of masculinity. *Marriage and Family Living,* 1957, **19,** 227–233.

Hartley, R. E. Sex-role pressures and the socialization of the male child. *Psychological Reports,* 1959, **5,** 457–468.

Hays, R. R. *The Dangerous Sex.* New York: Putnam, 1964.

Horner, M. Fail: bright women. *Psychology Today,* November 1969.

Kagan, J. Check one: __Male __Female. *Psychology Today,* July 1969.

Lehman, H. C. *Age and achievement.* Princeton, N. J.: Princeton University Press. 1953.

Life. Woman. August 13, 1971.

Mead, M. *Male and female: A study of the sexes in a changing world.* New York: William Morrow, 1949.

Montagu, A. *The humanization of man.* New York: Grove Press, 1962.

Montagu, A. *The natural superiority of women.* New York: Macmillan, 1970.

Queen, S., *et al. The family in various cultures.* Philadelphia: Lippincott, 1961.

Rader, D. The feminization of the American male. *Harper's Bazaar,* November 1971.

Ruitenbeek, H. M. *The male myth.* New York: Dell, 1967.

Sexton, P. C. *The feminized male.* New York: Vintage Books, 1969.

Slovic, P. Risk-taking in children: Age and sex differences. *Child Development,* 1966, **37,** 169–176.

Toby, J. Violence and the masculine ideal: Some qualitative data. In M. E. Wolfgang (Ed.), Patterns of violence. *The Annals,* 1966, **364,** 19–27.

Udry, J. R. Sex and family life. In E. Sagarin (Ed.), Sex and the contemporary American scene. *The Annals,* 1968, **376,** 25–35.

Ziegler, E. Payment by status. *Nation,* November 12, 1960.

chapter 12—the sexual revolution

Adelson, J. Is women's lib a passing fad? *The New York Times Magazine,* March 19, 1972.

Bartell, G. D. *Group sex.* New York: Peter H. Wyden, 1971.

Bettelheim, B. The commitment required of a woman entering a scientific profession in present-day American society. In *Woman and the scientific professions.* M.I.T. symposium on American women in science and engineering. 1965.

Brecker, E. M. *The sex researchers.* Boston: Little, Brown, 1969.

Broderick, C. B., & Fowler, S. C. New patterns of relationships between the sexes among preadolescents. *Marriage and Family Living,* 1961, **23,** 27–30.

Cantor, D. J. The homosexual revolution—A status report. In L. A. Kirkendall & R. N. Whitehurst (Eds.), *The new sexual revolution.* New York: Donald W. Brown, 1971. Pp. 85–95.

Chesler, P. Men drive women crazy. *Psychology Today,* July 1971.

Constantine, L., & Constantine, J. Where is marriage going? *The Futurist,* April 1970.

Degler, C. Revolution without ideology: The changing place of women in America. In R. Lifton (Ed.), *The woman in America*. Boston: Beacon Press, 1965. Pp. 193–210.

Denfield, D., & Gordon, M. The sociology of mate swapping: Or the family that swings together clings together. *Journal of Sex Research*, 1970, **6**, 85–100.

Deutsch, D. Woman's role: An Adlerian view. *Journal of Individual Psychology*, 1970, **26**, 122–123.

Ehrlich, P. R., & Ehrlich, A. H. *Population resource environment*. San Francisco: Freeman, 1970.

Erikson, E. H. Inner and outer space: Reflections on womanhood. *Daedalus*, 1964, **93**, 582–606.

Ferdinand, T. N. Sex behavior and the American class structure: A mosaic. In E. Sagarin (Ed.), *Sex and the contemporary American scene. The Annals*, 1968, **376**, 76–85.

Firestone, S. *The dialectic of sex*. New York: Bantam Books, 1970.

Ford, S., & Beach, F. A. *Patterns of sexual behavior*. New York: Harper, 1951.

Gagnon, J. H. There is no sex revolution. *Herald-Telephone*. Bloomington, Ind.: January 19, 1967.

Greer, G. *The female eunuch*. New York: McGraw-Hill, 1971.

Hardin, G. Sterilization—accepting the irrevocable. In L. S. Kirkendall & R. N. Whitehurst (Eds.), *The new sexual revolution*. New York: Donald W. Brown, 1971. Pp. 209–217.

Howe, I. The middle-class mind of Kate Millett. *Harper's*, December 1970.

Johnson, M. H., & Miller, C. The wives reconsider vasectomy. *Journal of Sex Research*. 1970, **6**, 36–40.

Kempton, S. Cutting loose. *Esquire*, July 1970.

Kinsey, A. C., Pomeroy, W. B., & Martin, C. E. *Sexual behavior in the human male*. Philadelphia: Saunders, 1948.

Kinsey, A. C., Pomeroy, W. B., Martin, C. E., Gebhard, P., *et al. Sexual behavior in the human female*. Philadelphia: Saunders, 1953.

Kirkendall, L. A. *Premarital intercourse and interpersonal relationships*. New York: Matrix House, 1966

Kuhlen, R. G., & Houlihan, Nancy B. Adolescent heterosexual interest in 1942 and 1963. *Child Development*, 1965, **36**, 1049–1052.

La Rue, L. Black liberation and woman's lib. *Trans-Action*, November-December, 1970.

Lawrenson, H. The feminine mistake. *Esquire*, January 1971.

Lester, J. Woman—the male fantasy. *Evergreen*, September 1970.

Limpus, L. The liberation of women: Sexual repression and the family. In H. Gadlin & B. E. Garskof (Eds.), *The uptight society: A book of readings*. Belmont, Calif.: Brooks/Cole, 1970. Pp. 435–441.

Mailer, N. *The prisoner of sex*. New York: Signet Books, 1971.

Marshall, D. S. Too much in Mangaia. *Psychology Today*, February 1971.

Masters, W. H., & Johnson, V. E. *Human sexual response*. Boston: Little, Brown. 1966.

McCandless, B. *Adolescent behavior and development*. New York: Dryden Press, 1970.

McLuhan, M., & Leonard, G. B. The future of sex. *Look,* July 25, 1967.

Messenger, J. C. The lack of the Irish. *Psychology Today,* February 1971.

Micossi, A. L. Conversion to women's lib. *Trans-Action,* November-December. 1970.

Millett, K. *Sexual politics.* Garden City, N. Y.: Doubleday, 1970.

Montagu, A. The pill, the sexual revolution, and the schools. *Phi Delta Kappa,* May 1968.

Morgan, R. (Ed.) *Sisterhood is powerful.* New York: Vintage Books, 1970.

O'Neill, C. C., & O'Neill, N. Patterns in group sexual activity. *Journal of Sex Research,* 1970, **6,** 101–112.

Palson, C. & Palson, R. Swinging in wedlock. *Society,* February 1972.

Pholman, E. Contraception in and out of marriage. In L. A. Kirkendall & R. N. Whitehurst (Eds.), *The new sexual revolution.* New York: Donald W. Brown, 1971. Pp. 183–196.

Reiss, I. L. *The social context of premarital permissiveness.* New York: Holt, Rinehart and Winston, 1967.

Reiss, I. L. How and why American's sex standards are changing. *Trans-Action,* March 1968.

Rheingold, J. *The fear of being a woman.* New York: Grune & Stratton, 1964.

Rimmer, R. M. *The Harrad experiment.* New York: Bantam Books, 1966.

Shainess, N. Abortion is no man's business. *Psychology Today,* May 1970.

Smigel, E. O., & Seiden, R. The decline and fall of the double standard. In E. Sagarin (Ed.), Sex and the contemporary American scene. *The Annals,* 1968, **376,** 6–17.

Smith, J. R., & Smith, L. G. Co-marital sex and the sexual freedom movement. *Journal of Sex Research,* 1970, **6,** 131–142.

Time. Legal abortion: Who, why and when. September 27, 1971.

Weisstein, N. Kinder, kuche, kirche as scientific law: Psychology constructs the female. In H. Gadlin & B. E. Garskoff (Eds.), *The uptight society: A book of readings.* Belmont, Calif.: Brooks/Cole Publishing, 1970. Pp. 427–434.

Whitehurst, R. N. American sexophobia. In L. A. Kirkendall & R. N. Whitehurst (Eds.), *The new sexual revolution.* New York: Donald W. Brown, 1971. Pp. 1–6.

Winick, C. The beige epoch: Depolarization of sex roles in America. In E. Sagarin (Ed.), *Sex and the contemporary American scene. The Annals,* 1968, **376,** 18–24.

Winthrop, H. Focus on the human condition: Sexual revolution or inner emptiness. Portents of Brave New World: The skin trade versus holistic balance in sexuality. *Journal of Human Relations,* 1970, **18,** 924–938.

chapter 13—marriage and the family

Bennett, J. W. Communal brethren of the Great Plains. *Trans-Action,* December 1966.

Bernard, J. Women, marriage and the future. *The Futurist,* April 1970.

Bettelheim, B. *The children of the dream: Communal child-rearing and American education.* New York: Macmillan, 1969.

Bronfenbrenner, U. *Two worlds of childhood: U.S. and U.S.S.R.* New York: Russell Sage Foundation, 1970.

Burgess, E. W. Economic, cultural and social factors in family breakdown. *American Journal of Orthopsychiatry*, 1954, **24**, 462–470.

Cantor, D. J. The right of divorce. *The Atlantic Monthly*, 1966.

Carter, E. Eight myths about divorce—and the facts. *The New York Times Magazine*, May 3, 1964.

Cutler, B. R., & Dyer, W. G. Initial adjustment processes in young married couples. *Social Forces*, 1965, **44**, 195–201.

Davids, L. North American marriage: 1990. *The Futurist*, October 1971.

Despert, J. L. *Children of divorce.* Garden City, N. Y.: Doubleday, 1953.

Dixon, R. B. Hallelujah the pill? *Trans-Action*, November-December 1970.

Eaton, J. W., & Weil, R. J. *Culture and mental disorders.* Glencoe, Ill.: Free Press, 1955.

Egleson, J., and Egleson, J. F. *Parents without partners.* New York: Dutton, 1961.

Field, M. G. The child as father to what kind of man? *Psychiatry and Social Science Review*, 1970, **4**, 2–6.

Goldman, R. K. Psychosocial development in cross-cultural perspective: A new look at an old issue. *Developmental Psychology*, 1971, **5**, 411–419.

Goode, J. Has the family circle come full circle? *Realites*, July 1966.

Hunt, M. The future of marriage. *Playboy*, August 1971.

Landis, J. T. The trauma of children when parents divorce. *Marriage and Family Living*, 1960, **22**, 7–13.

Langer, T. S., & Michael, S. T. *Life stress and mental health.* New York: Free Press, 1963.

Lasch, C. Divorce and the family in America. *Atlantic Monthly*, November 1966.

McNeil, E. B. *Human socialization.* Belmont, Calif.: Brooks/Cole, 1969.

Mead, M. Future family. *Trans-Action*, September 1971.

Miller, L. Child rearing in the kibbutz. In J. G. Howells (Ed.), *Modern perspectives in international child psychiatry.* New York: Brunner/Mazel, 1969. Pp. 321–346.

Orleans, M. & Wolfson, F. The future of the family. *The Futurist*, April 1970.

Pitts, J. R. The structural-functional approach. In H. T. Christensen (Ed.), *Handbook of marriage and the family.* Chicago: Rand McNally, 1964. Pp. 51–124.

Rabin, A. I. Infants and children under conditions of intermittent, mothering in the kibbutz. *American Journal of Orthopsychiatry*, 1958, **28**, 577–586.

Rabin, A. I. Kibbutz adolescents. *American Journal of Orthopsychiatry*, 1961, **31**, 493–504.

Rabin, A. I. Personality maturity of kibbutz and non-kibbutz Israeli boys. *Journal of Projective Techniques*, 1957, **21**, 148–153.

Rabin, A. I. Some sex differences in the attitudes of kibbutz adolescents. *The Israel Annals of Psychiatry*, 1968, **6**, 63–69.

Rabkin, Y., & Rabkin, K. Children of the kibbutz. *Psychology Today*, 1969, **3**, 40–46.

Rostow, E. G. Conflict and accommodation. In H. M. Ruitenbeek (Ed.), *Sexuality and identity.* New York: Delta, 1970. Pp. 146–173.

Scott, J. F. Marriage is not a personal matter. *The New York Times Magazine*, October 30, 1966.

Spiro, M. E. *Children of the kibbutz.* Cambridge, Mass.: Harvard University Press, 1958.

Steinzor, B. *When parents divorce.* New York: Pantheon Books, 1969.

Talmon-Garber, Y. The family in Israel: The kibbutz. *Marriage and Family Living*, 1954, **16**, 346–349.

Ungern-Sternberg, L. The marriage of the future. In H. Keyserling (Ed.), *The book of marriage.* New York: Harcourt, 1926. Pp. 263–270.

Yang, C. K. *The Chinese family in the communist revolution.* Cambridge, Mass.: Harvard University Press, 1959.

Young, K. *Personality and problems of adjustment.* (2nd Ed.) New York: Appleton-Century-Crofts, 1962.

Zimmerman, C. *The family and civilization.* New York: Harper, 1947.

chapter 14—the quest for identity

Adams, R. L., & Fox, R. J. Mainlining Jesus: The new trip. *Society*, February 1972.

Adelson, J. The mystique of adolescence. *Psychiatry*, 1964, **27**, 1–5.

Adelson, J. What generation gap? *The New York Times Magazine*, January 18, 1970.

Bach, M. *Strangers at the door.* Nashville, Tenn.: Abingdon Press, 1971.

Bealer, R. C., Willits, F. K., & Maida, P. R. The rebellious youth subculture—A myth. *Children*, 1964, **11**, 43–48.

Berger, B. M. Hippie morality—More old than new. *Trans-Action*, December 1967.

Berger, B. M. The new stage of American man—Almost endless adolescence. *The New York Times Magazine*, November 2, 1969.

Bingham, J. The intelligent square's guide to hippieland. *The New York Times Magazine*, September 24, 1967.

Blessitt, A. *Turned on to Jesus.* New York: Hawthorn Books, 1971.

Cannon, W. *The Jesus revolution.* Nashville, Tenn.: Broadman Press, 1971.

Clark, W. H. The psychology of religious experience. *Psychology Today*, February 1968.

Cooper, J. C. *Religion in the age of Aquarius.* Philadelphia: Westminister Press, 1971.

Davis, F. Haight-Ashbury's hippies and the future society. *Trans-Action*, December 1967.

Distler, L. S. The adolescent "hippie" and the emergence of a matristic culture. *Psychiatry*, 1970, **33**, 362–371.

Douglas, J. D. *Youth in turmoil.* National Institutes of Mental Health Center for Studies of Crime and Delinquency. Public Health Services Publication No. 2058. Chevy Chase, Md., 1970.

Feuer, L. *The conflict of generations: The character and significance of student movements.* New York: Basic Books, 1969.

Fischer, J. Four choices for young people. *Harper's Magazine*, August 1967.

Flacks, R. The liberated generation: An exploration of the roots of student protest. *Journal of Social Issues,* 1967, **23,** 52–75.

Friedenberg, E. Z. Current patterns of generational conflict. *Journal of Social Issues,* 1969, **25,** 21–38.

Graham, B. *The Jesus generation.* Grand Rapids, Mich.: Zondervan, 1971.

Greeley, A. M. *Come blow your mind with me.* New York: Doubleday, 1971.

Gustin, J. L. The revolt of youth. *Psychoanalysis and the Psychoanalytic Review,* 1961, **98,** 78–90.

Hadden, J. K. The private generation. *Psychology Today,* October 1969.

Halleck, S. You can go to hell with style. *Psychology Today,* November 1969.

Herst, P. Activist students challenge the social scientists. In F. F. Korten, S. W. Cook, & J. I. Lacey (Eds.), *Psychology and the problems of society.* Washington, D. C.: American Psychological Association, 1970. Pp. 395–405.

Howard, J. The groovy Christians of Rye, N. Y. *Life,* May 14, 1971.

Hurlock, E. B. American adolescents of today—A new species. *Adolescence,* 1966, **1,** 7–21.

Kalish, R. A. The old and new as generation gap allies. *The Gerentologist,* 1969, **9,** 83–89.

Kavanaugh, R. E. The grim generation. In *Readings in psychology today.* La Jolla, Calif.: CRM Books, 1969. Pp. 357–361.

Keniston, K. *The uncommitted: Alienated youth in American society.* (1st ed.) New York: Harcourt Brace Jovanovich, 1965.

Keniston, K. The sources of student dissent. *Journal of Social Issues,* 1967, **23,** 108–137.

Kneeland, D. E. Youth rebellion of the sixties waning. *The New York Times,* October 24, 1971.

Levitt, M., & Rubenstein, B. The children's crusade. *American Journal of Orthopsychiatry,* 1968, **38,** 591–598.

MacKay, C. *Extraordinary popular delusions and the madness of crowds.* New York: Noonday Press, 1932.

May, R. Love and will. *Psychology Today,* August 1969.

McNeil, E. B. *Human socialization.* Belmont, Calif.: Brooks/Cole, 1969.

Mead, M. *Culture and commitment.* Garden City, N. Y.: Doubleday, 1970.

Mead, M. Future family. *Trans-Action.* September 1971.

Miller, H. On hanging loose and loving: The dilemma of present youth. *Journal of Social Issues,* 1971, **27,** 35–46.

Miller, P. R. The Chicago demonstrators: A study in identity. *Bulletin of the Atomic Scientists,* 1969, **25,** 3–6.

Otto, H. A., & Otto, S. T. A new perspective of the adolescent. *Psychology in the Schools,* 1967, **4,** 76–81.

Palms, R. G. *The Jesus kids.* Valley Forge, Pa.: Judson Press, 1971.

Pederson, D. *Jesus people.* Pasadena, Calif.: Compass, 1971.

Plowman, E. *The Jesus movement in America.* Elgin, Ill.: David C. Cook, 1971.

Rafferty, M. Campus violence: A fascist conspiracy. In J. McEvoy & A. Miller (Eds.), *Black power and student rebellion.* Belmont, Calif.: Wadsworth, 1969. Pp. 212–221.

Reich, C. *The greening of America.* New York: Random House, 1970.

364

Revel, J. *Without Marx or Jesus: The new American revolution has begun.* New York: Doubleday, 1971.

Solisburg, W. W., & Solisburg, F. Youth and the search for intimacy. In L. A. Kirkendall & R. N. Whitehurst (Eds.), *The new sexual revolution.* New York: Donald W. Brown, 1971.

Slater, P. E. Cultures in collision. *Psychology Today,* July 1970.

Solomon, F., & Fishman, J. R. Youth and peace. A psychosocial study of student peace demonstrators in Washington, D. C. *Journal of Social Issues,* 1964, **20,** 54–73.

Sugarman, B. Involvement in youth culture, academic achievement and conformity in school. *The British Journal of Sociology,* 1967, **18,** 151–164.

Time. The new rebel cry: Jesus is coming! June 2, 1971.

Thomas, L. E. Family correlates of student political activism. *Developmental Psychology,* 1971, **4,** 206–214.

Walsh, C. *God at large.* New York: Seabury Press, 1971.

Ward, H. H. Are Detroit "children of God" hypnotized? *Detroit Free Press,* November 6, 1971.

Watts, W. A., Lynch, S., & Whittaker, D. Alienation and activism in today's college youth: Socialization patterns and current family realtionships. *Journal of Counseling Psychology,* 1969, **16,** 1–7.

Whittaker, D., & Watts, W. A. Personality characteristics associated with activism and disaffiliation in today's college-age youth. *Journal of Counseling Psychology,* 1971, **18,** 200–206.

Wylie, P. *Sons and daughters of mom.* New York: Doubleday, 1971.

Wyzanski, C. E. It is quite right that the young should talk about us as hypocrites; we are. *Saturday Review,* July 20, 1968.

Yablonsky, L. *The hippie trip.* New York: Pegasus, 1968.

Zoellner, R. Confessions of a middle-aged moralist. *Commonweal,* June 7, 1968.

chapter 15—psychology and utopia

Dahrendorf, R. Out of utopia: Toward a reorientation of sociological analysis. In G. Kateb (Ed.), *Utopia.* New York: Atherton Press, 1971. Pp. 103–126.

Dubos, R. *The dreams of reason.* New York: Columbia University Press, 1961.

Gobetz, G. E., & Frumkin, R. M. Teaching about utopian ideas and practices. *Improving College and University Teaching,* 1971, **19,** 26–32.

Huxley, A. *Brave new world.* New York: Bantam Books, 1932 and 1946.

Huxley, A. *Island.* New York: Bantam Books, 1962.

Huxley, A. *Brave New World Revisited.* New York: Harper & Row, 1965.

Laidler, H. W. *History of socialism.* New York: Thomas Y. Crowell, 1968.

Manuel, F. E. Toward a psychological history of utopia. In F. E. Manuel (Ed.), *Utopias and utopian thought.* Boston: Houghton Mifflin, 1965 and 1966. Pp. 69–98.

More, T. *Utopia.* Baltimore, Md.: Penguin Books, 1965.

Orwell, G. *1984.* New York: Harcourt, Brace, 1949.

Skinner, B. F. *Walden two.* New York: Macmillan 1948.

chapter 16—alternative societies: the communes

Atcheson, R. *The bearded lady*. New York: John Day, 1971.

Berger, B. M. The best things in life are free, or you can build them yourself. *The New York Times Book Review*, November 1971.

Diamond, S. *What the trees said*. New York: Delacorte Press, 1971.

Fairfield, D. Communes, USA. *The modern utopian*, Vol. 5 (1, 2, and 3). San Francisco: Alternatives Foundation, 1971.

Gardner, H. Your global alternative: Communes. *Esquire*, September 1970. P. 106.

Hine, R. V. *California's utopian communities*. New Haven, Conn.: Yale University Press, 1953.

Holloway, M. *Heavens on earth*. New York: Dover, 1966.

Houriet, R. *Getting back together*. New York: Coward, McCann & Geoghegan, 1971.

Kanter, R. M. Communes. *Psychology Today*, July 1970.

Laidler, H. W. *History of socialism*. New York: Thomas Y. Crowell, 1968.

Mungo, R. *Total loss farm*. New York: Dutton, 1971.

Reich, C. *The greening of America*. New York: Random House, 1970.

Slater, P. *The pursuit of loneliness*. Boston: Beacon Press, 1970.

chapter 17—encounter groups

Bell, R. L., Cleveland, S. E., Hanson, P. G., & O'Connell, W. E. Small group dialogue and discussion: An approach to police-community relationships. In H. C. Lindgren, D. Byrne, & F. Lindgren (Eds.), *Current research in psychology*. New York: Wiley, 1971.

Bindrim, P. Nudity. *Psychology Today*, May 1969.

Blanchard, W. H. Ecstasy without agony is baloney. *Psychology Today*, January 1970.

Blank, L. Nudity. *Psychology Today*, June 1969.

Burton, A. (Ed.) *Encounter*. San Francisco: Jossey-Bass, 1969.

Campbell, J. P., & M. D. Dunnette. Effectiveness of T-group experiences in managerial training and development. *Psychological Bulletin*, 1968, **70**, 73–104.

Cashdan, S. Sensitivity groups: Problems and promise. *Professional Psychology*, 1970, **1**, 217–224.

Dunnette, D. People feeling: Joy, more joy, and the "slough of despond." *Journal of Applied Behavioral Science*, 1969, **5**, 25–44.

Egan, G. *Encounter: Group processes for interpersonal growth*. Belmont, Calif.: Brooks/Cole, 1970.

Foulds, M. L., Wright, J. C., & Guinan, J. F. Marathon group: A six month follow-up. *Journal of College Student Personnel*, 1970, **11**, 426–431.

Goodall, K. Casualty lists from encounter groups. *Psychology Today*, July 1971.

Greening, T. C. Sensitivity training: Cult or contribution? *Personnel*, May –June 1964.

Heine, R. W. *Psychotherapy*. Englewood Cliffs, N. J.: Prentice-Hall, 1971.

Hoover, E. L. The age of encounter. *Human Behavior*, January/February 1972.

Howard, J. *Please touch*. New York: McGraw-Hill, 1970.

Hurewitz, P. Ethical considerations in leading therapeutic and quasi-therapeutic groups: Encounter and sensitivity groups. *Group Psychotherapy and Psychodrama*, 1970, **23**, 17–20.

Keen, S. Sing the body electric. *Psychology Today*, October 1970.

Lakin, M. Group sensitivity training and encounter: Uses and abuses of a method. *Counseling Psychologist*, 1970, **2**, 66–70.

Lamott, K. Marathon therapy is a psychological pressure cooker. *The New York Times*, July 13, 1969.

Maliver, B. T. Encounter groups up against the wall. *The New York Times Magazine*, January 3, 1971.

Mann, J. *Encounter*. New York: Grossman Publishers, 1970.

McNair, M. P. What price human relations? *Harvard Business Review*, March–April 1957.

McNeil, E. B. *Neuroses and personality disorders*. Englewood Cliffs, N. J.: Prentice-Hall, 1970.

Mehrabian, A. *Tactics of social influence*. Englewood Cliffs, N. J.: Prentice-Hall, 1970.

Morgan, C. T., & King, R. N. *Introduction to psychology* (4th Ed.) New York: McGraw-Hill, 1971.

Murphy, M. Esalen where it's at. *Psychology Today*, December 1967.

Perls, F. S. *In and out of the garbage pail*. Lafayette, Calif.: Real People Press, 1969.

Rogers, C. R. The group comes of age. *Psychology Today*, December 1969.

Ruitenbeek, H. M. *The new group therapies*. New York: Avon Books, 1970.

Sampson, E. E. *Social psychology and contemporary society*. New York: Wiley, 1971.

Schwartz, E. K. To group or not to group. *Contemporary Psychology*, 1971, **16**, 423–425.

Shepard, M., & Lee, M. *Marathon 16*. New York: Putnam, 1970.

Shostrom, E. L. Group therapy: Let the buyer beware. *Psychology Today*, May 1962.

Smith, R. J. A closer look at encounter therapies. *International Journal of Group Psychotherapy*, 1970, **20**, 192–209.

Tirnauer, L. The future of encounter groups. *The Futurist*, April 1971. Pp. 58–60.

chapter 18—behavior control

Andrews, L. M., & Karlins, M. *Requiem for democracy*. New York: Holt, Rinehart and Winston, 1971.

Avant, L. L. Vision in the ganzfeld. *Psychological Bulletin*, 1965, **64**, 246–258.

Bettelheim, B. *The informed heart*. New York: Free Press, 1960.

Bexton, W. H., Heron, W., & Scott, T. H. Effects of decreased variation in the sensory environment. *Canadian Journal of Psychology*, 1954, **8**, 70–76.

Bliss, E. J., & L. D. Clark. Visual hallucinations. In L. J. West (Ed.), *Hallucinations.* New York: Grune & Stratton, 1962.

Clarke, A. *Profiles of the future.* New York: Harper & Row, 1963.

Crutchfield, S. Conformity and character. *American Psychologist,* 1955, **10,** 191–198.

Eysenck, H. J. Behavior therapy as a scientific discipline. *Journal of Consulting and Clinical Psychology,* 1971, **36,** 314–319.

Fuller, P. Operant conditioning of a vegetative human organism. *American Journal of Psychology,* 1949, **63,** 587–590.

Gelfand, D. M., & Hartmann, D. P. Behavior therapy with children: A review and evaluation of research methodology. *Psychological Bulletin,* 1968, **69,** 204–215.

Goorney, A. Treatment of a compulsive horse race gambler by aversion therapy. *British Journal of Psychiatry,* 1968, **114,** 329–333.

Haggard, E. A., As, A., & Borgen, G.M. Social isolates and urbanites in perceptual isolation. *Journal of Abnormal Psychology,* 1970, **76,** 1–9.

Heath, R. Electrical self-stimulation of the brain in man. *American Journal of Psychiatry,* 1963, **120,** 571–577.

Heron, W. Cognitive and physiological effects of perceptual isolation. In P. Solomon *et al.* (Eds.), *Sensory deprivation.* Cambridge, Mass.: Harvard University Press, 1961.

Hunter, E. *Brainwashing in Red China.* New York: Vanguard, 1951.

Klein, M. H., Dittmann, A. T., Parloff, M. B., & Gill, M. M. Behavior therapy: Observations and reflections. *Journal Consulting and Clinical Psychology,* 1969, **33,** 259–266.

Krasner, L. Behavior control and social responsibility. *American Psychologist,* 1964, **17,** 199–204.

Kubzansky, P. E., & Leiderman, P. H. Sensory deprivation: An overview. In P. Solomon *et al.* (Eds.), *Sensory deprivation.* Cambridge, Mass.: Harvard University Press, 1961. Pp. 221–238.

Leites, N., & Bernaut, E. *Ritual of liquidation.* Glencoe, Ill.: Free Press, 1954.

Lifton, R. J. Home by ship: Reaction patterns of American prisoners of war repatriated from North Korea. *American Journal Psychiatry,* 1954, **110,** 732 –739.

Lifton, R. J. "Thought reform" of western civilians in Chinese communist prisons. *Psychiatry,* 1956, **19,** 173–195.

Lifton, R. J. *Thought reform and the psychology of totalism.* New York: Norton, 1961.

London, P. *Behavior control.* New York: Harper & Row, 1969.

McConnell, J. V. Criminals can be brainwashed—now. *Psychology Today,* April 1970.

Mendelson, J. H., Kubzansky, P. E., Leiderman, H. P., Wexler, D. E., Solomon, P. Sensory deprivation: A case analysis. In J. H. Kagan, M. Marshall, & C. Caldwell (Eds.), *Psychology: Adapted readings,* New York: Harcourt Brace Jovanovich, 1971.

Milgram, S. Behavioral study of obedience. *Journal of Abnormal and Social Psychology,* 1963, **67,** 371–378.

368

Patterson, G. R. Behavior techniques based upon social learning: An additional base for developing behavior modification technologies. In C. M. Frank (Ed.), *Behavior therapy appraisal and status*. New York: McGraw-Hill, 1969.

Penfield, W. The interpretive cortex. *Science*, 1959, **129**, 1719–1725.

Portes, A. On the emergence of behavior therapy in modern society. *Journal of Consulting and Clinical Psychology*, 1971, **36**, 303–313.

Rickett, A., & Rickett, A. *Prisoners of liberation*. New York: Cameron Associates, 1957.

Rogers. C. R. Freedom to become: Illusion or reality? In D. E. Hamachek (Ed.), *Human dynamics in psychology and education*. Boston: Allyn and Bacon, 1968. Pp. 540–548.

Rogers, C. R., & Skinner, B. F. Some issues concerning the control of human behavior: A symposium. In M. Karlins & L. M. Andrews (Eds.), *Man Controlled: Readings in the psychology of behavior control*. New York: Free Press, 1972. Pp. 239–263.

Rosenfeld, A. *Second Genesis*. Englewood Cliffs, N. J.: Prentice-Hall, 1969.

Ruff, G. N., Levy, E. Z., & Thaler, V. H. Factors in influencing reactions to reduced sensory input. In P. Solomon *et al.* (Eds.), *Sensory deprivation*. Cambridge, Mass.: Harvard University Press, 1961.

Samson, E. E. Social psychology and contemporary society. New York: Wiley, 1971.

Schein, E. H. The Chinese indoctrination program for prisoners of war: A study of attempted "brainwashing." In E. E. Maccoby, T. M. Newcomb, & E. L. Hartley (Eds.), *Social psychology*. (3rd. ed.) New York: Holt, 1958.

Schein, E. H., Schneier, I., & Barker, C. H. *Coercive persuasion*. New York: Norton, 1961.

Shirer, W. L. *The rise and fall of the Third Reich*. New York: Simon & Schuster, 1960.

Skinner, B. F. Freedom and the control of men. *The American Scholar*, 1955-1956, **25**, 47–65.

Skinner, B. F. *Beyond freedom and dignity*. New York: Alfred A. Knopf, 1971.

Walker, E. L., & Heyns, R. W. *An anatomy for conformity*. Belmont, Calif: Brooks/Cole, 1967.

Warren, J. Clark calls for research on drugs that would end "abuse of power." *A. P. A. Monitor*, October 1971.

Watson, J. *Behaviorism*. Chicago: University of Chicago Press, 1924.

Wheaton, J. L. Fact and fancy in sensory deprivation studies. *School of aviation medicine reports*. No. 5. Brooks Air Force Base, Texas, 1959. Pp. 59–60.

Wolpe, J., & Lazarus, A. A. *Behavior therapy techniques, A guide to the treatment of neuroses*. New York: Pergamon Press, 1967.

Zubek, J. P., Pushkar, D., Samson, W., & Gowing, J. Perceptual changes after prolonged isolation (darkness and silence). *Canadian Journal of Psychology*, 1961, **15**, 83–100.

Zuckerman, M., & Cohen, N. Sources of reports of visual and auditory sensations in perceptual isolation experiments. *Psychological Bulletin*, 1964, **62**, 11–20.

chapter 19—the quality of life

Bates, F. L. Social trends in a leisure society. *The Futurist*, February 1971.

Bennett, C. C. Secrets are for sharing. *Psychology Today*, February 1969.

Bernard, V. W., Ottenberg, P., & Redl, F. Dehumanization: A composite psychological defense in relation to modern war. In R. Perrucci & M. Pilisuk (Eds.), *The triple revolution—social problems in depth*. Boston: Little, Brown, 1968. Pp. 17–34.

Brenton, M. *The privacy invaders*. New York: Crest Books, 1964.

Campbell, A. Measuring the quality of life. *The Michigan Alumnus*, March 1971.

Clark, M. Patterns of aging among the elderly poor of the inner city. *Gerontologist*, 1971, **11**, 58–66.

Etzioni, A. Man and society: The inauthentic condition. In F. F. Korten, S. W. Cook, and J. I. Lacey (Eds.), *Psychology and Problems of Society*. Washington, D. C.: American Psychological Association, 1970. Pp. 451–459.

Fromm, E. *The revolution of hope–Toward a humanized technology*. New York: Bantam Books, 1968.

Jacobs, J. *The death and life of great American cities*, New York: Random House, 1961.

Josephson, E., & M. Josephson (Eds.), *Man alone*. New York: Dell, 1962.

Latane, B., & Darley, J. M. *The unresponsive bystander: Why doesn't he help?* New York: Appleton-Century-Crofts, 1970.

McNeil, E. B. 2001: A social science odyssey. In *A design for international relations research: Scope, theory, methods and relevance*, Mongraph No. 10. *American Academy of Political and Social Science*, October 1970. Pp. 154–158.

Miller, A. R. *The assault on privacy* Ann Arbor, Mich.: University of Michigan Press, 1971.

Sawyer, J., & Schlecter, H. Computers, privacy, and the National Data Center. *American Psychologist*, 1968, **23**, 810–818.

Schactel, E. G. On alienated concepts of identity. In E. Josephson and M. Josephson (Eds.) *Man alone*. New York: Dell, 1962.

Schwartz, T. Cargo-cult frenzy in the South Seas. *Psychology Today*, March 1971.

Seeman, M. Antidote to alienation—Learning to belong. *Trans-Action*, May/June 1966.

Slater, P. E. *The pursuit of loneliness*. Boston: Beacon Press, 1970.

Tilker, H. A. Socially responsible behavior as a function of observer responsibility and victim feedback. *Journal of Personality and Social Psychology*, 1970, **14**, 95–100.

U.S. News and World Report. 25 amazing years. November 15, 1971.

Westin, A. F. *Privacy and freedom*. New York: Atheneum, 1967.

Wiesner, J. B. The need for social engineering. In *Psychology and the Problems of Society*. Washington, D. C.: American Psychological Association, 1970.

Wrightsman, L. S., and Baker, N. J. Where have all the idealistic, imperturbable freshmen gone? *Proceedings of the 77th Annual Convention of the American Psychological Association*, 1969. Pp. 299–300.

chapter 20—psychology tomorrow

Bennis, W. G. A funny thing happened on the way to the future. *American Psychologist*. 1970, **25**, 595–608.

Brzezinski, Z. America in the technetronic age. In G. Kateb (Ed.), *Utopia*. New York: Atherton Press, 1971 Pp. 127–150.

Delgado, J. M. R. *Physical control of the mind*. New York: Harper & Row, 1969.

Grether, W. F. Psychology and the space frontier. *American Psychologist*, 1962, **17**, 92–101.

Kahn, H., & Wiener, A. J. *The year 2000*. New York: Macmillan, 1967.

McNeil, E. B. *Human socialization*. Belmont, Calif.: Brooks/Cole, 1969.

Michael, D. N. *The next generation*. New York: Vintage Books, 1965.

Mayer, E. Biological man and the year 2000. In D. Bell (Ed.), *Toward the year 2000: Work in progress*. Boston: Beacon Press, 1969. Pp. 200–204.

Miller, G. A. Psychology as a means of promoting human welfare. *American Psychologist*, 1969, **24**, 1063–1075.

Murphy, G. Psychology in the year 2000. *American Psychologist*, 1969, **24**, 523–530.

Platt, J. R. *The excitement of seeing*. Boston: Houghton Mifflin, 1962.

Platt, J. R. *The step to man*. New York: Wiley, 1966.

Ray, P. H. Human ecology, technology, and the need for social planning. *American Behavioral Scientist*, 1968, **2**, 16–19.

Rorvik, D. M. Brain waves. *Look*, October 6, 1970.

Schick, A. The cybernetic state. *Trans-Action*, February 1970.

Schwitzgebel, R. L. Electronic innovation in the behavioral sciences. *American Psychologist*, 1967, **22**, 364–370.

Schwitzgebel, R. L. Behavior instrumentation and social technology. *American Psychologist*, 1970, **25**, 491–499.

Skinner, B. F. *Beyond freedom and dignity*. New York: Knopf, 1971.